Drugs Politics

Iran has one of the world's highest rates of drug addiction, estimated to be between two and seven per cent of the entire population. This makes the questions this book asks all the more salient: what is the place of illegal substances in the politics of modern Iran? How have drugs affected the formation of the Iranian state and its power dynamics? And how have governmental attempts at controlling and regulating illicit drugs affected drug consumption and addiction? By answering these questions, Maziyar Ghiabi suggests that the Islamic Republic's image as an inherently conservative state is not only misplaced and inaccurate, but in part a myth. In order to dispel this myth, he skilfully combines ethnographic narratives from drug users, vivid field observations from 'under the bridge', with archival material from the pre- and post-revolutionary era, statistics on drug arrests and interviews with public officials. This title is also available as Open Access on Cambridge Core at doi.org/10.1017/9781108567084.

MAZIYAR GHIABI is an Italian/Iranian social scientist, ethnographer and historian, currently a lecturer at the University of Oxford and Titular Lecturer at Wadham College. Prior to this position, he was a Postdoctoral Fellow at the Paris School of Advanced Studies in Social Sciences (EHESS) and a member of the Institut de Recherche Interdisciplinaire des Enjeux Sociaux (IRIS). After finishing his BA and MA at the University of Ca' Foscari Venice, he obtained a Doctorate in Politics at the University of Oxford (St Antony's College) where he was a Wellcome Trust Scholar in Society and Ethics (2013–17). His interest falls at the crossroads of different disciplinary and intellectual fields, from medical anthropology to politics to modern social history across the Middle East and the Mediterranean. He is the editor of *Power and Illicit Drugs in the Global South* (Routledge, 2018).

Drugs Politics

Managing Disorder in the Islamic Republic of Iran

MAZIYAR GHIABI
University of Oxford

CAMBRIDGE
UNIVERSITY PRESS

University Printing House, Cambridge CB2 8BS, United Kingdom

One Liberty Plaza, 20th Floor, New York, NY 10006, USA

477 Williamstown Road, Port Melbourne, VIC 3207, Australia

314-321, 3rd Floor, Plot 3, Splendor Forum, Jasola District Centre, New Delhi - 110025, India

79 Anson Road, #06-04/06, Singapore 079906

Cambridge University Press is part of the University of Cambridge.

It furthers the University's mission by disseminating knowledge in the pursuit of education, learning and research at the highest international levels of excellence.

www.cambridge.org
Information on this title: www.cambridge.org/9781108466936
DOI: 10.1017/9781108567084

© Maziyar Ghiabi 2019

This publication is in copyright. Subject to statutory exception and to the provisions of relevant collective licensing agreements, no reproduction of any part may take place without the written permission of Cambridge University Press.

An online version of this work is published at doi.org/10.1017/9781108567084 under a Creative Commons Open Access license CC-BY-NC-ND 4.0 which permits re-use, distribution and reproduction in any medium for non-commercial purposes providing appropriate credit to the original work is given. You may not distribute derivative works without permission. To view a copy of this license, visit https://creativecommons.org/licenses/by-nc-nd/4.0

All versions of this work may contain content reproduced under license from third parties. Permission to reproduce this third-party content must be obtained from these third-parties directly.

When citing this work, please include a reference to the DOI 10.1017/9781108567084

First published 2019
First paperback edition 2021

A catalogue record for this publication is available from the British Library

Library of Congress Cataloging in Publication data
Names: Ghiabi, Maziyar, 1986– author.
Title: Drugs politics : managing disorder in the Islamic Republic of Iran / Maziyar Ghiabi.
Description: Cambridge, United Kingdom : Cambridge University Press, 2019. | Includes bibliographical references and index.
Identifiers: LCCN 2019001098 | ISBN 9781108475457 (alk. paper)
Subjects: LCSH: Drug control – Iran. | Drug abuse – Iran. | Drug abuse – Government policy – Iran.
Classification: LCC HV5840.I68 G48 2019 | DDC 362.29/15610955–dc23
LC record available at https://lccn.loc.gov/2019001098

ISBN 978-1-108-47545-7 Hardback
ISBN 978-1-108-46693-6 Paperback

Cambridge University Press has no responsibility for the persistence or accuracy of URLs for external or third-party internet websites referred to in this publication, and does not guarantee that any content on such websites is, or will remain, accurate or appropriate.

Every effort has been made to contact the relevant copyright holders for the images reproduced in this book. In the event of any error, the publisher will be pleased to make corrections in any reprints or future editions.

In memoriam Massimo Riva, javanmard, *for his love of living simply*

بود درد مو و درمانم از دوست
بود وصل مو و هجرانم از دوست
اگر قصابم از تن واکره پوست
جدا هرگز نگردد جانم از دوست

My pain and my cure is from the friend.
My closeness and my distance is from the friend.
Should the butcher peel off my skin from my body,
My soul will never depart from the friend.

Baba Taher-e Oryan

Contents

Acknowledgements	page ix
List of Figures	xiii
List of Tables	xv
Note on Transliteration	xvi
Persian Glossary	xvii
English Glossary	xix

	Prologue	1
	'Not the King but the Minister ... Not the Law but the Police ...'	3
1	The Drug Assemblage	16
	Part One	33
2	A Genealogy of Drugs Politics: Opiates under the Pahlavi	35
3	Drugs, Revolution, War	71
4	Reformism and Drugs: Formal and Informal Politics of Harm Reduction	98
	Interregnum	137
5	Crisis as an Institution: The Expediency Council	139
	Part Two	163
6	The Anthropological Mutation of Methamphetamines	165
7	The Art of Managing Disorder	189
8	Drugs and Populism: Ahmadinejad and Grassroots Authoritarianism	232

Epilogue 267
Power, Crisis, Drugs 269

Select Bibliography 289
Index 323

Acknowledgements

The Wellcome Trust provided the funding for my doctoral research under the Society & Ethics Doctoral Scholarship [Grant no. WT10988MA], which is the basis of this book. It did so within an intellectual framework and academic vision that is rare in today's funding landscape, especially for works related to Iran and the Middle East, where geopolitical interests overshadow any intellectual curiosity. Without this support, I would have not achieved my degree and this research would have not been written.

I am also grateful to the team at the *Ecole des Hautes Etudes en Sciences Sociales* and the *Institut de Recherche Interdisciplinaire en Sciences Sociales* in Paris, where I spent a beautiful eventful year as a postdoctoral fellow. Their humanistic kindness and intellectual overtures provided a stimulating, open-minded environment which made this book a less painstaking journey. I look forward to collaborating with them in the years ahead.

My fieldwork and primary research owes much to the United Nations Office on Drugs and Crime where I worked as an intern in Summer 2012. Gelareh, Setareh, Hamid-Reza Mitra, Ani, Negar and Maryam, as well as the country representative Antonino De Leo – and many others – shared with me all the contacts and information necessary to lay the ground for this research. In the addiction recovery centres, during outreach programmes and in methadone clinics, people made my daily encounters with the thorny issue of 'addiction' an enriching human experience. The many who shared their stories for the sake of my research were the engine of this whole work; without their kindness and human warmth, this work would have not been finished.

I wrote this book as a nomad: in Brussels' *Café Union* and *Bibliotheque Royale*; in Paris' *EHEES* and *SciencesPO libraries*; in Mantua, Sant'Omero and the Dolomites; in Tehran's National

Library and the *70 Qolleh* farm in Arak; and at the *Middle East Centre* in Oxford. I am grateful to the staff and workers in the libraries that enabled an ideal working environment. A special token of gratitude goes to Fariba Adelkhah for having hosted me at CERI as part of the Oxford-Sciences Po Exchange Programme in 2014/15; and to Stéphane Lacroix for having invited me to work at the Paris School of International Affairs in 2015/16 and in Menton in 2017/18.

I discussed ideas and approaches with a number of scholars who I am not exhaustively naming here: Jean-François Bayart, Beatrice Hibou, Edmund Herzig, Didier Fassin, Neil Carrier, Virginia Berridge, Michael Willis, Eugene Rogan, Alessandro Stella, Cyrus Schayegh, Roham Alvandi, Houchang Chehabi, Maasumeh Maarefvand, Rasmus Christian Eiling, Janne Bjerre Christensen (whose book inspired me many years ago), Federico Varese, Orkideh Behrouzan, Kevan Harris, Mitra Asfari, Dennis Rodgers, Jim Mills (for his advise on how to turn a thesis into a book), Isaac Campos, Walter Armbrust, Philip Robins, Marco Giacalone (who introduced me to Giorgio Agamben and Furio Jesi), Pietro Zanfrognini (the *pir-emoghan*), and many others. Matteo Legrenzi, from my former university in Venice, advised me throughout this journey and without his initial encouragement to apply at Oxford I would have never embarked on this mad plan. Simone Cristoforetti, also from Venice, shared with me part of the fieldwork time when he persuaded me to depart northward 'to capture the moment the Autumn Equinox's first light enters the Gonbad-e Kavus'. His vision is holistic. Colleagues at the Middle East Centre at St Antony's (Oxford) have been a constant support for me. Stephanie Cronin is the person who first suggested that I should apply to the Wellcome Trust and that is the genealogical origin of this book. Her intellectual guidance made my Oxford experience a most valuable one. I am truly grateful for this.

I thank Anne for her patience in reading through these pages, editing and clarifying what at times may have sounded more Latin than English. She has been a friend and a great host over these last years. My *broder* Rafa for his enthusiasm (the Greek etymology is revealing) and love for life. The chats and exchanges we had over the last seven years are at the heart of this book, together with what I learnt from his ethnographic gaze on Salvadorian gangs (and beyond). Massimiliano for his friendship and the pipe's smoke on his Venice veranda. We shall persevere in Belgrade one day soon. The farmhouse coop made up of Lupi, Fruk, Sara and Lorenzo and now Flora who cheered me up with their animal verses. Violetta for her

Acknowledgements   xi

magic of introducing new friends. Giò for making the seasonal stays in Mantua a semiotic trip. Shireen for teaching me how the internet and yoga are ethnographic fields. Minoo and Babak, and Nazila and Babak, Nazanin, Golnaz and Bahareh took care of me during my fieldwork in Tehran and I keep fond memories of these moments spent together. Kiana and Pietro for the ongoing discussions on Jalal Al-e Ahmad, Pier Paolo Pasolini, films, photography and culture across the invisible border between Italy and Iran. And the Parisian crew of 'Quartierino', *la commune de la Goutte-d'Or*.

Ideas and narratives in this book developed thanks to a number of academic encounters. Chapter 2 is inspired from a 'Global History Workshop on Pahlavi Iran' organised by Roham Alvandi at the LSE, published by Gingko Press in 2018. A modified, shorter version of Chapter 3 was awarded the Azizeh Sheibani Prize (2013) at Oxford and published in *Iranian Studies* (2015). I had the opportunity to reflect upon crisis politics and the role of the Expediency Council, discussed in Chapter 5, at a conference on the 'Implications of the Nuclear Agreement' hosted at the University of Copenhagen. Some of the materials appeared in an article published by *Middle Eastern Studies* (2019). I discussed material used in Chapter 6 in the seminar 'Consommation et Prohibition de drogue: approche transversal', organised by Alessandro Stella (CNRS) at the EHESS in Paris, and in a lecture at the London School of Hygiene and Tropical Medicine. Ideas and theories discussed in Chapter 7 emerged from a conference I organised in Oxford in Autumn 2016 on 'Drugs, Politics and Society in the Global South', which is part of the homonymous Special Issue published in *Third World Quarterly*.

But nothing has been as reassuring, gratifying and inspirational as the steady love of my family: my parents Faegheh and Gabriele, whose *mohabbat* and *forza* have been life-blood all the way through; Neli and Massimo, for a kind of love that only aunts and uncles can provide; Mahin and Habib, for being the true reason I first went back to my native country; Mammad, for our travels in villages, cities, mountains and islands and the fires and stars in Haftad Qolleh; and Ali and Afsaneh, who first convinced me that Oxford was worth the go and for being patient with my nonsense; Tara, Aryan, Dena and Yas, for we are brothers and sisters; and Carmen, Bob and Tim for their encouragement on the Abruzzo side. And in Tehran, Mohsen and Sasan, for poetic verses, anecdotes, commentaries and photos on the anthropological mutation of drugs in Iran. Altogether, their encouragement was one essential reason to give sense to an endeavour that, as time passed, shrank in meaning.

The daily existence of this book is shared with my partner Billie Jeanne. I thank her for her incommensurable patience for my highs and lows, and her perseverance of nomadism as a way of life. She is, after all, my drug of choice.

People at Cambridge University Press took care of the big and small details behind the publication: Maria Marsh, Natasha Whelan and others, as well as the copyeditor, Ursula Acton and Podhumai Anban. Without their help this book would look different and surely less scholarly. Nicola Zolin, a traveller friend, very kindly provided the cover image for the book.

The Wellcome Trust, again and finally, provided the funding to make this book open access. Good things must be shared. Errors are mine only.

Figures

2.1	Donkey Smoking Opium in a Suit	*page* 42
2.2	Hamid before Morphine (left) and after (right)	60
3.1	Awareness Campaign in Etela'at May 8, 1980	76
3.2	'War on Drugs' Martyrs (per year)	88
3.3	'War on Drugs' Martyrs	89
3.4	DCHQ Membership According to the 1988 Law	92
3.5	DCHQ Structure in the 2000s	94
3.6	Drug Prices from 1989 to 2006 (*tuman* per kg)	96
3.7	Narcotic Seizure (all type) (1987–2002) (kg)	97
4.1	Share of Narcotics as Global Seizures (1990–2001)	102
4.2	Morphine and Heroin Seizure (kg)	103
4.3	Prices of Illicit Drugs (*tuman* per kg)	104
4.4	Number of Drug-Related Deaths (1998–2006)	105
4.5	Drug-Related Crimes (1989–2005)	109
4.6	Methadone Clinics in Prisons	112
5.1	Structure of the Expediency Council	147
5.2	Policy Itinerary within the Expediency Council	150
5.3	Structure of Drug Policy Commission	155
6.1	Meanwhile in the Metro: Man Smoking *Shisheh*	177
6.2	Price of One Sut (1/10 of gram) of *shisheh*	178
6.3	Drug-Use-Related Deaths	187
7.1	Automatic Syringe, Condom Distributor, Harandi Park	218
7.2	'Every Day 8 Addict Die in Iran'	220
7.3	Members of the National Football Team	221
7.4	Marathon March, Tehran	222
7.5	'Give Me Your Hands, so We Can Walk in the Path of Purity'	223
8.1	Methadone Clinics (2009–13)	236
8.2	Methadone Maintenance Treatment Patients (2009–13)	238
8.3	Patients in Medical Facilities for 'Drug Abuse' (2013)	239
8.4	Number of People Admitted to Rehab Centres	240

8.5	Percentage of Drug Control Budget in 2014 (in millions of rials)	245
8.6	*Congress 60* Weekly Gathering in Park-e Taleqani	248
8.7	Gathering of Drug Users, Farahzad's 'Chehel Pelleh'	258
8.8	Sanitary Intervention by Outreach Programme	259
8.9	Outreach Team in Farahzad's *'Chehel Pelleh'*	260
8.10	Rhizomes and Grassroots Authoritarianism	263
E.1	Caricature of the Safe Injection Room Proposal	277
E.2	Changes in Drug Phenomenon in Iran (1800–2015)	278
E.3	Changing Regimes of Power and Treatment	279

Tables

2.1 Poppy Cultivation, Production and Consumption
     (1938–48) *page* 48
2.2 Registered Opium Addicts in the First Semester of 1974   67
3.1 Punishment According to the 1980 Drug Law   80
4.1 Opium Seizure, 1900–2001   104
6.1 Rates of Divorce in 2004–5   169
7.1 Public, Private and Illegal Camps   226
8.1 Budgetary Allocation (2014)   245
8.2 Comparison of Drug Addiction NGOs   249

Note on Transliteration

Throughout the text, I used a simplified version of the *International Journal of Middle East Studies* (Persian language) transliteration guidelines. For the *hamza* I have used ', whereas for *ayn* I have used '. I avoid diacritics and I have used the spelling of popular places as they are in use inside Iran. Names of people and place known in Western languages are translated with the most common form, e.g. Khomayni is Khomeini. For names such as 'Ali, I have dropped the ', since this is not generally pronounced in Persian. Local dialects (and slang) are transliterated as close as possible to the original pronunciation. The *ezafeh* is written as *-e* after consonants and as *-ye* after vowels and silent final *h*. The *tashdid* is transliterated by doubling the letter.

Persian Glossary

'attari	Traditional apothecary
Bangi	Hashish smoker
Basij-e Mosta'zafin	Voluntary Forces of the Disinherited
Camp (Kamp)	Rehabilitation centre
Daru	Medicine (slang for heroin)
Defa'-e Moqaddas	Sacred Defence
E'tiyad	Addiction
Estekbar-e jahani	Global Arrogance
Gart	Slang for 'heroin'
Gasht-e Esrshad	Moral police
Gharbzadegi	Occidentosis/Westoxification
Hakem-e shar'	Leading state prosecutor
Janbazan	War veterans
Jang-e Tahmili	Imposed war
Jonbesh	Movement
Kahesh-e asib/zayan	Harm reduction
Kamp	Camps (rehab camp), TC
Kerak (kerack)	Heroin-base drug, smoked and injected
Khomari	Withdrawal symptom/drunken state
Klinik	Clinic
Komiteh-ye Eslami	Islamic Committee
Komiteh-ye Mobarezeh ba AIDS	Committee to Fight against AIDS
Kopon	Coupon/voucher
Majles Shoura-ye Eslami (Majles)	National Assembly/Parliament
Majma'-e Tashkhis-e Maslahat-e Nezam	Council of the Discernment of the Expediency of the State (or Political Order)
Manqal	Brazier

xvii

Mo'tad	Addict
Mo'tadan-e Gomnam	Narcotics Anonymous (NA)
Namaz-e Jom'eh	Friday prayer
Niru-ye Amniyat-e Jomhuri-ye Eslami (NAJA)	Police
Nezam	System/state/order
Ordugah	Compulsory treatment centre
Pasdaran	Revolutionary Guards (IRGC)
Qachaq(chi)	Smuggling/(smuggler)
Qovveh Qazai'yeh	Judiciary
Sazman-e Behzisti-e Keshvar	Welfare Organisation
Sazman-e Zendan-ha-ye Keshvar	Prison Organisation
Seda va Sima	Radio and TV of the Islamic Republic
Setad	Headquarters
Shahid	Martyr
Shireh	Cooked opium residue
Shirehkesh-khaneh	Opium/*shireh* smoking den
Shisheh	Methamphetamine
Sukhteh	Opium residue (dross)
Sut	1/10 of *Shisheh*
Tajahor	Publicly intoxicated
Tarh-e jam'avari	Drug addict collection plan
Taryak(i)	Opium (opium addict)
Vafur	Opium pipe
Vaqf	Religious endowment
Velayat-e Faqih	Guardianship of the Jurist
Vezarat-e Behdasth va Darman	Ministry of Health and Treatment
Zarurat	Necessity, emergency (in Islamic Jurisprudence)

English Glossary

ATS	Amphetamine-type stimulants (e.g. ectasy, meth)
BMT	Buprenorphine maintenance treatment (aka BST)
DCHQ	Drug control headquarters (see *Setad*)
HRI (aka IHRA)	Harm Reduction International
INCAS	Iranian National Center for Addiction Studies
INCB	International Narcotics Control Board
IRGC	Islamic Revolution Guardian Corps (see *Pasdaran*)
IRIB	Islamic Republic of Iran Broadcasting (see *Seda va Sima*)
MENAHRA	Middle East and North Africa Harm Reduction Association
MMT	Methadone maintenance treatment (aka MST)
NAJA	Iranian National Police
NEP	Needle exchange programme
TC	Therapeutic communities (see *Camp*)
UNODC	United National Office on Drugs and Crime
WHO	World Health Organisation

Prologue

'Not the King but the Minister ... Not the Law but the Police ... '

It is only in the sharpest social and political crises that words, expressions, actions, and undertakings reveal their real meaning.[1]

Jalal Al-e Ahmad.

The true problem, the central mystery [*arcano*] of politics is not sovereignty, but government; it is not God, but the angel; it is not the King, but the minister; it is not the law, but the police – that is, the governmental machinery that they form and they keep moving.[2]

Giorgio Agamben

Summer 2012 was a typically turbulent period of Iranian contemporary history. President Mahmud Ahmadinejad was in the final year of his presidency, the revolts across the Arab world were matters of concern, interest and comparison in the streets and offices of Tehran, while everyone else was preparing for the European Football Cup in Poland and Ukraine. Arriving in Iran after a long first year at Oxford, I was getting ready for my first day of internship at the Tehran bureau of the United Nations Office on Drugs and Crime (UNODC). I was excited for many reasons, all of which speak rather clearly of my naiveté. Working for a UN office made me believe that perhaps once I finished my degree at Oxford, I could find employment back in Iran, or for that matter, anywhere in the world. The financial crisis that had struck Europe and the unholy competition for graduate jobs had made all of us students more desperate (including those at Oxford ...) and hopeful of the potential of an unpaid, uninsured internship at a UN office. Besides, the UNODC seemed the ideal place to start my research about drug policy; Iranian public institutions were unlikely to accept foreign-based interns at that time.

---

[1] *Safar be velayat-e Ezra'il [A journey to the land of Israel]*. (Majid, 1373 [1995]), 87.
[2] *Il Regno e la Gloria: per una Genealogia Teologica dell'Economia e del Governo: Homo Sacer, II, 2* (Bollati Boringhieri, 2009), 303.

A relative of mine, who hosted me upon my arrival, invited me after dinner to sit with him in the lounge, because he 'wanted to say a few words before my first day of work'. I took the invitation as a further sign of pride among my family at the fact that I was *working* (a euphemism for internship) at the UN. Instead, my relative's face became stern while he asked me, 'Do you know the two Iranian researchers – what was their name? – who worked on HIV programmes and were very famous here and in *Amrika*? Have you read what happened to them?' I was still a bit confused about the combination of his words and facial expression, when it came to my mind that only a year earlier, Arash Alaei, a doctor who had run a few HIV-prevention and treatment programmes in Iran, starting from the early 2000s, had been released after three years of incarceration in Tehran's Evin Prison. His brother, Kamiar, had been released the previous year. Both had been charged with collaborating with the CIA and acting against national security.

Of course, it was not the first time that I had been warned of the risks of doing research on Iran *in* Iran. Yet, I felt a shiver run up my spine and thought that maybe the fact that I was working on a difficult issue, based in a British university and a college which has had a global reputation for being, among other more scholarly things, 'a nest of spies', could have attracted understandable suspicion among the Iranian authorities.[3] Nonetheless, during the following six years of research, which included multiple visits over a cumulative period of roughly 15 months, I did not encounter any problem with the authorities, nor I was reminded formally or informally, of the red lines of fieldwork, despite having touched upon highly sensitive issues related to the politics of drugs in Iran. Perhaps not sensitive enough. A typical question from colleagues in the social sciences or Iranians in general runs, 'what did *they* [the Iranian authorities] tell you when you were *there* [Iran]? Were you interrogated about your research? Did they harass you?' Truth be told, the presence of intelligence officers and security apparatuses in the conducting of my fieldwork is remarkable by its absence, at least perceived absence. At no time was I interrogated,

---

[3] At the time, I was a student at St Antony's College, which has been accused over the last decades of being the training ground for Western intelligence. Following the 2009 elections in Iran, Mohammad Reza Jalaipour, head of Mir Hossein Musavi's electoral bureau, was accused of conspiring with foreign powers and arrested. See *The Guardian*, Friday 25, 2010, retrieved from www.theguardian.com/world/2010/jun/25/oxford-urges-iran-release-student.

nor did I ever meet people who warned me about what I was doing – apart from my family and friends. A fact, I should not hide, that triggered, in few occasions, accusations and suspicion of being a 'spy of the Islamic Republic' or an 'apologist' of the Iranian regime.

The subject that I had decided to investigate was an un(der)studied field, not only in the context of Iran but also in that of the Middle East and North Africa and, for that matter, the Islamic world.[4] The only other researcher who had paid heed to the issue of drugs, addiction and politics in Iran is Janne Bjerre Christensen, who had been expelled from the country in 2005 and not allowed back in until 2012.[5] Few researchers, especially anthropologists, had been able to work inside Iran between 2005 and 2015, especially to conduct studies of politics and the state. When the topic is discussed, often it occurs in the work of journalists, such as Ramita Navai's *City of Lies,* in which, for instance, narrative accounts take an overtly sensational turn at the expense of analysis, misleading readers towards Orientalist ideas such as the fact Iranians have a tendency to lie. This frame plays instrumentally in the geopolitical game and is very much in tune with Israeli and American rhetoric on Iran (see Bibi Netanyahu's big poster 'Iran Lies').[6] The axiom, Western countries speak truth, was never a serious assertion and less so in the aftermath of George W. Bush and Tony Blair's Weapons of Mass Destruction tirade, let alone in the era of Donald J. Trump.

On the other hand, there is an abundance of research on illicit drugs and addiction inside Iran. This body of knowledge is unfortunately dominated by epidemiological studies with narrow quantitative methods at the expense of qualitative, sociological and historical approaches. When social scientists engage in the study of illicit drugs, the tendency is to portray drugs through an ideological lens, turning them into all-encompassing

---

[4] With the exception of Philip Robins, *Middle East Drugs Bazaar: Production, Prevention and Consumption* (Hurst, 2016) and a few recent publications by myself: Maziyar Ghiabi, 'Deconstructing the Islamic Bloc: Middle East and North Africa and Pluralistic Drug Policy' in B. Stothard & A. Klein (eds.), *Collapse of the Global Order on Drugs? From UNGASS 2016 to the High Level Review 2019* (London: Esmerald Publication, 2018); and 'Drug Culture and Drug Policy across the Middle East and North Africa' in P. Gootenberg (ed.), *Oxford Handbook of Global Drugs History* (New York: Oxford University Press, 2020).

[5] Personal communication with the author.

[6] Noa Landau, 'Netanyahu: Iran Nuclear Deal is Based on Lies – Here is the Proof', *Haaretz*, April 30, 2018, retrieved August 21, 2018, from www.haaretz.com/middle-east-news/pm-expected-to-reveal-how-iran-cheated-world-on-nuke-program-1.6045300.

evils. There has not been a systematic treatment of illicit drugs from Iranian social scientists, perhaps with the exception of Said Madani's historical sociology, *Tarikh-e E'tiyad* (History of Addiction), which details the changing policies of drug control and addiction treatment from the Pahlavi monarchy up until 2005, the end of reformism. This book is currently out of print and its author sent in exile in the southern city of Bandar Abbas, for reasons unrelated to his research on addiction.

The dearth of scholarly work on illicit drugs prompted the project behind this book. With the generous support of the Wellcome Trust Doctoral Studentship in Society & Ethics at Oxford University's Department of Politics and International Relations, I was able to design a qualitatively rich and fieldwork-oriented study of drugs politics in Iran. The book uncovers the politics of illicit drugs in their historical trajectories and through ethnographic engagement. It does not deal with the object of illicit drugs as a separate dimension in modern society. Instead, it regards drugs as part of the larger state–society relations and power dynamics evolving throughout the twentieth and twenty-first centuries. Drugs are objects defining social and political life in a number of ways. People consume drugs, governments punish consumption and dealing of drugs, people seek sanitary and welfare support for drug dependencies, states intervene in facilitating, impeding or instructing public health measures on drug consumption. Drugs, hence, are part of a political game beyond the norms and regulations of drugs policy. This is what I refer to when discussing *drugs politics*.

In the case of Iran, illicit drugs are part of an underlying form of politics which assumes paradoxical outcomes. The Islamic Republic has systematically criminalised drug offenders and punished them with draconian measures, while it has also provided among the most progressive and controversial set of public health programmes (e.g. harm reduction) for drug (ab)users. Here, drugs politics works in a field of ambiguities and contradictions. In the book, these ethical contradictions and political articulations show how incongruities are essential to the maintenance and reproduction of political prerogatives, to the preservation of state interests. In doing so, the book dispels the idea of Iranian politics as a paradox and as exceptional.

Paradoxes are analytical venues for the understanding of modern politics in Iran, as elsewhere. For example, Iranian authorities, based on religious interpretation, allow and actively sponsor so-called *temporary marriages* (*sigheh* in Farsi, *mut'ah* in Arabic), while forbidding *de jure* and punishing premarital sex.⁷ In practice, this has resulted in the legalisation of prostitution and sex work, especially in sites of religious pilgrimage. But it is also used as an expedient for people willing to engage in a flexible union as for those engaged in *white marriages* (*ezdevaj-e sefid*), unmarried couples living together.⁸ Strict sexual codes and the adoption of normative sexuality intersect with the secular trends among younger generations, in defiance both of family and of state mores and norms.

Transgender identities in Iran are another apparently paradoxical situation. Since the late 1980s, the authorities have legislated in favour of gender reassignment surgery ('sex change'), legalising and providing welfare support for people who want to change gender, while denying legal status to homosexuals.⁹ In this way, the Islamic Republic has maintained an orthodox ban on same-sex desire through an unorthodox religious interpretation facilitated by the development and use of medical technology. In that respect, the status of transgender people is protected and legally safeguarded, potentially facilitating social and gender integration, while that of homosexuals remains unlawful and unrecognisable.

To these two cases, one could add the legal framework of organ donations, which in Iran operates under a legal, regulated market where individuals have the right to sell their organs to private citizens for a quantifiable amount of money. The law approved in 2000 regulates the private market of human organs in an attempt to curtail the mushrooming of the illegal organ trafficking market, as it has in other contexts such as India and other developing countries. Iran does not have a waiting list for transplant organs, especially for kidneys. Organised through public associations, under the control of the Ministry of Health, neither the transplant centre not the transplant physicians are involved in identifying potential vendors.¹⁰ Nonetheless,

---

⁷ Temporary marriage is a contractual agreement (as all marriage is according to Islamic jurisprudence) in which the two parties determine beforehand the duration of the marital bond.
⁸ Shahla Haeri, *Law of Desire: Temporary Marriage in Shi'i Iran* (Syracuse University Press, 2014).
⁹ Afsaneh Najmabadi, *Professing Selves: Transsexuality and Same-Sex Desire in Contemporary Iran* (Duke University Press, 2013). The cost of the entire process is covered by the Welfare Organisation.
¹⁰ Ahad J. Ghods and Shekoufeh Savaj, 'Iranian model of paid and regulated living-unrelated kidney donation', *Clinical Journal of the American Society of Nephrology* 1, 6 (2006).

this approach exacerbated the classist dimension of the legal organ market where economic hardship often compels individuals to resort to the sale of their organs for the benefit of wealthier people in need.

Another manifest paradox is the political structure of the Islamic Republic. The centre of gravity of this order stands in the coexistence and fluid balance between religious anointment, represented by the guidance of the Islamic jurist (in the shadow of god), with electoral representation of most major institutions. This systemic ambivalence is a rare thing in global politics and, thus, Iran seems a political exception of modernity. Uninterrupted national and local elections testify to the existence and endurance of democratic elements within the Iranian state, in spite of domestic and foreign challenges to which it had been exposed since the victory of the 1979 revolution. In this way, the political order, from a formal standpoint, adopts two diverging – incompatible – forms of legitimacy: a religious, theological one and a popular electoral one.

These are just a few examples of political paradoxes in Iran. It is no surprise, therefore, that the scholarship on Iran is also rife with references to 'paradoxes'.[11] A land of self-contradictory enigmas to which one cannot respond in a logical way, Iran's politics is regarded as being exceptional and differing from political trends as much in the West as in the East. In particular, the theocratic and republican paradox has been the object of countless academic publications, which in turn claim that the Islamic Republic is either a theocracy (and therefore implying that it is politically retrograde) or a faulty Islamic democracy, with potential of reform. Political practice is not part of the analytical picture. Scholarship of this type looks at paradoxes as opportunities for intellectual divagation and not as existing political reality. Instead of discussing modern Iranian politics and its inconsistencies as a paradox, my objective in this book has been that of dissecting this much appraised incongruence, the paradox itself, and bestowing meaning to it in the governmental practice of the state. The Iranian state cannot be explained simply by

---

[11] To mention a few: Mehrzad Boroujerdi, 'The Paradoxes of Politics in Postrevolutionary Iran' *Iran at the Crossroads* (Palgrave Macmillan, 2001); Hamid Dabashi, *Iran, the Green Movement and the USA: The Fox and the Paradox* (Zed Books, 2010); Azadeh Kian-Thiébaut, 'L'individu dans le Monde: Paradoxe de l'Iran Islamique' *Cahiers d'Etudes sur la Méditerranée Orientale et le monde Turco-Iranien*, 26 (1998); Hooman Majd, *The Ayatollah Begs to Differ: The Paradox of Modern Iran* (Anchor, 2009).

employing the metaphor of the paradox or, for that matter, that of a theocracy. Instead, the paradox has become the way power (and the state) operates, the mechanism through which it governs.

In the chapters of this book I do not argue that Iranian modernity is simply animated by paradoxes and self-contradictory phenomena, but that it is constituted by the oxymoron, and an oxymoronic dimension. The difference between these two figures of speech (paradox versus oxymoron) is capital: the etymology of 'oxymoron' indicates something that is 'sharp/pointed' (oxus) and 'dull/foolish' at the same time, as a 'wise fool', an 'eloquent silence'; in the realm of politics, the oxymoron reproduces the underlying, inescapable contradictions that animate political life and on which politics is ultimately constructed. Paradoxes, instead, remain simply a condition that defies logic and to which one cannot bestow political meaning. The examples of gender reassignment, organ donation and temporary marriage clarified situations of oxymoronic value. Oxymora are bearers of unusual meaning, which, beyond their poetic value, enable the formulation of new concepts and the opening of new intellectual avenues. In that, they hold chimeric value for they are not trusted at first glance, but make possible the overcoming of old habits, like that of getting used to words and ideas in the social sciences.

Observers often understand the harsh penalties for drug offences as a side effect of Islamic law. Indeed, following the Islamic Revolution in 1979, authorities adopted stricter rules and measures against drugs trafficking and drugs use. This strategy contributed to the militarisation of anti-narcotics, especially in the southeast region of Sistan and Baluchistan, but also in the adoption of the death penalty against drug traffickers up until 2017. However, a closer look at the history of drugs in Islam shows that Islamic law remains rather silent on the matter of narcotic drugs. Those expecting religion to be the driving force behind political decisions *vis-à-vis* illicit drugs will be disappointed. Only recently, following the appointment of clerical figures at the head of state institutions, have Islamic jurists taken a bolder, overt stance against narcotics. Even then, the clergy has often adopted a more nuanced and compromising approach on narcotic drugs compared to their civilian counterpart. Unrelenting calls for anti-drug operations comes from officials unconcerned with religious matters. For instance, once inquired about the medical and therapeutic use of substances such as cannabis, a number of Islamic jurists – often with highly influential followings – do not shy away from saying that, if scientifically proven, cannabis use is not against the rule of Islam for medical and therapeutic use.[12] This apparent paradox shows that regulation of illicit drugs does not derive from religious exegesis or persuasion, but rather from the workings of state. Religion could potentially be even a way towards reform of the current prohibitionist laws on illicit drugs. The book will not discuss the way religion treats the subject of drugs in the Islamic Republic. It avoids it with intent, for religion has little influence over the making of public policy on illicit drugs – or, for that matter, in most other fields of contemporary life. So, religion here is discussed by its absence in the thought and practice of drugs politics.

Following Gilles Deleuze's line of thought, the book does not question 'what is the nature of power', whether Iran is a theocracy, a republic or just another authoritarian state, but rather 'in what ways power is exercised, in what place it is formed and why it is everywhere'.[13] This new approach recasts the primacy of political practice over political rhetoric and formality. It privileges bottom-up analysis of social and political change as opposed to changes in political outlook and institutions. Paraphrasing Giorgio Agamben: this book is unconcerned with god and theology, but attentive to the intervention of its angels and agents; it leaves the king (or the Supreme Leader) aside and looks for the ministers; it reads the laws, but goes after the police.[14] Ethnographic observation and engagement, therefore, become a preferred method of study, instead of the classical use of discourse analysis and formal interviews. Practice over rhetoric, politics over policy, political order over the regime mean that the close-up narrative on Iran is seen transversally in light of political transformations globally.

This is a time when both illicit drugs and Iran are experiencing a surge in global interest. For the first time in a century, there is a direct challenge to the prohibitionist regime, with new models of drug regulation being discussed and proposed across the globe, the effects of which could be far-reaching in terms of social, cultural and

---

[12] Maziyar Ghiabi et al., 'Islam and Cannabis: Legalisation and Religious Debate in Iran', *International Journal of Drug Policy*, 56 (2018).

[13] Gilles Deleuze, *Due Regimi di Folli e Altri Scritti: Testi e Interviste 1975-1995* (Einaudi, 2010), 3.

[14] *Il Regno e la Gloria*, 303.

politico-economic futures.[15] The legalisation of cannabis adopted by Uruguay, Canada and a number of US States is a distinctive sign of the change in the global approach to illicit drugs to which the Iranian case is very much connected. And for the first time in several decades, in the wake of the nuclear negotiations in Vienna, Iran and the Western world are laying the hazardous ground for a broader rapprochement, an event that so far lives in the erratic environment of US president Donald Trump's foreign policy and in the regional confrontations across Eurasia and the Middle East. Regardless of the outcome of the current geopolitical earthquake, Iran is set to be a gravitational epicentre for regional and international politics, constructively or destructively. Although this book does not deal with either drug legalisation or post-nuclear-deal Iran, it pays attention to changes in Iran's drugs politics as a litmus test for larger societal and political transformations, in Iran as well as globally.

The study of drugs and politics also represents an unusual endeavour. No material product has been the object of systematic, global and unflatteringly ideological and practical interventions by the state as has illicit drugs. This has occurred with exceptional conformity, like no other global phenomenon. There is no country on the planet that has not adopted, in the last hundred years since the inception of international drug control, some sort of policy about illicit drug control. Regardless of cultural specificities or the economic and social importance of drugs (e.g. coca, opium, cannabis) states across the globe have adopted specific measures to bring under control, or to eradicate, these substances. The case of Iran, in particular, provides a paradigm of what has come to be known as the 'War on Drugs', in a political and cultural setting that has been characterised, by most of the area studies literature, by other investigations and scholarly questions. Iran, nevertheless, represents an outstanding case for the study of the War on Drugs; it is at the geopolitical crossroads of international drug routes, it has one of the world highest rates of drug 'addiction' – estimated at between 2–3 per cent and 6–7 per cent of

---

[15] Uruguay is the most significant case, but also in the USA, the case of Colorado, Washington, Oregon, California and Alaska. Similarly, Portugal has adopted a radical decriminalisation model while regulation of cannabis is being discussed in Italy, Spain and, interestingly, Iran. See *International Drug Policy Consortium*, retrieved from http://idpc.net/policy-advocacy/the-un-general-assembly-special-session-on-drugs-ungass-2016.

the entire population[16] – and it has progressively seen the rise of synthetic, industrial drugs, such as methamphetamines (*crystal meth*, aka as *shisheh*, 'glass'). Iran systematically reminds the international community that its anti-narcotics efforts are 'a price paid on behalf of the West', which would be otherwise overwhelmed by the sheer size of drug supply going westwards.[17] Because of its sheer quantitative dimension, the issue of drugs would deserve ample and in-depth scrutiny by scholars of Iran, the Middle East and the Islamic world as well as by those working on international drug policy. However, this subject of inquiry is almost absent not only from the radar of most area studies scholars, but also from those researching issues of the state and politics. Attention to Iran's role as a transit route for narcotics and the media focus on capital punishment – 80 per cent of sentences fell on drug traffickers up to 2017[18] – have obfuscated the political relevance of the drug phenomenon at a domestic level and its interaction with the transformation of Iranian politics over the past decades.

This book is divided into two Parts and an Interregnum. Diachronic narrative and synchronic analysis coexist throughout the chapters. Following this brief Prologue, I introduce the theoretical and methodological coordinates guiding the argument. The Introduction defines what I mean by 'drug assemblage' and 'apparatuses' of management of illicit drugs and what is 'addiction', where it comes from, and how it operates as a governmental category. In a cursory way, I take the opportunity to illustrate how I dealt with data in Iran, mapping the archival and ethnographic fieldwork, which, in the Iranian context, was a significant challenge for researchers.

Three historical chapters (Chapter 2, 3 and 4) constitute Part One. Chapter 2 looks at the origins of drugs politics and drug control in modern Iran, tracing the coordinates of the first drug laws in the 1900s and the modernising drugs legislation of the Pahlavi state. The fall of the Pahlavi state and the bouleversement of its drugs policy is the object of Chapter 3. The 1979 Revolution and the Iran–Iraq War determined

---

[16] *Financial Times*, January 2, 2015, retrieved from www.ft.com/cms/s/0/bcfb34ea-3e81-11e4-a620-00144feabdc0.html#axzz3VafleUT.
[17] DCHQ, 'Iran bearing heavy costs in fight against drug traffickers', retrieved from http://dchq.ir/en/index.php?option=com_content%26view=article&id=1468:iran-bearing-heavy-costs-in-fight-against-drug-traffickers-un-envoy&catid=90&Itemid=1144.
[18] *Sharq*, October 11, 2015, retrieved from http://sharghdaily.ir/News/75647.

a fundamental change in all political affairs and drugs were no exception. The chapter explores the populist call against drug trafficking and drug addiction and the way it intermingled with the war efforts during the 1980s. Chapter 4 discusses reformism and drugs. Rather than an overview of the way the reformist government of Mohammad Khatami (1997–2005) intervened *vis-à-vis* the drug assemblage, the chapter shows the way the drug crisis, both material and discursive, contributed to the adoption of reformist policies at the heart of the state. Legal reforms materialised through a coordinated engagement 'from below' among civil society agents, public officials and international consultants, and the opportunistic surfacing of an HIV/AIDS epidemic triggered by injecting drug use. The chapter demystifies the philosophical and intellectual take on reformism and shows how reforms work in practice.

Following Part One, the historical narrative leaves way to the Interregnum of Chapter 5. In this chapter, I analyse how crisis is institutionalised in the Islamic Republic and how it drives political machination. The case that I discuss is that of the Council for the Discernment of the Expediency of the State, known as Expediency Council. The chapter provides innovative accounts on how this institution has become the venue of crisis management and crisis politics in post-revolutionary Iran. It is not a coincidence that the Expediency Council is the only institution charged with the power to amend and reform drug laws, whereas all other laws are discussed and drafted in Parliament. Taken as a case study, the Expediency Council enables us to understand the micropolitics of crisis management in Iran's turbulent politics.

That is a theoretical introduction to Part Two, where I tackle Iran's contemporary drugs politics through ethnographic means. Few studies have tackled the period following 2005, and, especially 2009, through on-the-ground research. In Chapter 6, I introduce the epochal mutation characterising social and cultural life under the populist government of Mahmud Ahmadinejad. This period unveils the long-term transformation of Iranian society, a process akin to an 'anthropological mutation'. Rather than discussing this event in general terms, I privilege a situated analysis with an emphasis on consumption, psyche and sociality, visible in the manifestation of the drug phenomenon. The chapter accounts for the dramatic change in drug consumption starting from the 2000s, with the rise of *shisheh*, 'crystal meth', among large sections of society. These changes have substantial political effects, which I explain in Chapter 7. The chapter shows the logics behind governmental intervention *vis-à-vis* the new drug assemblage. The shift in popular consumption from narcotic to stimulant substances renders state-led programmes outdated and incapable of controlling the presence of drug consumers in the public space. A new governmental approach emerges, driven by 'the maintenance of disorder', a practice based on the outsourcing of drug control treatment and punishment to non-state, grassroots agents. The chapter discusses this new strategy through the paradigm of the addiction recovery 'camps', based on extensive ethnographic observation. The ethnographic narrative terminates with Chapter 8, where I engage with the role of non-governmental organisations (NGOs) and their relations to the populist government of Mahmud Ahmadinejad. The mushrooming of NGOs working on drug control and addiction recovery turned the field of civil society into a key partner of the government, especially in those terrains regarded as socially problematic. NGOs turn into 'twilight institutions': they are not the state but they exercise public authority. In this chapter, I argue that what is often labelled as authoritarianism is not necessarily the effect of a state-led ideology. There are forms of grassroots authoritarianism emerging from the work and ideas of social agents and ordinary citizens. They intervene in the social field with autonomous means, regardless of state ideology. At times, grassroots elements are the main obstacle in adopting progressive and humanitarian codes of conduct in drugs politics. These micropolitical manoeuvrings, instructed by fluid political logic, represent the art of managing disorder and governing crisis in the Islamic Republic. The Iranian case is part of a global process of contradiction and tension in which progress, change and setbacks are the outcome of infrapolitical, counterintuitive and historically rich developments.

The literature on contemporary Iran has laboured considerations of elite politics, institutional and theological/theoretical reform at the expense of studies of social and political transformation from below.[19] Nonetheless, there is an emerging trend of scholarly works attentive to the on-the-ground shifts characterising political life in contemporary Iran. Among these works, there is a symptomatic prevalence of studies based on ethnographic and historical approaches, which highlight issues related to public health, social policy and gender

[19] There are a few exceptions of course. See, for instance, the work of Asef Bayat and Fariba Adelkhah.

politics. Through the lens of public health, especially, this new scholarship has produced empirical knowledge on the way government rationalities have followed counterintuitive developments in social and political terms.[20] By discussing the phenomenology of drugs politics and addiction recovery, this book situates itself at the crossroads of these emerging debates. Its objective, rather than simply providing a historical or ethnographic narrative of the phenomenon, is to locate drugs politics within paradigms of government that have unfolded in the post-revolutionary era. This connects to broader critical issues that may be at work in political processes beyond the field of drugs.

The Iranian state has demonstrated unexpected flexibility in relation to these (and other) controversial issues, suggesting that its image as an inherently conservative, reactionary state is not only misplaced and inaccurate, but, in part, a myth. Instead, this book incites for a study of the Iranian state as a modern political machine, whose processes of formation and transformation do not necessarily differ from other, so-called liberal, and neoliberal, cases. Thus, the case of drugs politics brings Iran and the rest of the world closer, highlighting the art of managing disorder as a fundamental taxonomic imperative, which rests upon the use of crisis as a paradigm of government. The art of managing disorder, hence, comes forth as an analytical category for the interpretation of events and phenomena – for instance, corruption, security threats, immigration – which touch upon controversial and ambivalent questions across the Global South and North.

---

[20] Firoozeh Kashani-Sabet, *Conceiving Citizens: Women and the Politics of Motherhood in Iran* (Oxford University Press, 2011); Pardis Mahdavi, *Passionate Uprisings: Iran's Sexual Revolution* (Stanford University Press, 2009); Shahram Khosravi, *Young and Defiant in Tehran* (University of Pennsylvania Press, 2008). Keshavarzian, *Bazaar and State in Iran* (Cambridge University Press, 2007).

1 The Drug Assemblage

There are no rules in painting.
                    Francisco Goya, Spanish painter (1746–1828)

Introduction

In the social sciences, as in any scholarly endeavour, getting used to words is like acquiring a bad habit. And yet the necessity of adopting analytical categories remains paramount in the quest to interpret the world and, for that matter, politics. The history of the social sciences and, particularly, political science, has seen in the category of the 'state' a lasting frame of analysis, somehow bestowing on it a mythical unity and encompassing power.[1] Much of the theoretical gist of the deconstruction of the state is contained in Philip Abraham's seminal article 'Notes on the Difficulty of Studying the State'. Abrams proposes to abandon the category of state as a material object altogether and to take it as an ideological object, a 'unified symbol of an actual disunity'.[2] It is this inherently multifarious and, at the same time, amorphous feature of the state that begs for an interdisciplinary and process-oriented study of politics.

The usual object of investigation of political science, power, has been transformed by the theoretical contribution of the French philosopher Michel Foucault. Foucault's definition of power as a dynamic and omnipresent relational element contrasted starkly with the classical

---

[1] Even when other denominations have been in use; for instance, the use of the term 'political system' in Gabriel Abraham Almond and James Smoot Coleman, *The Politics of the Developing Areas* (Princeton University Press, 2015). For a thorough discussion of the developments of political science on the concept of 'state', see Timothy Mitchell, 'Society, Economy, and the State Effect' in George Steinmetz (ed.), *State/Culture: State-Formation after the Cultural Turn* (Cornell University Press, 1999).

[2] Abrams, 'Notes on The...', 75–6 and the quote in ibid., 79.

definitions of power – and the state – as legitimate source of authority. The reluctance of political science to look into other fields of the social to find the political was shaken by Foucault's methodological and theoretical invitation *to read everything*. Indeed, Foucault proceeded over the emergence of a study of politics (often not carried out by political scientists) that sought after the political in *topoi* traditionally prefigured as non-political.[3] The prison, the clinic, the school and the barracks became institutions entrenched with political value, and marginal categories – the 'dangerous class,' or the lumpenproletariat of Karl Marx – entered the scene of analysis. This *modus operandi* was not simply explicatory, to use Foucault's phraseology, of the mechanics of power and of the micropolitics of modern societies; its objective was to unearth more general and systemic questions around the state, government and power.

The study of political processes can only be accurate if taken through a historical lens, which captures the movements (however rhapsodic and multi-directional) of different events in time. In other words, genealogy is key to understanding politics and its changes. In genealogical quests, the flow of events may appear as a history of incongruity and discontinuity; it might manifest 'hazardous and broken trajectories' proceeding towards what Foucault labelled 'a barbarous and shameful confusion'.[4] Yet, it is a close-up analysis of how politics works as a productive force. In our case, it is a genealogy of drugs politics in Iran and its entanglement with crisis and state formation. In that, the narrative falls parallel with Foucault's invitation to take social, medical and cultural objects as political facts. That is also the case for drugs.

The American political scientist Paul Brass refers to the impact of Foucault's theories on the study of politics – and the discipline of political science – with his self-explicatory article 'Foucault Steals Political Science'. While most of the discipline has persevered in applying exogenous categories of analysis in order to re-enhance the taxonomic difference between Western states and the rest of the world, Foucault argued that, no matter the forms authority metamorphosed into, modern states share the trait of being 'police states', or in other

---

[3] Brass, 'Foucault Steals Political Science', *Annual Review of Political Science* 3, 1 (2000), 328.
[4] Mitchell Dean and Kaspar Villadsen, *State Phobia and Civil Society: The Political Legacy of Michel Foucault* (Stanford University Press, 2016), 65.

words, governmental machines of disciplinary mechanisms.[5] Although one should be aware of Hannah Arendt's warning that whatever the similarities between totalitarian (or, I dare add, authoritarian) regimes and democracies, their differences remain essential; the depiction of authoritarian states as more or less powerful unitary actors oversimplifies the complexities of processes of political formation. This reduction to a single all-powerful element within the realm of formal politics – the state – or, more recently with the rise of rational choice theory, the transformation into numerical data and statistics of any other material sign of power, has confined the study of multifaceted political phenomena to other disciplines of the social sciences, *in primis* political anthropology and political sociology.[6] Not particularly concerned with what disciplinary affiliation this research carries on board, this book discusses drugs through the lens of politics, of state formation and crisis intervention. Drugs as an ideological object remain ultimately tied to political formulations.

The life and history of illicit drugs is symbiotic with that of states. A weakening, a retreat, a dilution of the state is often announced in favour of the emergence of other international, or localised sub-state, forces. The withdrawal of the state manifests, instead, what Beatrice Hibou defined as a form of indirect government, or 'government at a distance', whereby processes of privatisation, delegation, outsourcing and devolution of state power are intended not to diminish, but to enhance political control at the expense of other terrains of state intervention, such as welfare, education, health, development and participation.[7] In this regard, neoliberal forms of bureaucratisation are not fixed, or clearly defined types of administration, but they are 'a point of entry, a microcosm ... around which and within which are played battles for power, [and] are expressed conflicts of legitimacy'.[8] State forms otherwise inconsistent with each other seem to represent similar modes of government when taken from the perspective of

[5] Ibid., 317.
[6] See Billie Jeanne Brownlee and Maziyar Ghiabi, 'Passive, Silent and Revolutionary: The "Arab Spring" Revisited', *Middle East Critique* 25, 3 (2016).
[7] Béatrice Hibou, *Privatizing the State* (Columbia University Press, 2004), 15–16. Cf. Renate Bridenthal, *The Hidden History of Crime, Corruption, and States* (Berghahn Books, 2013), 238.
[8] Béatrice Hibou, 'Introduction. La Bureaucratisation Néolibérale, Ou La Domination Et Le Redéploiement De L'état Dans Le Monde Contemporain' in *La Bureaucratisation Néolibérale* (La Découverte, 2013), 11.

practice, policy and grassroots political developments. That applies also to drugs politics.

Policy analysis, generally, has been understood as 'a quasi-scientific activity that requires a clinical approach'. Given that, the category of policy has not been interpreted as a political, ideological or hegemonic project, but rather as objects proclaimed in 'neutral, legal-rational idioms [which] appear to be mere instruments for promoting efficiency and effectiveness'.[9] Borrowing Steinmetz's definition, I refer to 'policy' as

cultural texts, as classificatory devices with various meanings, as narratives that serve to justify or condemn the present, or as rhetorical devices and discursive formations that function to empower some people and silence others ... [as] fundamental organizing principles of society, [which] contain implicit (and sometimes explicit) models of society.[10]

Policies are practices of government that work both along formal institutional lines – for instance, through the mediation and operations of public institutions – and along informal, societal repertoires – such as personal, clandestine connections and everyday public rhetoric.[11] They are a powerful illustration of how power intervenes and bear ideological and symbolic value. The coherence, effectiveness and, in Foucauldian parlance, disciplinary power of these political technologies (read 'policies') should not overstate the state's capacity to shape the social. Policies are the outcome of multiple scripts, inputs and lines of resistance: they can be produced through pressures from below – in spite of institutional resilience to change – by public officials, academics, NGO activists as well as a multitude of ordinary people.[12]

Health crises, of which drug crises are part, have been moments 'for the reconfiguration of the role of the liberal [and, I suggest, non-liberal] state'.[13] The concept of 'crisis' is key in framing political initiatives in terms of policymaking as much as in terms of practical intervention.

---

[9] Cris Shore and Susan Wright, *Anthropology of Policy: Perspectives on Governance and Power* (Routledge, 2003), 7.
[10] George Steinmetz, *State/Culture: State-Formation after the Cultural Turn* (Cornell University Press, 1999), 6.
[11] Javier Auyero, 'Introductory Note to Politics under the Microscope: Special Issue on Political Ethnography', *Qualitative Sociology* 29, 3 (2006), 4–6.
[12] Cf. Asef Bayat, *Life as Politics: How Ordinary People Change the Middle East* (Stanford University Press, 2013); Adam White, *The Everyday Life of the State: A State-in-Society Approach* (University of Washington Press, 2013), 16.
[13] Jon E. Zibbell, 'Can the Lunatics Actually Take over the Asylum?: Reconfiguring Subjectivity and Neo-Liberal Governance in Contemporary

Crises operate in such a way that allow societal forces to push for change in certain fields, where governments have previously been unwilling or reluctant to intervene. Thence, how does politics diagnose a crisis? And how are social groups, especially marginal ones, treated by political institutions when they are under (invented or material) conditions of crisis? The Italian philosopher Giorgio Agamben argues that in contemporary governance the use of 'emergency' is no longer provisional, but 'constitutes a permanent technology of government', and has produced the non-juridical notion of crisis.[14] It is the engendering of 'zones of indistinction' between the law and its practice to which Agamben applies the notion of the 'state of exception'. In the words of the author himself,

> [the state of exception] defines a 'state of the law' in which, on the one hand, the norm is in force [*vige*] but is not applied (it has no 'force' [*forza*]) and, on the other, acts that do not have the value [*valore*] of law acquire its 'force'.[15]

The prognosis of crisis is rooted in the modern conceptualisation of politics and the political;[16] and because crisis operates as a narrative device regulating the framing of the present (or of history), it functions also as an analytical category, a prism of understanding of complex phenomena throughout historical progress. It is therefore a central interpretative category for studying state formation and state–society relations, in the West as much as globally.

Apparatuses (*dispositifs*) are a key dimension of crisis politics and crisis management. Social service organisations, medical personnel, gangs, charity workers and volunteers, as well as ideological machine and media tools, all embody different forms of apparatuses.[17] According to the definition, apparatus is a 'device of population control and economic management composed of disparate elements that coalesce in particular historical conjectures, usually moments identified as "crises"', composed of 'discourses, institutions, architectural arrangements, policy decisions, laws, administrative measures, scientific statements, moral and philosophical

---

British Drug Treatment Policy', *International Journal of Drug Policy* 15, 1 (2004), 56.
[14] Giorgio Agamben, 'For a Theory of Destituent Power', *Kronos* (2013).
[15] *Stato Di Eccezione* (Torino: Bollati Boringhieri, 2003), 38.
[16] Janet Roitman, *Anti-Crisis* (Duke University Press, 2013), 22.
[17] See Michel Foucault, 'Il Faut Défendre La Société'. *Cours Au Collège De France*, 1976 (1997).

propositions'.[18] Seen as such, crisis and apparatus live in a symbiotic relation. Crisis justifies the existence of apparatuses, whereas apparatuses give shape to the perception and materialisation of crisis.

This brings us to the subject matter of this book: Because the framing of the 'drug problem' has rhetorically and materially produced and reproduced multiple lines of crises – health, social, ethical and political – both globally and locally, an array of different, and often apparently incoherent, apparatuses have emerged over the course of a hundred years.[19] I shall now consider some of these apparatuses.

Apparatuses: Addiction, Treatment, Harm Reduction

It is an unattainable task to arrive at a definition of 'drug' in today's parlance. Linguistic references are ambiguous and refer to multiple *things* at the same time; or, perhaps, language is precise enough and the problem lies in the politics of definitions. After all, 'drug' in the English language refers to a large variety of 'substances', which have, or might not have, therapeutic, alimentary or other psychophysical effects. The use of adjectives such as 'narcotic', 'stimulant', 'illicit' or 'psychoactive' is intended to clarify the ethereal nature of words such as drugs and substance. The words drugs and substances can only be temporarily discharged of their ambiguity with the use of an attribute: illicit or illegal. That confirms to us that the nature of drugs in modern societies is inherently political, for drugs are tied to a political classification enunciated through legal means: the prohibitionist regime.

Despite the recent debates about changes in the global policy on illicit drugs – exemplified by cannabis legalisation in Canada, a number of US States, and Uruguay – most of the world's states adopt rules and regulations which prohibit, limit and outlaw a rather uniform set of

---

[18] Gregory Feldman, 'Illuminating the Apparatus: Steps toward a Nonlocal Ethnography of Global Governance' in *Policy World*, 34.
[19] For a journalistic account of drug crises in the West over the last century, see Johann Hari, *Chasing the Scream: The First and Last Days of the War on Drugs* (Bloomsbury Publishing, 2015). For an intellectual analysis of Western drug prohibitions, see David Musto, *The American Disease: Origins of Narcotic Control* (Oxford University Press, 1999); David Courtwright, *Forces of Habit* (Harvard University Press, 2009).

substances.[20] These, to be brief, include, narcotic drugs such as opiates (opium, heroin), cannabis (marijuana, weed, hashish) as well as amphetamine-type stimulants (ATS: ecstasy, MDMA ...), hallucinogens (LSD, 'magic mushrooms' ...) and a set of pharmaceutical products considered controlled substances (methadone, morphine, Ritalin, etc.).

When one studies drugs politics, it becomes inevitable to define a key question about drugs: addiction. It is often considered as a chronic disease by the medical community, which has bolstered this reading within the policymaking community.[21] However, one could argue, along with Toby Seddon, that addiction is de facto a governmental concept, whose historical roots cannot be traced beyond two hundred years ago.[22] As a governmental concept, addiction has been instrumental in defining limits of morality regarding public and private behaviour. Individuals develop neurotic, chronic relationships with such different things as food, sex, gambling, internet shopping and any other material or immaterial object.

Drug addiction is a definition with a public life – but weak scientific legitimacy. Public authorities, NGOs, medical and welfare workers use it to refer to a broad spectrum of human situations. I refer interchangeably to this definition of addiction as drug (ab)use. By using the idiom (ab)use, I want to suggest the malleability of the concept of addiction, which is both dynamic and ambiguous. It is a practice deemed problematic, but the boundaries of which are not clearly defined and, as such, leave room for interpretation of what is addiction. Although it is beyond the scope of this book to treat the issues around the definitions of addiction, I invite a look at addiction as a total social fact – *un fait social total*, as Marcell Mauss would say – that echoes through the legal, economic, religious and individual fabric of life.[23]

---

[20] See LSE Ideas, 'Ending the Drug Wars: Report of the LSE Expert Group on the Economics of Drug Policy' (May 2014), retrieved from www.lse.ac.uk/IDEAS/Projects/IDPP/The-Expert-Group-on-the-Economics-of-Drug-Policy.aspx.

[21] Addiction has been a term in use for several decades, preceded by 'habit' and followed by 'dependence' or 'drug dependence'. See Virginia Berridge and Alex Mold, *Concepts of Addictive Substances and Behaviours across Time and Place* (Oxford University Press, 2016).

[22] Toby Seddon, *A History of Drugs: Drugs and Freedom in the Liberal Age* (Routledge, 2009), 27–8.

[23] See Marcel Mauss. 'Essai sur le don forme et raison de l'échange dans les sociétés archaïques.' *L'Année sociologique (1896/1897–1924/1925)* 1 (1923): 30–186.

When faced with growing complexities of social facts, states react through forms of governmentalisation. Seen through phenomenological forms, by *seeing like a state*, drugs (ab)use affects and is affected by political transformation.[24] How do governments *treat* drug (ab)use? And what does this treatment signify in political terms?

Multiple apparatuses partake in the drug assemblage made of consumption, treatment and punishment. Methadone is a device that illustrates the many dimensions of the assemblage. A synthetic drug first produced in late-1930s Germany, methadone is a substance that mirrors the effect of opiates. Included by the World Health Organisation in the List of Essential Medicines, methadone is a cost-effective substitute of opium, morphine and heroin. For this reason, it is administered in clinics or through other medical facilities, under so-called methadone maintenance treatments (MMT). These programmes administer methadone as a substitute substance to drug (ab)users over a prolonged period, sometimes indefinitely. The introduction of methadone into the technologies of treatment remains nonetheless contested, for methadone induces a strong dependency in the patients. For the medical community, it is considered a pharmaceutical product, a medicine and it is prescribed as such in case of opiate dependency. Among law enforcement agencies (LEAs), however, it has been widely considered as an illegal substance and, indeed, methadone is currently scheduled as a 'narcotic drug' under the Single Convention of Narcotic Drugs (1961), the modern regulatory base of international drug control.[25] Civil society groups supporting abstinence-based treatment (aka 'cold turkey') – the most famous being *Narcotics Anonymous* – cast it as a drug both dangerous and unethical, as do many religious groups that do not make distinction between methadone and other narcotics.[26] An increasing number of drug (ab)users consume methadone as their primary intoxicant drug, buying it in the illegal market. Supporters of MMT argue that its benefits outdo its harms: by substituting dangerous drugs, such as opium and heroin, with a legal, prescription drug, methadone produces a positive change in drug (ab)users. Yet rather than causing a positive transformation in the medical condition of the drug (ab)user,

---

[24] See James Scott, *Seeing like a State: How Certain Schemes to Improve the Human Condition have Failed* (Yale University Press, 1999).
[25] See 'Methadone and Buprenorphine and International Drug Control Conventions', retrieved from www.ncbi.nlm.nih.gov/books/NBK143176/.
[26] Philippe Bourgois and Jeffrey Schonberg, *Righteous Dopefiend* (University of California Press, 2009), 284.

methadone prevents the subject from entering the world of illegality, with all its obvious harms, the most remarkable of all being, perhaps, the threat of the police and the prison. In fact, its pharmacological effects are similar to heroin and morphine, as is its addictive (dependence inducing) nature. But the normalising effect, the power to transform unruly individuals into 'docile bodies', accounts for methadone's status as a privileged technology of government, beside its cost-effectiveness given that methadone remains a relatively inexpensive product. Often labelled as 'liquid handcuffs', methadone treatment produces immediate biopolitical effects on its target subjects. By stopping the cravings for narcotic drugs and hooking the patient onto a controlled substance, methadone produces stability and legibility within the disorderly community of drug (ab)users. One should not avoid saying that, for injecting drug users, methadone treatment can prevent the risk of intravenous infectious diseases, notably HIV/AIDS and hepatitis caused by shared needles and paraphernalia. That said, methadone is an apparatus, a technology of government, political in nature and medical in its unwrapping, with underlying political effects. In the words of anthropologist Philippe Bourgois, methadone is 'a pernicious and intense exercise of biopower, an attempt by a hostile state' – which after all condemns the use of narcotic drugs – 'to control unruly misuse of pleasure' and to 'reform unproductive bodies'.[27]

But methadone is not the only device in the drug assemblage. Drug policy in general, and treatment technologies in particular, are updated with changing paradigms of government. This does not imply that previously accepted treatment forms are substituted by new models amid political change; more often, it implies a coexistence of multiple forms of treatment technologies that apply at different times, to different political contexts and for different purposes. Coexistence of multiple techniques is the key to the state objective of management of risk. Harm reduction is a case in point. A set of 'policies, programmes and practices that aim to reduce the harms associated with the use of psychoactive drugs in people unable or unwilling to stop', harm reduction's defining features 'are the focus on the prevention of harm, rather than on the prevention of drug use itself, and the focus on people who continue to use drugs'.[28] The provision of clean needles and injection paraphernalia – known also as Needle

---

[27] Bourgois cited in Helen Keane, 'Foucault on Methadone: Beyond Biopower', *International Journal of Drug Policy* 20, 5 (2009), 450.
[28] See HRI website at www.hri.global.

Exchange Programmes (NEPs) – as well as condoms, account for the main, but not exclusive, practices of harm reduction. A highly controversial practice, harm reduction has faced great obstacles since the start of its journey as a public policy approach to drug consumption. Conceived in the 1980s, amidst the HIV epidemic that had struck Europe and North America, harm reduction called for a pragmatic understanding of the public health and welfare challenges represented by people using drugs. Over the years, harm reduction encompassed different ideological strands, which turned it into a spectrum of ideas rather than a clear public policy plan. It included radical harm reduction activism which called for toppling down the prohibition, law enforcement regime against drug users – therefore guaranteeing their rights to safe and protected drug consumption – to state-led forms of harm reduction, which coexist with clearly punitive drug policy. Despite this inconsistency, harm reduction policies have been introduced as a legitimate public policy approach by an increasing number of countries. Initially in Western and Northern Europe, the discourse of harm reduction is currently discussed and considered as a viable policy on drug consumption in several MENA countries. Harm reduction, thus, turns into an apparatus of management of drugs crisis which coexists with apparently incompatible forms of drug control, such as incarceration, police control, forced treatment and prohibition of drug consumption. The Islamic Republic of Iran is among the countries implementing one of the most comprehensive harm reduction strategies at a global level, as explored in Part Two of this book.

Despite harm reduction's prominence in the public debate around illegal drugs, the most widespread approach to treatment of drug (ab)use remains that of 'therapeutic communities' (TCs), which in the context of Iran, are called addiction rehab camps, or simply *kamp*. Developed in the early 1950s in the United States, this model of treatment reached global diffusion in a matter of decades and today more than sixty-five countries operate TCs. These are centres where people with substance abuse issues refer to kick their habit and find psychological and physiological stability. The spectrum of different activities and philosophies of treatment is great, but detoxification through peer-to-peer support is its defining trait. Based on a democratic, grassroots and participative model of self-help, one of the basic tenets of these communities was the refusal to accept that people with substance-use disorders (addicts – but also, generally, heterodox social categories) need to be institutionalised in formal, hierarchical centres.[29] The TC method is not uncontroversial. Their ideology espouses strict prohibition. At times, TCs appropriated the violence of state prohibition onto their own treatment of drug (ab)use. Their target continues to be marginal and impoverished individuals, the condition of which is never understood in political, social or economic terms, but exclusively through the prism of their medical(ised) condition, addiction. In Chapter 7, I provide an ethnographic analysis of how these centres work and how they reproduce a grassroots government of the drug crisis that is in tune with state interests.

Dealing with Data: Allegories, Disorders, Methods

Apparatuses work on multiple levels, in the micropolitical dimension as much as in the realm of discourse and ideology. The study of the drug assemblage – and its many apparatuses – demands careful methodological consideration. Methods must uncover how the machine of politics intervenes, in praxis, on illegal drugs. To do so means to subordinate the methods to the questions being studied. The hermeneutic approach I adopted instructed that all situations are complex, but complexities can be dissected and re-ordered through an inductive approach, echoing the multi-vocal dimension of politics.[30]

To start with, I had to make sense of the dissonant statistics, which populated the world of drugs policy. In Iran, statistics as such did not explain the transformation of the drug phenomenon. They remained both static and monolithic, an image of the state itself in its outer mask. After all, it is telling that the official number of drug addicts (*mo'tadan*) since the 1979 Revolution up to 2017 had been, unchangeably, 1.2 million, despite the doubling of the country's population, from roughly forty million to eighty in 2016, and the appearance of new drugs and drug cultures. In 2017, *ex abrupto*, the Drug Control Headquarters (DCHQ), the umbrella organisation on all illicit drug matters, announced that the number of addicts had reached 2.8 million

---

[29] NIDA, 'What Is a Therapeutic Community', retrieved from www.drugabuse.gov/publications/research-reports/therapeutic-communities/what-therapeutic-communitys-approach; and Angela Garcia, *The Pastoral Clinic: Addiction and Dispossession along the Rio Grande* (University of California Press, 2010).

[30] White, *The Everyday Life*, vii.

people.[31] Before then, state officials themselves had repeatedly and insistently declared that the number of drug addicts was 'going up' every year.[32] It is clear that the numbers do not hold water in this realm.

I situated the statistics and the discourses that emerged from public institutions within a puzzle – the assemblage, one might say – which I then followed throughout my fieldwork. Javier Auyero suggests, 'scientific objects are conquered in the field' and often by identifying, tracing and following 'puzzles, enigmas and paradoxes'.[33] In the case of Iran, the enigma was the political effect of drugs over the process of (trans)formation of the state after the 1979 revolution. Consequently, this generated a *state effect* on the phenomenon of drugs. For instance, how did an Islamic Republic secularise its fight against drugs and drug (ab)use? And how did it legitimate and promote controversial programmes of harm reduction (such as needle exchange in prisons and methadone substitution) on a national scale? How can this paradox be followed in the field, given agency, image and voice? What does drugs politics reveal about government and power?

The paradox as such is not a sufficient metaphor, because it does not explain a 'situation'. That is why I refer throughout the book to another figure of speech to cast light on the case: the oxymoron. The juxtaposition of otherwise apparently (and allegedly) incongruent elements can be explained by the acceptance that reality has (and perhaps must have) an oxymoronic dimension. I observed and studied the subject in the form of an allegory, 'the art of meaning something other and more than what is being said'.[34] In fact, where information is controlled and confined or distorted – as in Iran and on Iran and, if there was any doubt, in light of recent revelations of media distortion (e.g. Facebook), also in the West – allegory becomes a prime form of expression and materialisation of events that would otherwise not be

---

[31] BBC, June 25, 2017, retrieved from www.bbc.co.uk/news/world-middle-east-40397727.
[32] For instance, *Hamshahri*, June 23, 2015, retrieved from www.hamshahrionline.ir/details/298952/Society/socialnews.
[33] Javier Auyero, 'Ethnography at the Margins: Warrants, Puzzles and Narrative Strategies', Latin American Centre Weekly Seminar, St Antony's College, Oxford, November 27, 2016. George E. Marcus, 'Ethnography in/of the World System: The Emergence of Multi-Sited Ethnography' *Annual Review of Anthropology* (1995), 109-10.
[34] Law, *After Method*, 88.

coherent.³⁵ In this way, I describe and situate how, for instance, the Iranian state could apply severe punishment towards drug (ab)use but at the same time accept a comprehensive system of welfare and public health support for drug (ab)users. This line of inquiry conducted to the art of *managing disorder*. To understand how to manage disorder instead of disposing order, one needs to tackle a condition that is sharp and foolish at the same – an oxymoron – the image aptly fitting the situation through which the drug war in Iran – and differently elsewhere – is reproduced.

From a practical point of view, I adopted a variety of methodological tools in carrying out this project. One of the most conventional ways of expanding research data is that of interviewing stakeholders. I decided to do so, aware, however, of the limits that the Iranian political context put in front of researchers. Government officials need their superiors' approval before any declaration to a national or foreign researcher. It also did not seem the best strategy on qualitative grounds; public officials and state representatives have a bureaucratic tendency to reproduce the official position of the state, about which I was all too aware given also my rich archive of public declarations in the newspapers. To gain fresh insight from state representatives I needed to be accepted as a member of the drug policy community – an endeavour that fell naturally in my academic profile. My connection with the UNODC proved instrumental. As an intern at the office in Tehran, I participated in meetings with many officials from the various ministries, the DCHQ, NGO workers and medical advisors. As a prohibitionist organisation, the UNODC has enjoyed positive relations, compared to other international agencies, with the Iranian government, a fact that helped my integration into the drug policy community. As an Oxford doctoral student, I was received with respect and my views were taken more seriously than I probably deserved. Between 2013 and 2017, I participated in drug policy conferences in Tehran (Addiction Science Conferences), Beirut (MENAHRA conferences), Bogotá and Rome (ISSDP Conferences) where many of Iran's drug policy scholars and policymakers took part. By that time, I was an active member of this

---

³⁵ Allegory is a central device in Iranian cinema. See, for instance, Michelle Langford, 'Allegory and the Aesthetics of Becoming-Woman in Marziyeh Meshkini's *The Day I Became a Woman*,' *Camera Obscura* 22, 1 64 (2007); Negar Mottahedeh, *Displaced Allegories: Post-Revolutionary Iranian Cinema* (Duke University Press, 2008).

community, I was included in the selective mailing list and newsletters, including the social media venues (i.e. Telegram app) in which issues where often debated. In other words, I developed a certain familiarity with the people who I wanted to interview, a fact that I believe positively shaped the exchange of information.

The core of my personal archive for this research, however, is represented by a collection of newspaper articles, reports, official documents, unpublished material and images dating between 1978 and 2015. It also includes around three thousand articles in Persian from leading national newspapers (*Iran, Kayhan, Resalat, Jomhuri-ye Eslami, Etela'at, Jam-e Jam, E'temad-e Melli, Sharq*, but less systematically also others) published in Iran over that period.[36] I capitalised on a peculiarity of the Iranian press: newspapers have a tendency to report direct quotes and declarations of political agents, experts, civil society groups and representatives of the government; at times, a dialogue becomes visible between diverging views that can be read through the press, in different locations. Not only does this feature enable us to *follow the allegory* of the drug phenomenon in the public discourse, it also facilitates the ethnographic use of newspapers, especially when political debates are grounded in state intervention in the field. Content analysis and deconstruction were central in this process.

Familiarity with the UNDOC office put me in a privileged position in finding technical material on drug policy programmes implemented or discussed in Iran between 1999 and 2015. I had the opportunity to read internal reports, unpublished and published statistics, and communications between the Iranian ministries, the DCHQ and the UN office as well as international reports. The publications of the DCHQ also proved an important source for data on policy implementation, as well as a rich and readily available collection of proposals, views and ideas about drug policy.

As I was conducting fieldwork in Iran, I learnt and tuned my skills as an ethnographic observer/participant, educating myself in the arts of

---

[36] *Iran* is the official daily newspaper of the government of Iran and is owned by the Iran News Agency (IRNA), the *Pravda* of the Islamic Republic. Yet it has been closed at least a couple of times in the last fifteen years, due to court rulings. *Kayhan, Resalat, Etela'at* and *Jomhuri-ye Eslami* are conservative newspapers in decreasing order; *Jam-e Jam, E'temad-e Melli* and *Sharq* are reformist-oriented, in increasing order.

immersion, mimesis, and 'thick description' in/of the field.[37] I convinced myself that I had reached an acceptable level of ethnographic immersion, when, while visiting a drop-in centre (DIC: a centre which provides low-threshold support to drug users) in southern Tehran, the psychologist with whom I had spoken on the phone mistook me for a homeless drug user and started interrogating me with the ordinary questions, in a dismissive tone. I found myself in the position for long enough to be immersed in the role I was mistakenly given – thus gaining original insight in what it means to be a drug user in that part of the city – before taking out my business card with the Oxford logo and handing it to the very embarrassed doctor. Mimesis and immersion can be of great value – and reward – in the field.

In my ethnographic fieldwork, which focused on the presence/latency of the state rather than individual subjects, I visited and worked in multiple sites, as opposed to the traditional ethnographic experience that tends to restrain the research to a community, a village, or a setting. Political ethnographies, in fact, need to be multi-sited for the simple reason that politics has no clear boundaries and the processes that produce the political are often not confined to an office, a ministry, a group of individuals or a certain geographical area. They are uncontained and uncontainable. Conference venues have been a surprisingly telling site of observation and participation of ethnographic narratives. There, given the participation of officials of the state, civil society groups, activists, medical experts and advisors, as well as international guests and organisations, I followed the people and the allegory of 'drugs/addiction' in the public display of opinions among speakers.

More narrowly ethnographic was my experience as observer/participant in therapeutic communities (TCs), generally referred to in Persian as *camp*. They number in the thousands and did not allow me a systematic coverage. Nonetheless, I attempted to visit as many as I could, multiple times, and to be attentive to the different type, geographical location and gender. Overall, I personally visited fifteen camps. As for female treatment camps, they represented a harder site of fieldwork as access is often denied or restricted to female visitors. Yet, I had the opportunity to access a female treatment camp half a dozen

---

[37] Clifford Geertz, 'Thick Description: Toward an Interpretive Theory of Culture'. *The Interpretation of Cultures* (1973), 3–30.

times. Although this represents a single case, I made sure to compare the observations that I had in the female camp with that of other sources, including newspapers, reports, and accounts of women who have been interned in other camps.

Conclusions

This Introduction is an analytical compass to aid in reading the book. Here, I situated interpretative categories such as oxymoron, assemblage, crisis, state formation, drugs, addiction and harm reduction. I also provided a synthetic description of the means I used to carry out fieldwork in Iran and on the ways research was done on the sensitive subject of drugs (ab)use. History and ethnography were two guiding tools in deconstructing drugs politics and its 'crisis' in modern Iran. A set of questions guided the discussion: what is the effect of crisis on the (Iranian) state and its formation? And how does crisis operate throughout different regimes of power and in different political environments? How to study politics in practice rather than on formal grounds?

The book assesses the potential of crisis as an idiom (and time) for reform. Crisis, it seems, produces responses that can be understood and explored in the form of assemblage. By deconstructing the drug phenomenon into its multiple parts – repression, treatment and make-believe worlds – the book discusses the way power and politics went through remarkable and unexpected transformations amidst crises. The case in point is limited, but at the same time, is one that falls at the crossroads of key institutional and societal axes. Drugs as epiphenomenon of state-society unfold the challenges that government and political orders face when the crisis acquires multiple faces – medical, ethical, security and social – in that the drug crisis remains an ultimately political fact, whereby all responses are produced, *in nuce*, through a political scheme.

While countries bolstering a secular, technically oriented paradigm of government, such as the United States, Russia and China, have regularly adopted a moralising – even religious – approach to drug policymaking, the clerical and political establishment in the Islamic Republic of Iran has felt at ease with the scientific, medical and technical lexicon of drug policy. Both can be affiliated to two diverging aspects of contemporary governmentality, often labelled as neoliberal: the increasing religious, moralising approach to social questions (e.g.

Pentecostalism in the United States; Christian Orthodoxy in Russia) and the dominance of technical experts and knowledge on social *problematiques*, as in the case of Iran.[38]

A fundamental demystification needs to be done regarding the study of drugs politics. Dominated by a highly ideological and distorted debate, drugs are used as a public enemy to discredit opponents or to indicate something standing outside all moral boundaries. Ironically, the subject of drugs shares its status of anathema – especially in the West – with that of the Islamic Republic of Iran. It is telling that both drugs and Iran have been labelled as evils against which the righteous should move in combat. At a time of epochal changes in international drug policy and Iran's place in the world (dis)order, this double demystification, I believe, is a worthwhile endeavour.

The failure of security responses to the drug problem – across the globe – has become an unshakable datum among scholars of drug policy. Toby Seddon points out that 'it is very difficult to study drug policy for any length of time without coming to the conclusion eventually that the prohibition paradigm is fatally flawed'.[39] It is with this in mind that one can say the study of politics has become such that no scholar who studies it for any length of time can deny that the discipline craves for an interdisciplinary, fieldwork-oriented engagement, and is in search of *topoi* that have hitherto been regarded as the turf of others, lest it be complacent and complicit with the current *state* of affairs.[40] It seems that in research, as sometimes in everyday life, trespassing is key to any advancement.[41]

---

[38] Cf. Jarrett Zigon, *'HIV Is God's Blessing': Rehabilitating Morality in Neoliberal Russia* (University of California Press, 2010).

[39] Seddon, *A History*, 102.

[40] For a philosophical digression on how to reconstruct political understandings, see Gilles Deleuze and Félix Guattari, *Mille Plateaux: Capitalisme et Schizophrénie* (Paris: Minuit, 1980), 5–7.

[41] Cf. Pierre Bourdieu and Loïc Wacquant, *An Invitation to Reflexive Sociology* (University of Chicago Press, 1992).

Part One

2 | *A Genealogy of Drugs Politics: Opiates under the Pahlavi*

Prohibition [of opium] was motivated by prestige reasons. At a time of modernization, which in most developing countries means imitation of Western models, the use of opium was considered a shameful hangover of a dark Oriental past. It did not fit with the image of an awakening, Westernizing Iran that the Shah was creating.[1]

Jahan Saleh (Iran's Ministry of Health in 1955)

Introduction

What does the history of drugs consumption tells us of the life and place of Iranians in the modern world?[2]

Narcotics, themselves a quintessential global commodity, figured prominently in the history of Iran. It all started with opium in ancient times. Panacea painkiller, lucrative crop, poetic intoxicant and sexual inhabitant, in the course of the twentieth century traditional opium users found themselves in a semantic landscape populated by the announcement of modernity. A 'psychoactive revolution' had happened worldwide, in which Iranians participate actively: people acquired the power to alter their state of mind, at their will and through consumption of psychoactive substances. Availability of psychoactive drugs had become entrenched in the socio-economic fabric of the modern world, complementing the traditional use of drugs, opium in particular, as a medical remedy.[3] With high drug productivity and faster trade links at the turn of the twentieth century, narcotics became widely available across the world. Iran, for that matter, produced large

---

[1] *New York Times*, February 11, 1973.
[2] In Persian, the words used for drugs are *mavadd* and *mavadd-e mokhadder*, which stand for 'substance' and 'narcotic substance'.
[3] Courtwright, *Forces of Habit*, Introduction. This does not mean that psychoactive substances were not used prior to the twentieth century. It is the consumeristic dimension of drugs use that is unique to this period.

amounts of opium since the commercialisation of agriculture, which occurred in the late nineteenth century.

Old rituals turned into modern consumption, which was technological, through the use of hypodermic needles and refined chemicals; stronger, with more potent substances; and, crucially, speedier.[4] This 'psychoactive revolution' did not proceed unnoticed by political institutions. Although nameless characters in modern history, drug users have been an object of elites' concerns in the political game of disciplining, modernisation and public order.[5] Spearheaded by the United States' reformist momentum, a new regime of regulation of psychoactive substances, initiated in the early 1900s, reshaped the world into a more moral, read sober, one.[6] By the mid 1950s, consumption of intoxicants found narrow legitimate space and it was clamped down on by the police. Orientalised as a cultural practice of enslaving 'addiction' and pharmacological dependency, the use of drugs outside the West emerged in dialogue with global consumption trends and not simply as a tale of mimicry of Western consumption.[7]

This chapter provides the background to the transformations that drug policy experienced before the 1979 Islamic Revolution. It describes processes of state formation, drugs politics and addiction during the pre-1979 period.[8] As in the case of other state policies during this era, 'abrupt reversals, sudden initiatives and equally sudden retreats'

---

[4] Smoking itself is a practice requiring sophistication, compared to eating. It enables speedier intake of the substance. More technological are pills and needles, which emerge over the twentieth century. Cf. Courtwright, *Forces of Habit*, p. 4.

[5] For an account of how US and UK policies on drugs have made 'use' of the figure of the drug user in modern history, see Merrill Singer and J. Bryan Page. *The Social Value of Drug Addicts: Uses of the Useless* (Routledge, 2016).

[6] Ian Tyrrell, *Reforming the World: The Creation of America's Moral Empire* (Princeton University Press, 2010).

[7] For accounts of other cases in the Global South, see James Mills, 'Decolonising Drugs in Asia: the case of cocaine in colonial India', *Third World Quarterly* 38, no. 2 (2018). For instance, cocaine was feared in the US southern states because 'Negro cocaine users might become oblivious of their prescribed bounds and attack white society'. A similarly argument was made for the Chinese immigrant community in California. In Musto, *The American Disease*, p. 6.

[8] I avoid discussing pre-modern history of drugs in Iran, which would necessitate a whole other chapter. See Rudi Matthee's excellent work, *The Pursuit of Pleasure: Drugs and Stimulants in Iranian History, 1500–1900* (Princeton University Press, 2005).

characterise drugs politics.⁹ Iran adopted the whole range of policies with regard to narcotic drugs – from *laissez-faire* legalisation to total ban – since the inception of the first prohibitionist agenda in 1909 and, especially, over a period of four decades, between 1941 and 1979, when drug prohibition became a central element of the domestic and international discourse. Before streaming into this historical trajectory, the chapter discusses briefly the birth of the category of 'addiction' (*eti'yad*) in its global-local nexus. This is situated in a period of great political transformation, corresponding to the Constitutional Revolution (1906–11) and the slow demise of the Qajar dynasty (1780–1925). The birth of 'addiction', one could argue, coincided with the naissance of modern political life in Iran.

Modernity and Addiction

American sociologist Harry Levine argues that the category of addiction is an invented concept dating back to the late eighteenth century. Its immediate relation is not to the idea of inebriation, as one might think, but to that of individual freedom, and therefore, to liberal governance.¹⁰ The word 'addiction' itself has its etymological root in the Latin *addicere*, which refers to the practice of enslaving someone. In Persian, the Arabic-origin term *e'tiyad*, suggests the chronic return, relapse or familiarity to something. Both terms express the impossibility of being 'free' and, therefore, the inability to make judgements or take decisions (especially in the case of *addicere*). This idea, generated in the medical knowledge of late nineteenth century Europe, gained prominence in Iran when foreign-educated students returned to their country and started using the lexicon, images and aetiology of Western medicine. Incidentally, Iranian intellectuals had relied almost exclusively on the accounts of foreign travellers in order to narrate the history of drugs, thus orientalising the life of the drug itself.¹¹

---

⁹ Stephanie Cronin, *Tribal Politics in Iran: Rural Conflict and the New State, 1921–1941* (Routledge, 2007); cf. Cyrus Schayegh, *Who Is Knowledgeable Is Strong: Science, Class, and the Formation of Modern Iranian Society, 1900–1950* (University of California Press, 2009), 3.
¹⁰ Harry Levine in Seddon, *A History*, 27.
¹¹ How 'addiction' became a diagnostic lens in Iran is a question that deserves a separate research project, which goes beyond the scope of this book. Cf. Schayegh, *Who Is Knowledgeable*, 191; Matthee, *The Pursuit of Pleasure*.

The emergence of a discourse on prohibition signed a moment of modernity in the political life of the early twentieth century, a modernity which was, nonetheless, at odds with the everyday life of Iranians. There, opium was the unchallenged remedy of the masses; it was administrated by local apothecaries (*'attari*) as painkiller, sedative for diarrhoea, lung problems, universal tonic or, simply, a panacea for just about everyone who manifested symptoms, however vague, of physical or psychological malaise. The *hakim* – a traditional doctor – would dispense it 'when challenged by an illness that he could not treat'.[12] British doctors travelling in Iran reveal that 'to practice medicine among Persians means constant contact with the subject of addiction to opium. It crops up a dozen times a day ...'.[13] Rather than being only a medical remedy, opium also had its place in everyday rituals and practices. Opium smoking, using a pipe (*vafur*) and a charcoal brazier (*manqal*), usually occurred in front of an audience – either other opium smokers or just attendees – the interaction with whom encouraged the reciting of poetry – Sa'adi, Ferdowsi and Khayyam being main poetic totems – and inconclusive discussions about history and the past in general. Opium had the reputation of making people acquire powerful oratorical skills. This circle, *doreh*, enabled ties of friendship and communality to evolve around the practice of smoking, especially among middle and upper classes, with opium being 'the medium through which members of a group organized'.[14] In the course of the twentieth century, people habituated to this practice were referred to, somewhat sarcastically, as the *pay-e manqali*, 'those who sit at the feet of the brazier'. Conviviality, business, relaxation and therapy converged in the practice of opium smoking.

---

[12] Amir Afkhami, 'Compromised Constitutions: The Iranian Experience with the 1918 Influenza Pandemic' *Bulletin of the History of Medicine* 77, 2 (2003), 386; Gerald T. McLaughlin and Thomas M. Quinn, 'Drug Control in Iran: A Legal and Historical Analysis', *Iowa Law Review* 59 (1973), 481.

[13] Anthony R. Neligan, 'The Opium Question with Special Reference to Persia' (JSTOR, 1929), 1. See also Hormoz Ebrahimnejad, *Medicine, Public Health, and the Qājār State: Patterns of Medical Modernization in Nineteenth-Century Iran*, vol. 4 (Brill, 2004), 154; and Shireen Mahdavi, 'Shahs, Doctors, Diplomats and Missionaries in 19th Century Iran', *British Journal of Middle Eastern Studies* 32, 2 (2005), 185.

[14] Hamid Mowlana, 'The Politics of Opium in Iran: A Social-Psychological Interface' in Simmons and Said, *Drugs, Politics, and Diplomacy* (1974), 79.

Opium was a normative element of life in Iran. At the end of the day of fasting or before the sunrise hour in the month of Ramadan, ambulant vendors would provide water and, for those in need, opium pills by shouting in the courtyards and in front of the mosques, 'there is water and opium! [*ab ast va taryak*]'.[15] In northern Iran, mothers would give small bits of opium to their children before heading to the fields to work. Later, before bedtime, children would be given a *sharbat-e baccheh* (the child's syrup), made of the poppy skin boiled with sugar, which would ensure a sound sleep.[16] These stories have global parallels; in for instance popular narratives in southern Italy, under the name of *papagna* (papaverum), and in the UK under the company label of Godfrey's Cordial. At the time of modernisation, such practices contributed to the demonization of the popular classes (workers and peasants) in the public image, describing their methods as irresponsible and not in tune with modern nursing practices.[17] Individual use, instead, would be later described by modernist intellectual Sadegh Hedayat through his novels' narrators, whose characters dwelled, amid existential sorrows and melancholies, on opium and spirit taking.[18] By 1933, Sir Arnold Wilson, the British civil commissioner in Baghdad, would be adamant arguing that '[t]he existence in Western countries of a few weak-minded drug addicts is a poor excuse for under-mining by harassing legislation the sturdy individualism that is one of the most enduring assets of the Persian race'.[19] The frame of addiction as inescapably connected to opium use, however, had already been adopted by Iranian intellectuals and political entrepreneurs in the early days of the Constitutional Revolution. The demise of the old political order, embodied by the ailing Qajar dynasty, unleashed a reformist push that affected the social fabric – at

[15] Jahan -'alì Azarkhosh, *Afat-e Zendegi* (Tehran: Chapp-e Gohar, 1956 [1334]), 367–8. Also Neligan, 'The Opium Question', 25.
[16] A. A. Alemi and M. N. Naraghi, 'The Iceberg of Opium Addiction an Epidemiological Survey of Opium Addiction in a Rural Community', *Drug and Alcohol Dependence* 3, 2 (1978), 109; Elgin Earl Groseclose, *Introduction to Iran* (Oxford University Press, 1947),198; Neligan, 'The Opium Question', 16.
[17] Virginia Berridge and Griffith Edwards, *Opium and the People* (ABC, 1982), 98–101. Berridge interestingly shows how these practices were widespread also among upper class families, but this never became a concern in the public debate; 105.
[18] Sadeq Hedayat, 'Zende Be Gur' (Tehran: Amir Kabir, 1930); 'Buf-E Kur' (1952).
[19] Groseclose, *Introduction to Iran*, 208.

least in the urban areas – and models of governance, with their far-reaching influence over individuals' public life.

Reformists and radicals in the early twentieth century, either inspired by the Constitutionalist paradigm or because they effectively took part in the upheaval, called for a remaking of Iranian society and of national politics, starting from the establishment of a representative body, the Parliament (*Majles*) and the adoption of centralised, administrative mechanism in health, education, language, social control and the like. Constitutionalists represented a wide spectrum of ideas and persuasions, but their common goal was reforming the old socio-political order of Qajar Iran. Modernisation, whatever its content implied, was the sole and only medium to avoid complete subjugation to the imperial West.

By then, opium had come to play an important role in the economy of Iran, known at the time as Persia. In the Qajar economy, the poppy was a cash crop that provided steadfast revenues in a declining agricultural system. With commercialisation of agricultural output, opium became omnipresent and with it the habit of opium eating, supplanted since the early 1900s with opium smoking. Constitutionalists referred to opium addiction as one of the most serious social, political ills afflicting the country. They were actively advocating for a drastic cure of this pathology, which metaphorically embodied the sickness of late Qajar Iran.[20] Hossein Kuhi Kermani, a poet and reformist intellectual active over these years, reports that when Constitutionalists conquered Tehran, they started a serious fight against opium and the *taryaki* (aka, *teryaki*, the opium user), with missions of police officers and volunteers in the southern parts of Tehran with the objective to close down drug nests.[21] These areas would be theatres of similar manifestations a hundred years later, under the municipal pressure of Tehran's administrations.[22]

The Constitutionalists' engagement with the problems associated with opium coincided on the international level with the first conferences on opium control. The first of these meetings happened in Shanghai in 1909,

---

[20] In 1947, Arthur C. Millspaugh, American director of Iran's finances, wrote a book divided into a section titled 'Report from the Clinic', with sub-chapters 'Can Persia Save Herself?', 'Suggestions for a Prescription' and 'How Shall the Doctoring Be Done?' See Arthur Chester Millspaugh, *Americans in Persia* (Brookings Institution, 1925).

[21] Mohammad Hossein Shahidi, *Mavadd-e Mokhadder, Amniyat-e Ejtema'i va Rah-e Sevvom* (Tehran: Entesharat-e Ettela'at, 2010 [1389]), 67.

[22] See Harandi Park, in Chapter 7.

the milestone of the prohibitionist regime in the twentieth century. In Shanghai, Western powers attempted to draw an overview of the world's drug situation in a bid to regulate the flow of opium and instil a legibility principle in terms of production and trade, with the ultimate objective to limit the flow of commercial opium only to medical needs. Iran participated in the meeting as part of its bid to join the global diplomatic arena of modernity. Ironically, the Iranian envoy at this meeting, Mirza Ja'far Rezaiof, was himself an opium trader, disquieted by an appointment which could have potentially 'cut his own throat', given that opium represented Iran's major export and his principle business.[23]

Amidst the momentum of the Constitutionalists' anti-opium campaigns, Iran became the first opium-producing country to limit cultivation, and to restrain opium use in public.[24] On March 15, 1911, a year before The Hague Convention on Opium Control, the *Majles* approved the Law of Opium Limitation (*Qanun-e Tahdid-e Tariyak*), enforcing a seven-year period for opium users to give up their habit.[25] This provision also made the government effectively accountable for the delivery of opium to the people, with the creation of a quota system (*sahmiyah*), which required the registration of drug users through the state administrative offices and the payment of taxes against the provision of opium. In other words, the law sanctioned public/state intervention in the private sphere of individual behaviour – i.e. consumption – and granted the inquisitor's power to the officials of the Ministry of Finance. Even though this decision did not mean prohibition of the poppy economy, it signified that the new politics triggered by the Constitutionalist Revolution followed lines tuned with global trends towards the public space and therefore with modern life (style).

Whether opium prohibition was inspired and reproduced under the influence of Western countries or it had indigenously emerged, is a debate that extends beyond the scope of this chapter.[26] What can be

---

[23] Ram Baruch Regavim, 'The Most Sovereign of Masters: The History of Opium in Modern Iran, 1850–1955' (University of Pennsylvania, PhD Thesis: 2012), 151. On the first drug conventions, see William B. McAllister, *Drug Diplomacy in the Twentieth Century: An International History* (Psychology Press, 2000).
[24] Groseclose, *Introduction to Iran*, 208.
[25] Said Madani Qahrfarkhi, *E'tiyad* Dar Iran [Addiction in Iran] (Tehran: Nashr-e Sales, 2011), 144.
[26] Cf. Isaac Campos, *Home Grown*; James Windle, *Suppressing Illicit Opium Production: Successful Intervention in Asia and the Middle East* (IB Tauris, 2016).

Figure 2.1 Donkey Smoking Opium in a Suit
The small statue dates back to the late 1950s, early 1960s. Courtesy of Antonio Mazziatelli, former UNODC representative in Iran.

discerned here however, are the effects of state-deployed control policies on the social fabric. The formation of modern Iranian state machinery made possible a steady intrusion, though fragmentary, into the life of opium users and of opium itself. In the pre-twentieth-century period, in fact, Iranian rulers had at different times ruled in favour of or against the use of opium and other drugs (including wine), but at no time had they had the means to control people's behaviour and so affect the lives of multitudinous drug users. The Shahs themselves have been known, in popular narratives, as divided into those fighting against, or those indulging in, the use of opium. At times, the rulers would indulge in drug use so heavily as to destabilise their reign.[27] By the time of the Constitutional

---

[27] Shahidi, *Mavadd-e Mokhadder*, 28–29, Matthee, *The Pursuit of Pleasure*.

Revolution, the idea of a ruler whose mind and body is intoxicated by opium or other substances had become a central political theme, fuelling, among other things, an Orientalist portrayal of power in the Eastern world. The reformers of this period used the failure of past sovereigns to warn against the danger of intoxication, marking clearly that modernity did not have space for old pastimes. Genealogically, reformers interpreted opium and addiction to it as the cause of national backwardness, a *leitmotif* among revolutionaries during the Islamic Revolution of 1979 (Figure 2.1).

State Building on Drugs

When the old Qajar monarchy fell apart and the military autocrat Reza Khan rose to power, the priorities of the Constitutional Revolution narrowed down to the imperative of state building, centralisation, control over the national territory and systematic taxation. For this and other reasons, the poppy maintained its firm place as a key asset in the national economy. Opium represented a major source of state building for the newly established Pahlavi state from 1925 onwards. It contributed directly to the creation and upgrading of the national army, a fact that, by 1928, pushed Reza Shah to create the Opium State Monopoly.[28] By that time, Iran was producing 30 per cent of the world's opium, exporting enormous, unregistered quantities towards East Asia.[29] Although the government intended to restrain opium consumption, they were neither capable, nor willing to give up an important share of their revenues, some years as high as 9 per cent of the total gross domestic product.[30] As a strategic asset, opium never came under full state control; resilient farmers, including nomadic tribes threatened by the encroachment of the state and its anti-tribal/sedentarisation policy, continued to harvest and bargain with the authorities, at times successfully, at others contentiously. Emblematic of the contentious nature of opium politics, even before Pahlavi modernisation, was the *bast* (sanctuary) taken by the people of Isfahan in the city's Telegraph Compound in 1923, which, in a matter of days, if not hours, turned into a full seven-thousand-person demonstration against attempts by the central government to gain full control, with hefty taxation, over

---

[28] Qahrfarkhi, *E'tiyad*, 147.   [29] Groseclose, *Introduction to Iran*, 212.
[30] Bradley Hansen, 'Learning to Tax: The Political Economy of the Opium Trade in Iran, 1921–1941', *The Journal of Economic History* 61, 1 (2001), 97.

the production of opium.[31] Members of the clergy participated, not least because considerable portion of *vaqf* lands (religious endowments) in Iran's southwest were cultivated with the poppy. Opium, as such, constituted a vital source of capital, which made poppy growers (or better, their capitalist patrons) the wealthiest class.[32] Inevitably, this led to an economy of contraband of vast proportions, which had few equals globally and which supplied the market at its bottom and top ends, respectively petty merchants in the many ports connecting Bushire to Vladivostok, and legitimate pharmaceutical houses which used Persian opium 'because of its superior quality and high morphine content'.[33] Capital accumulation over the first half of the twentieth century among a circumscribed class of landowners might have well occurred because of opium production.[34]

Beside the international trafficking networks, the opium economy produced a social life of its own, one in which, well into the Pahlavi era, the presence of the state remained a latency. With the creation of the Opium Monopoly, the state required all the opium produced locally to be stocked into governmental warehouses, which were administrated by state officials. Yet, much of the opium sap never reached these locations or, when it actually did, it did so only at face value, with quantities much inferior to the actual production. Concealed during the harvest period, opium was then sold at a higher price to smugglers who would resell abroad at higher rates.[35]

The list of those involved in the opium economy was not restricted to landowners, cultivators and smugglers. Labourers, commission and export merchants, brokers, bazaar agents, chiefs, clerks, manipulators, packers, porters, carpenters, coppersmiths, retailers, and mendicants

---

[31] See Stephanie Cronin, 'Resisting the New State: Peasants and Pastoralists in Iran, 1921–41', *The Journal of Peasant Studies* 32, 1 (2005).

[32] W. MacCormack, Moses Khan, and Muḥammad K. Amiri. *Memorandum on Persian Opium: Prepared for Dr. Ac Mispaugh, Administrator General of the Finances* (Parliament Press, 1924), 11.

[33] Iranian opium was known as having a higher morphine value (12 per cent) compared to Indian, Turkish and Balkan opium. See Azarkhosh, *Afat-e Zendegi*; Groseclose, *Introduction to Iran*, 108; Neligan, 'The Opium Question', 37.

[34] The shift in favour of commercial agricultural production was, in part, driven by expanding poppy cultivation; see Shoko Okazaki, 'The Great Persian Famine of 1870–71'. *Bulletin of the School of Oriental and African Studies* 49, no. 1 (1986): 183–92.

[35] Groseclose, *Introduction to Iran*, 108–9.

were part of this line of production. During harvest time, they were often accompanied by a motley crowd of dervishes, story-tellers, musicians, owners of performing animals and a whole industry of amusement providers who were paid for their company or 'given alms by having the flat side of the opium knife scrapped on their palms'.[36] An observer of such events reports from 3,000 to 5,000 strangers in a single area during the harvest season. The village mullahs, who might have blessed the event with a *salavat* (eulogy to the prophet and his family) were given sap of premium opium as tokens of gratitude. In the first decades of the century, among the 80,000 inhabitants of Isfahan, about one quarter gained their living directly or indirectly in the opium economy.[37] The front store of shops advertised the narcotic with signs as such 'Here the best Shirazi and Isfahani Opium is sold!'[38] Stephanie Cronin indicates that, in certain regions of the country, opium had even become a local currency in times of political instability.[39] When the modernising state increased its effort at controlling the opium economy, the effect was that the large number of middlemen and beneficiaries of this economy remained unemployed or saw their revenues decline significantly. It is plausible to think that many of these categories joined forces with the widespread associations of smugglers which had enriched the informal economy ever since. The risk of 'moral reputation' and 'moral isolation' compelled Iranian policy-makers to cooperate with the international drug control regime.[40] For the first time in Iranian history, the crime of smuggling (*qachaq*) was also included in a new legislation. It is reported that between the late 1920s and the early 1930s, more than 10,000 traffickers were arrested per year, prompting the government to acknowledge that there were more people smoking contraband opium than government opium.[41] Yet, while signing the Geneva Convention on Opium Control (1925), a diplomatic agreement that provided statistical information on the production and trade of opium, the Iranian delegation maintained its reservations on the key issue of certification and restriction of

[36] Arthur C. Millspaugh, *The American Task in Persia* (Century Company, 1925), 190–1.
[37] Ibid., 190. Neligan, 'The Opium Question', 37.
[38] Azarkhosh, *Afat-e Zendegi*, 373.
[39] Stephanie Cronin, *Soldiers, Shahs and Subalterns in Iran: Opposition, Protest and Revolt, 1921–1941* (Springer, 2010), 191.
[40] MacCormack et al., *Memorandum on Persian*, 1–2.
[41] Hansen, 'Learning to Tax', 103.

exports to those countries in which opium trading was illegal.[42] Smuggling flourished as never before, a historical fact that deserves a more accurate account than that provided here.

Reza Shah himself was a regular user of opium, although it is said, perhaps hagiographically, that he smoked twice a day standing on his feet – as opposed to those laying on their side indulging in poetry, conversation and day-dreaming.[43] In this image, one can interpret the difference between the traditional Shahs of the pre-Pahlavi period – several of them known opium users – and the moderniser Shah who used opium without losing his mental alertness and bodily stamina. Together with the Islamic veil, the traditional hat, nomadic life and *sufi* practice (*tasavvof*), opium smoking was in fact seen as a habit that would have little space in the making of modern Iran.[44] Its place, even within the practice of apothecaries, had to be substituted by modern science and Western medicine. Restrictions started to be applied to opium, as other allegedly customary elements such as ethnic attire, the veil and traditional hats were banned from being used in public. Reza Shah banned the use of opium for those in the army and in the bureaucracy.[45] Nevertheless, the *Majles* itself reportedly had a lounge in which deputies could ease their nerves and discuss issues of concern over an opium pipe.[46] It was the façade of the life of opium, particularly when confronted by Western observers, which preoccupied the Shah. To demonstrate that the real concern of the government was alignment with Western models of governance and behaviour, in 1928 the government approved the Opium Restriction Act, which made opium cultivation legitimate only after government certification through the State Opium Organisation. The Organisation supervised all opium exports as agreed by the 1925 Geneva Agreement; together with the Ministry of Finance, it collected the opium residue (*sukhteh*) from public places and managed the sale of cooked opium residue (*shireh-ye matbukh*) to the smoking houses (*shirehkesh khaneh*).[47] The idea that the government was keen to purchase the residue of smoked opium

[42] League of Nations, 'Records of the Second Opium Conference', vol. I (Geneva, November 17, 1924 – February 19, 1925), 122.
[43] Ali Akbar Alimardani, 'Mavadd-e Mokhadder va Rejim-e Pahlavi', *Faslnameh-ye Motale'at-e Tarikh* 25, 114.
[44] Interestingly enough, *sufism* has regularly been associated with drug taking and often vilified on this ground.
[45] McLaughlin, 'Drug Control', 486.   [46] *New York Times*, February 11, 1973.
[47] Azarkhosh, *Afat-e Zendegi*, 404–5.

contributed, indirectly, to the shift from traditional opium eating – as it had been diffused in Iran from times immemorial – to smoking, which was a practice emerging at the turn of twentieth century, under the influence of Chinese opium culture. This shift in governmental policy had a lasting effect on drug consumption over the following decades.

Under the order of the Allied forces and with the Anglo-Soviet Occupation of Iran, Reza was sent into exile in 1941. Earlier that year, the government had, in a populist push, banned opium production in twenty-two regions – but not Isfahan – in a move that would have had drastic consequences were Iran not occupied by the Allied Forces.[48] *De facto*, the ban was a complete failure. Cultivators in these regions protested by selling their opium at very cheap prices, in order to empty their stock so that the government had to allow cultivation again in order to refill the national opium reservoir, a strategic asset in periods of conflict.[49] The resilience and tactics of the farmers exemplified well the influence that these non-elites could have on policymakers. However, the consequences of their defiance were catastrophic; cheap prices combined with the perception of opium as an essential source of relief from pain and protection against illnesses, incited large numbers of Iranians to consume it and, in some cases, to set up small opiate factory-shops to cook and sell the opium residue.[50]

It is with the setting up of these small opium-cooking factories that an opium derivate gained popularity among the working class: *shireh*. Considered more detrimental and addictive than opium, with a higher morphine content, *shireh* was sought by longer-term smokers. Mostly smoked by working-class men in specific factory-shops, it had a greater stigma, often making it comparable to that of the brothels in the moralising public narratives.[51] Interestingly enough, these places were called *dar-ol-'alaj*, the Arabic expression for 'clinic' or 'treatment house', which hints at the inseparability of recreational and self-medicine in opiate use over this period.[52] In Tehran alone, there were more than a hundred *shirehkesh-khaneh* spread across the city from south to north. In one instance, a bus operated as a peripatetic smoking house on the Karaj road to avoid police raids aimed at closing

[48] Groseclose, *Introduction to Iran*, 215.
[49] In times of war, morphine reservoirs represent a strategic asset for their analgesic virtue.
[50] Qahfarkhi, *E'tiyad*, 190–1. [51] See Azarkhosh, *Afat-e Zendegi*, 404.
[52] Ibid., 373.

Table 2.1 *Poppy Cultivation, Production and Consumption (1938–48)*[56]

Year	Area of Cultivation (hectare)	Production (kg)	Consumption (kg)
1938	26,963	704,000	269,000
1939	24,543	672,000	300,000
1940	28,036	789,000	307,000
1941	37,113	761,000	263,000
1942	11,820	210,000	211,000
1943	1,068	215,000	122,000
1944	12,740	131,000	66,000
1945	9,287	182,000	64,000
1946	18,400	516,000	28,000
1947	187	5,600	0
1948	1,17	34,100	0

them. The driver's aid shouted the slogan, 'we take away dead, we bring back alive [*morde mibarim, zendeh miyarim*]'.[53] But the widespread use of opium and *shireh* reached a climax during the allied occupation (1941–46), due to the unsettling conditions in which most people lived, especially in the central and northern regions.

War, Coups d'État and International Drug Control (1941–55)

In 1944, the government of the United States circulated a joint resolution signed by Congress among all opium-producing countries, which urged these countries to effectively eradicate or reduce poppy cultivation and to limit their opium production to legitimate medical needs.[54] One of the primary reasons was the seizure of opium in the United States, three-quarters of which had allegedly originated in Iran and crossed the Pacific thanks to Chinese merchants heading to San Francisco.[55] Thus, a global network of opium smuggling had been born before the coming of organised criminal groups, although the Iranian authorities maintained that they had progressively eradicated poppy cultivation (Table 2.1). The reality on the ground, in fact, spoke

---

[53] Ibid., 510. [54] Groseclose, *Introduction to Iran*, 216.
[55] Ryan Gingeras, 'Poppy Politics: American Agents, Iranian Addicts and Afghan Opium, 1945–80', *Iranian Studies* 45, 3 (2012), 318–19.
[56] Data extrapolated from *Bulletin of Narcotics* 1, 1 (1949).

of a stupendous flow of opium out of Iran, much to the concern of Western powers – a concern that was mostly an expression of concern (the threat of opiate addiction against the nation), without real concern (the embeddedness of opiates in popular practice).

By the end of World War II, a small number of US narcotics officials, many of whom had been previously working as intelligence officers, helped the Pahlavi state to re-produce a prohibitionist regime in Tehran, which, in their strategy had to embody a global model for the rest of the region and beyond.[57] Through this collaboration, US influence within Iran increased significantly, especially for what concerned the repressive, coercive institutions of the Pahlavi state: police, intelligence and the army. For their part, the Iranian authorities had repeatedly played the opium card to convince the United States to provide development assistance funds, by highlighting the threats of opiates and Soviet communism. In this setting, Iranian authorities remained purposefully ambivalent, refusing to provide clear information to the FBN officials, convinced also of the geopolitical relevance that Iran had acquired in respect to the Soviet anathema. Knowledge about the drug situation came mostly from non-governmental sources, which at times concocted a distorting image of opium consumption and culture in Iran.[58]

The emergence of the Society for the Fight against Alcohol and Opium, created in 1943, proved tactical to this situation. It campaigned aggressively for the prohibition of all alcoholic spirits and opiates and announced astonishing data on 'addiction'. In its first three years, it distributed around 80,000 information leaflets, participated in more than a hundred public meetings and intervened regularly on national radio.[59] Members of this organisation belonged exclusively to the elites, among whom were members of parliament, judges, prominent public figures and their wives. Their influence operated in a discursive way towards the public, but it also affected the perception of the drug *problematique* among the authorities, including American officials. They circulated statistics, for instance, with the purpose of engendering a sense of crisis:

---

[57] Gingeras, 'Poppy Politics', 16. On the US prohibition regime, see Musto, *The American Disease*.
[58] John Collins, 'Regulations and Prohibitions: Anglo-American Relations and International Drug Control, 1939–1964' (LSE: PhD Thesis, 2015), 92.
[59] Qahrfarkhi, *E'tiyad*, 149.

two million grams of opium used daily ... six million *rial* lost every day ... 5,000 suicide attempts with opium [women's figuring prominently] ... one thousand-three hundred *shirehkesh-khaneh* operating in the country, one hundred thousand people dying every year for opium use and fifty thousand children becoming orphans.[60]

Furthermore, the Society arranged theatre pieces about opium which often depicted a caricatured opium smoker as the sources of all social and family evils, from which the expression *khanemansuzi* (burning one's household) gained popularity. On November 22, 1946, the Society organised a public ceremony of the *vafursuzan* (opium pipe burning, literally 'those burning the *vafurs*') – antecedent to the Islamic Republic's opium-burning ceremonies – to which foreign dignitaries would participate, praising their moral prohibitionist effort.[61] In its manifesto, this society declared, 'it seems that the question of the effects of opium and alcohol has reached a point where the extinction of the Iranian race and generation will take place ... In the name of the protection of the nationality, this committee has been created'.[62] This mixture of Persian nationalism and sense of crisis tainted the official discourse on drugs and pushed lawmakers to adopt tough measures on drug consumption.

The Society's stance on drugs ignored the extent to which opium was part of the cultural norms and everyday customs of Iranians. Instead, it was instrumental in introducing legislations that targeted public intoxication among the popular classes. The new anti-drug propaganda described opium as a primary impediment to labour, although Iranian workers had traditionally used opium for its tonic effect.[63] Coincidently, the government issued, first, a ban on the fifteen-minute work break for opium smokers, and then circulated a communiqué pointing out that 'workers should not use opium on their jobs'.[64] Employment of officials had to be based on their avoidance of opium use, a behaviour that could have cost them their place at work.[65] Modernisation of the national economy, which had to move conjunctly with social behaviour, passed through the progressive abandoning of opium in favour of other habits, such as alcoholic drinks. The *teriyaki* was inherently weak and its place in the post-1941 public discourse

[60] Ibid. [61] Ibid., 149–50. [62] Shahidi, *Mavadd-e Mokhadder*, 80.
[63] Cf. Schayegh, *Who Is Knowledgeable*, 186–7. On cannabis as tonic for Jamaican workers, cf. Courtwright, *Forces of Habit*.
[64] Groseclose, *Introduction to Iran*, 215; *New York Times*, February 11, 1973.
[65] Azarkhosh, *Afat-e Zendegi*, 450–1.

condemned as underserving. Associated with lying, the addict was unreliable in the workplace, a perception that was widespread in the rural as much as the urban centres.[66]

The new bureaucratic apparatuses of the state, bolstered by the ideological and logistical support of the US anti-narcotic officials endowed the Anti-Opium Society with unprecedented clout over this issue. On January 28, 1945, hence, a deputy from Hamadan, Hassan Ali Farmand, who had previously opposed the Opium Monopoly in 1928, introduced a bill for the total prohibition of cultivation of poppies and use of opium.[67] Between 1941 and 1953, the *Majles* approved a number of legislative acts: the creation of a 'coupon system' for registered drug users; the prohibition of opium cultivation in 1942–43; a ban on opium consumption in August 1946 under Prime Minister Ahmad Qavam, which lasted only ten months; and, under the government of Mohammad Mosaddeq (1951–53), a law amendment banning production, purchase and sale of opium and its derivatives and the consumption of alcoholic drinks.[68] Over this period the government declared a war on coffeehouses, which were either to be closed or to cover up the use of opium within the building; enforcement of laws against public intoxication (*tajahor*) incremented, enshrining a legal framing which would prove durable up to the new millennium.

Prohibitionist rhetoric gained further momentum during the oil nationalization under Mosaddeq when the parliament voted unanimously to ban alcohol and opium use within six months.[69] The move, however, was largely a populist tactic to gather support (including that of the clergy: alcohol ban) at a time when economic sanctions and international isolation were crippling the life of Iranians. Even government officials had very little belief in the effectiveness of this law. Asked by a journalist whether one could get a drink in Tehran six months from the entry in force of the law, a government official laughed and responded, 'Yes, and six years from now, too'.[70] At the same time, with state finances shrinking because of the stalemate in the oil industry, Mossadegh, in agreement with the *Majles*, had pushed for a steady increase in opium production in order to compensate for the drop in oil exports. The strategy had its limited results and 'the

---

[66] Schayegh, *Who Is Knowledgeable*, passim. Lois Beck, *Nomad: A Year in the Life of a Qashqa'i Tribesman in Iran* (University of California Press, 1991), 401.
[67] Groseclose, *Introduction to Iran*, 216. [68] Qahrfarkhi, *E'tiyad*, 153–6.
[69] *New York Times*, May 7, 1952. [70] *New York Times*, February 15, 1953.

government reported opium revenues of over 200 million *rials* a year from 1951 to 1954, about 20 percent of the total'.[71] In 1952, the United Nations accused Iran together with Communist China of smuggling opium, following a period of poor cooperation between the country and the US-led international drug control regime.[72] The British government also attempted to delegitimise the nationalist government in Tehran, ahead of the planned coup, by, among other methods, 'spreading the rumor that Mosaddeq reeked of opium and "indulged freely" in that drug'.[73] But, paradoxically, while the United States and the United Kingdom planned to topple Iran's democratically elected prime minister, the United States purchased, both legally and illegally, large amounts of Iranian opium, out of the fear that the 'Soviet bomb' and the outbreak of a nuclear confrontation amid the Korean War (1950–53) would bring unprecedented levels of casualties.[74] Opiates endured as the global painkiller, while the Cold War mentality required the primacy of strategic calculi over other diplomatic objectives, including that of international drug control.[75]

Opium Prohibition and Westoxification: (1955–69)

With the CIA-orchestrated coup d'état that brought Mohammad Reza Pahlavi back to the peacock throne, the United States gained greater influence over Iran's domestic politics. For the FBN and its chief Anslinger, this meant that Iran had to become a global model of the prohibitionist regime. The decision to cooperate with Washington's *in fieri* War on Drugs, writes Ryan Gingeras, provided an essential model for future agreements, 'should America's global campaign against narcotics proceed successfully'.[76]

Jahan Saleh, Minister of Health under Mohammad Reza Shah, promotor of the ban, conceded that, 'Prohibition [of opium] was motivated by prestige reasons. At a time of modernization, which in

---

[71] Hansen, 'Learning to Tax', 109.
[72] Qahrfarkhi, *E'tiyad*, 155. New York Times, May 7, 1952.
[73] Ervand Abrahamian, *The Coup: 1953, the Cia, and the Roots of Modern US–Iranian Relations* (The New Press, 2013), 101. In a similar vein with the contemporary use of 'fake news'.
[74] See McAllister, *Drug Diplomacy*, 171. Collins, 'Regulations and Prohibitions', 213.
[75] Pierre-Arnaud Chouvy, *Opium: Uncovering the Politics of the Poppy* (Harvard University Press, 2009), 97.
[76] Gingeras, 'Poppy Politics', 323.

most developing countries means imitation of Western models, the use of opium was considered a shameful hangover of a dark Oriental past. It did not fit with the image of an awakening, Westernizing Iran that the Shah was creating'.[77] Prohibition worked instrumentally in the securitisation of domestic politics, while it steadily aligned the monarchy with the US-led camp. Thus, in November 1955, Jahan Saleh pushed for the approval of the Law Prohibiting Poppy cultivation and Opium Use. He argued that there were around 1.5 million drug addicts out of a population of 19 million.[78] Given the embeddedness of the opium economy and culture, the legislative process encountered obstacles from a variety of social groups, such as coffeeshop owners, opium traders, apothecaries, landowners in poppy-cultivated regions and those who thought that the poppy was an inalienable part of Persian culture and backbone of its people's economy.[79] Yet, the public perception of drug (ab)use as a social liability and danger to people's health outplayed the economic benefits of the poppy. Reports were widespread that the number of opiate (ab)users – the term used was inevitably 'addict' – had reached two million; in areas such as Gorgan, the Caspian region, it was said that 90 per cent to 100 per cent of the population was addicted (addiction in these cases probably signifying opium consumers).[80] Evidently, some exaggeration was at play and instrumental in causing a public crisis about opium, a feature that would prove long lasting.[81]

In his speech in front of the Senate, the proposer of the prohibition bill, Jahan Saleh, first downplayed the financial value of opium for the economy, then made clear that the health of people had no monetary price and that 'people's productivity would consequently increase by hundredfold'.[82] This did not convince his opponents, who requested the bill to be discussed in all the relevant committees, which were numerous. The request however was rejected by senator Mehdi

---

[77] *New York Times*, February 11, 1973.
[78] A. E. Wright, 'The Battle against Opium in Iran: A record of progress', *Bulletin of Narcotics* 10, 2 (1958): 8–11.
[79] Samin Fasihi and Farideh Farzi, 'Mas'aleh-ye Tariyak dar Jame'eh-ye 'asr-e Reza Shah', *Tarikh-e Eslam va Iran* 25, no. 25 (2015).
[80] Shahidi, *Mavadd-e Mokhadder*, 116.
[81] On the imperative to create a 'moral public', see Darius Rejali, *Torture & Modernity: Self, Society, and State in Modern Iran* (Westview Press, 1994), 101–12.
[82] Azarkhosh, *Afat-e Zendegi*, 513.

Malekzadeh, who with emphatic sentiment and a trembling voice, reacted, 'I am a staunch supporter of this bill, I know every bit of it, there is not a single section of this bill that does not have a financial or judicial aspect, but this is a health bill and when confronted with health questions other questions have no value. This is a bill on the lives and wellbeing of people'.[83] By prioritising the public health dimension of the opium crisis, the proponents intended to bypass challenging political questions. After all, health crises are moments of reconfiguration of the political and social order.

Following the debate, the bill passed to the *Majles*, which approved it and added to its text an article on the prohibition of alcohol sale and procurement, much to the astonishment of the royal court and the modernist elites. Negotiations ensued to remove reference to alcohol; the Shah himself, during a meeting with the members of parliament, stated that 'one of the significant undertakings that have been made is the outset of the fight against opium, which must be fulfilled with attention', leaving out any reference to the issue of alcohol and spirits.[84] By October 30, 1955, the text was amended in reference to alcohol and approved as the 'Law on Prohibition of Poppy Cultivation and Opium Use'.[85] The law envisaged heavy penalties for producers, traffickers and consumers. If found with fifty grams of opium or one gram of any other narcotic, the offender could face up to ten years of solitary confinement, and later the death sentence. For the 'addict', a six-month period of grace was conceded to kick her/his habit. Opium use in public places, such as cafes and hotels, could incur hefty fines and between six months to one year imprisonment, with recidivists seeing the weight of the sentence increased.[86] It was a moral onslaught accompanied with the machinery of policing, which caused a drastic rise in the adulteration of opium, causing, according to an observer, 'deleterious effects' on consumers.[87]

The target of this new policy was not the international drug networks that operated throughout Iran. Instead, subaltern groups, such as paupers, sex workers, vagrant mendicants and members of tribes that operated smuggling routes, paid the highest price, in the guise of prison and stigmatisation. It is no coincidence that the institutionalisation of

---

[83] Ibid., 514.   [84] Ibid., 517.   [85] Ibid., 514.
[86] McLaughlin, 'Drug Control', 492.
[87] Adulteration reached 90 per cent in major urban centres; see Wright, 'The Battle'.

a national system of incarceration took place during these years.[88] The prison regime did not specifically punish drug consumption by that time; rather it focused on inebriation and the breach of public morality, with an emphasis on other drugs such as hashish, understood as heterodox by the religious establishment and 'left leaning' by the police, similarly to how FBN director Harry J. Anslinger regarded cannabis as the drug of the perverted jazz milieu.[89] Two years after the entry into force of the law, the government had to declare an amnesty for drug offenders, because of the overcrowding of the facilities. Shahab Ferdowsi, then advisor to the Ministry of Justice, revealed that 'poor people are paying the price of this policy'.[90] Imposed as a modernising programme, prohibition targeted those categories that were at odds with the Pahlavi view of what Iranian society should look like. That meant targeting – unsystematically – a good many outside the modernist city-dwellers.

The state discourse promoted, by indirect means, 'useful delinquency' as opposed to political opposition, the effects of which can be seen in Tehran thugs' participation during the coup against Mossadegh.[91] The words of Michel Foucault come timely for this claim: 'Delinquency solidified by a penal system centred upon the prison, thus represents a diversion of illegality for the illicit circuits of profit and power of the dominant class'.[92] It is clear that the creation of a moral public, whether in political terms (anti-Communism, Westernised), or in social terms (productive, healthy and law-abiding), was among the central concerns of the Pahlavi state, while at the same time it was also a tactical expedient. Besides, there was also 'appetite for medicine'.[93] The *Bulletin of Narcotics* reports, 'Iran, in a special programme inaugurated in November 1955, established treatment centres in its several provinces to provide withdrawal and short-term rehabilitation for addicts'.[94] But it later adds, 'those addicts who

---

[88] See Naser Rabi'i, *Ta'rikh-e zindan dar 'aṣr-e qajar va pahlavi* (Tehran: Qaqanus, 2011).
[89] Hari, *Chasing the Scream*, 19–21; on the police in London, see Mills, *Cannabis Nation*.
[90] Shahidi, *Mavadd-e Mokhadder*, 119.
[91] Ali Rahnema, *Behind the 1953 Coup in Iran: Thugs, Turncoats, Soldiers, and Spooks* (Cambridge University Press, 2014), 79 and 139.
[92] Michel Foucault, *Discipline and Punish: The Birth of the Prison* (Vintage, 1977), 280.
[93] Ibid., 304.   [94] *Bulletin on Narcotics*, 1958, 2 (5).

are convicted of crime usually receive no special treatment, and are sent to prison as are other law violators'.[95] In the words of the Iranian Minister of Health Amir Hossein Raji, the objective was:

> to cure those who can be cured and to remove by imprisonment those who cannot be cured; to stop the supply of drugs from external and from internal sources, to fill the place of the poppy crop in the agricultural economy of the country; to create a social climate in which the use of drugs is reprehended.[96]

The discretion of treatment, the diagnosis of curability and the necessity of punishment coalesced in the governance of illicit drugs. The stated formed new powers in the terrain of social control, citizens' well-being and public health. In 1959, the law was further tightened, outlawing the possession of poppy seeds with punishments of up to three years, despite these seeds being widely used in foodstuff, including bread.[97] Beside the heavy sentences, the prohibitionist regime of 1955 reproduced itself by funnelling the monies generating by drug confiscations (including property) to the anti-narcotic machinery.[98] By the early 1960s, the government was allocating a five million dollar budget for anti-narcotics, while the United States provided around 250,000 USD for Iran's contribution to international drug control, including military hardware, planes, helicopters and training.[99] It is evident how anti-narcotics went hand in hand with the expansion of the intelligence service: in 1957, coincidentally, Garland Williams, one of the influential FBN supervisors, arrived in Tehran to set up a narcotic squad, while the CIA and the Mossad were establishing the SAVAK, Iran's infamous secret service.[100]

Concomitant to the militarisation of the drug assemblage (here an anti-narcotic assemblage), in 1961, a cabinet decree re-instated the capital penalty for those engaging in drug trafficking following the signing of the Single Convention on Narcotic Drugs (1961). The international agreement 'exhorted signatory states to introduce more punitive domestic criminal laws that punished individuals for

---

[95] Ibid.
[96] Amir H. Radji, 'Opium Control in Iran: A New Regime', *Bulletin on Narcotics*, 1959, 1 (1), retrieved from www.unodc.org/unodc/en/data-and-analysis/bulletin/bulletin_1959–01-01_1_page002.html.
[97] McLaughlin, 'Drug Control', 494.   [98] Ibid.
[99] *New York Times*, April 2, 1964.
[100] Douglas Valentine, *The Strength of the Wolf: The Secret History of America's War on Drugs* (Verso, 2004), 169.

engagement in all aspects of the illicit drug trade, including cultivation, manufacture, possession, transportation, sale, import, export or use of controlled drugs for non-medical purposes'.[101] The international drug control machinery advised governments to incarcerate users; it also threatened to apply an embargo against those countries which held non-transparent attitudes on illicit drugs.

Over this period, the number of sentences in Iran increased substantially, concomitantly with the announcement of the state-led 'White Revolution' in 1963. Announced by the Shah as the new deal for Iranian agriculture, the reform sought to overhaul the century-old pattern of land possession and cultivation. Beside manoeuvring limited land redistribution to middle and small land-owners, the White Revolution facilitated the creation and expansion of large agribusiness, at detriment of all other cultivators. Mohammad Reza Shah's call for social renewal found large-scale opposition, led by sections of the clergy, including Ayatollah Ruhollah Khomeini. The protest went down in history under the name of the 'June 5 Revolt (*Panzdah-e Khordad*)'. It was severely repressed and Khomeini was sent into exile, the start of a long journey that would see him return to Iran only in February 1979. In his book, *Islamic Government*, Khomeini also writes about the Shah's approach to illicit drugs and the adoption of the death sentence for drug offences:

> I am amazed at the way these people [the Pahlavi] think. They kill people for possessing ten grams of heroin and say, 'That is the law' ... (I am not saying it is permissible to sell heroin, but this is not the appropriate punishment. The sale of heroin must indeed be prohibited but the punishment must be in proportion to the crime). When Islam, however, stipulates that the drinker of alcohol should receive eighty lashes, they consider it 'too harsh.' They can execute someone for possessing ten grams of heroin and the question of harshness does not even arise![102]

More royalist than the king, more catholic than the pope, the Iranian state was also more prohibitionist than the leader of drug prohibition,

---

[101] Julia Buxton, *The Political Economy of Narcotics: Production, Consumption and Global Markets* (Zed Books, 2006), 57.
[102] Ruhollah Khomeini and Hamid Algar, *Islamic Government: Governance of the Jurist* (Alhoda, UK, 2002), 12. A change of mind occurred when Khomeini came to power. See Maziyar Ghiabi, 'Drugs and Revolution in Iran: Islamic Devotion, Revolutionary Zeal and Republican Means', *Iranian Studies* 48, 2 (2015).

the United States. The authorities turned this model into a special Iranian fetish, a model for the supporters of ever-harsher punishments against drug consumers worldwide. The side effects surfaced promptly. With harsher punishments against opium (and drugs in general), harder drugs gained popularity, with their accessibility, too, widening. As an old drug policy motto says, 'the harder the enforcement, the harder the drugs'. With stricter control, harder drugs became available to the public at the expense of traditional drugs such as opium, a rationale that goes also under the name of the 'Iron Law of Prohibition'.[103] In 1957, two years after the entry into force of the prohibition, a man was hospitalised for heroin abuse after being found in the Tehran's Mehran Gardens.[104] It is the first reported case of heroin 'addiction' in Iranian history. The appearance of heroin signalled the changing social life of drugs over this period and in the following years.

Heroin was more difficult to detect, easier to transport for long distances, more lucrative with higher margins of profit and at the same time, with a much stronger effect than opium. It required no specific space for its use and, unlike opium, did not have a strong smell, which could attract unsolicited attention. Yet, heroin had no place in popular culture, neither as a medical nor recreational product and its repercussions on the user's health were far more problematic than opium and *shireh*. If opium had an ambiguous status within Iran's table of values and social habitus, being simultaneously medical, ritual and indigenous, heroin incarnated the intrusion of global consumption behaviours in the pursuit of pleasure and modernity.

By that time, the state regarded the question of 'addiction' as an epidemic that had to be isolated, as if it were cholera or the plague. Heroin instead instantiated, in the vision of the critics of the Pahlavi regime, a paradigmatic case of what intellectual Jalal Al-e Ahmad would call 'Westoxification [*gharbzadegi*]'. The words of Jalal Al-e Ahmad, without referring to heroin directly, echoed the way heroin gained popularity among the urban modernist milieu. 'Gharbzadegi is like cholera', he writes, 'a disease that comes from without, fostered in an environment made for breeding diseases'.[105] The environment to

[103] Richard Cowan, 'How the Narcs Created Crack', *National Review* 38 (1986).
[104] Qahrfarkhi, *E'tiyad*, 157.
[105] Jalal Al-e Ahmad and Robert Campbell, *Occidentosis: A Plague from the West* (Mizan Press, 1983), 166.

which the author refers, was the modernisation programmes promoted by Mohammad Reza Shah during the 1960s and 70s, which, along with globalising trends in cities, produced a changing flow of time: faster transportation, less reliance on the land-based economy, exposure to Western industrial modes of consumption, with technology acquiring an ever-more-dominant role in people's lives, and individuality as the meter of being in the world. Life changed, together with a change in epoch, and life, at least for those exposed more directly to these changes.[106] To this contributed Shah's so-called 'White Revolution' starting from 1963; the mass exodus from villages to urban centres, Tehran predominantly, signified an epochal change in the life of Iranians, at all levels, and the acquaintance with forms of sociability, consumption and recreation that differed substantially from that of rural communities. Inevitably, consumption patterns (including that of psychoactive, narcotic substances) changed in favour of modern substances.

According to Al-e Ahmad, Westoxification occurred through the impotency of indigenous models of consumption and production faced with Western supremacy in technology, industry and trade. Upper-class young people often embraced the nascent counterculture of the 1960s, where it also coincided with the ascent of heroin culture in Europe and North America. Heroin use in Iran did not enter into the practice of the ordinary people at least up to the end of the Pahlavi era, but remained a rather elitist pastime, given the higher price and its availability in urban areas.[107] Examples of this genre of life are provided by films such as Mohammad Ali Ja'fari's *The Plague of Life, or Morphine* (*Afat-e Zendegi ya Morphine*, 1960), which portrays the life and fall of a wealthy, modern(ist) man, Hamid, well-respected by family and society, and deceived by a beautiful cabaret singer (Shahla Rihali) to collaborate with a drug trafficking organisation, because once he injects morphine (or heroin), he is at the mercy of his dealers and meets all their requests just for another shoot. Hamid, who prior to the encounter with morphine used to wear impeccable black suits, suddenly metamorphoses into a southern Tehrani *luti*, with an unclean shirt and facetious mannerisms. From being a gifted classical piano

[106] Mohammed Reza Pahlavi, *The White Revolution of Iran* (Imperial Pahlavi Library, 1967).
[107] Central Treaty Organisation (CENTO), 'Seminar on Public Health and Medical Problems Involved in Narcotics Drug Addiction' (Tehran: CENTO, April 8–12, 1972), 25–6.

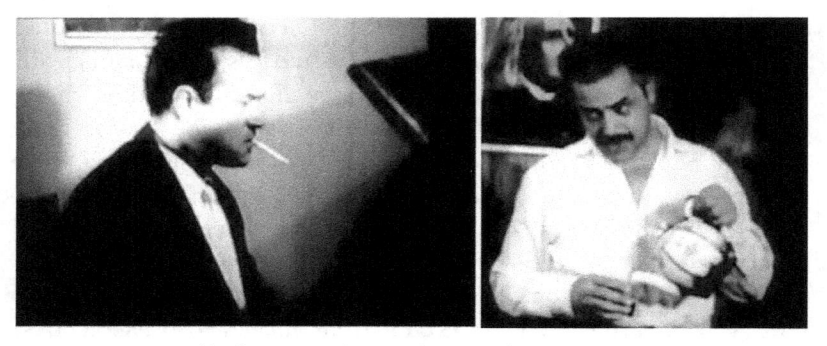

Figure 2.2 Hamid before Morphine (left) and after (right)

player, he is transformed into a moustached *baba karam*, who drinks black tea and plays only folk music (Figure 2.2).[108]

During this period, the problem of drug (ab)use experienced an evolution and a complication. New drugs and new social groups entered the illegal economy, blurring the boundary of legality. Following the 1955 prohibition law, organised criminal groups entered into the world and mythology of Iran's drugs politics. Secret laboratories mushroomed across the country, with the northwest Tabriz and Malayer, becoming a key production zone. Prohibition made the business of opiates highly profitable and persuaded groups of ordinary people who previously had little contact with the opium economy to set up production lines of morphine and heroin. In the police accounts, bakers, butchers and other ordinary workers used their workplace, house or farmhouse to produce amounts of opium derivatives and to sell it to traffickers.[109] By using opium smuggled into Iran from Afghanistan, or morphine base coming southward from Turkey, 'heroin chemists' developed underground networks of procurement and production.[110] A contemporary commentator acknowledged that the process of transformation 'is not more complex than making a bootleg

---

[108] A *baba karam* is a folkloric character in vogue during the Pahlavi period, *and* since the late 1990s, which derives its notoriety from a popular dance (*raqs-e baba karam*) usually performed by moustached men in the bazaar or around fountains.

[109] See Shahidi, *Mavadd-e Mokhadder*, 121.

[110] McLaughlin, 'Drug Control', 477. Gootenberg shows, similarly, how cocaine production skyrocketed in Peru after it coca cultivation was made illegal; see Paul Gootenberg, *Andean Cocaine: The Making of a Global Drug* (University of North Carolina Press, 2008).

of whiskey in the United States', a similarity that recalls the early days of US prohibition and the production of moonshine. At times, heavy armed confrontations occurred, especially when the traffickers were members of tribes or Afghans. For example, in 1957, an eleven-hour shooting battle broke out between the Gendarmerie (in charge of antinarcotics) and the Kakavand Tribe, in the Kurdish town of Kermanshah, leaving eighteen tribesmen dead and forty-five wounded.[111] These outbursts of war-like violence heightened the sense of crisis that characterised the world of drugs, unprecedented for the Iranian public. Increased confrontation signified also that the financial bonanza of heroin trafficking had soon established international connections between local drug business and a transnational network of associates that reached the wealthy markets of the West.

The road to hell is paved with good intentions. That is not the case for the Pahlavi state. At the time when FBN advisors advocated in favour of Iran's 'selfless effort', the American intelligence was also well informed about the Shah's acolytes' role in the international narcotic trade.[112] Gingeras reports that among the families directly involved in the narcotic affairs, apart from the Pahlavi, the CIA had mentioned the 'Vahabzadeh, Ebtehajh, Namazee and Ardalan families'.[113] The shah's twin sister, Princess Ashraf Pahlavi, had been allegedly involved in cases of narcotics trafficking and critics of the Pahlavi regime associated her with international criminal organisations. It was reported that in 1967, while on her way out of Geneva airport, Ashraf's luggage was searched by the Swiss antinarcotics police, who allegedly found large amounts of heroin. Because of her diplomatic immunity, she was not prosecuted, but the international media covered the event in-depth, causing a scandal. Swiss and French newspapers spread the news about the incident, although official accounts have so far remained contested, especially by supporters of the Pahlavi monarchy. Ashraf sued *Le Monde* for these allegations and eventually won her libel case, having the story retracted.[114]

[111] *New York Times*, June 17, 1953; *New York Times*, January 12, 1958.
[112] Ryan Gingeras, 'Istanbul Confidential: Heroin, Espionage, and Politics in Cold War Turkey, 1945–1960', *Diplomatic History* (2013), 25.
[113] 'Poppy Politics', 319.
[114] This claim is made especially in Fardust's memoires, published posthumously. Hossein Fardoust, *The Rise and Fall of the Pahlavi Dynasty* (Hadis Publishing House, 1995). While the materials provided by the SAVAK documentation on the regime appears to be reliable, albeit at times with lacunae, some of the

Two other high-ranking officials had already been involved in a similar case. In 1960, the Swiss authorities warned of an Iranian national, Hushang Davvalu, suspected of shipping heroin into Europe. Ten years later, the police searched his house in Switzerland, where they found narcotics. Davvalu, who suffered from heart problems, was allowed to return home to Tehran.[115] Shah's two brothers, too, were seemingly embroiled in the trafficking business. Hamid-Reza Pahlavi, the younger brother, is described in the account of the SAVAK as 'having established in Takht-e Jamshid Street a headquarter, which used air companies to smuggle drugs, especially opium from outside the country into Iran, to produce heroin and then distribute it in Tehran and other cities'. The document describes also the involvement of high officials in the army who at times escorted the prince in his business trips. Hamid-Reza reached considerable fame to the point that the best heroin available in Tehran, in the 1960s, was known as *heroin-e hamid-reza*.[116]

The other brother of the Shah, Mahmud-Reza, had also been caught up in the business. A *bon vivant* with a habit for opium and heroin, his relation with the Shah was strained and he was forbidden to participate in events at the royal court.[117] Since 1951, American officials have also been observing the movements and affairs of Mahmoud-Reza across the Mediterranean Sea and the Atlantic Ocean. In February of that same year, Charles Siragusa, an experienced investigator of the FBN, spotted the prince 'in a purple Cadillac with two beautiful women' in Hamburg. The FBN discovered that Mahmud-Reza, under the alias Marmoud Kawa, smuggled heroin between Tehran, Paris, New York

claims in the above-mentioned memoires remain dubious. For methodological consideration of these sources, see 'About the Sources' in Charles Kurzman, *The Unthinkable Revolution in Iran* (Harvard University Press, 2009). For this purpose, Ashraf also requested support from the US government. See 'Telegram 64317 From the Department of State to the Embassy in Iran', April 14, 1972, and 'Telegram 2080 From the Embassy in Iran to the Department of State', April 11, 1972, in M. Belmonte (ed.), *Foreign Relations of the United States, 1969–1976, Volume E–4, Documents on Iran And Iraq, 1969–1972*, Washington, DC 2006, Documents 177 and 178. See Ashraf's memoire, Pahlavi, A., *Faces in a Mirror: Memoirs from Exile* (Englewood Cliffs, 1980), 188–91; See CIA, PA/HO Department of State E. O. 12958, as amended June 21, 2006. Pol 15–1 Iran.
[115] Alimardani, *Drugs and the Pahlavi*, 119.
[116] *Parvandeh-ye enferadi-ye Hamid-Reza*, 17/06/1341 cited also in Ivi, 125.
[117] Alimardani, *Drugs and the Pahlavi*, 125.

and Detroit, but the United States never followed up the lead in this case and instead arrested an Armenian associate of the prince, who operated a network, among whom were part also Iran's counsels in Brussels and Cairo.[118] Thence, Iran's diplomatic corps acquired the reputation of a drug trafficking network, despite attempts to cover up the scandals.

As previously said, US regional interest in the Middle East and the ongoing Cold War priorities prevented the FBN from disclosing the vast network of international heroin trafficking that operated under the Pahlavi family. The state itself remained in a paradoxical position: it hardened its drug laws, it militarised its drug control strategy and expanded its intelligence networks through anti-narcotic cooperation with the USA, but it acquiesced in not interfering with high-calibre heroin trafficking networks, often connected or known to the royal court. Iran became the regional machinery of US anti-narcotic strategy, through intelligence and information sharing, but also one of the main hubs for illegal narcotics in the region.[119]

The means of enforcement of the drug laws improved steadily, the number of people punished for drug offenses increased dramatically, and prison populations reached unprecedented levels with administrative costs becoming a burden in budgetary allocations. Welfare for drug rehabilitation remained weak and the promise to uproot drugs from society sounded like a farce. In 1969, however, the government overturned the 1955 opium prohibition and established a regulated system of opium distribution and poppy cultivation. This occurred, most symbolically, when newly elected US president Richard Nixon declared the beginning of the 'War on Drugs'.

Iranizing Prohibition?

The second half of twentieth century saw prohibition of drugs turning into a central issue in the global political debate. Intermingling of domestic and foreign affairs in drugs politics was the rule. Nixon's call for a 'War on Drugs' influenced the discourse on illicit drugs across the globe. Indeed, US domestic politics had its leverage over international narcotics control. In his bid to win the US election, Richard Nixon had to defeat two enemies: the black voter constituency and

[118] Valentine, *The Strength*, 117–119.   [119] *Bulletin on Narcotics*, 1960, 4 (4).

the anti-war left, both galvanised by the vibrant movements of the late 1960s. As his former domestic policy advisor revealed in 2016, 'we couldn't make it illegal to be either against the war or black, but by getting the public to associate the hippies with marijuana and blacks with heroin, and then criminalizing both heavily, we could disrupt those communities'.[120]

As the United States embraced a more systematic prohibition, its close ally the Shah seemed to go in another direction. Counter-intuitively, the Iranian government introduced a groundbreaking policy, which had few systematic precedents globally and which apparently defied, on its own terms, the prohibitionist regime. In 1969, the Iranian government re-introduced state-supervised poppy cultivation and opium production and, crucially, opium distribution programmes on a mass-scale. The move occurred for several reasons, the main being the refusal by Iran's neighbours, Turkey, Afghanistan and Pakistan, to eradicate their local production of opium, most of which passed through Iran, with a considerable part of it being turned into smoke by Iranians. In the words of the former Minister of Health Saleh, 'gold goes out, opium comes in',[121] with capital flight becoming a serious threat to economic development. Payment for opium depleted the gold reserves over the 1960s. Moreover, the government sought to decrease the economic burden of its anti-narcotic strategy, which had caused hardships for families whose breadwinner had been incarcerated for drug offences. An eightfold increase in heroin confiscation occurred between 1964 and 1966, prompting the government to reconsider the feasibility and effectiveness of the prohibition of opium. Heroin, a more dangerous substance but easier to transport and to consume, had become popular among an increasing number of citizens.

The government considered the 1969 drug law reform as a fresh start for the country's drug strategy. The judicial authorities granted amnesty to people condemned under the 1955 drug law and the government introduced a vast medical system of drug treatment and rehabilitation, a model that resembled in its vision the 'British model' of heroin maintenance, but which differed radically from it in its quantitative scope.[122] It also made the promise to the United States that Iran

---

[120] Dan Baum, 'Legalize it all', *Harper's Magazine* (April 2016), retrieved from https://harpers.org/archive/2016/04/legalize-it-all/.
[121] *New York Times*, February 11, 1973.
[122] McLaughlin, 'Drug Control', 497–8.

would reintroduce opium prohibition once Turkey and Afghanistan had done the same.[123] But despite the Turkish ban on opium between 1969 and 1974 – which occurred under heavy US pressure on Ankara – poppy fields flourished undisturbed in Iran up to the fall of Shah in 1979.

The legendary 'coupon system', which is still recalled by many elderly Iranians, permitted the issue of vouchers to registered opium users. The new law granted consumption rights to two main groups. The first one was that of people over the age of sixty who would receive their ration after approval of a physician. The other group was that of people between the age of twenty and fifty-nine, who manifested medical, psychological symptoms for which opium could be used or who could not give up their opium use, for which the state assumed the responsibility to supply them with opium. The symptoms for which one could receive the coupon, included headache, rheumatism, back pain, depression, arthritis, etc., assessed by a governmental panel under the Ministry of Health. A consumer could purchase a daily dose of opium (between two and ten grams) from a licenced pharmacy or drug store.[124] The GP or the pharmacy then issued an ID card with a photograph, personal particulars, the daily amount of opium, and the pharmacy from which he/she should secure the opium ration. The public had access to two kinds of opium. One of a lower standard, which the government took from opium seizures of illicit traffic, coming mostly from Afghanistan and to a lesser extent Pakistan, costing six rials per gram; and the other, known for its outstanding quality – sometimes recalled as *senaturi* ('senatorial') – produced in the state-owned poppy farms, priced at seventeen and a half rials per gram.[125]

With the comfort of guaranteed availability of opium, the registered user could walk to a convenient pharmacy and, at a price intended to annihilate the competition of the illegal market, purchase the highest quality of opium, worldwide. By 1972, there were about 110,000 registered people out of an estimated total population of ca. 400,000 opium users; in 1978, about 188,000 with 52 per cent of those

---

[123] Chouvy, *Opium*, 20.
[124] CENTO, 'Seminar', 112. See Iradj Siassi and Bahman Fozouni, 'Dilemmas of Iran's Opium Maintenance Program: An Action Research for Evaluating Goal Conflicts and Policy Changes', *International Journal of the Addictions* 15, 8 (1980).
[125] Ibid., 113–14.

registered under the age of sixty.[126] Those who did not register could buy opium, illegally, from registered users, who often had amounts in excess of their need and could re-sell it, or access the illicit market of Afghan and Pakistani opium, which remained in place especially in rural areas. The figure of the 'patient-pusher' appeared in the narrative of opium,[127] with an intergenerational mix where elderly opium users would register for the coupon in order to avoid younger users having to rely on the illegal market, or to make some marginal profit from reselling the coupons.[128] To have opium at home, after all, was part of the customs of greeting hosts and a *sine qua non* in areas such as Kerman, Isfahan and Mashhad.[129]

The illegal market did not disappear overnight; in areas in which the state had limited presence, people kept on relying on their networks. People living in villages, for instance, witnessed very little change after the 1969 policy or, for that matter, any previous policy. Distances were great, physicians few and distribution networks weak. Women, too, had a tendency not to register (although they did in some case), mostly due to the negative perception of female opium smokers, especially when young.[130] The public perception was that working classes registered for the coupons, given that opium dispensaries stood in less wealthy areas, especially in Tehran. In reality, bourgeois classes benefited from the distribution network too. But only a small proportion of the total population registered.

Treatment and rehabilitation facilities were also insufficient. The main hospital for the treatment of drug abuse in Tehran, the *Bimarestan-e Mo'tadan* (Addicts' Hospital), had only 150 beds in 1970, while in the rest of the country lack of infrastructures was even more blatant.[131] The private sector provided treatment services, including psychiatric and psychological support, but mainly addressed the urban bourgeois class, who could afford their higher fees.[132] The oil boom of the early 1970s – the grand leap forward of Iranian politico-economics – produced limited

---

[126] See A. H. Mehryar and M. R. Moharreri, 'A Study of Authorized Opium Addiction in Shiraz City and Fars Province, Iran' *British Journal of Addiction to Alcohol & Other Drugs* 73, 1 (1978).
[127] Siassi, 'Dilemmas of Iran's', 1133.
[128] Several accounts of elderly users living in Arak, Isfahan, Kerman and Tehran.
[129] Joanna de Groot, 'Kerman in the Late Nineteenth Century: a Regional Study of Society and Social Change' (University of Oxford, DPhil Thesis, 1978).
[130] Mehryar, 'A Study of Authorized', 97. [131] Qahrfarkhi, *E'tiyad*, 163.
[132] *Bulletin on Narcotics*, 1976, 3 (3).

Table 2.2 *Registered Opium Addicts in the First Semester of 1974*

REGIONS	REGISTERED DRUG USERS
Tehran	44.000
Khorasan	18.400
Mazandaran	17.700
Gilan	17.000
Kerman	11.900
Isfahan	6.700
Yazd	2.000
Kurdistan	1.100
Sistan & Baluchistan	1.000
Persian Gulf Ports	300

Data sampled from Qahrfarkhi, *E'tiyad*, 161.

effects on state intervention. The majority of registered users were in the urban centres of the north, in particular in Tehran and the Caspian region, whereas areas with a historical connection to opium and the poppy economy had significantly lower numbers of registered patients (see Kerman). People with access to opium without the mediation of the state opted for the illegal market.

By the mid-1970s, drugs and politics intertwined because the royal court had firstly been accused of operating an illegal network of drug trafficking and, now, had become the main legitimate provider of narcotics to the population (Table 2.2). Socially and culturally, the presence of drugs was also conspicuous. The International Conference of Medicine, which took place in the northern city of Ramsar in 1971, dedicated its entire convention to the issue of addiction. Its proceedings advised the government to ban poppy cultivation or to keep it at a minimum required for essential medical needs for the certified drug addicts. Moreover, it suggested stopping the coupon system out of the risk of opium diversion to the general population and the widespread over-prescription practiced by doctors.[133] The government refused to take either of these suggestions and the coupon system lived up to the days of the Islamic Revolution in 1979.

[133] Shahid, *Mavadd-e Mokhadder*, 129.

The 1969 drug law, however, was not dissonant with global prohibitionist discourse. Since the 1920s, UK doctors had prescribed heroin to patients who were dependent on the substance. In 1967, the Ministry of Health instructed doctors to continue this practice to prevent the spread of heroin trafficking in the UK, despite increasing pressures against it.[134] The model allowed an opiate abuser to seek medical support in special clinics, housed in hospitals and under the supervision of psychiatrists. The fundamental difference in the 1970s was the quantitative dimension of the Iranian programme, which numbered hundreds of thousands of people, compared to the UK model which accounted for a mere 342 in 1964.[135] Similarly to the UK, addiction was reframed as a disability and not simply a disease, with its consequences bypassing the simple individual and being borne by family and society.[136] The Iranian government made the National Iranian Society for Rehabilitation of the Disabled the institution in charge of treatment and maintenance of drug users.[137] In this regard, the programme was not a niche attempt to control a marginal population, but a vast societal endeavour with the purpose of addressing a public health concern. Neither it was a move towards drug legalisation or comprehensive medicalisation of the drug use. Instead, it embodied a *different* form of prohibition, the effect of which touched mostly on poorer communities.

The 1969 law disposed that drug trafficking crimes needed to be judged, not by civilian courts, but by military courts. This upgrading of the security sensitivity on the narcotic issue can be partly interpreted as the Shah's signal to his closest ally, the United States, of Iran's sincere pledge to stop the flow of heroin; and partly as a means to buttress coercive means against those operating in a terrain which was exclusively the turf of the state, namely opium production.[138] A CIA memorandum reported that 'Tehran has embarked on a stringer smuggling

---

[134] Sarah G. Mars, *The Politics of Addiction: Medical Conflict and Drug Dependence in England since the 1960s* (Springer, 2012), 27.
[135] Ibid., 8.   [136] Berridge, *Concepts of Addictive*, 73.
[137] Amir A. Afkhami, 'From Punishment to Harm Reduction: Resecularization of Addiction in Contemporary Iran' in Ali Gheissari, *Contemporary Iran* (Oxford University Press, 2009), 189.
[138] After 1979, military courts ceased to judge drug crimes. Their role was overtaken by the new revolutionary courts established under the Islamic Republic judicial reform. Maziyar Ghiabi, 'Drugs and Revolution in Iran: Islamic Devotion, Revolutionary Zeal and Republican Means', *Iranian Studies* 48, no. 2 (2015): 139–63.

eradication program', with more than ninety smugglers executed between 1969 and 1971.[139] In 1975, it was estimated that there were 6,000 prisons spread throughout Iran, with drug offenders being still the largest population.[140] Instead of establishing a system of regulation, with an underlying non-prohibitionist mindset, the Iranian state adopted a double form of intervention aimed ultimately at the exclusive control of the narcotic issue by itself, both on domestic distribution and production. In practice, competing groups with close ties to the state – one could call them *the rhizomes of the state?* – such as corrupted elements of the court, transnational elites connected to smugglers, and drug producers inside and outside Iran outplayed the state's drug strategy to their own benefit.

Conclusions

Timothy Mitchell writes that 'the essence of modern politics is not policies formed on one side of this division being applied to or shaped by the other, but the producing and reproducing of these lines of difference'.[141] In this regard, Mitchell's historicisation is reminiscent of Foucault's genealogical approach: it is not a 'quest for the origins of policies or values, neither is 'its duty to demonstrate that the past actively lives in the present'.[142] The task of genealogy, paraphrasing the French philosopher, is to record the history of unstable, incongruent and discontinuous events into a historical process that makes visible all of those discontinuities that cut across state and society.[143] This chapter traced a genealogy of prohibition in modern Iran and its relation to the process of modern state formation. The birth of the drug control machinery in Iran dates back to the aftermath of the Constitutional Revolution (1906–11) and forms part of the wider global inception of prohibitionist policies in the early twentieth century. Sponsored by the United States, the Shanghai Conference in 1909 represented a first global effort to draw homogenising lines of

---

[139] 'Memorandum for the CIA heroin coordinator', US State Department, July 1, 1971, retrieved from http://2001-2009.state.gov/documents/organization/70 647.pdf.
[140] Rejali, *Torture & Modernity*, 55.   [141] Mitchell, 'Society, Economy', 184.
[142] Michel Foucault, *Language, Counter-Memory, Practice: Selected Essays and Interviews* (Cornell University Press, 1980), 146.
[143] Ibid., 150–4 and 162.

behaviour (sobriety, temperance, order: legibility) – haphazardly – into the body politic of the world system. Opium, as such, symbolised an anti-modern element, a hindrance in the modernisation destiny of any country. Opium, and addiction as its governmental paradigm, embodied a life handicapped by dependence, impotency, apathy and above all, slavery. Within a matter of decades, the adoption of this discourse produced apparatuses of narcotic control and prohibition. Accordingly, Iran went through a period of inconsistent experimentation, both for the state as a governmental machinery, and the people as interlocutors of and experimenters with the phenomenon of illegal drugs. In detailing these processes, the chapter unmasked the Pahlavi state's relation to social and political modernisation through an analysis of this period's drugs politics. This setting provided the contextual prelude to subsequent socio-political and cultural transformations that accompanied and followed the Islamic Revolution of 1979.

In the opium popular mythology, an apocryphal story narrates the discontinuities described at the close of this chapter. Four public officials, connoisseurs of opium (*tariyak shenas*) and professional opium users (*herfei*), would go every morning in the Opium Desk within the Office of the Treasury (*dara'i*) to test the quality of the state opium, before attaching the government banderole to those opium cakes up to standard for national distribution. With the revolution in 1979 and the closure of the Opium Desk, all four of them died because of *khomari* (hangover for the lack of opium).[144]

---

[144] Referred to the author in several instances by long-term opium smokers.

3 | *Drugs, Revolution, War*

I have nothing to do with addiction, I deal with the fight against drugs, in this fight I confiscate their opium, I tear up their coupons; now whatever the government intends to do is none of my business.

Ayatollah Khalkhali, Head of Anti-Narcotics (1980)

The most important question after the war is addiction.

Ayatollah Ruhollah Khomeini

Introduction

'Give me three months and I will solve the problem of addiction in this country', declared the newly appointed head of the Anti-Narcotics Bureau in Tehran, Ayatollah Sadegh Khalkhali on the eve of the victory of the Islamic Revolution.[1] The ousting of the Shah and the coming to power of the revolutionaries had profound effects on the ideas, policies and visions that the Iranian state had *vis à vis* illicit drugs and addiction. Narcotics, in the eyes of the revolutionary state, did not simply embody a source of illegality, physical and psychological deviation and moral depravity, as was the case for the Pahlavi regime during its prohibitionist campaigns. Narcotics were agents of political and, indeed, counter-revolutionary value/vice to which the new political order had to respond with full force and determination. In times of revolution, there was no place for drug consumption. Criticism against the previous political establishment – and its global patron, the United States – adopted the lexicon of anti-narcotic propaganda; the idea of addiction itself, in some ways similarly to what had happened during the 1906–11 Constitutional Revolution, implied sympathy for the *ancien régime* of the Shahs and their corrosive political morality.

---

[1] Reported in *Tabnak*, December 21, 2015, retrieved from www.tabnak.ir/fa/news/555470.

Under this rationale the period following 1979 saw the systematic overturning of policies laying at the foundation of the Pahlavi's drug control strategy in the decade preceding the revolution. But it would be incomplete to describe the developments over the 1980s as a mere about-face of previous approaches. The Islamic Republic undertook a set of interventions that speak about the intermingling of drugs and politics in the context of epochal events in Iranian history, especially that of the eight-year war with Iraq and the transition from revolutionary to so-called pragmatic politics. This chapter explores the techniques that the revolutionary state adopted to counter the perceived threat of narcotic (ab)use and drug trafficking. Three major moments characterise this period: the revolutionary years (1979–81), the war years (1981–8) and the post-war years (1988–97).

Tabula Rasa: the Islamic Paladin Ayatollah Sadegh Khalkhali

On 27 June 1979, Ayatollah Khomeini declared, 'drugs are prohibited';[2] their trafficking, consumption and 'promotion' were against the rules of Islam and could not take place in the Islamic Republic. This ruling, although informal in nature, sanctioned a swift redirection of Iran's previous approach to narcotic drugs, in terms of both control and consumption. As had happened in 1955, Iran seemed ready to go back to a policy of total prohibition and eradication of opiates, this time under the banner of Islam rather than that of the international drug control regime. It was not the concern of alignment with international conventions of drug control that guided the decision of the Iranian leaders, but rather the obligation to build a body politic detoxified of old habits, enshrined in a new ethics of sobriety in politics as well as in everyday life. This revolutionary vision had to come to terms with the existing programmes of opium maintenance and treatment started in 1969. What was going to be the lot of the registered opium users under the Pahlavi coupon system? In the *zeitgeist* of the first years of the revolution, between the return of Ayatollah Khomeini in February 1979 and the outbreak of the war in September 1980, the question acquired sensitive political value well beyond the technical considerations of medical management and opium production. Illicit

[2] *Jomhuri-ye Eslami*, June 27, 1979.

drugs and their consumption reified a field of political contention and intervention, which went hand in hand with the legitimacy and vision of the newly established Islamic Republic and which would have lasting presence in its political transformation in later years.

On 25 August 1979, Iran's interim president Mehdi Bazargan, who espoused a liberal orientation for the new political order, signed the ministerial cabinet act giving permission to registered opium users to purchase opium from the state at a fixed rate of thirty *rials*. The concession was meant to be an exceptional permission lasting for a period of six months, after which all opium users were required to kick their habit. Those who continued to use opium would have to rely on the black market and would be considered criminals. But given that Khomeini had already declared that the poppy had to be eradicated from all cultivated lands, the government allowed the Opium Transaction Organisation (*Sazman-e moʿamelat-e tariyak*) – previously charged with the approval and provision of opium 'coupons' – to purchase a hundred tons of opium from India, a major legitimate producer of pharmaceutical opium.[3] Intended to assist those who had been under the previous regulated opium distribution system, the one-off transaction enabled the new political order to find alternatives in the field of drugs policy. Ayatollah Sadegh-e Khalkhali best emblematised the vision of this new model.

A mid-ranking cleric loyal to Ayatollah Khomeini prior the revolution, the Imam appointed Khalkhali as Iran's first *hakem-e sharʿ*, the leading state prosecutor. Just a few days after the victory of the revolutionary camp against the Shah, in mid-February, Khalkhali had taken up the demanding post of Islamic Robespierre.[4] Unsettled by the burdensome appointment, Khalkhali wrote to Khomeini, 'I am thankful, but this job has blood and it is very demanding ... I fear that my name ['face', *chehreh*] in the history of the revolution will be stained in blood and that the enemies of Islam will propagate [stories] against me, especially since I will need to judge the perpetrators of vice and corruption and crime in Iran'.[5] The assessment of his predicament, indeed, was correct, and Khalkhali's name remained associated with the reign

---

[3] 'Law Bill on Permission to Buy Opium for Legitimate Addicts in the Country', Governmental Paper [scanned document], June 9, 1980.
[4] Ayatollah Hajj Shaykh Sadegh Khalkhali [hereafter Khalkhali], *Ayyam-e Enzeva* (Tehran: Nashr-e Saye, 2010), 290.
[5] Ibid.

of terror of the revolution. As the supreme judge heading the Revolutionary Courts, Khalkhali fulfilled the task of annihilating the old guard of the Pahlavi regime in a reign of terror that also represented the cathartic moment of the revolution. What often goes unmentioned is that at the same time Abolhassan Bani Sadr, Iran's first elected president, nominated Khalkhali as the first head of the Bureau of Anti-Narcotics.[6] Prohibition of drugs (and alcohol) became a new religion, with its punitive apparatuses of inquisitions. Khalkhali's duty as Iran's drug tsar lasted less than one year, but its effects were historically and genealogically profound.

Under Khalkhali, Iranian authorities eradicated the poppy crop for the first time in the country's modern history. The endeavour, promised at different historical stages equally by Iranian Constitutionalists, anti-drug campaigners, the Shah and the United States, was eventually carried out with no international support in a matter of two years. After having called on producers to cultivate 'moral crops' such as wheat, rice and lentils, the authorities banned opium production on 26 January 1980.[7] Khomeini declared 'smuggling' and 'trafficking' *haram*, a statement which had no precedent in Islamic jurisprudence, and which signalled a shifting attitude and new hermeneutics among the clerical class.[8] Along with him, prominent clerics expressed their condemnation of drug use in official *fatwas*. Up until then Islamic jurisprudence had remained ambivalent on opium, maintaining a quietist mode of existence about its consumption.

Khalkhali personally oversaw the files of the convicted drug offenders in collective sessions. In several instances, charges against political opponents were solidified with accusation of involvement in drug dealing or drug use, thus making manifest the narratives, mythologies and suspicions that had characterised anti-Shah opposition during the 1970s. For instance, the prosecutors accused the leftist guerrilla movement of the *Fadayan-e Khalq* of harbouring massive amounts of opium (20 tons), heroin (435 kg) and hashish (2742 kg) in its headquarters, a finding that led to the execution (and public delegitimation) of the group apparatchik.[9] Similarly, high-ranking officials of the previous regime were found guilty of *mofsed-fil-'arz*, 'spreading corruption on earth',

[6] *Etela'at*, May 10, 1980. [7] *Jomhuri-ye Eslami*, October 25, 1979.
[8] *Farhang News*, June 30, 2015, retrieved from www.farhangnews.ir/content/130464.
[9] *Etela'at*, January 7, 1981.

a theological charge that contemplated as its prime element the involvement in narcotics trafficking, drug use and broadly defined 'debauchery'.[10]

Within this scenario, one can locate the role of revolutionary tribunals, heir to the Shah's military tribunals, now headed by Khalkhali in the purification process. These courts judged drug cases together with crimes against the state, religion and national security, as well as those of prostitution, gambling and smuggling. Revolutionary courts brought public executions and TV confessions to prominence and into the societal eye as a means to legitimise the new political order and deter deviance from it. Khalkhali's role in this narrative was central: as head of the Anti-Narcotics Bureau he was a regular presence in the media, with his performance being praised for its relentless and merciless engagement against criminals. On special occasions, he would personally visit large groups of drug addicts arrested by the Islamic Committees and Gendarmerie and gathered in parks and squares. Those arrested had their hair shaved in the middle and on the sides of the head, a sign of humiliation in a manner combining pre-modern punishment with modern anti-narcotics stigmatisation. A person's appearance as a 'drug addict' would land him/her a criminal charge, with confiscation of drugs not being strictly necessary for condemnation. In video footage taken during one of Khalkhali's visit, a man, one of the arrested offenders, says, 'I am 55 years old and I am an addict, but today I was going to the public bath – everyone knows me here – I had no drugs on me, I was taken here for my appearance [*qiyafeh*]. No to that regime [the Pahlavi]! Curse on that regime, which reduced us to this'.[11] His justification hints at two apparently inconsistent points: he pleads guilty to being an addict, but also a person who did not commit any crime on that day; and he puts the burden of his status on the political order that preceded Khalkhali's arrival, that of the Pahlavis.

The fight against narcotics and, in the rhetoric of this time, against its faceless patrons of mafia rings, international criminals and imperialist politicians produced what Michel Foucault defined in *Discipline and Punish* 'the daily bulletin of alarm or victory', in which the political objective promised by the state is achievable in the short term, but

---

[10] Khalkhali, *Ayyam*, passim.
[11] Video footage retrieved from YouTube at www.youtube.com/watch?v=Zntek j5l_lM [retrieved on 20 August, 2018].

کلیه معتادین کشور به جزیره خارک و در جنوب منتقل میشوند

Figure 3.1 Awareness Campaign in Etela'at May 8, 1980

permanently hindered by the obscure forces that undermine the revolutionary zeal (Figure 3.1).[12] As an Islamic paladin in a *jihad* (or crusade) against narcotics, Khalkhali applied heavy sentences, including long-term incarceration and public execution, against drug traffickers involved at the top and bottom of the business hierarchy. He also targeted commercial activities involved, laterally, in the trade, including truck drivers, travellers' rest stations (*bonga-ye mosaferin*), coffeehouses, and travel agencies.[13] Confiscation of the personal possessions of the convicted to the benefit of the law enforcement agencies or the Foundation of the Addicts (*bonyad-e mo'tadan*) was standard practice. The Foundation, instead, dispensed the funds for detoxification programmes and medical assistance, most of which had a punitive character.[14] Albeit celebrated by some, Khalkhali's *modus operandi* fell outside the legalistic and procedural tradition of Islamic law, especially regarding matters of confiscation of private property and the use of collective sentences. To this criticism, however, he responded with revolutionary zeal: 'On the Imam's [Khomeini] order, I am the *hakem-e shar'* [the maximum judge] and wherever I want I can judge!'[15]

Again, as in 1910s and then 1950s, the Iranian state preceded American prohibitionist efforts and their call for a War on Drugs. It was under the fervour of the Islamic revolution and the challenge to extirpate, in the words of public officials, 'the cancer of drugs', that Khalkhali undertook his mission. Counter-intuitively, this call anticipated the US President Ronald Regan's pledge for a 'drug free world' in the 1980s. Anti-narcotic and reactionary religiosity animated the

[12] Michel Foucault, *Discipline and Punish*, trans. Alan Sheridan. New York: Vintage, 1977, p. 286.
[13] *Enqelab-e Eslami*, October 30, 1980; May 11, 1980.
[14] *Kayhan*, January 5, 1981.
[15] Said Madani Qahrfarkhi, *Bar-resi-ye tajarob-e modiriyyat-e kahesh-e taqaza-ye suye masraf-e mavvad-e tey-ye dou daheh-ye akhir* (1358–1380) (Tehran: UNODC, 2004, unpublished research [pdf]).

ideology of the Iranian and the American states, though at different ends of the spectrum.

On the occasion of the execution of a hundred drug traffickers, Khalkhali declared: 'I have nothing to do with addiction, I deal with the fight against drugs, in this fight I confiscate their opium, I tear up their coupons; now whatever the government intends to do is none of my business'.[16] Yet, his undertakings did not go without criticism; widespread accusations of corruption among his anti-narcotic officials and ambiguity over the boundaries of his powers tarnished his image as an Islamic paladin. Allegations of torture against drug (ab)users and mass trials with no oversight cast a shadow on the other side of 'revolutionary justice'.[17] On May 12, 1980, three months after his appointment, Khalkhali submitted his resignation, which was initially refused by then-president Bani Sadr, who had to clarify in the newspaper *Enqelab-e Eslami* what the 'limits of Khalkhali's duties' were.[18] By December of that same year, however, Khalkhali resigned from his post amid harsh criticism from the political cadres and fear throughout society.[19]

His methods had broken many of the tacit and explicit conventions of Iranian culture, such as the sanctity of the private space of the house and a respectful demeanour towards strangers and elderly people. His onslaught against drugs, initially welcomed by the revolutionary camp at large, terrorised people well beyond the deviant classes of drug (ab)users and the upper elites of the *ancien régime*. Traditional households, pious in the expression of their religiosity as much as conservative in respect of privacy and propriety, had seen anti-narcotic officials intervening in their neighbourhoods in unholy and indignant outbursts. The disrespect of middle class tranquillity animating Khalkhali's anti-drug campaign prompted Khomeini's intervention on December 29, 1980. Aimed at moderating the feverish and uncompromising tone and actions of his delegate judge, Khomeini stated: 'Wealth is a gift from God' in a major public updating of revolutionary fervour. The eight-point declaration had to set the guidelines for the new political order:

---

[16] *Kayhan*, July 6, 1980.
[17] Abrahamian, Ervand, *Tortured Confessions: Prisons and Public Recantations in Modern Iran* (University of California Press, 1999), 128.
[18] *Enqelab-e Eslami*, May 15, 1980.   [19] Qahrfarkhi, *E'tiyad*, 188.

Law Enforcement officers who inadvertently find instruments of debauchery or gambling or prostitution or other things such as narcotics must keep the knowledge to themselves. They do not have the right to divulge this information since doing so would violate the dignity of Muslims.[20]

This statement also coincided with the dismissal of Khalkhali as head of anti-narcotics and the appointment of two mid-ranking clerics in his stead. The means of eradication of narcotics shifted with Khalkhali's withdrawal from the drug battle. It also contributed a change in the phenomenon of illicit drugs.

The Imposed Wars: Iraq and Drugs (1980–88)

The Iraqi invasion of the southwestern oil-rich region of Khuzestan exacerbated the already faltering security on the borders, leaving the gendarmerie and the police in disarray. Easier availability of illicit drugs coincided with a qualitative shift. The trend that had started during the 1960s, which had seen upper-class Iranians acquiring a taste for heroin, was democratised in the years following the revolution, also as an effect of urbanisation. Despite Khalkhali's total war on drugs, his means had remained ineffective and fragmentary, and his strategy relied on fear and the unsystematic searches for drugs. The prospect of eradication of illicit drugs in this ecology, with opium geographically and historically entrenched, was unrealistic. It soon coincided with the spread of heroin within Iran's borders.

With tougher laws on drug trafficking, heroin had a comparative advantage on opium and other illegal substances. It was harder to detect both as a smuggled commodity and as a consumed substance. It guaranteed a much higher return on profits with smaller quantities, with European markets keeping up the demand for all the 1980s. Clinical records from this period point at a generational, geographical shift in the phenomenon of drugs: a majority of younger urban-origin (including recently urbanised) groups shifted to heroin smoking, with rural elderly people maintaining the opium habit.[21] In the absence of

[20] Abrahamian, *Tortured Confessions*, 39.
[21] Shahin Dalvand, Cyrus Agahi, and Christopher Spencer, 'Drug Addicts Seeking Treatment after the Iranian Revolution: A Clinic-Based Study', *Drug and Alcohol Dependence* 14, 1 (1984).

reliable data, this shift suggests a fall in the cost of heroin, whereas prior to 1979 heroin had remained an elitist habit. On the eastern front, the insurgency in Soviet-occupied Afghanistan had resulted in skyrocketing poppy production, with very large quantities of opium and refined heroin making their way through Iran. The sale of opiates across the world, and their transit through Iran, financed the *mujahedin* fight against the Red Army, a business model allegedly facilitated by the CIA in a bid to bog down the Soviet Union into a new Vietnam. Without adequate intelligence and with the bulk of the army and volunteer forces occupied on the Western front against Iraq, Iran's War on Drugs had to rely on a different strategy.[22]

By end of 1981, the Islamic Republic faced several crises: the invasion of its territories by Iraq (September 1980), the US embassy hostage crisis (November 1979–January 1981), the dismissal of the elected president Bani Sadr (June 20, 1981), and the concomitant purges carried out by Ayatollah Khalkhali since 1979. Heroin was not top on the agenda of the revolutionaries, but, by the 1980s, it turned into a visible trait of urban life. Its devastating effects were undeniable in the post-war period.

The authorities could not establish a new moral order free of narcotics. Hence, they recalibrated their focus towards the war and clamped down on political deviancy. *Vis-à-vis* drugs, the government's rationale became *governing the crisis* through different sets of techniques. These techniques intermingled with those of the war front, buttressing the interpretation of the anti-narcotic fight as a second 'imposed war' (*jang-e tahmili*), the first one being Saddam Hussein's invasion backed by imperialist forces. The Central Islamic Committee formulated the legal framework of both the war against Iraq and the war against drugs in November 1981 (Table 3.1). The Committee assigned the duty of drug control programmes to 'Headquarters' (*setad*) and their regional representatives, operating in direct contact line with the government executive. The law punished possession of quantities over one kg of opiates by the death sentence, even on the first offence; then it applied the death sentence also for minor repeated offences (more than three offences). Addiction, per se, was a criminal offence even without possession of drugs, a legal interpretation object of polemics up until the late 2010s.

[22] In the 1980s, approximately 60 per cent of the world's opium was produced in Afghanistan; by the mid 2000s, this had reached over 88 per cent. See Hermann Kreutzmann, 'Afghanistan and the Opium World Market: Poppy Production and Trade', *Iranian Studies* 40, 5 (2007).

Table 3.1 *Punishment According to the 1980 Drug Law*

Quantity	Punishment
≤50 gr. opiates	1–3 years prison sentence, or monetary and corporal punishment
50 gr. ≥ and ≤ 1 kg of opiates	2–10 years prison sentence
≥ of 1 kg of opiates (or repeated offence).	Death penalty
Cultivating opium	Destruction of cultivation; 3–15 years prison; if repeated, death penalty

Data extrapolated from Qahrfarkhi, E'tiyad, 181–2

This period also brought with it the imprimatur of later years and, as such, has genealogical value. Repressive practices of drug control did not terminate suddenly; instead, a shift in their practice occurred under different disciplining priorities: keeping addiction 'out of the public gaze'; mobilising societal elements in the fight against narcotics; integrating the rhetoric of conspiracy and suspicion into the war on drugs. One could see this shift as the transition from revolutionary zeal in favour of republican means.

The Quarantine

Once the six-month period allowing drug users to kick their habit came to an end, the priority became 'to prevent addiction from being visible from the outside and from becoming a showcase [*vitrini*]'.[23] Governing the crisis of drug use – and the management of public disorder – occurred through the quarantine. Hojjatoleslam Zargar, Khalkhali's successor at the head of the Anti-Narcotics Bureau, remarked that 'when arrested, the addict is considered a criminal and punished; then he is hospitalised and put under treatment and also condemned'.[24] This combination of incarceration and forced treatment could be observed in the massive entry of drug (ab)users into the penal/welfare system. The number of people arrested for drug (ab)use increased from 19,160 in 1982 to 92,046 in 1988.[25] The authorities set up state-run labour

---

[23] Ibid., 261–2.   [24] *Kayhan*, January 8, 1982.   [25] Qahrfarkhi, *E'tiyad*, 252.

and detoxification centres across the country, some with the capacity to take in thousands. Conceived with little scientific acumen or medical knowledge, these centres forced interned people to work on land-reclaiming projects, construction sites and other manual activities while detoxifying. Their effectiveness would often depend on the skills and personality of the management cadres, driven mostly by amateur devotion rather than experience in treating addiction. Shurabad, located in southern Tehran, was to be the model of these centres. Here, lectures in 'Islamic ideology', sessions of collective prayer and forced labour would occupy the period of internment, which could last up to six months. Accounts of violence were numerous, with an unspecified, but considerable, number of deaths.[26]

Quarantine was also carried out through other techniques, the most emblematic being that of the 'islands'. Drug (ab)users, especially the poor and homeless, would be sent to unpopulated islands in the Persian Gulf, the *jazirah*.[27] Under extremely difficult physical and psychological conditions, they were forced into outdoor manual labour, in the desolated landscapes of the south. This 'exile' – indeed, the southern coast had been used in lieu of exile in modern Iranian history – enabled the authorities to cast off from the public space those unaligned with the ethical predicaments of the Islamisation project.

Quarantining drug (ab)users preserved the façade of moral purity and social order dear to the Islamist authorities and had also the objective of instilling fear into all drug consumers. Yet, by 1984, rather than a decline in drug use, categories hitherto thought of as pure and untouched by drugs seemed to be involved in it. In Mashhad, the local authorities inaugurated the first Women's Rehabilitation Centre, while several hospitals across the country opened ad hoc sections for children dependant on opiates.[28] This would often come as a side-effect of the husband/father's opium smoking and/or the consequences of arrests, which inevitably caused hardships on poorer families and the resort to illegal means of economic sustenance, such as drug dealing, smuggling, and sex work. The most affected geographical areas were Khorasan, Baluchistan and the southern districts of Tehran. There, widespread drug (ab)use coexisted with the dominant position of drugs in the economy and, consequently, with the devastating effect of anti-narcotic operations on the local population. Heroin consumption

[26] Ibid.   [27] *Etela'at*, April 24, 1983.   [28] Qahrfarkhi, *E'tiyad*, 286.

increased even in rural communities once known only for opium and shireh smoking. A small village in Khorasan, for instance, was reported to have '118 of 150 families addicted to heroin'.[29] The authorities associated public vagrancy with drug (ab)use, a feature of drug policy for the following decades. Several national campaigns against vagrants and street 'addicts' took place throughout the 1980s.[30] While solidarity with the *mosta'zafin* (downtrodden) was expressed in the public discourse, the authorities were also eager to reorganise the public space, Islamising its guise, a process which did not tolerate the unruly, undisciplined category of the homeless.

Not all the efforts were detrimental to marginalised communities. A study of clinical access to addiction treatment carried out in 1984 in the city of Shiraz indicates that 'government clinics, after the revolution, are now seeing a broader range of addicts than before'.[31] The rural population and working class men visited the public clinics in larger percentages than prior to 1979, suggesting that the revolution's welfarist dimension had its inroads into the treatment of addiction too. Treatment was to some extent socialised over the 1980s, but this was potentially a consequence of the changing pattern of drug (ab)use – rise in heroin use – and of the pressure of state criminalising policies towards drug (ab)users. In other words, access to treatment among poorer communities came as part of the long-term effect of Khalkhali's shock therapy. Although public deviancy – embodied by drug (ab)use – undermined the ethical legitimacy of the Islamic Republic, the narrative of narcotics fell within the local/global nexus of revolution and imperialism. In this nexus, world power, the global arrogance (*estekbar-e jahani*), plotted to undermine the Islamic Republic through the Trojan horse filled with drugs.

Drug Paranoia and the Politics of Suspicion

'Everyday drugs and in particular heroin are designed as part of a long term programme by the enemies of the revolution, who through a wide and expensive network aim at making young people addicted'.[32] Thus read the first page of the newspaper *Jomhuri-ye Eslami* on August 5, 1986. The War on Drugs was the second chapter of the 'Imposed War',

---

[29] Madani, *Bar-resi*, 47.
[30] *Kayhan*, May 21, 1981; *Jomhuri-ye Eslami*, May 13, 1980.
[31] Dalvand, 'Drug Addicts', 90. [32] *Jomhuri-ye Eslami*, August 5, 1986.

the name which the Iranian leadership had used to describe the conflict with Saddam's Iraq. Not only held up by the upper echelons of power, the population at large espoused this interpretation of drugs politics. The alignment of US and Soviet interests – together with Europe and much of the rest of the world – in support of Saddam's Iraq spoke too clearly to the ordinary people in Iran: the world could not accept a revolutionary and independent Iran. A grand geopolitical scheme depicted drug traffickers and their victimised disciples, drug users, as pieces of a global chess game masterminded by the United States and Israel.

The language used in reference to drug offenders (especially narco-traffickers) was eloquent: *saudageran-e marg* (merchants of death), *saudageran-e badbakhti* (merchants of misery), *gerd-e sheytani* (Satanic circle), *ashrar* (evils).[33] These went together with references to the conspiracy that worked against Iran's anti-narcotic efforts: *tout'eh-ye shaytani* (diabolic conspiracy) and *harbeh-ye este'mari* (colonial weapon).[34]

The lexicon became an enduring feature of anti-narcotic parlance for years to come. There were certainly reasons for blaming international politics for the flow of drugs through Iran. With the Soviet Red Army involved in the Afghan war, the *mujahidin* took advantage of poppy cultivation as a profitable source of cash and people's sole means of survival. Afghanistan became the leader in the opium trade, a position it still maintains uncontested. This trade moved through the territory of the Islamic Republic in alarming numbers – between 50 and 90 per cent of all opiates worldwide. In less than a decade, the price of heroin had decreased by five times in the streets of Tehran, establishing itself as a competitive alternative to opium.[35] Despite reiterated calls for stricter border control, the Iranian authorities were not able to divert their strategic focus eastwards until the end of the war. Geopolitical constraints made the central anti-narcotic strategy – based on supply reduction – in large part futile. Futility, however, did not mean irrelevance. Since the early 1980s, the Islamic Republic came top in opium and heroin seizure globally, an endeavour carried out against the grain of international isolation and lack of regional cooperation with opium producing countries such as Afghanistan and Pakistan.

---

[33] *Etela'at*, August 28, 1986.   [34] *Etela'at*, January 27, 1986.
[35] *Jomhuri-ye Eslami*, August 5, 1988.

By 1990, almost three million Afghans lived across Iran, many in Tehran and Baluchistan, both locations key to the drug network.[36] Of course, the social and ethnic networks connecting Afghan refugees with their social milieu across the border might have helped the smuggling of drugs (as everything else) into Iran. Poverty and lack of economic opportunities had their impact on the reliance of members of these communities on the political economy of the black market. Against this picture, Afghan refugees were object of sporadic episodes of suspicion which depicted them as 'fifth column' of international drug mafia aiming at destabilising the Islamic Republic.

The Baluch and the Kurds, both historically involved in the smuggling and illegal economy, including that of drugs, had a similar fate. The drug economy represented a major financial resource of their separatist agendas, which the government regarded with mistrust and open antagonism. For instance, in 1984–5 'of the 25,000 kg of drugs confiscated at the national level, 10,000 kg were seized in Sistan and Baluchistan alone'.[37] The flow of narcotics from the southeast prompted the government to install spatial security barriers between central Iran and regions bordering Afghanistan and Pakistan. The authorities built a security belt in the area of Kerman and across the surrounding desert, with several check points along the highway route. Military and intelligence was deployed to counter the drug flow, with limited success. Aimed at protecting Tehran from the influx of drugs, the barrier had to undercut revenues of those groups that opposed the central government. On the western border, a similar build up took place on the route through the Iranian Kurdistan region leading to Turkey. This spatial intervention localised the burden of the anti-narcotic combat along Iran's geographical borders, which coincided in part with the ethnical and economic frontiers.[38]

Popular Mobilisation against Illicit Drugs

The experience of the war against Iraq proved instrumental in the fight against narcotics. Revolutionary institutions and parastatal organisations provided a military dimension to the implementation of anti-narcotics operations, which brought in *pasdaran* (IRGC, aka

---

[36] Elaheh Rostami-Povey, *Afghan Women: Identity and Invasion* (Zed Books, 2007), 80.
[37] *Etela'at*, August 28, 1986.   [38] *Etela'at*, January 23, 1988.

revolutionary guards), appointees of Revolutionary Courts, *basij* forces (volunteers), and the many foundations that operated at the ambiguous margins of Iran's state-led economy. The 'call on duty' of this decade also honed in on the narcotics combat. The propaganda machinery, tested with revolution and war, rolled fast on the topic of drugs too. Mosques had a primary role in this scheme. The fulcrum of moralisation programmes in neighbourhoods, they worked in close contact with the local Islamic Committees. In the case of arrests for 'moral crimes' (drug use, breach of gender code, gambling), the local committee would bring the offenders to the nearest mosque and, after an impromptu investigation, they could be taken to the Islamic court. State representatives held sermons in mosques, in particular during the officially sanctioned Friday prayers. For instance, in 1988 the national organisation of the Friday Prayers' Leaders 'signed a declaration in staunch support of the fight against drugs and the officials involved in the fight' and called for the involvement of the clergy in the combat.[39] Pledging allegiance to the war on drugs was as important a duty as the obligation to support the troops on the Iraqi front.

The combat also developed real operational tactics; a number of military plans tackled both drug trafficking and public addiction throughout the national territory. The Revolutionary Guards and the Ministry of Interior conducted operation *Val'adiyat* in the region of Hormozgan, which brought to justice 'more than 2,400 addicts'.[40] Other operations involved naval units in the Strait of Hurmuz or security forces in urban centres, often with large deployments of troops.[41] The veneer as well as the structure of these plans bore profound similarities to the simultaneous military operations on the southwest border. Tactically, these operations did not rely exclusively on military personnel and regular forces. Instead, as has been a hallmark of the republican era, a large number of entities connected to parastatal foundations and local committees participated in the operations. The *Basij-e Mostaza'fin Organisation* committed 500,000 volunteers to the war on drugs, with representatives being present (but perhaps not particularly active) across most of the urban and rural towns of the country.[42] Even in the urban

[39] *Etela'at*, January 10, 1988.
[40] Named after the 100th *Surah* of the Quran; *Jomhuri-ye Eslami*, November 6, 1988.
[41] *Etela'at*, July 24, 1989.
[42] *Etela'at*, January 27, 1986. *Jomhuri-ye Eslami*, January 23, 1989.

fringes of the capital, such as the *gowd*, IRGC Committees had established councils and operational units where 'the morally deviant elements in the community, e.g. gamblers and drug dealers, were identified and isolated'.[43]

In the framing of the Islamic Republic leadership, the war on drugs was as existential an issue as the war against Iraq. President Ali Khamenei, echoing Khomeini's slogan, circulated a statement pointing out that 'the most important question after the war is the question of addiction'; his Prime Minister and later rival Mir Hossein Mousavi also stated, 'we must give the same importance that we give to the war to the fight against drugs and addiction'.[44] After the resignation of Khalkhali, the anti-narcotics apparatus progressively shifted its focus to intelligence gathering, although this process did not fully materialise before the early 1990s. The Ministry of Information, the equivalent of intelligence and secret services, issued a communiqué to the public requesting full collaboration and information sharing about drug use and drug trafficking. It activated a special telephone number, the 128, and set up local mailboxes so that every citizen could contribute to the fight against narcotics. Newspapers published regular advertisements and distributed leaflets with slogans inviting people to stay alert and cooperate with the police regarding drug consumption.[45] This societal mobilisation produced a level of public engagement in that many families, whether under the influence of fearmongering propaganda or by the experience of 'addiction' in the lives of their cohorts, wanted to see the government succeed in the anti-drug campaign. Yet, it also had its counter-effects: collaboration with the authorities meant that discord and infighting could emerge within communities, where local jealousies, deep-seated hatreds or petty skirmishes could justify referral to the authorities with the accusation of drug (ab)use or drug dealing. To settle the score with one's enemies, the catchall of 'drugs' proved instrumental. This also targeted the lower stratum of the drug market, with petty-dealers and ordinary users being identified instead of the bosses and ringleaders.

---

[43] 'A virtually underground settlement created by the brick-making industry in South Tehran' in Asef Bayat, *Street Politics: Poor People's Movements in Iran* (Columbia University Press, 1997), 92. For a history of slums in Iran, see Bernard Hourcade, 'L'émergence Des Banlieues De Téhéran' *Cahiers d'études sur la méditerranée orientale et le monde turco-iranien*, 24 (1997).

[44] Qahrfarkhi, *E'tiyad*, 248.   [45] *Jomhuri-ye Eslami*, January 11, 1988.

Mobilisation also meant that the military engaged in armed confrontation with the drug cartels that managed one of the most lucrative and quantitatively significant trades worldwide. Equipped with sophisticated weaponry and organised along ethnic, tribal lines – especially in the Zahedan region, along the border with Pakistan – drug traffickers would often outnumber and outplay the regular army units. When not confronting the army, traffickers would use un-manned camels loaded with drugs to cross the desert and reach a designated area where other human mules would continue the journey towards Tehran and from there to Turkey and Europe. The value of any drug passing an international border would double *ipso facto*.[46] Once stock reached the western border of Iran, it would be transferred via Iraq or Turkey towards richer European countries, with its value increased by a ratio of a hundred. The lucrative nature of this business made it extremely resilient and highly flexible in the face of any hindrance. Corruption ensued as a logical effect of the trade – as it has been the rule worldwide – and the Islamic Republic was no exception. In several instances, public officials were charged with accusations of drug corruption. The authorities did not take these accusations lightly, the punishment for collaboration with drug cartels being merciless, the death penalty for officials of higher ranking. In 1989, the head of the Anti-Narcotic Section of the Islamic Committee of Zahedan – the capital of opiates trafficking in Iran – was found guilty of 'taking over 10 million [*tuman*] bribe from a drug trafficker';[47] the head of the Drug Control Headquarters (DCHQ) in Mashhad, later in 1995, was judged for his 'excessive violations in his administration'.[48] The Judiciary applied the maximum sentence. Both officials were hanged.

The Iranian state upheld its moral standing *vis à vis* these accusations by showcasing the human cost that its war on drugs had had since 1979. The number of soldiers and volunteers who lost their lives in anti-narcotic operations (or while on duty attacked by drug traffickers) increased from 7 in 1979 to more than 155 in 1988 and 264 in 1992. It steadily increased over the years of the Iran–Iraq War, reaching a maximum after the reforms of law enforcement in the early 1990s.

The government bestowed the title of 'martyrs', *shahid*, to all those who lost their lives on anti-narcotic duty (Figure 3.2). The families of

---

[46] Robins, *Middle East Bazaar*, Introduction. [47] *Etela'at*, January 19, 1989.
[48] *Etela'at*, July 12, 1995.

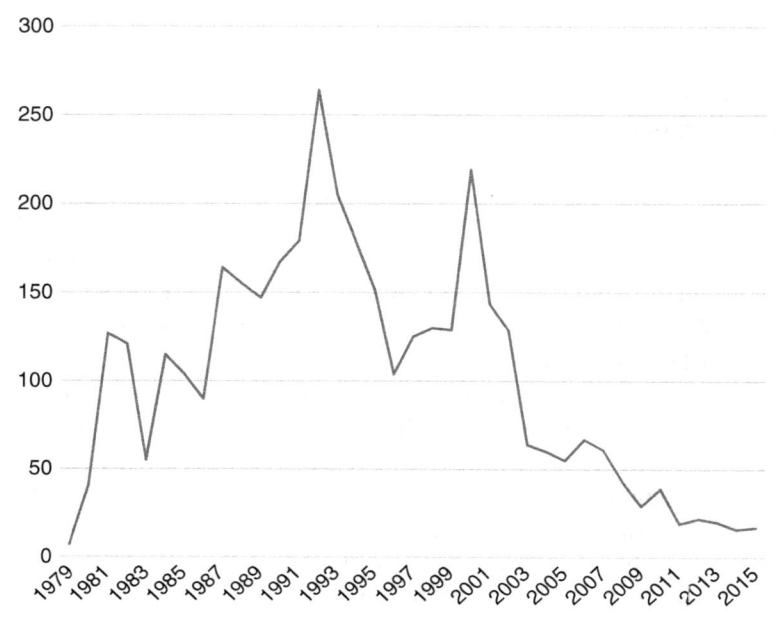

Figure 3.2 'War on Drugs' Martyrs (per year)
DCHQ, 'Unpublished data', undated.

the drug war martyrs had all the attached economic and social benefits that the title of martyr carried, approximately equivalent to that of the soldiers who fought and perished on the Iraqi front.[49] They entered the sacred semantic body of the Islamic Republic. While the Sacred Defence ended in 1988, the War on Drugs continued unhampered up to the present day, and with it the drug war martyrs, reaching a peak in the early 1990s, when narcotic combat topped the list of security priorities following the end of the Iran–Iraq War.

Of the 3,766 security and army members who perished between 1979 and 2015, the greatest share (66 per cent) is represented by the police (NAJA), followed by the IRGC and the Basij (both 11 per cent).[50] The numbers speak, in fact, of the mobilisation character of the 'War on Drugs', at least up to the mid 2000s. They also provide raw data on overall levels of drug-related violence in the

---

[49] *Jomhuri-ye Eslami*, April 17, 1983.
[50] The police and gendarmerie were merged under the name of NAJA after 1991.

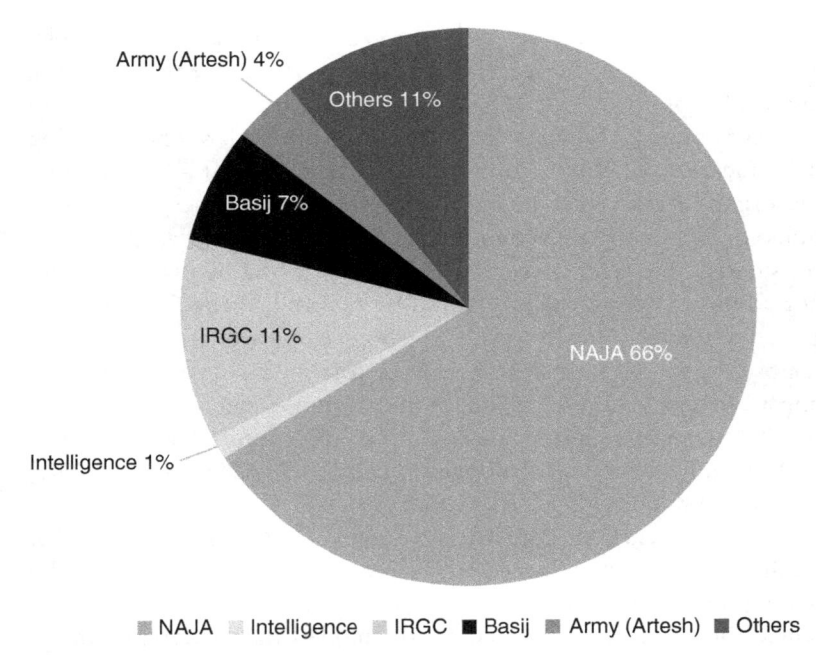

Figure 3.3 'War on Drugs' Martyrs
DCHQ, 'Unpublished data', undated.

Iranian context, which confirms that despite the four-decade War on Drugs, Iran has lower levels of violence when compared with other drug-torn contexts, such as 2010s Mexico, 2000s Afghanistan and 1980s Colombia (Figure 3.3).[51]

Although prevalent, the military/security mobilisation techniques operated alongside a number of more localised, civic and humanitarian initiatives that took place throughout the 1980s and indeed represented a first step towards broader programmes in the following decades. Here too, official and informal institutions worked alongside each other. The Construction Jihad (*Jahad-e Sazandegi*), for instance, launched autonomous programmes of treatment for female drug (ab)users and their children.[52] Islamic Associations (*anjoman-e eslami*) built large treatment camps across Tehran and other cities, often overlapping and exchanging patients with state-run centres mentioned above.

[51] An issue that I intend to explore in future research projects.
[52] Qahrfarkhi, *E'tiyad*, 199.

The Komeyl Hospital was another important example. The hospital actively undertook addiction treatment under the financial support of twelve benefactors from the medical and scientific community. Patients received psychological support during detoxification, at the price of 12,500 rials. Without state support, the organisation relied on the patients' contribution or the donations of sympathetic supporters.[53] Once the medical personnel considered the drug user recovered and stable, he (women were not admitted here initially), would be referred to the Construction Effort Organisation in order to find employment. In case of relapse, he would be sent to prison or a labour/treatment camp for imprisonment.[54] A system of treatment/punishment surfaced over the 1980s and connected a network of institutions, organisations, centres and people who belonged and did not belong to the state, allowing limited addiction treatment.

This coexistence of state and non-state support, at the fringes of legality, has an oxymoronic dimension, a feature that would fully develop in the following decades. This experience in the 1980s represented the genealogical ground for the models that materialise in the post-war period, at least *in nuce*.

After the War (1988–97): Policy Reconstruction and Medicalisation

With the end of the eight-year war against Iraq, the Islamic Republic entered a new phase of its politics, a period labelled 'Thermidorian' or 'Second Republic'.[55] The Islamic Revolution of 1979 intertwined, intrinsically, with the 'Sacred Defence', bearing on the evolution of institutions and policies. Questions of political structure and constitutional legitimacy were put on hold for several years during the war, allowing for the adoption of short-term mechanisms of political management. It was not the end of war with Iraq – the war itself having been 'normalised' in the lives of Iranians (at least those living away from borders) – but the death of the Supreme Leader that represented the greatest moment of instability for the still-young Islamic Republic. A moment of unprecedented crisis, the political order faced its greatest challenge, for which, however, it had been

[53] Ibid., 213–14.   [54] Ibid., 199.
[55] See Jean-François Bayart, 'Thermidor En Iran', *Politique étrangère* (1991).

prepared long before the event. Under the guidance of Khomeini himself, the leading figures of the state had taken a set of institutional measures to manage the post-Khomeini transition.

By the end of the war, the state moved from deploying the politics of religion to being more religiously political. End of the war also prompted the end of popular mobilisation targeted at an external threat (i.e. Iraq), and the need to refocus state formation towards domestic issues, including the rebuilding of infrastructures, of the war economy amidst low oil prices, and the redistribution of resources to those social classes who had selflessly supported the war effort. The coexistence of formal and informal institutions (e.g. the *bonyad*, the Islamic Committees), which had characterised the war years, needed readjustment for the necessity of post-war recovery.[56] Welfare policies and institutions had to be recalibrated and progressively formalised into readable bureaucratic and administrative machinery.

Institutionalisation and bureaucratisation occurred also in the field of drug policy. The creation of the Drug Control Headquarters (*setad-e mobarezeh ba mavadd-e mokhadder*) is the most significant development in the country's drug policy structure, introduced following the approval of the text of the 1988 anti-drug law emanating from the Expediency Council.[57] Public officials' experiences during the years of the war forged the mentality and practical undertakings of the post-war drug strategy. A distinctive signature of the war, the *setad* was a venue where officials of different political persuasions, institutional affiliation and expertise would meet and discuss matters of management in politics, security as well as economics, in collective terms. As an executive body, under the command of the president, the drug control *setad* advised the government and pushed in favour of structural reforms in drugs policy. The *setad* was also a model of intervention beyond the field of the drug war or, for that matter, the war. The number of governmental and intra-governmental bodies set up under the *setad* model has been a hallmark of Iranian politics since the 1980s. Among these, the

---

[56] Kevan Harris, 'A Martyrs' Welfare State and Its Contradictions: Regime Resilience and Limits through the Lens of Social Policy in Iran' in *Middle East Authoritarianisms: Governance, Contestation, and Regime Resilience in Syria and Iran* (2013), 67–8. And Mahmood Messkoub, 'Social policy in Iran in the twentieth century', *Iranian Studies* 39, 2 (2006), 251.

[57] While the text of the law is discussed in the *Interregnum*, the role of the DCHQ is relevant to the analysis of the post-war period.

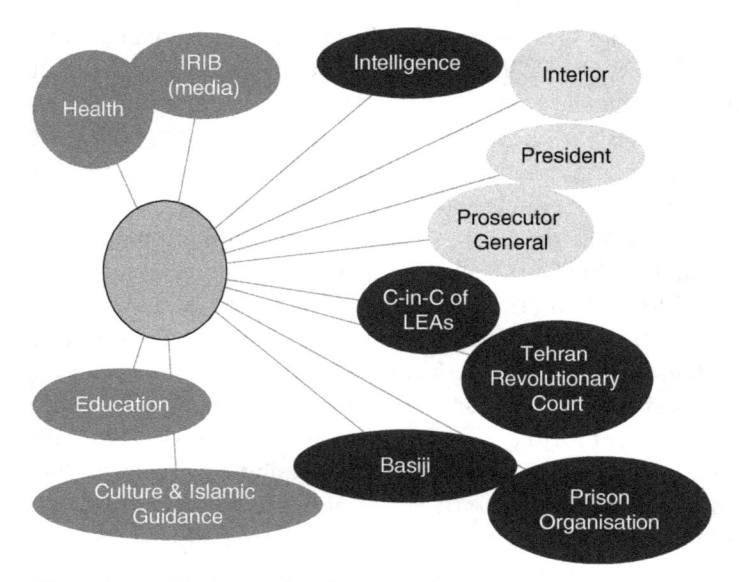

Figure 3.4 DCHQ Membership according to the 1988 Law

Drug Control Headquarters has been the most powerful and financially significant, but others should not be left aside: the Irregular War *setad*,[58] the Moral Code *setad* ('*amr be-ma'ruf nahi' bil-monker*), the Anti-Smuggling and Counterfeit Goods *setad*, the National Elections *setad*.

During the war, the headquarters became the most reliable and fastest way to respond to the urgencies of the front or to domestic problems, such as food shortages and security threats. With the conclusion of the war, however, the government dismantled the war headquarters. The drug war *setad*, however, had expanded and never ceased to operate since its creation. Its field of intervention spanned from anti-trafficking, intelligence gathering and judicial oversight – in other words, everything related to drug supply reduction – to rehabilitation, treatment (or drug demand reduction), international relations, prevention and research programmes. According to the 1988 law, the DCHQ is the place 'where all the [drug] related executive and juridical operations shall be centred' (Figure 3.4).[59]

---

[58] *Fars*, November 26, 2010, retrieved from www.farsnews.com/newstext.php?nn=8908241792.
[59] See Chapter 5 for a discussion of the law.

Heir to the Office for the Coordination of the Fight against Addiction, headed by Khalkhali in 1980, the DCHQ had the task of coordinating and executing the drug war nationwide. Weighted towards security-oriented programmes, with law enforcement, intelligence and judicial officials being more prominent, the DCHQ adopted a less security-oriented outlook from the 2000s. Its funding has increased constantly since its inception, as have its duties, which cover all the provinces in the country where the Local Coordination Council (*shoura-ye hamahangi*) of the DHCQ operate.

Its standing, nonetheless, has remained ambiguous. Because its place within the organs of the state is uncertain, the DCHQ is involved in every drug-related matter but does not hold responsibility and its presence at times remains incoherent and ineffective.[60] As a coordination body between different ministries, it rests upon a fragile compromise, which in practice is a coexistence of inconsistencies. The DCHQ works as an oxymoron, a site where otherwise incompatible mechanisms of political intervention find a place to operate (Figure 3.5). By bringing public agents with different approaches on drugs under the same roof, the DCHQ acted as the agency promoting, opposing, criticising and defending all and nothing in national drugs politics. It is both an institutional showcase for Iran's War on Drugs and the engine of policies that, as I discuss in Part Two, have diverging political objectives.

Despite its inconsistencies, the DCHQ had a significant impact on the first half of the 1990s. Under the directorship of Mohammad Fellah, a former intelligence and prison official, two important developments took place.

Deconstruction of scientific and medical expertise characterised the period following the Islamic Revolution in 1979. Instead, the war helped to reintegrate previously undermined professional categories, in particular scientists and doctors, who in the 1990s received renewed state support and encouragement for their activity.[61] The medical community gained influence in the making of the post-war approach to illicit drugs and, significantly, drug (ab)use. Mohammad Fellah seconded this trend and pushed tactically towards the medicalisation of 'addiction', with the

---

[60] Reported in several interviews with public officials, including DCHQ ones.
[61] Farhad Khosrokhavar and Amin Ghaneirad, 'Iran's New Scientific Community', *Iranian Studies* 39, 2 (2006), 262.

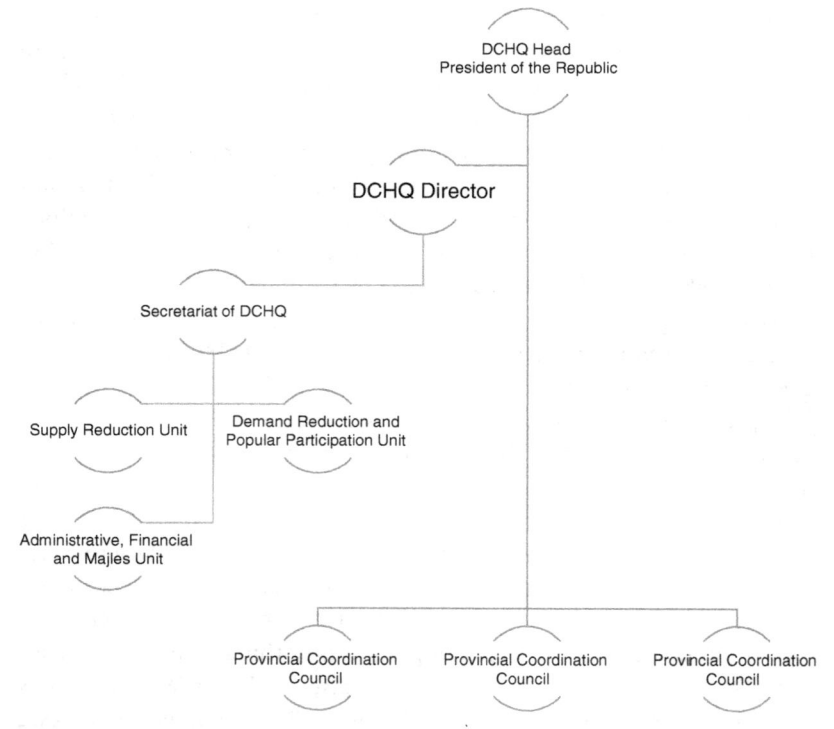

```
                    DCHQ Head
                President of the Republic
                          │
                    DCHQ Director
                          │
        ┌─────────────────┤
   Secretariat of DCHQ    │
        │                 │
   ┌────┼─────────┐       │
Supply        Demand Reduction and
Reduction Unit   Popular Participation Unit
        │
Administrative, Financial
   and Majles Unit
                          │
            ┌─────────────┼─────────────┐
     Provincial       Provincial     Provincial
    Coordination    Coordination    Coordination
       Council         Council         Council
```

Figure 3.5 DCHQ Structure in the 2000s

objective of de-emphasising the crime-oriented weight of the drug laws. An outspoken critic of the 1980s policies, he argued for a medical approach and the abandonment of punitive measures. His push eventually succeeded in 1997 when the Expediency Council ruled that addiction was not a crime and could be therefore treated without punishment. Fellah's other most significant endeavour was more covert. As head of the DCHQ, he facilitated the creation of NGOs in the field of addiction. In line with the mindset of these years, his attempt signalled the need to unburden the social weight of addiction through the inclusion of non-state organisms in tackling drugs. Not coincidentally, one of the subsections of the DCHQ is specifically dedicated to 'popular participation' (*mosharekat-e mardomi*) in provision of welfare according to the drug laws. The seeds of this strategy, however, would be visible and effective only later in the 2000s.

Conclusions

Revolutions, combats and wars are events that dictate the rhythm of history. Less visible is the way these events impinge upon phenomena such as drugs consumption, drug production and the illegal economy. Drastic political change results in changing worldviews *vis-à-vis* drugs. This chapter accounted for the epochal transformation that drugs politics underwent from the fall of the Pahlavi dynasty – and its unconventional drug control programmes – to the populist and revolutionary onslaught against narcotics under the newly established Islamic Republic. Drugs acquired the value of political objects, charged with ideological connotation. They were anti-revolutionary first and foremost, only secondarily anti-Islamic. Part of an imperialist plot to divert the youthful strength of the revolution from its global goals, drugs coalesced all that was rotten in the old political order. Victory against illegal drugs was the ultimate revolutionary objective.

From the point of view of political practice, the combat against narcotics borrowed from those same methods used in the crisis management approach of the Iran–Iraq War. Mobilisation of popular forces, creation of multiple headquarters (the *setadisation* of politics) and the adoption of a language borrowing from the war discourse and its Manichean worldview. As the war ended, drugs politics shifted towards new methods and objectives. The inauguration of the 'reconstruction era' under president Ayatollah Hashemi-Rafsanjani (1989–97) meant that economic issues and the concerns of the middle class over security and public space became more central in policymaking. Since multiple competing agencies operated in law enforcement, in 1991 the government approved the merging of the City Police and the Gendarmerie and the Islamic Revolutionary Committees into the NAJA, the Islamic Republic Law Enforcement.[62] The centralisation of law enforcement increased the capacity of the police to control the public space, which resulted in a massive number of arrests, among which those for drug-related offences figured as the absolute highest. Similarly, it led to increasing number of drugs seizures, although this did not have a noticeable effect on drug price. By the late 1990s, drug prices stabilised – even considering Iran's high inflation – and the public

---

[62] NAJA, 'Tarikhcheh', retrieved from http://police.ir/Portal/Home/Default.aspx?CategoryID=1e3abacf-2e74-46da-ae12-f3f7511572cf.

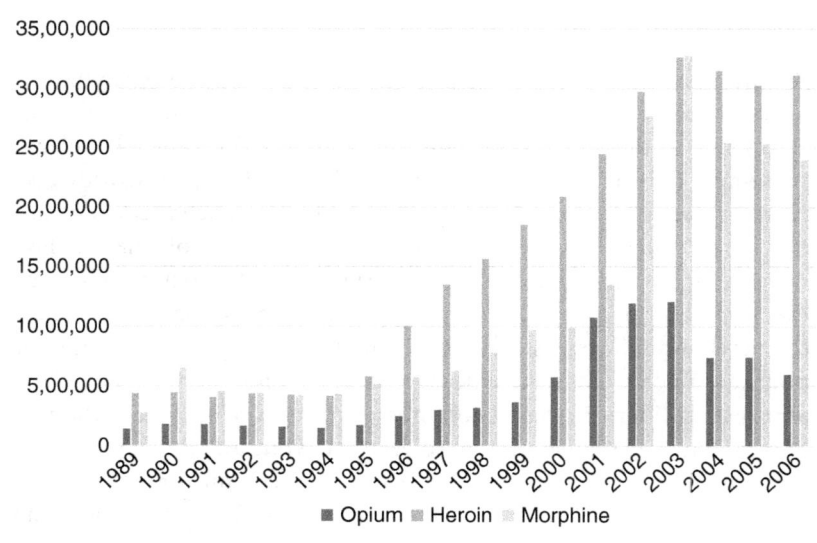

Figure 3.6 Drug Prices from 1989 to 2006 (*toman*/kg)

considered drugs as the third social problem after unemployment and high cost of life (Figure 3.6 and Figure 3.7).[63]

The shift from the external threat (Iraq) to the internal management of (dis)order had its direct effects on drug policy. With a government that pursued a smaller role for itself in the public life of Iranians and which sought the privatisation of some sectors of the economy, the management of the drug problem also faced transformation. The state-run treatment camps, amid the criticism of violence, abuse and mismanagement, were progressively closed, including that of Shurabad. There was an attempt to shift the provision of services for drug (ab) users to their families or, for that matter, to the private sector. In this, the reintegration of the medical professions was timely and instrumental.

By the end of the 1990s, there was a boom in private practice of treatment for middle-class drug (ab)users; their practice was not concealed from the public gaze and actually took place through advertisements in newspapers and on the radio, as well as posters on walls and in shopping malls. Although the government intervened to restrain the

[63] *Keyhan*, June 14, 1998.

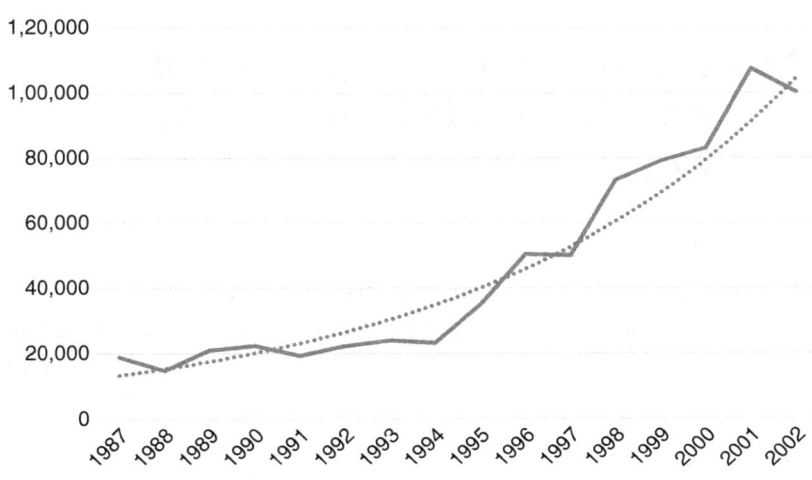

Figure 3.7 Narcotic Seizure (all type) (1987–2002) (kg)
Data extrapolated from DCHQ quoted in 'Research Study on Drugs, Crime and Terrorism in the I.R. of Iran', UNODC (Tehran, January 2006, unpublished report [word file]).

illegal market of treatment, private practices of cure and pseudo-treatment remained a vibrant sector of Iran's addiction paramedicine. It was part and parcel of the socialisation of drug 'addiction' and the shift towards the privatisation of treatment that ensued in the later decades. Demobilisation, a key aspect of Rafsanjani's politics, worked equally in the field of drugs politics. A new technocratic class gained legitimacy and asserted the right to manage the challenging environment of post-war Iran. It also promised to make this environment stable, prosperous and profitable for those operating in the private sector. These elements distinguished the basis for a new pragmatic approach to government, which set the stage for the emergence of reformism and post-reformism.

4 | Reformism and Drugs: Formal and Informal Politics of Harm Reduction

We have one national *crisis* every nine days of government.[1]
Mohammad Khatami, President of the Islamic Republic of Iran
(1997–2005)

Introduction

Just below the surface of post-war president Hashemi Rafsanjani's demobilisation process (1989–97), new political and social groups had made an appearance in Iranian society, bringing forth new interpretations about religion and politics, as well as up-to-date ideas about social and political reforms. They contested, constructively, the relationship between religion and state, asking for increasing political participation in the country's domestic affairs. In other words, they demanded more representation in the institutions and the acknowledgment by the political order (*nezam*) of the changing nature of Iranian society. Securing the support of these new constituencies, Mohammad Khatami, the soft-spoken and intellectually sophisticated cleric, received plebiscitary support in the presidential elections of 1997, sanctioning the birth of a pluralistic and civil society-oriented political agent, the second *Khordad* movement (*jonbesh-e dovvom-e Khordad*). The birth of the reform movement left a lasting signature on the public politics of the Islamic Republic, despite its demise and cornering, up until today.

The movement, which takes its name from the victory date of Khatami's first election, aimed to 'normalise' state–society relations; in the words of Ehteshami, 'to overhaul the Islamic Republic; modernize its structures; rationalize its bureaucracy; and put in place a more

---

[1] Ghoncheh Tazmini, *Khatami's Iran: The Islamic Republic and the Turbulent Path to Reform* (IB Tauris, 2009), 127.

Introduction

accountable and responsive system of government'.² Normalisation, in other words, meant downplaying the revolutionary rhetoric and opening new space for the categories side-lined since the early 1980s. Making tactical use of media, in particular newspapers, the reform movement opened up new spaces of confrontation and debate, and called for wide-scale updating at a level of policy *and* polity. It did so not without serious backlash.³

Younger generations constituted the backbone of the *eslahat* (reforms). Composed largely of the urban, educated, young spectrum of people, among whom women played an active and influential role, they called for a rejuvenation of revolutionary politics. Support came also from a multifaceted, if not very theoretical, group of post-Islamist intelligentsia, disillusioned with the static orthodoxy of state ideology and keen to foster an understanding of religion and politics which was dynamic, attuned with the post-Cold War context, ready to settle with liberal and neoliberal compromises. While intellectual circles – known as 'new religious intellectuals' (*roshan-fekran-e dini*) – espoused a theoretical, elitist and rather esoteric strategy to redesign and reform the Islamic Republic, often by appealing to the cultural and philosophical antecedents of Iran's history, women and social activists attempted to introduce change by practice.⁴ Thus occurred the curious and quantitatively important expansion of Iranian civil society, which fomented the success of, and was later fomented by, the reformist president Khatami. To use the words of political scientist Ghoncheh Tazmini, civil society needed 'to bridge the conceptual gap that existed between society and the state – a state increasingly lacking in civic input'.⁵ Hence, civil society became also a governmental instrument to circumnavigate the many hazards along the path of societal reforms. As a member of the *Majles* said by the end of the Khatami mandate, 'If you interpret reform as a movement within the government, I think yes, this is the end. But if you regard it as a social phenomenon, then it is still very much alive'.⁶

---

² Anoushiravan Ehteshami and Mahjoob Zweiri, *Iran and the Rise of Its Neoconservatives: The Politics of Tehran's Silent Revolution* (IB Tauris, 2007), 6.
³ See Mehdi Semati, *Media, Culture and Society in Iran: Living with Globalization and the Islamic State*, vol. 5 (Routledge, 2007).
⁴ Farhad Khosrokhavar, 'The New Intellectuals in Iran', *Social Compass* 51, 2 (2004).
⁵ Tazmini, *Khatami's Iran*, 61.
⁶ Jim Muir, 'Analysis: What Now for Iran?', February 24, 2004, retrieved from http://news.bbc.co.uk/2/hi/middle_east/3514551.stm.

The change in Iran's political atmosphere brought about by Mohammad Khatami's election, combined with the influence of experts' knowledge, opened up an unprecedented, and rather unrestrained, debate about how to deal with social dilemmas and, especially, with the problem of drug (ab)use. This chapter intends to discuss the changes preceding Iran's harm reduction reform – the set of policies that enable welfare and public health interventions for drug (ab)users – through an analysis of the social and political agents that contributed to its integration in the national legislation. The period taken into consideration coincides with that of the two-term presidency of Mohammad Khatami (1997–2005), but with some flexibility. After all, the timeframe is intended to give a conceptual system in which reformism *à la iranienne* overlaps with a broader movement in support of harm reduction. As such, the two phenomena never coincided, but they interacted extensively.

Without dwelling on the actual narratives of the reform movement, which have been thoroughly studied elsewhere, one can infer that with the onset of the reformist era, the field of drug policy entered concomitantly with higher polity into the playground of revision and reassessment. Most of the reforms promoted by the presidency had ended in resounding failure, the most evident case being Khatami's debacle of the 'twin bills' in 2003 and the limitations on freedom of expression that were powerfully in place at the end of his presidency. The first one refers to two governmental proposals that would have bolstered the executive power of the president and curbed the supervising powers of veto of the Guardian Council. The latter institution oversees eligibility criteria for the country's elections and it has repeatedly been a cumbersome obstacle to reforms. Targeted by the judiciary throughout the early 2000s, the reformist camp had been cajoled into helplessness and disillusionment towards the perspective of institutional reforms and change within the higher echelons of the Islamic Republic.

After introducing reformism and the contextual changes taking place over this period, the chapter sheds light on the changing phenomenon of drug (ab)use and how it engendered a situation of multiple crises. It analyses the process by which the Iranian state introduced reforms within the legislation. These changes were not the result of instantaneous and abrupt political events, rather they followed a fast-paced, directional shift in attitude among expert knowledge, the policymaking community *and* the political leadership. Although the Chapter travels through the historical events of the reformist government, it does so only with the aim of casting analytical light on the how harm reduction became a legitimate public policy. Thus, it scrutinises the interaction between public institutions, grassroots organisations and the international community in their bid to introduce a new policy about illicit drugs. Key to the proceeding of this chapter is the conceptualisation of 'policy'. As discussed in Chapter 1, policy identifies a set of events, in the guise of processes, relations, interventions, measures, explicit and hidden actions, declarations, discourses, laws and reforms enacted by the state, its subsidiaries or those agents acting in its stead. It also includes medical statements, webs of meaning, semantic spaces with a complex 'social life', agency and unclear boundaries. This holistic understanding of policy fits the definition of 'apparatus', a device that coalesces during times of crises and which is composed of 'resolutely heterogeneous' categories, as in the case of Iranian reformism.[7]

Crisis as an Idiom for Reforms

Since the successful eradication of poppy cultivation during the 1980s, most of the opiates entering into Iran originated in Afghanistan. Between 1970 and 1999, Afghan opium production increased from 130 tons to 4600 tons annually. This stellar increase is justified as a counter-effect of the ban in Iran and Turkey and the spike in demand for opiates, especially heroin, in Europe and North America.[8] Opium flow had been steady over the course of the 1980s and the 1990s, but the advance of the Taliban since 1996 and the capture of Kabul by their forces in September of that same year, signalled important changes for Iran's drug situation. In control of almost the entire opium production in Afghanistan, the regime in Kabul negotiated with the international community – in particular the antecedent to the UNODC, the UNDCP, a ban on the cultivation of poppies in all the territories it controlled – in exchange of international development aid. Scepticism being the rule *vis à vis* the Taliban among international donors, most of the funds for alternative farming were held back and Afghanistan produced a record of 4,600 tons in 1999.[9] Funded by Saudi and Sunni radical money, the Taliban forces put up strong anti-Iranian opposition.

[7] Cf. Shore, *Policy Worlds*, 1–3, 32, 125 and 169.   [8] Chouvy, *Opium*, 150–1.
[9] Ibid., 49.

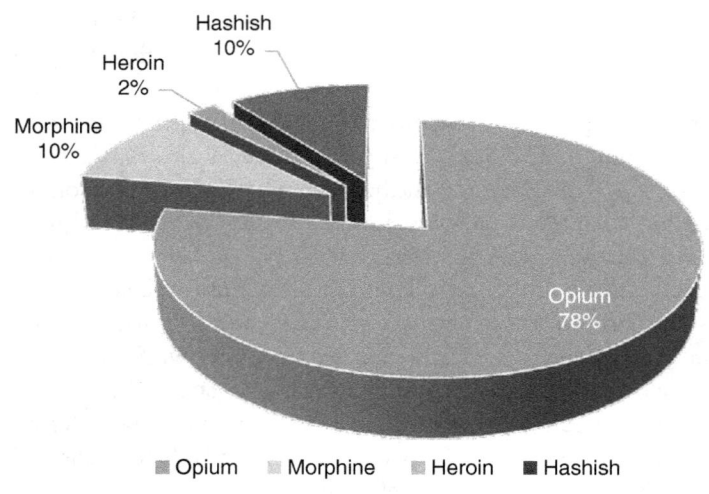

Figure 4.1 Share of Narcotics as Global Seizures (1990–2001)

The drug flow meant Iranian authorities' strategy on illicit drugs bore little results. Iran's long-term ally in Afghanistan, the Northern Alliance, had previously agreed to a ban of the poppy in June 1999, but with no effect on the actual opium output because most flowers grew in Taliban-controlled lands. The following year, though, an order of the Mullah Omar, the Taliban's political leader, abruptly banned poppy cultivation and 99 per cent of opium production stopped, with only 35 tons being produced.[10] The effects of this were immediate on the Iranian side: an upward spiral in the price of opium (more than 400 per cent rise)[11]; and a lack of supply to Iran's multitudinous opium users signified a shock in the drug market (Figure 4.1, Figure 4.2).

Many older drug users recall the effect of the Taliban opium ban with tragic remembrance. Many had seen their friends falling sick, or worse, dying.[12] With opium out of the market and heroin both impure and exorbitantly costly, people who had previously smoked, sniffed or

---

[10] Ibid., 53. And Graham Farrell and John Thorne, 'Where Have All the Flowers Gone?: Evaluation of the Taliban Crackdown against Opium Poppy Cultivation in Afghanistan', *International Journal of Drug Policy* 16, 2 (2005).
[11] Interview with Fariba Soltani, via Skype, July 11, 2014.
[12] While interviewing people in rehab camps and clinics, many referred to the abstemious days of early 1380 (2000–1) when opium had become '*sakht-ul-vosul* (hard to find)'.

Crisis as an Idiom for Reforms   103

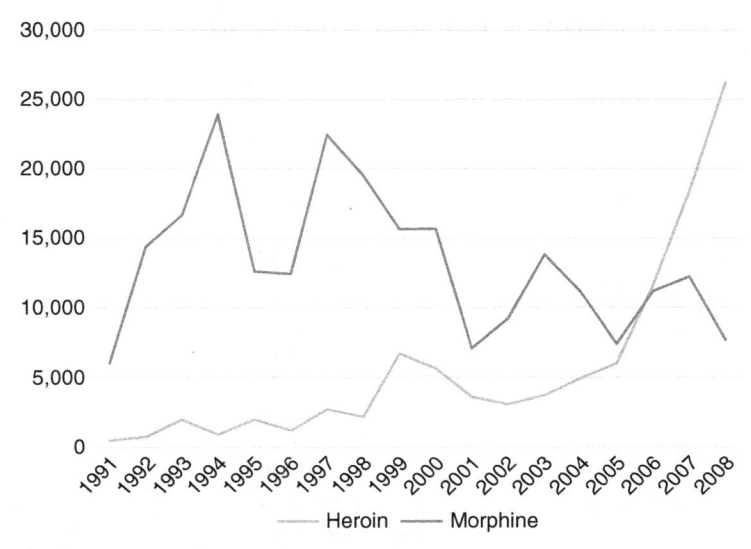

Figure 4.2 Morphine and Heroin Seizure (kg)

eaten opium, shifted first to smoking heroin (as this had been the most common form of use in Iran, because of the high purity) and then to injecting it.[13] The death toll due to drug (ab)use reached record levels and confirmed the risk of a massive shift among drug users to heroin (Figure 4.3). It was the production of another crisis within the discursive crisis of drug phenomena (Table 4.1).

DCHQ Officials had previously tried to compel the Taliban government to reduce opium production, but they had not envisioned the crisis that a sudden fall in opium supply could cause among Iranian drug (ab)users. With skyrocketing prices and increasing adulteration of the drug, many opium users opted to shift to heroin, which was more available and, comparatively, cheaper. Heroin, because of its smaller size and its higher potency, had been easier to smuggle in, despite the harsher penalties that this faced. Small quantities of the drug produced more potent effects on the body, reducing withdrawal symptoms (Figure 4.4).

---

[13] Qahrfarkhi, *E'tiyad*, 148–9. Morphine is also used among many users interchangeably with opium, *kerak* and heroin.

Table 4.1 *Opium Seizure, 1900–2001*

	Opium (kg)
1990	20,800
1991	23,483
1992	38,254
1993	63,941
1994	117,095
1995	126,554
1996	149,577
1997	162,414
1998	154,454
1999	204,485
2000	179,053
2001	79,747
Total	1,319,857

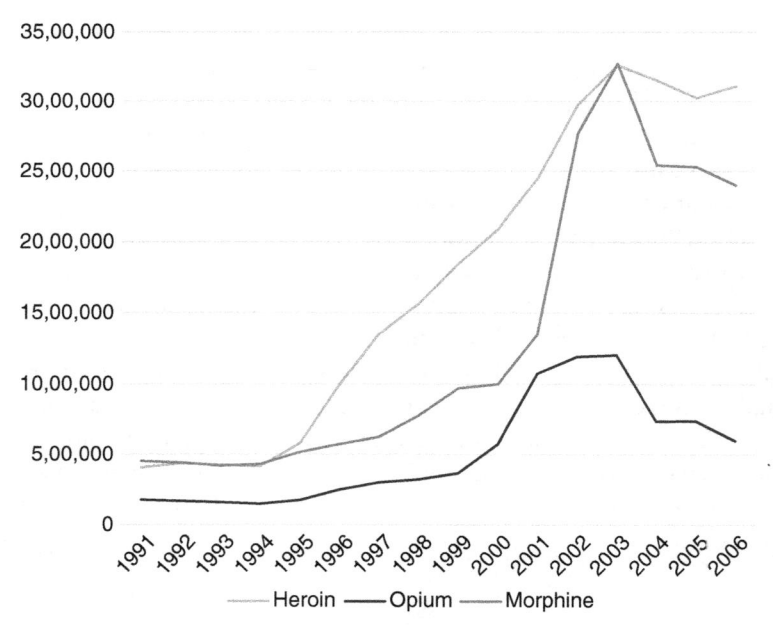

Figure 4.3 Prices of Illicit Drugs (*tuman* per kg)
DCHQ, 'Statistics' (UNODC, unpublished, undated, [Excel File]).

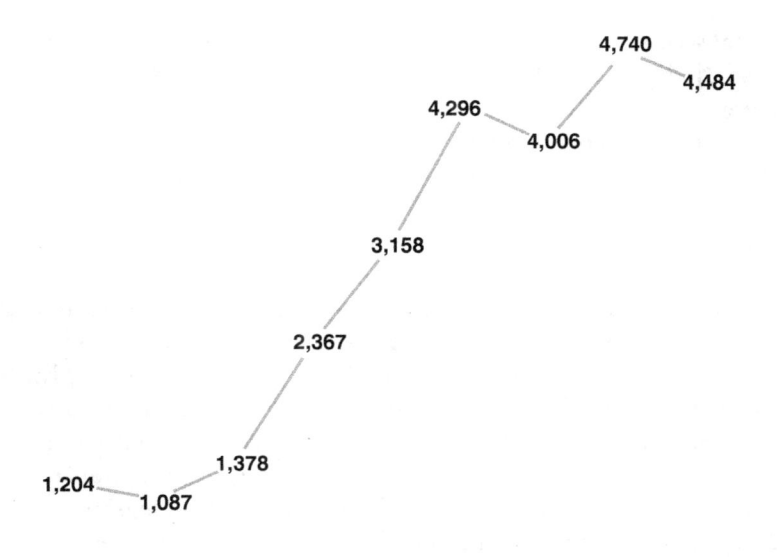

Crisis as an Idiom for Reforms 105

```
                           4,740
                              4,484
              4,296
                     4,006
          3,158

     2,367


       1,378
1,204
   1,087


1998  1999  2000  2001  2002  2003  2004  2005  2006
```

Figure 4.4 Number of Drug-Related Deaths (1998–2006)
DCHQ, 'Statistics' (UNODC, unpublished, undated [Excel File]). It is unclear whether the increase is related to the increase in the numbers of drug users. It may indicate the higher impurity of opiates or a general shift towards injecting opiates which trigger a higher risk of overdose.

Heroin posed a greater threat than opium; the latter had maintained its status as a traditional substance and had further regained authority – as a miraculous painkiller – among many war veterans who suffered from chronic pain and post-traumatic effects and 'mental distress'.[14] Heroin use among larger sections of the population signalled the shift towards more modern consumption habits, with many complexities and challenges such as the risk of HIV-AIDS, hepatitis and other infectious diseases. Injecting, hence, bears twice the negative mark of drug use. It is culturally seen as exogenous and estranged from the

[14] See Janne Bjerre Christensen, *Drugs, Deviancy and Democracy in Iran: The Interaction of State and Civil Society*. vol. 32 (IB Tauris, 2011); and R. Elling, *Minorities in Iran: Nationalism and Ethnicity after Khomeini* (Springer, 2013), 76.

traditional style of use (e.g. eating, smoking), which incorporates sharing as an essential part of the drug-use culture, and can therefore be interpreted as Westernised, if not Westoxified.[15] Although within injecting-drug-user communities sharing also signifies commonality and mutuality, it is cast as dangerous and socially harmful in mainstream society, as it symbolises both destitution and HIV risks. In Iran, the stigma on injection embodied the bottom-line of drug use, the *tah-e khatt* (endline).

The increase in heroin use engendered a situation of perceived crisis throughout Iran's policymaking community. State officials discussed the need to manage the Afghan opium market and to intervene directly in Afghanistan to secure the supply of opium, preventing drug users from shifting to substances that were more dangerous. Iran entered in negotiations with international partners concerning possible Iranian involvement in Afghanistan at the end of 2000, aimed at purchasing the entire Afghan opium harvest and transforming it into pharmaceutical morphine. This proposal was turned down due to international opposition, allegedly by the United States.[16] At that point, Seyyed Alizadeh Tabatabai, who acted as advisor to Khatami in the DCHQ and was a member of the Tehran City Council, put forward the bold proposal of trading Iranian wheat for Afghan opium.[17] He also suggested that for those addicts who could not be treated, the government should provide state-sponsored opium in order to 'reduce harm' for society, while also exporting the excess quantities in the form of morphine.[18] Despite the failures of these initiatives, the change in attitude indicated a new pragmatism towards the drug problem, one which did not concentrate exclusively on drugs per se, but attempted to read them within the broader social, political and economic context of late 1990s. The discursive shift was also a symptom of the reformist officials' unease with the country's stifled and uncompromising 'War on Drugs'. The remarks of public officials implied a 'harm reduction' mentality broader than the field of drugs policy, permeating a new vision (and ideology) of state–society relations. It was also the litmus test about Iran's willingness to introduce reforms in the field of drugs, as a matter of urgency. At the heart of the reformist camp infatuation with a new approach to drugs and addiction

---

[15] On the notion of 'Westoxification', see Chapter 2.
[16] Interview with Antonio Mazzitelli, via Skype, October 29, 2014.
[17] *Resalat*, October 20, 2000. [18] *Keyhan*, February 13, 2001.

was a quest for *reforming* society at large; not simply agreeing to change a technical mechanism within the drug policy machinery.

There were discussions in the medical community about the immediate necessity of a substitute for opium, which was becoming costly and hardly available. Meetings took place in different settings – within the DCHQ, the Ministry of Health and in workshops organised by the UNODC.[19] Discussions started about introducing methadone into the Iranian pharmacopeia to offer it to all opium users as a legal substitute.[20] The medical community urged the government to act rapidly to prevent a massive shift towards heroin use, an event which could have had lasting consequences for the country's health and social outlook. There were strong disagreements about the introduction of methadone,[21] but methadone was recognised as a substance embodying useful features in the management of the opiate crisis. Its pharmacological effects had the potency to perform as a synthetic substitute to opium and heroin, without compelling the government to reintroduce the cultivation of poppies (which was deemed morally problematic after the prohibition campaigns of the 1980s). Methadone created a strong dependence in the patient under treatment, at times stronger than heroin's, but without its enduring rush of pleasure and ecstasy, which was seen as one of the deviant aspects of heroin use by the authorities. Moreover, it was relatively cheap to produce since Iran had already developed its pharmaceutical industry in this sector.

By the time the authorities discussed the introduction of methadone, in the early 2000s, there were reports about a new drug, *kerak*.[22] Not to be confused with the North American *crack*, the Iranian *kerak* (aka *kerack*) is a form of compressed heroin, with a higher potency. *Kerak* was cheaper, stronger and newer, appealing also to those who wanted to differentiate themselves from old-fashioned opium users and the stigmatised heroin injectors.[23] Its name reprised the North American drug scene of the late 1980s and the 'crack epidemic', but it had no chemical resemblance to it. Iran's *kerak* had a higher purity than street heroin and was dark in colour, while US crack was cocaine-based and

---

[19] Interview with a Sefatian, Tehran, April 9, 2014.
[20] Interview with Bijan Nasirimanesh, via Skype, October 29, 2014.
[21] Interview with Sefatian; Mostashahri.
[22] Ali Farhoudian et al., 'Component Analysis of Iranian Crack: A Newly Abused Narcotic Substance in Iran', *Iranian Journal of Pharmaceutical Research* 13, 1 (2014).
[23] Discussions with long-time drug users in the cities of Tehran and Arak, 2012–15.

white. The name, in this case, operated as a fashion brand among users who regarded *kerak* as a more sophisticated substance, which, despite its chemical differences, connected them to American users and global consumption trends. It soon became evident that *kerak* consumption had similar effects to that of heroin, despite it being less adulterated during the early 2000s.[24]

Meanwhile, public officials hinted at the average age of drug (ab)use falling. In a country where three quarters of the population were under thirty, it did not take long before the public – and the state – regarded the *kerak* surge as a crisis within the crisis, a breeding ground for a future generation of addicts. By 2005, *kerak* was already the new scare drug. With the rise in drug injecting and an ever-rising prison population, Iran was going downhill towards a severe HIV epidemic. In discourse, doctors, experts, and political authorities were contributing to a new framing of the crisis.[25] The medical community had tried to sensitise the government about the dangerous health consequences of injecting drug habits in prison, but prior to the reformist government, the normative reaction among decision-makers was denial. Mohammad Fellah, former head of the Prison Organisation (*Sazman-e Zendan-ha-ye Keshvar*) and knowledgeable about the challenge represented by incarcerating drug (ab)users, on several occasions demonstrated his opposition to the anti-narcotic model adopted over those years. Overtly, he maintained that prison for drug crimes is ineffective.

Iran's prison population had increased consistently since the end of the war, with the number of drug offenders tripling between 1989 and 1998 (Figure 4.5). In 1998, drug-related prisoners numbered around more than 170,000. The situation became so alarming that the head of the Prison Organisation publicly asked the NAJA 'not to refer the arrested addicts to the prisons'.[26] For a country that had declared an all-out war on narcotic drugs since 1979, and paid a heavy price in human and financial terms to stop the flow of drugs, availability of drugs in prisons – a presumably highly secure institution – meant that the securitisation approach against drugs had failed. If denial had been the usual reaction of the authorities in the 1980s and early 1990s, the HIV and hepatitis crises of late 1990s had prevented any further camouflage.

[24] Interview with Hamid-Reza Tahernokhost, Tehran, September 2014.
[25] *Radio Free Europe/Radio Liberty*, April 6, 2006, retrieved from www.rferl.org/content/article/1067452.html.
[26] *Nouruz*, October 11, 2000.

Crisis as an Idiom for Reforms 109

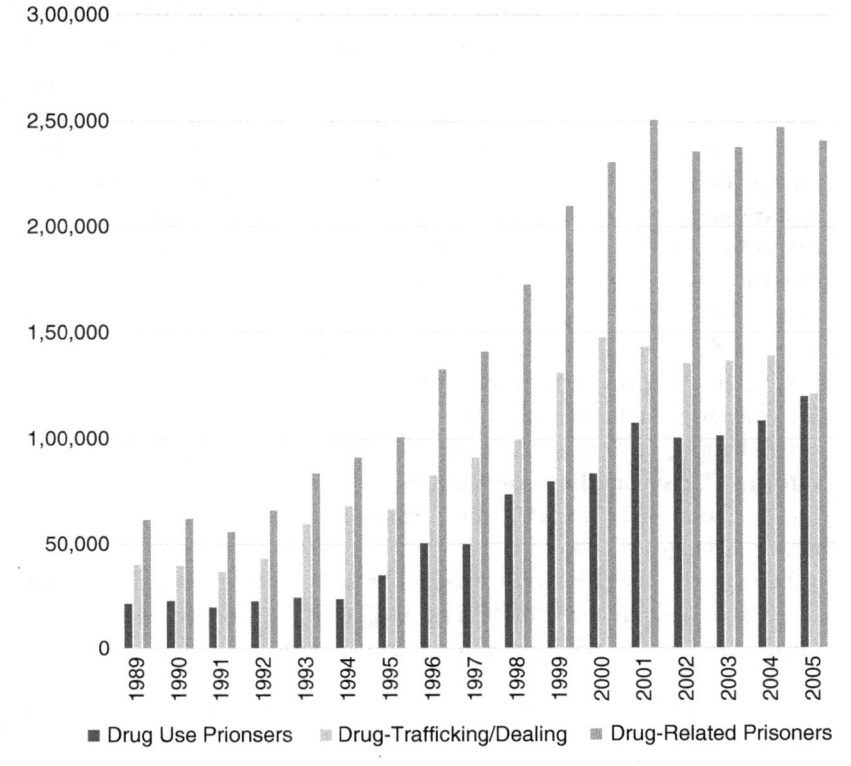

Figure 4.5 Drug-Related Crimes (1989–2005)
DCHQ, 'Statistics'.

As Behrouzan holds, 'understanding the role of prisons in the spread of HIV and AIDS was critical to the policy paradigm shift that occurred in the 1990s'.[27] Although there had been some attention to the issue of HIV in the early 1990s, this had never turned into an explicit and comprehensive policy with regard to HIV prevention. It was only in 1997, that the government commissioned, under pressure from the National Committee to Combat AIDS (set up in 1987), the first study of HIV prevalence in three provincial prisons: the Ab-e Hayat prison in Kerman province, the Abelabad prison in Shiraz and the Dizelabad prison in Kermanshah. The results were disturbing. Almost

[27] Orkideh Behrouzan, 'An Epidemic of Meanings: HIV and AIDS in Iran and the Significance of History, Language and Gender', *The Fourth Wave: Violence, Gender, Culture and HIV in the 21st Century* (Paris: UNESCO, 2011).

100 per cent of drug-injecting prisoners were HIV-positive, many of them married.[28] Kermanshah had seen the number of HIV infected people going up from 58 cases in 1996, to 407 cases in 1997 and 1,228 cases in 2001.[29] Crisis took the form of an epidemic semantically and ideologically associated with so-called Westoxified behaviours (sexual promiscuity, homosexuality, injecting drugs). For a state governed under imperatives of ethical righteousness, moral orthodoxy and political straightness, the HIV epidemic bypassed the frontiers of public health and touched those of public ethics and politics. The reactions oscillated between silent denial among some and hectic alarmism among others. The governmental team of the reformist president tipped the balance in favour of forward-looking approaches to the HIV epidemic and allowed civil society organisations to intervene in this field. Failure meant necessity for reforms. Crisis in the moral coding of the Islamic Republic confirmed the need to update, to reform the political order in line with new challenges.

During the Twenty-sixth Special Session of the United Nations General Assembly on HIV/AIDS in 2001, the deputy Minister of Health declared to the international community,

the epidemic has been given due attention during the past years in order to stem and combat its spread ... we believe that international assistance, particularly through relevant agencies, can certainly help us to pursue the next steps.[30]

Iran's HIV epidemic, generally caused by shared needles, spread rapidly in the country's western provinces that had suffered the effects of the eight-year war with Iraq. There, the psychological and physiological traces of the war materialised in the form of massive drug (ab)use. HIV prevalence was highest (more than 5 per cent) among prisoners in Khuzestan, Hormozgan, Kermanshah and Ilam.[31]

[28] Interview with Kamiar Alaei, via Skype, October 20, 2014.
[29] WHO, 'Best Practice in HIV/AIDS Prevention and Care for Injecting Drug Abusers: The Triangular Clinic in Kermanshah, Islamic Republic of Iran' (Cairo: Regional Office for the Eastern Mediterranean, 2004).
[30] 'Twenty-Sixth Special Session of the UNGA on HIV/AIDS', retrieved from www.un.org/ga/aids/statements/docs/iranE.htm.
[31] Ali-Akbar Haghdoost et al., 'HIV Trend among Iranian Prisoners in 1990s and 2000s: Analysis of Aggregated Data from HIV Sentinel Sero-Surveys', *Harm Reduction Journal* 10, 1 (2013).

In south-western cities, large-scale displacement, destruction of dwellings and infrastructures and psychological unsettledness during the 1980s was followed by paucity of employment opportunities and lack of adequate life conditions (lack of infrastructure, air pollution) from the 1990s onwards.

The ground for reforms developed through local experimentation. Policymakers implemented these experimentations in policy on the social and spatial margins. These margins were both geographical and ethical, overlapping with the most unstable disorderly categories among Iran's millions-strong drug-using population. The first group of people was that of the homeless, vagrant heroin and *kerak* users on the outskirt of the cities and in the once-known *gowd* of Southern Tehran.[32] Other categories included rural men who had moved into the urban centres, mostly Tehran's peripheries, in search of occupation, which often resulted in desultory jobs, further marginalisation and the adoption of more sophisticated style of drug use (heroin, *kerak* use versus traditional opium smoking). The second category was that of the prisoners. The two categories had mostly overlapped in the country's modern history, where the main target of systematic police repression has been the street drug (ab)users.

In particular, the epidemiology of HIV transmission among drug-consuming prisoners had a far-reaching influence on the policy outcomes. The journey of the virus from inside to outside the prison describes the genealogical trajectory of Iran's harm reduction. As the crisis originated inside prisons, the policy had to be subject to experiment first in the prison context, evaluated and then propagated outside (Figure 4.6).

The introduction of harm reduction programmes in prisons followed a broader reform project within the Prison Organisation. In 2001, the head of the Prison Organisation submitted a letter to the Head of the Judiciary to request his opinion and support for the prison reform. This included the abolition of prison uniform which 'humiliates the criminals, [and it] is contrary to the correctional purposes of prisons',[33] increased training and free time for prisoners, and providing

---

[32] The *gowd* are informal residential areas once mostly inhabited by brick makers in Moulavi and Shush Squares.
[33] *Yas-e-no Daily*, 2 December 2003.

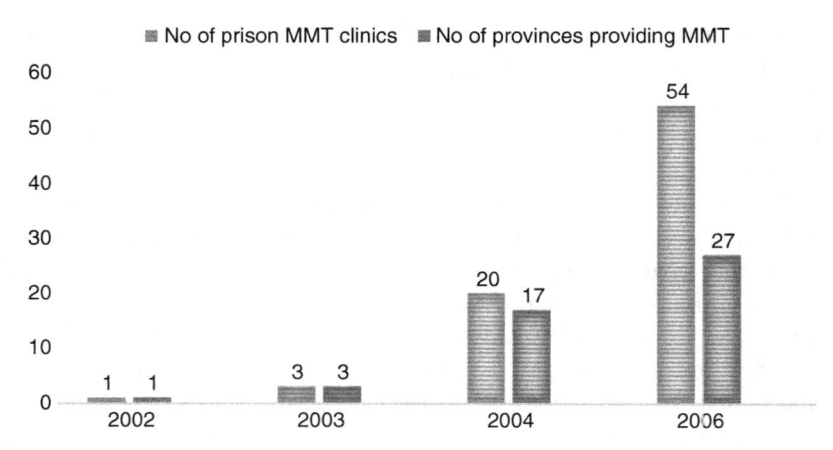

Figure 4.6 Methadone Clinics in Prisons
DCHQ, *Annual Report 2009* (Tehran, 2010). The year 1381 corresponds to 2002–3 in the Gregorian calendar.

alternatives to incarceration.[34] The latter was the object of complex debate within the institutions. Although the topic did not exclusively relate to drug offenders, the issue of drug policy reform was the panacea for the prison system. In 2005, a group of seventeen MPs requested abrogation of the 1980 'Law for strengthening sanctions for drug crimes' – the major pillar of post-revolutionary policy about drugs – to enable the judge to take into consideration elements such as age, gender, social and family condition, to avoid harsher sanctions and, tactically, the overcrowding of prisons. By 2005, drug offenders made up about 60 per cent of the prison population, the great majority men (90 per cent).[35] Drug users represented 50–60 per cent of prisoners, many of whom had started injecting in prison, usually with shared needles. The push towards a reform of the criminal law, with reference to alternatives to incarceration, was envisioned within the idea of state–society reforms promoted during Khatami's presidency as much as in response to a critical stage in prison management.

---

[34] *Ma'vi*, May 10, 2006. *Ma'vi* is the internal newspaper of the Islamic Republic's Judiciary.
[35] UNODC, *Research Study on Drugs, Crime and Terrorism in the I.R. of Iran* (unpublished, January 2006 [word file]).

A reality of crisis, both symbolic (ethical legitimacy of the Iranian state) and material (the epidemics of HIV, prison plus injecting drug use) triggered policy change and political reforming. It was the manifestation of a politics of crisis rooted in the post-revolutionary, post-war ideology of government, and governmentality. In the years after the war, social categories such as war veterans, women and young people were increasingly using drugs, with the signs of this phenomenon being more evident in public by the day. Comparisons with the pre-revolutionary period revealed a worsening of the drug phenomenon, despite the material and rhetorical efforts of the political leadership. Those who had lived during the Pahlavi regime's years, recalled the issue of drugs as mostly a weekend vice among elderly people, while a glance at the 2000s situation showed every social strata, and all generations, affected by illicit drugs. A legitimacy crisis for the Islamic Republic was on the way, through the historicisation of political/social phenomena, by which people and politics interpreted the crisis. With two decades having passed since the Islamic Revolution, policies were being disposed within a frame that contemplated a historical chronology. The adoption of crisis as an idiom of reform became part of this historisation process.

To respond to the failures of the present, public agents from different official and civic venues initiated a reformist bid in the field of drugs policy. Their concerted tactics resulted in Iran's harm reduction strategy.

Harm Reduction: Underground, Bottom-Up and 'Lights Off'

Towards the end of the 1990s, public discourse hinted at the failure of Iran's two-decade war on drugs, but statements by officials were only moderately critical, with a few exceptions.[36] The state sought the way out of the impasse through collaboration with non-state organisations, in order to intervene without directly being involved in the thorny question. Evidently, drugs and HIV had political underpinnings that could mire the reformist government. Public officials promoting reformist methods on drug (ab)use and the HIV epidemic adopted medical,

---

[36] *Keyhan*, September 30, 1999; *Enqelab-e Eslami*, October 16, 2001.
   The accusations came almost exclusively from conservative newspapers, as part of an attempt that Khatami described as *siyah-nemai*, 'showing the dark side of the things'. Semati, *Media, Culture*, 65.

pathological frames. Rooted in the way social sciences and scientists in general discuss societal and sociological matters, the social pathology inclination is deep-rooted in Iranian politics. Through this lens, unorthodox behaviour, anger, crime and other 'deviant realities' are read as pathologies of society, of modernity, of the city, of globalisation and so on. This historical inclination overlapped with the reintegration of the medical community in the post-war period resulting in a new place for medicine – and, hence, pathological frames – in politics.

Medicine and pathological frames had a productive effect too. Legitimated by their 'scientific' discourse, doctors had more leeway to intervene in the public debate. Their arguments resonated positively also with Islamic law, where the priority of individual and public health justify unorthodox interpretation of the law – and of government. Their criticisms remained within the realm of public policy, of mechanism, of management and of community welfare. It did not discuss changes in the political order, in politics at a higher level. Medicine became a malleable tool for supporters and antagonists of reforms, a venue to express resentment and critical thoughts regarding contemporary Iran, its social and political failures, without endangering the political order and its ethical primacy.

In this socio-political ecosystem, the synergies between public officials, medical professionals, civil society groups and international drug experts coalesced around the need to reform Iran's drugs policy. Individuals in the anti-drug administration made good use of their clout 'from below' in the law-making machinery of the state; civil society groups intensified their grassroots operations, helped by financing and knowledge provision of international organisations inside Iran. This assemblage of forces gave birth, rather rapidly – in about four or five years – to a structured and multi-sectorial harm reduction system operating countrywide. These practical steps in the making of a legalised harm reduction field preceded the Head of the Judiciary Ayatollah Mahmud Hashemi-Shahrudi's approval of 'harm reduction'. In January 2005, the judicial branch issued a decree supporting needle exchange programmes and warning against interference by state organisations (e.g. police and judiciary) with these 'needed and fruitful public health interventions'.[37] On June 8, 2005, after a process of

---

[37] 'Decriminalisation Bill in the Drug and Treatment of Drug Abusers Law' (UNODC: dated 24 July 2006 [pdf scanned file]).

several years, President Mohammad Khatami's ministerial cabinet, at the suggestion of the Head of the Judiciary, approved the bill of 'Decriminalisation of treatment of those suffering from narcotic drug abuse'. The law entrusted 'the Ministry of Health and the Ministry of Social Security with all the duties and responsibilities of prevention, treatment and harm reduction of narcotic and psychoactive drug use'.[38] Those operating in drug policy regarded the move as an effective decriminalisation of addiction' and an Islamic juridical backing of substitution and maintenance treatment, exemplified by methadone treatment and needle exchange programmes.

For the first time, the notion of harm reduction was included in the national legislation of the Islamic Republic of Iran.[39] By providing drug (ab)users with clean and sanitised paraphernalia (needles, condoms, etc.), harm reduction support centres do not require drug users to give up drug use. From an ethical standpoint, the approval of harm reduction signified the acceptance that drug consumption is an inescapable aspect of human life, to which governments need to respond by *reducing harms* and not by ideological opposition. Harm reduction was a realistic response, with pragmatic underpinning. How did a conservative juridical branch turn in favour of contentious practices of needle exchange programmes and methadone substitution inside and outside prisons, when it had previously taken up a total ideological combat against drug consumers?

Civil Society as the Government by Practice

It is often argued that Bijan Nasirimanesh, a GP interested in addiction treatment, started the first harm reduction centres in Iran.[40] Nasirimanesh had started an experimental, underground needle exchange programme in the mid 1990s, in Marvdasht, located in the province of Shiraz. Later this experiment was given the name of *Persepolis* NGO Society for Harm Reduction and worked as a semi-

---

[38] Ibid.
[39] The progressive nature of this reform is evident when one considers that the United Nations failed to include harm reduction in their general texts up to 2018.
[40] Confirmed by a number of interviews with harm reduction experts, whom I met in Iran during spring 2014.

legal drop-in centre (DIC). A DIC is a space where vulnerable individuals can seek low-threshold, welfare support. They often address the very basic needs of pauperised drug (ab)users, homeless and mendicant people, or sex workers.

While operating the DIC, Nasirimanesh lobbied to get his activity recognised and legalised by the authorities. 'I was a very junior doctor but they took it seriously' he says in an interview. 'They didn't want to implement these things themselves, so having a nongovernmental organization like Persepolis ready to do whatever – it was a perfect match. They didn't say no to a single thing!'[41] Persepolis NGO obtained a license from the Ministry of Health in 2001 to operate within the legal framework. The process, once initiated, did not encounter hindrances or administrative obstacles and, according to the NGO founder, 'was actually facilitated and encouraged by governmental institutions'.[42] Following the success of the first DIC, Nasirimanesh established another DIC in Tehran, with outreach programmes in the more destitute areas of the city, around the area of Darvaz-e Ghar, between Moulavi and Shush Squares. Participation of the local community and of the people treated was key to the philosophy of action promoted in the DICs. The outreach workers recruited from the drug using communities in the areas of interest would head off to the *patoqs* (drug using/dealing hotspots) once or twice a day, distributing condoms, clean syringes and giving basic medical care to largely, but not necessarily, homeless drug users. Their encounters with drug users introduced public health measures in a community previously ignored by public institutions. Outreaching drug users enriched knowledge about the drug phenomenon, reordering what the public simply cast as disorderly groups and helpless people.

By the early 2000s, the *patoqs* had become part of the urban landscape of Tehran and other major cities. Often also labelled 'colonies' (*koloni*) of drug users, the *patoqs* of the early 2000s embodied the material face of marginality in the urban landscape. Large groups of destitute, sun-burnt men and women gathered in 'nomadic' settlements, in parks, alleys and sidewalks, living in an economy of petty dealing, garbage collection, sex work, petty robberies and barter of goods and favours – including sexual ones. The historical antecedents of this informal economy can be found in the sites of the

---

[41] Rosenberg, 'How Iran Derailed'. [42] Interview with Nasirimanesh.

shirehkesh-khaneh in the south of the capital or in the gathering of opium users in the Park-e Marivan, a hotspot of popular drug culture in the 1960s discussed in Chapter 2.

Working in these settings meant facing several challenges. The law enforcement agencies (LEAs) represented the most immediate threat to the work of support and outreach in harm reduction. Police operations were a regular feature of the working class neighbourhoods, especially those neighbourhoods notorious for drug dealing (e.g. Khak-e Sefid, Darvazeh Ghar). Their consequences were twofold: firstly, drug (ab) users could be arrested and sent to prison, with all the negative effects on their individual health and well-being. After all, the risk of HIV contagion remained highest in the prison. A longer-term damage was the sentiment of distrust and suspicion that police operations cast on harm reduction programmes.[43] Drug arrests made the efforts of harm reduction workers difficult and unstable, especially in winning the trust of local communities in favour of an alternative to the punishment model. Given that Persepolis preached a peer-to-peer model, the NGO employed former, or in some cases current, drug users in support programmes. Its objective was not simply to recover the addicts, but to dissipate, through praxis, the stigma of homelessness, HIV and drug (ab)use. This grassroots model fell in line with the state's approach to social questions, especially with the drug phenomenon. The Ministry of Health, through the expertise network of the UNODC, helped Persepolis establish Iran's first methadone substitution centre in 2000.

Persepolis was not unique in the harm reduction landscape of the 2000s. Other meaningful experiences emerged from the city of Kermanshah. The outbreak of the HIV epidemic in the city's major prison pressed the government for an immediate response. The first survey of HIV in Kermanshah took place in 1995. Although the results were not alarming, a member of the Majles from Kermanshah requested the opening of a national AIDS hospital in the city. Once approved, the proposal faced the unwelcoming reaction of the local population, which took to the streets and damaged governmental buildings, impeding the inauguration of the work. Popular opposition to the plan confirmed the top-down nature behind it. Kamiar Alaei, a local physician who, together with his brother, started the first harm reduction activities in Kermanshah, suggests that the government plan

---

[43] Interview with Shirazi.

ignored cultural sensibilities and people's perception of the problem. 'People realised that HIV patients would be referred to the city and Kermanshah would be tagged by HIV'.[44] The city of Hamadan in Western Iran had had a similar reaction to the establishment of a large mental health hospital (popularly known as *timarestan*) in the early 1990s. The fear was that it would become the medical centre of all of Iran's mental health problems, therefore acquiring the fame of the city of the fools.[45] To cope with the HIV epidemic in Kermanshah, the government needed the support of local groups.

By the year 2000, local authorities in the Kermanshah managed establishing Triangular Clinics supported by the University of Medical Sciences. Triangular clinics provided three kinds of services: sexually transmitted disease testing and treatment; HIV/AIDS testing, treatment, counselling, and housing; and harm reduction materials and methadone maintenance.[46] Collaboration between the state, the university and local groups sought to respond to the spread of HIV through practical means, starting from the prison population and their families. These two groups had the highest infection rate among all. By relying on civic groups, the government kept out of the thorny business of addiction and HIV. It opened the field for non-state groups to manage the HIV crisis, while it acquired insight into the crisis itself through the knowledge network and information gathering built up by civil society organisations. The Alaei brothers fit this role in every respect. Fluent *Kirmanshani* speakers, they had been active in the Kermanshah province for several years prior the opening of the Triangular Clinics.[47] Their project spoke a language, synthetically as much as semantically, familiar to the local population. At the same time, through their affiliation and activism in the medical and drug policy community, they had working connections with the political centre, a fact that legitimated their endeavours in the first years of work.

Like the experience of Persepolis, the Triangular Clinics focused on social perception of drug use and HIV as they attempted to cast away

---

[44] Kamiar Alaei, 'I Was Jailed for My Work on HIV in Iran, but the Tide Is Turning', *The Conversation,* retrieved from http://theconversation.com/i-was-jailed-for-my-work-on-hiv-in-iran-but-the-tide-is-turning-21144.
[45] Interview with Kamiar Alaei, via Skype, October 20, 2014.
[46] Pardis Mahdavi, 'Who Will Catch Me If I Fall? Health and the Infrastructure of Risk for Urban Young Iranians', in *Contemporary Iran,* 184.
[47] *Kirmanshani* is the Kurdish language spoken among the Kurds in the region of Kermanshah.

stigma and reintegrate their patients back into their normal lives. In Maziar Bahari's documentary *Mohammad and the Matchmaker*, the Canadian/Iranian Newsweek journalist follows an HIV-positive and former injecting drug user in his search for a new wife.[48] The matchmaker in question is Arash Alaei, the younger of the two Alaei brothers, who has been Mohammad's doctor for many years. Through his network of HIV-positive people in Kermanshah, the doctor finds Fereshteh, a twenty-one-year-old woman who contracted HIV from her heroin-injecting ex-husband. Tension is palpable in the meeting, but more importantly, the two are willing to show their faces and talk to the camera without shame. By talking to the camera, they also talk to policymakers, make a potential contribution to the cause of HIV-positive people in Iran, and give legitimacy to the civil society projects of the Alaei brothers.

Getting rid of the stigma of drug (ab)use and, especially, HIV was an important passage because 'the leading cause of death among former prison inmates living with HIV and AIDS was not from AIDS-related diseases but, instead, from suicide'.[49] Long years of state propaganda and public outcry against drug (ab)users had instilled deep contempt and fear towards them, especially those infected with HIV and those whose drug dependence was visible in public. Stigma represented a harder enemy to overcome. Having HIV meant being cast out of society, with adverse psychological repercussions as well as material consequences. An employer could fire an HIV-infected person for being HIV-positive. Parents could disown their children and deny them support and inheritance rights. Public debates and media rhetoric reiterated feelings of guilt and unfitness of those infected by the virus. At times, the virus itself became emblem of Western moral corruption and corporal destituteness. With stigma alive in the public understanding of HIV, prevention and treatment programmes could not succeed and expand up to required needs. Opposition against harm reduction stayed strong within political pockets, especially among conservatives and security-oriented groups. The general population, for the most, maintained the view of the drug (ab)users as undeserving individuals, with tougher punishment being the only response to drugs.[50] As such,

---

[48] Maziar Bahari, 'Mohammad and the Matchmaker' (2003), retrieved from www.idfa.nl.
[49] Behrouzan, 'An Epidemic of Meanings', 325.
[50] Harsh comments against drug addicts are the rule when discussing my research with ordinary people in informal settings.

harm reduction remained unpopular and far from people's priorities, partly due to the decades-long propaganda against narcotics which accused drugs of all possible earthly evils and partly due to the lack of adequate explanation to the public of what harm reduction meant. Introducing a new language, for a new understanding of social realities, was a daunting task.

Beside the work of civil society groups, other personalities contributed to a change in attitude towards HIV and drug (ab)use. Minoo Mohraz is one of the most significant of all. A leading figure in Iran's Committee to Combat AIDS and an internationally respected scholar, she worked together with the Alaei brothers in several nationwide awareness campaigns. A regular contributor to the media and a prolific public lecturer, she would spell out, breaking all taboos, the situation of HIV as related to sexual behaviours outside the marriage and to drug injection. In her own words, her mission '[was] to bring an awareness of AIDS to every Iranian household through television, newspapers and magazines'.[51] Her authoritative profile convinced members of the government to promote destigmatising policies. She recalls that in 2003, 'one of Khatami's deputies had proposed a resolution that prevented those afflicted by AIDS from getting fired from their jobs, however it was not passed'.[52] Despite the failure to achieve policy recognition on this particular occasion, the government supported the activities and tactics of civil society groups in the field of prevention and awareness of HIV. In this way, the government partly circumvented the obstacles put in the way by those attempting to slow down the process of social reforms. Newspapers expanded their coverage about HIV stories, dipping down into the human stories of infected people. By casting light on everyday aspects of HIV-positive people, they also succeeded in 'normalising' the topic of HIV in the public's eye and paved the way for the inclusion of HIV-patients into the acceptable boundaries of society.

By mid-2000, Kamiar and Arash Alaei's efforts expanded into a nationwide programme. The Prison Organisation introduced the Triangular Clinic model inside the prison. The Khatami government was a vocal support of the plan and the Ministry backed it enthusiastically. The international community, too, recognised the efficacy of the

---

[51] *Rooyesh*, June 09, 2007, retrieved from http://rooyesh.blog.com/2007/06/09/inside-iran-increasing-aids-awareness/.
[52] Ibid.

Iranian model and awarded the project the 'Best Practice in HIV prevention and care for injecting drug users' for the MENA region.[53] By 2006, the two brothers operated in sixty-seven cities and fifty-eight prisons, cooperating with international organisations (e.g. WHO, UN) and neighbouring countries (Afghanistan, Pakistan) to set up similar programmes in Central Asia and the Muslim world.[54]

Going international was not only a matter of prestige and humanitarianism. Despite the reformist government's readiness to provide the financial resources for the Triangular Clinics and other prevention programmes, the civil society organisations active during this era understood the importance of being financially independent from the government. With opposition to harm reduction never properly rooted within the political order, a change in government could have proved fatal to the harm reduction process. The flow of money for the projects could have easily been stopped and the scaling up of the programmes would have risked being only piecemeal and, hence, insufficient.[55] Where all state-led policies and plans had failed, civil society activism and networks succeeded in shaking the status quo, eventually influencing public policy.

Nonetheless, the role of civil society groups should not be overstated. They were neither independent nor autonomous, and their strategy was synchronic with that of governmental plans. Khatami's push for the entry of civil society in participatory politics also meant that the Islamic Republic could manage (*modiriyat*) areas of high ethical sensibility through cooperation with non-state groups, such as NGOs. Interaction between government and civil society, which came about in overlapping ways, occurred through intra-societal and clandestine manoeuvrings of public officials, without which the practices of harm reduction (initially underground and semi-legal) would have never seen the light as state policies, regulations and laws. The overlapping of HIV crisis, massive drug consumption and the expansion of civic groups interested in harm reduction enabled the progressive policy shift. I shall now discuss how the state worked through clandestine, off-the-record practices in the field of harm reduction.

---

[53] *Radio Free Europe/Radio Liberty*, October 3, 2006, retrieved from www.rferl.org/content/article/1071768.html.
[54] Ibid. [55] Interview with Alaei.

The State – Driving with the Lights Off

One should not overestimate the capacity to produce change in the highly resilient environment of Iranian public policy. Opposition to policy reform remained staunch despite the sense of emergency and crisis propelled by the HIV epidemic.

Informal, semi-legal practices of harm reduction coexisted, for the initial years, with a set of regulations that, *de jure*, outlawed them. Criminalisation of drug (ab)users, particularly those visible in the public eye (e.g. homeless and poorer drug consumers), remained steadfast. Policing loomed large over the heads of social workers, outreach personnel and drug consumers seeking harm reduction services. Started in very marginal zones of the urban landscapes of Iran's growing cities, harm reduction kept working with hidden (to the security state's eye) and underground programmes. Hooman Narenjiha, former director for prevention and advisor in addiction treatment to the Drug Control Headquarters (DCHQ), claims that 'in order to approve harm reduction and institutionalise this new approach, harm reduction programmes had to be initiated *cheragh khamush*, [lights off]'.[56]

Lights off required direction from those in the administration of drugs politics. High and mid-ranking officials in the Ministry of Health, Welfare Organisation, and the DCHQ laid the groundwork for the harm reductionists. From behind the scenes, public officials backed the work of civil society groups, opening a sympathetic space within their own institutions *vis-à-vis* harm reduction, before harm reduction's approval in the national legislation. A group of people within the public institutions lobbied in favour of legal reforms in drug policy, while civil society groups pushed the boundaries in practice. Among them, Said Sefatian, former head of drug demand reduction in the DCHQ, played a fundamental role. Over the more than eight years of his mandate at the DCHQ, Sefatian witnessed the country's rapid shift in favour of harm reduction.[57] Speaking about the outset of harm reduction during an interview, he said,

It wasn't easy, I had to bear heavy pressures at the time. Thinking about needle exchange programmes or MMT programmes was controversial.

---

[56] Interview with Hooman Narenjiha, Tehran, April 4, 2014.
[57] The length of his mandate is considerable compared to the *short-termism* of most public officials, especially when change in government is concerned.

When we started in 2001, in this country, addiction, more or less, was not considered a crime, and it was not considered a disease either ... You could open a treatment centre, where you would accept addicts and you provide services to them, and then there would be the police and there would be the officials of the Judiciary, who would simply come to the centre and close it down. They would collect all the addicts. If we had 50 addicts, they would collect all of them, put them on a bus, and arrest them. Sometimes, even the personnel would be targeted and I had to intervene![58]

This account points to the persistent criminalisation coexisting with the introduction of harm reduction practices. The endurance of security-oriented approaches epitomises deep-rooted elements within state power. *Driving with the lights off* was the methodology of action in order to escape institutional, ideological obstacles. It was based on the synergy between public officials who supported the promotion of harm reduction and civil society groups operating on the ground. For instance, Bahram Yeganeh, who acted as the director of Iran's AIDS committee during the reformist period, explains that when there were talks about needle exchange programmes within prisons, the top authorities of the Prison Organisation declared their opposition, but with 'the collaboration of mid-ranking officials [*modiran-e miyaneh*] we carried it out, while the upper level was against it'.[59] The *mesostrata* of the state acted as a practical ground between civil society and the state, somehow bypassing the formal hierarchy existent in ordinary situations.

Sefatian refers to the actual group of people, within and without the state, whose synergies worked in favour of harm reduction. He refers to this group as an alliance of people who had similar concerns about addiction and shared values in how to respond to the crisis.

There were several reasons why we succeeded. The first was that we had a *great team*. In the DCHQ, the Ministry of Health's office for addiction, the Welfare Organisation, the Prison Organisation, the NGOs and in the UNODC ... This group had a great alliance, every week we would meet in my office at the DCHQ and we would discuss how to carry out and push forward programmes [towards harm reduction] to respond to the *crisis*.[60]

This group of people, who belonged to different institutions often in competition with each other, was key in connecting the practices of

[58] Interview with Sefatian, Tehran, April 9, 2014. [59] Qahrfarkhi, *E'tiyad*, 488.
[60] Interview with Sefatian, April 2014. Emphases added.

non-governmental organisations with the judiciary, the policy community in the Majles and the negotiating body with regard to drugs policy, the Expediency Council.[61] Because the police intervened in many cases to stop the activities of the DICs, Sefatian thought of an expedient, a way to turn this repression into a positive force.[62] He opted to *go public*:

> As soon as the police would go to make trouble for the DICs and the treatment centres, I would call the newspapers and send journalists to that centre to report on the event. For instance, if Dr [X]'s centre has been targeted by the police, I would immediately call a journalist to report about it and it would be published on the website and on the newspapers.[63]

Through the media, the harm reductionists brought the contention to the public sphere and to the attention of the judiciary and the government. The 'proximity' with the often security-oriented judicial authority, in particular, represented another opportunity to introduce the advantages (and values) of harm reduction within the order of state law-making. As Sefatian recounts, once called in front of the Attorney General to explain his remarks about the worsening condition of 'addiction', he took advantage of the circumstances to speak about the benefits that Iran could obtain from going all the way forward in implementing harm reduction. His argument was similar to those that the Alaei brothers and Bijan Nasirimanesh used with clerics and ordinary citizens in order to break the taboo of providing clean needles to drug users and prisoners. Although Sefatian did not coordinate his actions and statements with civic groups, and vice versa, the dialogue and exchange of ideas informed their engagement with the higher layers of drugs politics.

This situation generated, *ipso facto*, a common idiom of 'crisis' and a common set of argumentation around it to adopt when discussing reforms and harm reduction with those opposing them, first and foremost with the state. Sefatian's role and his connections with on-the-ground groups is revealing of the scope of 'politics from below' within

---

[61] As referred to by Sefatian himself, the Welfare Organisation and the Ministry of Health would not openly support these initiatives and were actively against harm reduction during the meetings. This aspect also emerged in the interview with Gelareh Mostashahri, Tehran, April 8, 2014.
[62] Unlike the police and the judiciary, the anti-narcotic police did not interfere, instead concentrating its operations on large-scale trafficking.
[63] Interview with Sefatian, April 2014.

Iranian public policy. Elements within the governmental machinery operated, persuasively and materially, in order to produce, firstly, practical change in the field of drug policy and, eventually, formal recognition of this change in the laws. Politics from below played along with the HIV epidemics and the shifts towards more dangerous drug consumption patterns in the early 2000s. The harm reduction assemblage made of public officials, informal networks and civic groups built up its own apparatuses of crisis management.

The judicial authority and the clergy as a whole needed to clarify their official stance, and to confront those critics who blamed them for being unresponsive on this issue. To find an acceptable and pragmatic solution, language had to hint at simple wisdom, with a loose Koranic justification: *between bad and worse, one is required to opt for bad.*[64] According to the mainstream interpretation of the Koran, if a Muslim's life is in in danger of death, he or she is *required* to survive even when survival is dependent on committing sinful acts (*haram*), such as drinking alcohol if alcohol is the only available beverage in the desert, eating dead bodies if that is the only available food, or providing clean needles to pathological drug users, if that is the only way one can prevent deadly HIV infections for them and their families. Connected to the notion of *zarurat* (necessity/emergency), which I shall discuss in the next Chapter, this hermeneutical vision allowed the clergy to adopt a flexible position *vis-à-vis* matters of governance. This further justified reform-oriented approaches to drug laws, for the Expediency Council had already prefigured drug phenomena as part of the state *maslahat* (interest) and a primary field of management of crisis.

As for the media, the coverage of controversial programmes for addiction had no immediate favourable return for the harm reduction movement. Most of the reportage was negative and critical; public opinion maintained its traditional dislike for drug (ab)users, addicts, as dangerous subjects, associating them with criminal behaviour and moral deviancy. The role of the media, nonetheless, was not aimed at changing, in the first place, public opinion, but at creating a public debate about illicit drug and public health. As revealed by Sefatian himself:

At the time, I took five journalists to come and report on our pilot experiments ... Positive and negative coverage played in our favour, regardless of their criticism. Why? Because I wanted to open up the view of the

---

[64] See also Christensen, *Drugs, Deviancy*, 146.

public officials, I wanted to start a public debate about alternatives. And it worked. I noticed that the Majles representatives, the courts and the LEAs had already taken the lead to attack our programmes. On the other hand, some people were praising it, so I moved the fight away from me and I made it public. It was not my personal opinion anymore. It became a public question![65]

For the harm reductionists, it was crucial to introduce their arguments into the public debate. A famous aphorism comes to mind: 'the only thing worse than being talked about is not being talked about'.

Can this be regarded as a distinguishing method of action in a political environment resistant to change, such as that of Iran? By counterbalancing the soft means of the press and the defiant practices of NGOs, to the coercion of the police and the law, public officials supporting harm reduction opened up a political space for discussion and change. The case in question also defines an established tactic among policy reformers, which has had its precedents in recent history. In 1998, then-director of the DCHQ, Mohammad Fellah, had attempted shifting the way people discussed and thought of addiction. In an interview, he revealed:

In order to change the maxim 'addiction is a crime' ... I asked the [DCHQ] director for news and communication to give me a journalist so that I could work with him on a series of tasks and I could ask him to do some stuff [sic]. They sent me a *brother*[66] from the newspaper *Iran*[67] and we went together to interview the Ministry of Interior, the Attorney General ... In the meantime, in the newspaper we would write 'addiction is not a crime'. Then I would ask the Ministry of Welfare to send a letter to the Head of the Judiciary and to ask him whether addiction was a crime or not. The answer was not positive, but we started again from scratch and sent another letter after three months ... After we had done this a few times, the attitudes started changing'.[68]

---

[65] Interview with Sefatian, April 2014.
[66] *Baradar* (brother) is the Islamic Republic equivalent of 'comrade' in Soviet Russia.
[67] Interesting enough, *Iran* is the official daily newspaper of the government of Iran and is owned by the Iran News Agency (IRNA). Yet it has been closed at least a couple of times in the last fifteen years, due to court rulings.
[68] Qahfarkhi, *E'tiyad*, 457. Emphasis added.

Considering that at the time of this interview, addiction *was* a crime, Fellah's expedient is paradigmatic of repertoires entrenched in the mechanism of power and reform. Indeed, it might well be that it was the legacy of Mohammad Fellah in the DCHQ that provided the tools and tactics of action among the harm reductionists, as in the case of Sefatian. Fellah and Sefatian's tactics exemplify similar acts of politics from below within the policymaking community.

Strategic resistance met opposition to harm reduction; public debates, clandestine connections, semi-formal networks worked in favour of reforms. The use of the media in the policy 'game' is a bearer of great significance when contextualised in the mechanisms of power during the reformist governments. It is, in the words of Gholam Khiyabani, the press which carries the burden and acts as 'a surrogate party'.[69] Newspapers and journals become the arena for new proposals indirectly (or explicitly) related to a particular political group or faction. It is no coincidence that both NGOs and press publications incremented their output and coverage from Khatami's election in 1997 onwards. In this regard, one could argue that civil society, too, had become a 'surrogate party', an indirect government for the reformist, or to put it more crudely, civil society performed as the *government in practice.* Support for groups outside government, such as the NGOs, was instrumental to the government itself, for it had the objective to push for reforms otherwise unspeakable by the government itself.

Contextually to the rise of the harm reduction, rogue (more or less) members loosely associated with the anti-reformist camp discredited, accused or, worse, physically harmed several high-profile ministers and officials.[70] These individuals paid the price for demanding more daring reforms in the political order. Reformism meant that the 'red lines' of politics blurred, with the risks and stakes higher than ever. Harm reductionists too faced challenges from those who deemed their push for reforms as incompatible and threatening the Islamic order or the

---

[69] Gholam Khiabany, *Iranian Media: The Paradox of Modernity* (Routledge, 2009), 25.

[70] The most notorious cases are those of Saeed Hajjarian, the ideologue of the reformist camp and an early-days revolutionary in 1979, who was attacked by rogue security agents; and Abdollah Nouri, a leading reformist and former Minister of Interior, who was sentenced to five years in prison.

security of the state. On several occasions, the authorities seemed on the verge of turning back and stopping all harm reduction programmes. Gelareh Mostashari, senior expert in drug demand reduction at the UNODC office in Tehran, speaks about it in these terms:

When I was working at the Ministry of Health, the head of the police, which at the time was Mohammad Baqer Qalibaf [former mayor of Tehran and presidential candidate][71], wrote a project out of the blue, saying, 'Let's bring all the addicts to *Jazireh* [island] and confine them'. An island! We were talking about harm reduction and he put forward the option of the island? The Qalibaf report became like a bombshell, all those who had disputes under the surface started opposing Qalibaf's project, and it was consequently withdrawn thanks to the mediation of the DCHQ'.[72]

The diatribe referred to immediately went public in the Tehran-based newspaper *Hamshahri* on October 22, 2003, with the title 'Favourable and Contrary Reactions to the Maintenance of High-risk Drug Addicts in *Jazireh*', where several members of the DCHQ argued in favour of harm reduction, criticising those who wanted to look backward, implicating Mohammad Baqer Qalibaf, then Head of the Police.[73] Qalibaf had been putting more than a spanner in the NGOs' works. He repeatedly targeted Persepolis outreach programmes in Darvazeh Ghar, attacked the DIC of another NGO in Khak-e Sefid (an infamous gangster nest in Eastern Tehran) and continued generally to stand against the medicalisation of drug (ab)use.[74]

Harm reduction found itself stranded between health and welfare on the one hand, and law and order on the other. Lack of cooperation between different branches of the state exacerbated the idiosyncrasy of reformism, caught between government and the securitising state. Crisis helped getting out of the impasse, with civil society groups turning to the device of crisis management and its technology of intervention amidst the impossibility of action. This process involved pressures, resistance to diktats, promotion of sympathetic projects and informal connections, including with international organisations, *in primis* the UNODC.

---

[71] Mayor Qalibaf has changed his opinion and today supports harm reduction policies.
[72] Interview with Mostashari.   [73] *Hamshahri*, October 22, 2003.
[74] Interview with Shirazi.

The UNODC as a 'Bridge' between the State and Society

It is not a coincidence that the emergence of the harm reduction discourse took place contemporaneously with the establishment of the UNODC headquarters in Tehran in July 1999. The establishment of the UN office in Tehran was part of the broader rapprochement between Iran and the West, led by the reformist government and the international community. The event was facilitated, partly by the activism of the Khatami government, partly by the EU need to counter the flow of drugs into its territories. The international organisation occupied (and still does) a six-storey building in a busy, commercial area of Tehran, Vanak Square, where it had its headquarters separated from other UN offices. The personnel was mostly composed of Iranian nationals and a handful of foreign experts, among which was the Italian representative of the UNODC. Overall, the office numbered a couple of dozen people operating full-time, in three main sections: Drug Demand Reduction; Drug Supply Reduction; and Crime, Justice and Corruption. On the one hand, the UN had historically provided technical and financial support for the expansion of civil society organisations in the developing world; cooperation with Iranian institutions in the field of drug policy was arguably easier than working in the field of human and gender rights.[75] On the other hand, the cadres of the Islamic Republic perceived the UNODC as a historically prohibitionist organism, which did not pose strong ideological barriers with Iran's own prohibitionist discourse. Since 1997, Pino Arlacchi, a well-known Italian sociologist, had been appointed head of the UN anti-narcotic body, with the promise to eradicate or sensitively reduce drug supply and demand within ten years.[76] To do so, the international organisation needed full cooperation from Iran, which, in turn, was seeking to reignite the diplomatic track at the international level. Iran and the UNODC had prohibitionist credentials and a stake in expanding their collaboration. In fact, they both campaigned around Pino Arlacchi's (in)famous slogan of the late 1990s, 'a drug-free world'.[77]

---

[75] For a similar argument, see Janne Bjerre Christensen, 'Human Rights and Wrongs in Iran's Drug Diplomacy with Europe', *The Middle East Journal* 71, no. 3 (2017).
[76] Chouvy, *Opium*, 11.
[77] Often attributed to Antonio Maria Costa, the slogan was actually first used by Arlacchi.

However, the role of the UN body went beyond that of partner in fighting drug trafficking, or, in drug policy parlance, supply reduction. In the Iranian context, the UNODC supported policies which were still taboo in its headquarters in Vienna. While there were discussions about harm reduction in Tehran, with the UNODC coordinating meetings between international experts and national authorities, the Vienna-based body preached a neutralist, if not opposing, stance on harm reduction policies elsewhere. This was specifically due to the United States' decade-long opposition to harm reduction. As the UN drug control body received most of its international funding from the United States, there was a tacit understanding that UN strategic programmes should focus on the supply reduction side, and downplay harm reduction. In line with that, Antonio Maria Costa, the UNODC high representative, warned that 'under the guise of "harm reduction", there are people working disingenuously to alter the world's opposition to drugs ... We neither endorse needle exchange as a solution for drug abuse, nor support public statements advocating such practices'.[78] So, how can one explain UNODC's constructive role with Iranian harm reductionism in the light of its overt opposition to harm reduction globally?

The answer needs to look at the strained relations between the United States and Iran during this period, despite the partial defrosting during Khatami's diplomatic push under the slogan of *Dialogue among Civilisations*. The text of the Third Development Plan stressed the need to establish foreign and international partnerships in the field of research and development. This was partially successful and, by the turn of the millennium, Iran could benefit from the partnership of 'various international and foreign organizations, including various developmental agencies of the United Nations such as UNDP, UNICEF, UNFPA, UNODC and UNESCO since 1999, the World Bank since 2000, and the British Council since 2001'.[79]

Lack of diplomatic relations between the United States and Iran signified that UNODC undertakings inside Iran would have to be financed (and therefore influenced) by other countries. It was mostly European money, with Italy (for drug use issues) and the United

---

[78] 'UN does not support harm reduction', May 19, 2007, retrieved from www.encod.org/info/UN-DOES-NOT-SUPPORT-HARM-REDUCTION.html.

[79] Maryam Borjian, 'The Rise and Fall of a Partnership: The British Council and the Islamic Republic of Iran (2001–09)', *Iranian Studies* 44, 4 (2011), 548.

Kingdom, Germany and Switzerland (for drug trafficking) that promoted UNODC programme in Tehran. Contrary to UN practice in most of the developing world, the office in Tehran employed almost exclusively national staff.[80] This had several advantages, in terms of capacity to influence the harm reduction process, and some dangers. Most of the staff had previously worked or researched within state ministries and had an existing network of associates. They had extensive knowledge of the cultural, social and administrative peculiarities of the country. In other words, the staff was acquainted with the red lines of Iranian politics and knew how to, tactically, deal with them. They also had more legitimacy *vis-à-vis* national authorities, which have been historically (and somewhat correctly) suspicious of foreign meddling into the country's domestic affairs. Within the UNODC, this also left more leeway of manoeuvring to promote approaches which clashed with US guidelines. On the other hand, being Iranian exposed them to a possible backlash from the authorities, given that drugs was a highly sensitive matter.[81]

Based on these potentialities, the UNODC acquired a status of relevance in a short period and secured an influential role in the faltering and precarious terrain of Iranian drugs politics. In the words of Fariba Soltani, who acted as demand reduction officer at the time, 'the UNODC functioned as a *bridge* with the international community, providing contacts and networking opportunities for Iranian national experts. It later facilitated funding for travels to conferences, workshops'.[82] Then-UNODC representative Mazzitelli confirmed that the leading task with regard to civil organisations was to 'to *bridge*, to support and to give visibility and credibility to initiatives'.[83] The *Nouruz* Initiative of the UNODC financed two demand reduction projects, *Darius* and *Persepolis*, for civil society. The choice of the names bore political significance. The projects were named after key elements of Iran's pre-Islamic history, which had been mostly ignored, if not opposed, by the governments of the Islamic Republic prior the election of the reformist president Khatami.[84]

---

[80] Interview with Mazzitelli. [81] Ibid.
[82] Interviews with NGO director, April, 2014. Emphasis added.
[83] Interview with Mazzitelli. Emphasis added.
[84] The supply reduction project was named *Cyrus*, after the Cyrus 'the Great', king of the Achaemenid Empire.

The funding promoted the establishment of the DARIUS Institute, focused on prevention programmes, and Persepolis NGO, which provided harm reduction services. Another UNODC official, Gelareh Mostashari notes:

> [The UNODC] *bridged* this movement [*jonbesh*] with the outside. At the time, I was not working at the UNDOC, but I was involved in the events and processes from my post in the Ministry of Health. It must be said that many of the processes initiated were done by the people inside Iran, but they used the *bridge* [*pol*] that the UNODC provided to connect with the outside.[85]

By directly involving the medical community and experts in the field of drug policy, the UNODC managed to establish an informal, yet proactive, forum of debate within the institutions. 'It was the first time', Soltani recalls, 'that we had such a comprehensive discussion about drug policy and HIV in Iran. People were talking around a table, overtly'.[86] Regularly, civil society groups would take part in these events and would share their bottom-up experience of the drug phenomenon. On some occasions, a triad of medical expertise, grassroots organisations and the UNODC would hold workshops for the NAJA and the Judiciary, advocating for harm reduction measures.[87] For example, in October 2004, members of the Mini Dublin Group,[88] the DCHQ and several dozen NGOs participated to a two-day workshop on demand reduction and advocacy. On this occasion, Arash Alaei asked if the UNODC could play a coordinating role between the NGOs and the government.[89] The bridge of the UN body facilitated communication with state organs, often engaged only half-heartedly in implementing a more humanitarian approach to drug (ab)use.

The UNODC, by means of providing institutional backing for Iranian officials' country visits, introduced them to alternative models of drug policy and successful examples for the implementation of harm reduction. Among the several country visits that the UNODC supported, Sefatian refers to one visit in particular: Italy. 'Italy was the

---

[85] Interview with Mostashari, 2015. Emphasis added.
[86] Interview with Soltani.
[87] Ibid. Confirmed also by the interviews with Nasirimanesh and Alaei.
[88] The Mini Dublin Group is a donor-coordination group of countries.
[89] UNODC. *Participatory workshop with the NGOs to identify joint strategies on Drug Demand Reduction* (unpublished report, November 2004 [Word file]).

first country I visited and looked at in order to change Iran's drug policy in 2001', he says and adds, 'I re-used many of the things I learnt in Italy from their experience for our work in Iran'.[90] The role of Italy in mediating between Iran's bid on reformism and the international community was not coincidence. When the United Nations inaugurated the year 1999 as the Year of Dialogue among Civilisations – giving clout to president Khatami's diplomatic effort – Giandomenico Picco, an Italian UN official who had been, *inter alia*, behind the negotiations of the Iran–Iraq War and US hostage crisis in Lebanon, was nominated the Personal Representative of the Secretary General for the United Nations Year of Dialogue among Civilizations.[91] The UNODC representative Antonio Mazzitelli suggests indeed that 'it was not Italy perhaps, but Italians that activated a channel of communication between Iran and the international community during the reformist period. Drugs were part of a bigger, ongoing dialogue'.[92]

In the early 2000s, Iran obtained international support for its pilot harm reduction plan, which, in turn, convinced the authorities that the right path had been taken. Given the fact that one of Khatami's greatest concerns was international recognition, international cooperation in the field of drug policy was all the more significant and welcomed. The UNODC had created the neutral venue for civil society and state officials to share ideas and promote new strategies. The prestige of collaborating with the United Nations added legitimacy and strength to the voice of the participants.[93] In drug matters, cooperation with the international order seemed easier and more productive. Many believed it could be a model in other fields in which Iran sought recognition and rapprochement.

The establishment and consolidation of diplomatic ties with international partners is among the most effective – and yet short-lived – moves that the Khatami government undertook. The relationship with the international community in the field of drug diplomacy not only enhanced the chances for a progressive move domestically, it also resulted in being a durable and solid element of cooperation between

---

[90] Interview with Sefatian, April 2014.
[91] See Giandomenico Picco and Kamal Aboulmagd, *Crossing the Divide: Dialogue among Civilizations* (Seton Hall University, 2001).
[92] Interview with Mazzitelli.   [93] Interview with Soltani.

Iran and the rest of the world, even during the darkest periods of Iran–West confrontation, namely after US president George W. Bush's 'Axis of Evil' speech. Khatami's *Dialogue among Civilisations* was built mostly through intellectual fora and through symposia, but its most practical achievements were in the field of international cooperation on drug control and drug trafficking which were of immediate concern to Iran's European counterparts, more than Khatami's philosophising interpretation of civilisation and religions.

Conclusions

As the reformist government initiated a reflexive moment with regard to the role, reach and regulations of the state, it also acknowledged the limitations proper to the agency of its government, which were also due to the conflictual nature of inter-institutional dynamics during the period 1997–2005. The lost hegemony of state apparatuses, on the one hand, brokered an opportunity for 'co-regulation' and pilotage *in tandem* with civil society organisations.[94] The flow of opium, first, then its sudden drop, coalesced with the increase of injecting as a mode of consumption, which in turn contributed to the spread of the virus HIV. The drug assemblage constituted by the multiple crises around illicit drugs – health, ethical, social and political – opened up opportunities for co-working between competing apparatuses. Informal civic workers, medical professionals, prison officials, international donors, bureaucrats and politicians were all part in the great game of drugs politics. Their inroads, often informal if not illegal, enabled change by practice and, finally, recognition of reforms. The developments of the reformist period, in fact, did not result from the enunciation of governmental policies 'from above'. The government never took the lead in changing the content of drug control programmes. Instead, a pluralistic alliance of diverse groups, which acted not always in coordination with each other and rarely in overt political terms, took the lead. This secular alliance introduced the spark of change, lobbied for it and secured the support of public officials and key regime stakeholders. From this

---

[94] Cf. Mirella Landriscina, 'Professional Performances on a Well-Constructed Stage: The Case of an Institutionalized Advocacy Organization' in *New Perspectives*. 183–4.

perspective, one can see why and how civil society was the *leit motif* of the reformist era.[95]

This assemblage of groups that belonged to different public and private organisations, including state representatives, medical experts, NGO workers and activists as well as international donors, contributed to the birth of the harm reduction system in a matter of less than a decade. Diachronic to this synchronic moment – the 'great team' referred to by a drug policy official – was the phenomenon of drugs and addiction in Iran, itself the result of global changes in the drug ecosystem. First with the ban of opium by the Taliban and then with its unprecedented expansion in the wake of the US-led invasion of Afghanistan, the Iranian state experienced a transformative and unpredictable reality to which it responded through a combination of security measures and technical knowledge. Both, one could argue, defied the image of the Islamic Republic as a religiously driven political machine and, instead, categorised a governmental approach, which adopted profane means and a secular mindset in dealing with issues of critical importance, *with crises*.

The making of the harm reduction policy is situated in a grey area between formal state institutions and societal (including international) agents. The case of harm reduction elucidates otherwise shady mechanisms of formulation of (controversial) policies, while also revealing meaningful aspects of Iran's governmentality on crises. Crisis is an ordinary event in Iranian politics. Partly, the perpetual crisis is contingent of the revolutionary nature of the Iranian state; and partly, it is a loophole to quicken or slow down the process of reforms. President Khatami, whose government adopted the idiom of 'reforms', described his mandate as a period during which the government faced 'a national crisis every nine days of government'.[96] His reforms, too, adopted the idiom of the crisis, especially in the field of drugs policy.

---

[95] BBC, August 10, 2005, retrieved from www.bbc.co.uk/persian/iran/story/2005/08/050801_pm-khatami-presidency.shtml.
[96] Tazmini, *Khatami's Iran*, 127.

Interregnum

5 | *Crisis as an Institution: The Expediency Council*

From your comments during the Friday prayers it would appear that you don't believe it is correct [to characterize] the state as an absolute trusteeship which God conferred upon the noble Prophet ... and that the state is the most important of God's ordinances and has precedence over all other derived ordinances of God.[1]

Khomeini in response to Khamenei (Friday Sermon, January 1, 1988)

Where, in the history of Islam, could you find a parliament, a president, a prime minister, and a cabinet? Indeed, 80% of what we do actually does not have anything to do with the history of Islam![2]

Hashemi-Rafsanjani to the Majles

Introduction

The first part of this book dwelt on the trajectories that animated the history of narcotic drugs and state-led attempts at drug control. This *interregnum* – a time in between two eras – stops the historical flow to reflect on one especial institution, the Council for the Discernment of the Expediency of the State (*majma'-e tashkhis maslahat-e nezam*), which was established during a transitional phase at the end of the 1980s. Through the example of this institution, I bring under scrutiny some of the important structural changes of the post-war era. The *interregnum* also enables a pause on the broader question of what is crisis and how crisis works in the context of Iran (and of drugs politics). Many see the Reformist period as a breakthrough in Iran's post-revolutionary history, a moment when a new language on politics and an alternative way of organising society comes into being.

[1] Asghar Schirazi, *The Constitution of Iran: Politics and the State in the Islamic Republic* (IB Tauris, 1998).
[2] Jean-François Bayart, *L'Islam Républicain: Ankara, Téhéran, Dakar* (Albin Michel, 2011), 240; also in Abrahamian, *Khomeinism*, 15.

Yet, what *follows* reformism is truly unprecedented, a breakaway from the way government worked since 1979. This *interregnum* comes as a prelude to Part Two, where the book discusses crisis and drugs politics under the post-reformist state, headed by Mahmud Ahmadinejad (2005–13). To understand where crisis stands in post-revolutionary politics, one needs to start from its institutional organ: the Expediency Council.

On the theoretical level, the Expediency Council embodies the governmentality of the Islamic Republic on issues of crisis. Its importance stems from its role in the framing and governmental intervention in disputes, conflicts and situations that, in the words of Khomeini himself, 'could not be solved through *normal* means'.[3] The birth of this institution – which is unique to the Islamic Republic – opens up a phase where the *art of managing disorder and governing crisis* is the overarching governmental paradigm.[4]

The case of drugs policy is of especial importance to this institution, which simultaneously performs executive, legislative, and consultative tasks. All Iranian legislation is debated and, initially, formulated in the parliament (*Majles*), except for drug laws that are debated and formulated in the Expediency Council. From a political standpoint, after 1988, and more clearly since reformism, this contributed to the making of the 'drug problem' into a permanent crisis for the Islamic Republic. A permanent crisis which the state governs and manages through this unique political organ.

Without tackling the complex and sophistic arguments arising from the interpretation of religious law and state formation, this chapter discusses the notion of crisis in the establishment of the Expediency Council. It examines the structure and powers of the Council within the political order and analyses a few paradigmatic interventions. Finally, it considers the Council's role and effect on drug policy, a sphere so far absent in the scholarly literature. Indirectly, the arguments presented in this *Interregnum* (Chapter 5) provide an alternative interpretation to the classical interpretation of the Islamic Republic's politics as characterised by the rivalry between two poles of power: Ali Khamenei *versus* Hashemi Rafsanjani. By going beyond the politics of political

---

[3] Seyfollah Sarrami, *Ahkam-e Hokumati va Maslahat* (Tehran: 'abeir, Center of Strategic Studies, 2001 [1380]). Emphasis added.
[4] A similar institution might be the French *Conseil d'état*.

leaders, the chapter unveils processes of state formation that are at odds with the reading of Iran's politics as divided into personalities belonging to the reformist, moderate/pragmatist and fundamentalist camps.[5] Instead, it unpacks the state's logics on crisis and its political practice, the way power operates in laws and society. In this way, the chapter provides a new frame of reference to discuss how politics works in Iran, one that goes beyond the factional frame dividing personalities into 'conservatives' and 'reformists', 'the regime' and the rest.

Where Does Expediency Stand? Constitutional Revisions and Governmental Ordinances

It is unclear when the Expediency Council was first established. Complex but less ambiguous – albeit ambiguous nonetheless – is its place within the institutional framework of the Islamic Republic starting from the post-war period. In synopsis: the maximum authority in the Islamic Republic is the Supreme Leader and *vali-ye faqih*, who oversees all branches of the state; the head of the executive branch – the president – is elected through popular vote whereas the elections are scrutinised and 'filtered' by the Guardian Council. The latter is also charged with evaluation of all laws voted in the legislative branch, the parliament (*Majles-e Shura-ye Eslami*). The composition of the Guardian Council is made of six clerics appointed by the Supreme Leader and six jurists selected by the Parliament. When the legislative process is bogged down by a clash between the laws proposed by the Parliament and the Guardian Council – as has historically happened – the matter is referred to the Expediency Council. Although conflict resolution between Parliament and Guardian Council was the initial duty of the Expediency Council, the latter have expanded its authority to other influential domains, which include executive, legislative and supervisory powers. I shall trace how the Council acquired such powers:

The constitutional changes that took place at the end of the 1980s exemplify the political transformation occurring at the heart of the Islamic Republic. On April 24, 1989, forty days before his death, Khomeini sent a letter to the then-president of the Republic Ali Khamenei requesting the creation of

---

[5] With all the variations of the case depending on the lexicon adopted by different authors. See Anoushiravan Ehteshami and Mahjoob Zweiri, *Iran and the Rise of Its Neoconservatives: The Politics of Tehran's Silent Revolution* (IB Tauris, 2007).

a Council for the Revision of the Constitution (*shura-ye baznegari qanun-e asasi*). Khomeini's decree addressed two main questions: leadership; and constitutional recognition of the Expediency Council of the State, the latter having been created in 1986 as a temporary institution to solve the stalemate between the Parliament and the Guardian Council.[6]

The revisions of the Constitution included cosmetic/ideological changes, such as the re-labelling of the Parliament from *majles-e shura-ye melli* (national council) to *majles-e shura-ye eslami* (Islamic council), to more structural amendments, such as the abolition of the post of Prime Minister and the transfer of the latter's duties to the Presidency. In addition, the Supreme Judiciary Council, tasked with all matters related to justice, was replaced by the Head of the Judiciary, directly appointed by the Supreme Leader.[7] The highest political authority in the Islamic Republic remained the Supreme Leader, who just before Khomeini's death had seen its office strengthened with new powers, upgrading it to the *velayat-e motlaq-e faqih*, 'absolute guardianship of the jurist'. This new attribute allowed the leadership to issue 'governmental ordinances' (*ahkam-e hokumati*) when the political order (*nezam*) experienced instability, crisis or disorder.[8]

Since the Parliament could not legislate outside the remit of the Constitution *and* of the official religion (i.e. Islamic law as interpreted by the Guardian Council), the governmental ordinances were meant to address those situations in which standard political intervention was problematic. The ordinances were based on two key elements: 'the *ejtihad-e mostamerr* (permanent interpretative effort of the jurist), expected to update its interpretation of religious laws according to the changing of times'; and 'the acknowledgment of advanced sciences [*'olum*], arts [*fonun*] and experiences [*tajarob*] of mankind and their effort towards progress'.[9] In other words, the governmental power

---

[6] Said Amir Arjomand and Nathan J Brown, *The Rule of Law, Islam, and Constitutional Politics in Egypt and Iran* (SUNY Press, 2013), 33. While Arjomand refers to this institution as 'Maslahat Council' and Schirazi calls it 'Assessment Council', I prefer to adopt the official jargon used by the Iranian authorities. In Persian, politicians and commentators usually refer to this institution simply as *majma'* (Council) or *maslahat-e nezam* (State Expediency).
[7] Ibid.
[8] *Nezam* is the Persian/Arabic word for 'system'. Its etymological origin however hints at the Arabic root 'nzm', indicating 'order'. As such, the word *nezam* could be interpreted as 'political order'.
[9] Sarrami, *Ahkam-e Hokumati*.

brought in by the constitutional revision institutionalised the short-term political expediency that had characterised the management of the war and its politics of crisis, to which the creation and institutionalisation of the Expediency Council was the most paradigmatic response. I shall now provide a timeline of the birth of the Expediency Council and its relation to the idea of 'state' and 'crisis'.

The Genesis of the Expediency Council

Not much has been said about the Expediency Council in the academic literature. Generally, reference to this institution is limited to a few lines, or a paragraph, detailing its birth in the late 1980s and its role as mediator between the *Majles* and the Guardian Council. Nonetheless, in the hierarchy of the Islamic Republic, the Expediency Council stands at the very top of the political machinery, in a symbiotic relationship with the Office of the Supreme Leader (*daftar-e maqam-e mo'azzam-e rahbari*), and has affected processes of state formation at fundamental historical junctures.

Schirazi holds that, in practice, the Expediency Council had existed since 1981 as 'an authority that can go over the head of the official government and decide on the most important questions of policy'.[10] Its *modus operandi*, behind the scenes, might have paralleled that of other unelected councils with legislative power in the early 1980s, such as the Supreme Council of the Cultural Revolution and the Supreme Council supporting the War and that of Reconstruction.[11] If this is the case – plausible given the practice of holding informal high-ranking meetings outside government venues – the Council started its activities coterminous to the critical period of state formation after the revolution. One could interpret it as the materialisation of state prerogatives amid the multiple moral and political constraints of the early 1980s.

It is worth noting that, up to the end of the war, the state-making approach accentuated, haphazardly, the notion of 'rule of emergency' in order to circumvent religious impediments. Based on the Koranic assumption that 'emergencies make it permissible to do what is forbidden', the Iranian state resorted, on a number of occasions, to this ploy to bring forth crucial political projects, not dissimilar to the way harm reduction would be introduced in the 2000s.[12] The rulings approved by the Parliament through this process were considered

[10] Schirazi, *The Constitution*, 95.   [11] Cf. Ibid., 64–5.   [12] Ibid., 175.

zarurat, 'necessity', and implemented as an experiment without going through the vetting process of the Guardian Council.[13] Yet, the use of emergency as a device of governance lacked institutional venues and it addressed mostly the demands, expectations and social vibrations following the revolution and the war efforts.[14] Other issues remained blocked amid the stalemate between the Guardian Council and the Parliament. The three branches of the state eventually sent a letter to Khomeini requesting further clarification on how to enact a governmental ordinance. Khomeini, after having upheld that 'government ... is one of the principle rules [*ahkam*] of Islam and it stands above all other rulings including prayer, fasting and hajj',[15] responded with a groundbreaking paragraph in which he paved the way the establishment of the Expediency Council. The letter concludes with these lines:

bear in mind that the interest of the political order [*maslahat-e nezam*] is among the important issues that, if ignored, can cause the failure of our dear Islam. Today the world of Islam considers the Islamic Republic of Iran a universal sign for the solution of its problems. The interest of the political order and the people [*maslahat nezam-e va mardom*] is a fundamental issue that if opposed ... might leave way to the American Islam of the arrogant and powerful with all the billions from within and without. (February 5, 1988)[16]

Khomeini, as such, claimed that governance was the core element of Islam, acknowledging the centrality of politics to the government especially in an *Islamic* state.[17] This implied, as Saeed Hajjarian holds, acknowledging 'the dynamicity of religious thought in its applicability with the requirements of the historical era and to the solution of problems and insufficiencies of society'.[18] One could add that there is an apparent

---

[13] *Majmu'e Mosavabat-e Majma'e Tashkhis-e Maslahat-e Nezam* [Collection of Decrees of the Expediency Council], Directory of the Expediency Council (Tehran: Expediency Council, 1388 [2009]). I leave aside, begrudgingly, the political theological side of this debate, which is increasingly a matter of research. See Rejali, *Torture & Modernity*, 137–9.

[14] Examples of these are the call for radical interpretation of Land Reform, Rent Reform, Domestic and Foreign Trade. See Schirazi, *The Constitution*, 185–202.

[15] *Majmu'e Mosavabat*, 13. The passage is quoted, similarly, in Arjomand, *The Rule of Law*, 33.

[16] *Majmu'e Mosavabat*, 13.

[17] Cf. Naser Ghobadzadeh, *Religious Secularity: A Theological Challenge to the Islamic State* (Oxford University Press, 2014), 27.

[18] Saeed Hajjarian, *Jomhuriyat; Afsunzodayi Az Qodrat* (Tehran: Tarh-e Nou, 1379).

oxymoronic value in this statement: in order to save Islam from the danger of the secular world (the *American Islam*), the Islamic Republic needs to think outside Islam. It needs to become profane, in the etymological sense of *pro-fanum* that is: 'to stand out of the temple' (of religion), in the form of a secular Islam, or of a religion that engages with the world and its time.

If one pays heed to the Articles of the Constitution as revised in 1988, references to the Expediency Council occur in sections in which a situation of urgency or crisis is contemplated. Article 112 legitimises its establishment and defines its main duties:

Upon order of the Supreme Leader, the Expediency Council should meet at any time the Guardian Council judges a bill proposed by the Majles to be against the principles of *shari'ah* or the Constitution ... Also the Council should meet for consideration on any issue forwarded to it by the Supreme Leader.[19]

Article 110 lists the responsibilities of the Supreme Leader, among which stands out 'the resolution of the political order's problems which are not solvable in a normal way (*az tariq-e 'adi*), through the Council for the Discernment of the Expediency of the Political Order'.[20] This article enshrined the primacy of political reason in matters of statecraft and policymaking, the implication being that Islam *cannot* alone be the solution to all problems, very much opposite to what Islamists have historically held (e.g. 'Islam is the solution'). To further strengthen the contingency/crisis nature of the council, Article 111 establishes that,

If the leader is incapable of governing ... a council is formed with the president, head of Judiciary, one of the jurists of the Guardian Council as chosen by the Expediency Council ... If for any reason one of the members of this temporary council cannot fulfil his role, the Expediency Council will appoint another in his place, maintaining the majority of clerics in the council.[21]

Finally, Article 177 allows the revision of the Constitution only when the Supreme Leader, *after consultation with the Expediency Council*, indicates which parts of the text need to be amended.[22] With the enshrining of this institution within the structure of the Islamic Republic, the state acquired the capacity to intervene in spheres that were religiously controversial, beside making space for a conflict management institution. More importantly, Khomeini did not bestow the

[19] Sarrami, *Ahkam-e Hokumati*.   [20] *Majmu'e Mosavabat*, 42–4.   [21] Ibid.,
[22] Ibid.

institution of the *velayat-e faqih* (and religious law more generally) with the ultimate power to rule over all matters of urgency that regard the state. It had made the state itself, through the Council, the ultimate authority on all matters.[23] Inevitably, this epochal transformation triggered criticism and a debate around the legitimacy of this paradigm of government.[24]

'Gazing Eye, Thoughtful Brain': Structures & Powers

The Expediency Council can be described as the regime in a nutshell. It comprises the leading figures of the political order from all branches of the state. Every member is directly appointed by the Supreme Leader and holds a post for a renewable five-year term. There has been continuity in the membership of the Council, with a progressive increase of its size, although members who were at odds with the regime (e.g. Mir-Hossein Musavi) have not seen their posts renewed. Presidents of the republic have regularly been appointed to the Council, as well as the Heads of Judiciary, members of the Guardian Council, influential IRGC commanders, Directors of the National Security Council as well as Speakers of Parliament. Inevitably, clerical elements dominated the Council, although laymen have seen their numbers on the rise.[25] Read against the grain of its principle task – the interest of the political order (and not simply that of mediating conflicts between different state branches) – the presence of clerics may have contributed to a further secularisation of their attitudes when faced with political contingency of the profane type.[26] The Council's interventions, too, are indicators of consistency and political logics governing the Iranian state over several decades and through different political

---

[23] Ayatollah Azari Qomi points to a similar dynamic when discussing the transformation brought about by the installation of the Council. See Schirazi, *The Constitution*, 231.

[24] See Sarrami, *Ahkam-e Hokumati*, 149, 291; and *Fars*, November 30, 2015, retrieved from www.farsnews.com/13940908001164.

[25] It is no surprise that women have been excluded from the council's assembly, since women have yet to occupy top offices such as the presidency, the judiciary, etc. Female ministers, judges and vice-presidents have taken part in the specialised meetings; female experts have also been invited to advise the Council on specific issues.

[26] The Council appointed by Khamenei in 2011 is made up of fourteen clerics and twenty-two lay members. Two of its non-clerical members have passed away since, reducing the number of laymen to twenty. See Expediency Council, 'Shura-ye Majma'e' http://maslahat.ir/DocLib2/Irec%20Pillars/Irec%20council.aspx.

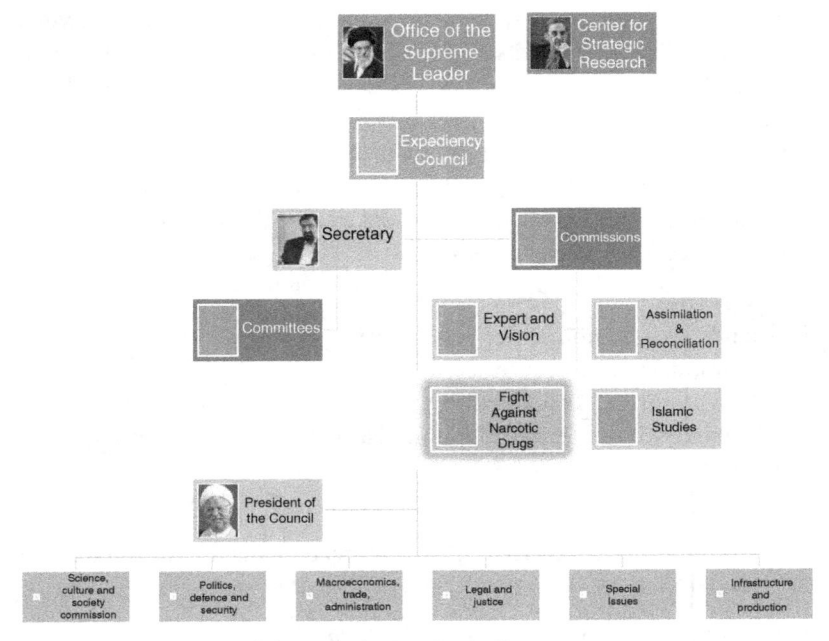

Figure 5.1 Structure of the Expediency Council
The current president of the Council is Sadegh Ardeshir Amoli Larijani, who succeeded Mahmoud Hashemi Shahroudi, appointed following Hashemi-Rafsanjani's death in 2017 and deceased in December 2018. The Table includes Hashemi-Rafsanjani's picture because he has been the longstanding figure at the head of the Council.

environments: reformism (Khatami), populism (Ahmadinejad) and centrism/pragmatism (Rouhani).

On February 20, 1997, Khamenei issued a decree in which he outlined the new duties of the Expediency Council, adding to the constitutional duties, 'the powers to determine the general policies of the state and major questions of the country; tackling of important issues on request of the Leadership as well as advising the Leadership'.[27] Since then, the Expediency Council has operated as a Leadership Headquarters on all political matters. In the words of its general secretary Mohsen Rezaei, 'the Leadership needs an expert institution *with a gazing eye* and *a thoughtful brain*',[28] and the Council has been unavoidably regarded as the only institution capable of operating as such (Figure 5.1).

[27] Hajjarian, *Jomhuriyat*, 414.   [28] Ibid., 417. Emphasis added.

The Council adopts a secular structure divided into the following: presidency (Hashemi Rafsanjani: 1989–2017; Hashemi Shahrudi: 2017–2018; Amoli Larijani 2019–); secretary (Mohsen Rezaei: 1997–) under which operate several specialised commissions; six permanent commissions; and the Centre of Strategic Studies acting as a research tool to the Council.[29] Each permanent commission has a chairman, a deputy and a secretary, and is expected to examine bills and proposals from the specialised commissions.

They are divided according to the following fields:

1 Science, culture and society commission;
2 Politics, defence and security;
3 Infrastructure and production;
4 Macroeconomics, trade and administration;
5 Legal and justice.
6 Special Issues.[30]

Four specialised committees operate instead under the Secretariat of the Council:

1 Experts and Visions/Prospects (*cheshmandaz*);
2 Assimilation/Reconciliation (*taifiq*);
3 Fight against Smuggling and Narcotic Drugs;
4 Islamic Studies.[31]

Overall, the only independent specialised committee dealing with a specific social and political urgency within the Expediency Council is the Drug Policy Commission. Beside the above-mentioned duty to solve those problems of the Islamic political order that cannot otherwise find a 'normal' solution, the Council performs its multiple duties according to an internal regulation which stresses, repeatedly, the use of 'the most updated findings of expertise', 'the use of practical, developmental and foundational researches within the country's research centres', and 'the use of experts from public and private sectors' in the determination of its decisions.[32]

---

[29] After Hassan Rouhani's election to the presidency in 2013, Khamenei appointed his long-term advisor on foreign policy, Ali Akbar Velayati, as director of the Centre, before dismantling the Centre in 2017.
[30] *Majmu'e Mosavabat*. An additional commission is named 'Special Affairs'.
[31] Expediency Council, 'Dabirkhane-Ye Majma'e' http://maslahat.ir/DocLib2/Irec%20Pillars/Irec%20Secretariate.aspx.
[32] Respectively Article 4 and 15 of the Internal Regulations of the Expediency Council.

Khamenei himself highlighted these aspects of the policymaking process at the heart of the Council. After the end of the war and the death of Khomeini, Khamenei revealed, the leadership sought to make use of the Council as 'a collection of thoughts, interpretative efforts [*ejtehad*], expertise [*karshenasi*], experiences and adherence to the traditions and observance of the interest [*maslahat*]'. The Leader invited those taking part in it 'to go beyond *factions* in the meeting of the Council. Here the question is the interest of the country'.[33] If one goes beyond the rhetorical aspects of this message, the lack of any direct or indirect reference (apart from an opening eulogy) to Islam, religion or, for that matter, moral codes is emblematic of the mechanisms embodied in this institutional body. Operating as profane venue of confrontation among long-term political figures of the Islamic Republic, the Council also enjoys especial powers in terms of policymaking, beyond that of resolving conflicts between the Guardian Council and the Parliament.

Between the year of its establishment and its formalisation in the Constitution, the Expediency Council was authorised to pass laws without mediation from other state institutions, including the main legislative body of the country, the *Majles*.[34] Thus, the Council entrusted itself with fundamental legislative powers, as an extension to the Supreme Leader's authority to solve problems *unconventionally*. The body had potentially far-reaching powers, exploited, however, only in times of policy bottleneck, urgency and crisis. Neither the Parliament nor the Guardian Council can modify laws approved by the Expediency Council. Once the Council approves a legislation, the only procedure through which the law can be updated, cancelled or reformed is another deliberation of the Council itself. Other state institutions cannot audit and investigate the Council's work without the Leader's consent, a fact that represents a strong exception given Iran's parliament *de jure* comprehensive auditing powers.[35] The Council being unelected, these issues hint at a fundamental democratic and republican deficit, which gains momentum in times of political crisis, and highlight the negligible checks and balances structure. But it also guarantees systemic harmony when the political order is under pressure.

---

[33] Ibid. Emphasis added.
[34] Silvia Tellenbach, 'Principle of Legality in the Iranian Constitutional and Criminal Law' in Arjomand, *The Rule of Law*, 104–6.
[35] Farideh Farhi, 'Constitutionalism and Parliamentary Struggle for Relevance and Independence' in Arjomand, *The Rule of Law*, 129.

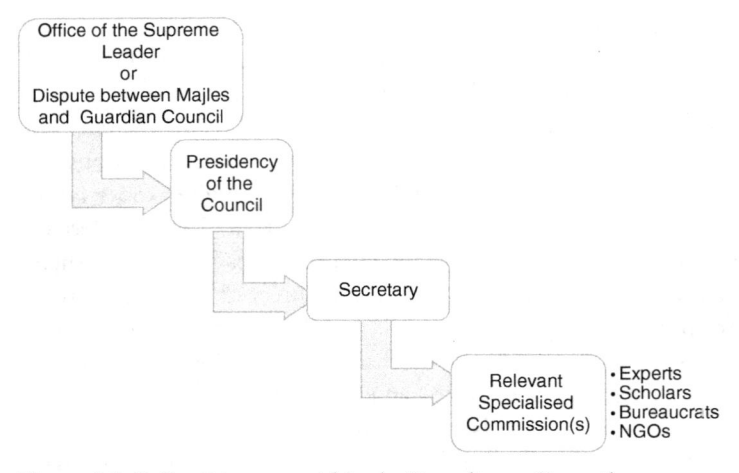

Figure 5.2 Policy Itinerary within the Expediency Council

But how does the actual process of policy formulation work within the Expediency Council?

At receipt of a request for intervention, whether by the Leader or by the Parliament (in case of stalemate), the presidency of the Council refers the dispute or the question to the secretary, which then introduces the matter to one of the relevant specialised commissions (under the Secretariat). The latter investigates the request in collaboration with the specialised independent committees (such as the Drug Policy Committee), which expresses its opinion after evaluation and assessment by inviting experts on the issue; it then sends back the issue to the permanent commission of the Council. The latter evaluates it and, if it deems the proposal relevant and solid, the question is sent to the Council's assembly for a final vote (Figure 5.2). The deliberations of the Council are on nominal majority vote and need the endorsement of the Supreme Leader, a procedure that has hitherto been a formality. The Expediency Council, indeed, is the arena of confrontation at the core of the Islamic Republic. The lower-level investigative commissions and committees operate through a bureaucratic apparatus made up mostly of officials connected through personal and/or professional networks to ministries and other institution of the state. In addition, each step of the evaluation happens with the participation of officials and personnel of relevant ministries, which can intervene even in the final vote of the Council. In this, the Council is characterised by a certain flexibility in terms of its structure, membership and content of debate.

This fluidity and breadth of intervention has caused, as mentioned earlier, disapproval by members of the executive. For instance, president Hassan Rouhani criticised the interference of the Expediency Council, in which he is also an experienced member, on the drafting of the 6th Development Plan, which he argued was a priority of his government.[36] Similarly, the *Majles* repeatedly expressed concern over its incapability of legislating in areas in which the Council has already intervened, because other legislative branches cannot amend laws approved by the Council. Accused of having become a sort of upper house, a Senate – which in Iran's political parlance is inherently pejorative and illegitimate (despite a revival of this idea amid the governance crisis of 2018) – the ambiguity of the Expediency Council (and its General Policies) within the political order are often questioned. At the same time, these accusations fall short when one considers the use of expert knowledge and scientific research in the justifications of the Expediency Council's decisions. This gives further credit on the institutional consistency of the Council in spite of changing political environments from the 1990s to the 2010s.

One sector in which the Council has been permanently active and in charge is that of drug laws and drug policy.

The Expediency Council on Drug Policy

Between 1988 and 2001, the Expediency Council intervened in eight different circumstance on drug laws, marking drug legislation as the exclusive turf of this institution. While the Council has legislated on a wide spectrum of issues over the course of the last three decades, law-making has been ordinarily and legitimately carried out by the Parliament. For drug laws, in contrast, this exception has effectively been the rule. Towards the end of the 1980s, Khomeini spelled out clearly that 'after the war, the most important question for the Islamic Republic is the problem of drugs'.[37] With the end of the war, state-making efforts and social intervention shifted towards the other

[36] *Fars*, December 20, 2015.
[37] Visible on posters and graffiti around the country.

'imposed war', that of drugs. As an epiphenomenon, drugs embodied a fundamental, political crisis. Instead of undertaking a standard legislative path through the *Majles*, which perhaps could have engendered mutual accusations of corruption, laxity, hypocrisy and anti-revolutionary behaviour, the Council, headed by then to-be Leader Ali Khamenei, presided over the first comprehensive draft of drug laws. It is emblematic that a most profane, yet ethically problematic, issue such as drugs became a question of *raison d'état* or *maslahat*.

On May 29, 1988, the Council approved the first Anti-Narcotics Law. This became a milestone determining the architecture of Iran's strategy on drugs for the years to come. The text included initially forty articles that systematically addressed issues of illicit drugs trafficking (opiates, cannabis, etc.), punishments and fines as well as measures of intervention for drug addicts. The text of the law did not produce a radical change in terms of measures against drug use and trafficking, but it reified a 'security and social necessity' for the state.[38] The objective was not to overhaul the security-oriented, punitive approach that had come into being following the Revolution. Instead, it was enshrining a legal frame for the state-led strategy on illicit drugs, updating the early 1980s approach characterised by great revolutionary zeal, but little systemic engagement. Even on this occasion, the Council's intervention was meant to be temporary and the Anti-Narcotics Law had a validity of only two years. Instead, six months after its approval, the Expediency Council abrogated the two-year validity and entrusted the execution of all drug-related matters to a newly created institution, the Drug Control Headquarters (DCHQ), established by Article 33 of the law.

According to the 1988 law, 'addiction' remained a crime punished with incarceration and fines. The law did not envisage major changes from the previous sanctions. It enhanced and reaffirmed heavy sanctions for drug trafficking, cultivation and possession (above certain quantities), it maintained the death penalty for recidivist offenders (three times) of major drug crimes, and it legitimised confiscation of property for drug dealers. Those who introduced drugs into military barracks and prisons could see their penalties augmented severely, amid reports of widespread drug (ab)use among conscripts, veterans and prisoners.

[38] Qahrfarkhi, *E'tiyad*, 332.

As during the 1980s, drug crimes were judged by the Revolutionary Courts, together with blasphemy and crimes against the revolution, national security and the Islamic Republic. Among the features of the revolutionary court, there is the fact that its deliberations cannot be reassessed and revised. Inevitably, this has led over the years to harsher punishments, with a weak judgement process, even in the cases that lead to death sentences. Although this provision has never been uprooted in the national drug laws, over the 1990s and, especially the 2000s, the Council introduced a number of revisions to the drug laws, with important changes regarding sanctions and welfare provisions. Because the laws approved by the Expediency Council can be revised *only* by the Council itself, the issue of drugs – and drug policy – situated itself in a condition of permanent crisis. In other words, drugs became an especial question of political consideration for the Islamic Republic, one with which elected bodies could not interfere directly, and where the highest echelons of the state needed strategic evaluation and inter-institutional compromise. This condition can be called 'dead-end law making (*qanungozari-ye bon-bast*)'. Among the key features of this model is the necessity of reproducing crisis in order to allow for the reconsideration of previously sanctioned laws. An interview with a long-term member of the Expediency Council's bureaucratic machinery unveils this condition:

At times, a social question [*mo'zal-e ejtema'i*] is not so relevant to people up to when it is transformed into a social phenomenon [*padideh-ye ejtema'i*] which grows and grows. When its limits go further, it becomes a concern to everyone ... Sometimes, the worse it gets [*kharab-tar besheh*], the more it is to our advantage because it gets to a point at which we have to take a decision and when the situation looks, or is, critical then we can actually make decisions that are innovative. At that point, in political terms, you can transform the threat into an opportunity.

In 2004, the Council modified the status of the Committee on Drug Policy into a Commission given additional tasks and duties. Today, the Commission is made up of four specialised committees dedicated to drug supply reduction, drug demand reduction, strategic policies, and international and transnational relations.[39] The Council's meetings on

[39] Expediency Council, 'Pishineh', retrieved from http://maslahat.ir/Commissions/AntiDrug/DocLib/History.aspx.

drug policy, too, have increased from one meeting every two-to-three months to meetings on a fortnightly basis.[40] The commission for drug policy is headed by former IRGC commander Mohsen Rezaei, and the secretary/director is former DCHQ official Ali Hashemi who supervises the work of the four sub-committees, the most important ones being drug supply and drug demand reduction (Figure 5.3).[41] Rezaei has been member of the Council since 1997, where he acts as Secretary General with duties of supervision of the various committees and commissions as well as referral of their findings to the president of the council during general discussions and voting. Appreciated as a military commander – his 2015 return to the IRGC was a clear sign of this – he made a good case for his pragmatism when, in 1981, amid the confrontation against superior Iraqi military forces, he stated, 'We should accept that we are involved in a great revolution in which all the world has created an alliance against us, so we can't overcome the war issue only by praying, we ought to increase our military science and technological power'.[42] In 1988, he sent an open letter to Supreme Leader Khomeini affirming that the war against Iraq could not be won and that Iran should prepare itself for a negotiated settlement. As a director of the Council, he has given prominence to these same characteristics by coordinating the evaluation process in the lower committees with expert members of the research community. Known to be a pragmatist in the Western scholarly discourse, the interesting elements rest on the emphasis that Rezaei has put throughout his career on scientific and technological advancement, something that has been largely utilised in drug policy approaches.

His closest advisor in the Drug Policy Commission is Ali Hashemi, formerly at the head of the DCHQ. Hashemi is a high-ranking bureaucrat who has acted over the course of the last decades as advisor to President Mohammad Khatami (1997–2005), member of the National Security Council (1986–97) and member of the IRGC (1979–86). His contribution to the field of drug policy is guided by public health considerations and an understanding of national security, inclusive of public health matters. Indeed, under the reformist presidency, he actively supported the expansion of humanitarian and reform-oriented

---

[40] Interview with Said Sefatian, Tehran, September 20, 2015. This Commission has been headed by Ali Hashemi, formerly Director of the DCHQ.
[41] 'Rezaei Returns to His Military Roots', *Al-Monitor*, May 13, 2015. [42] Ibid.

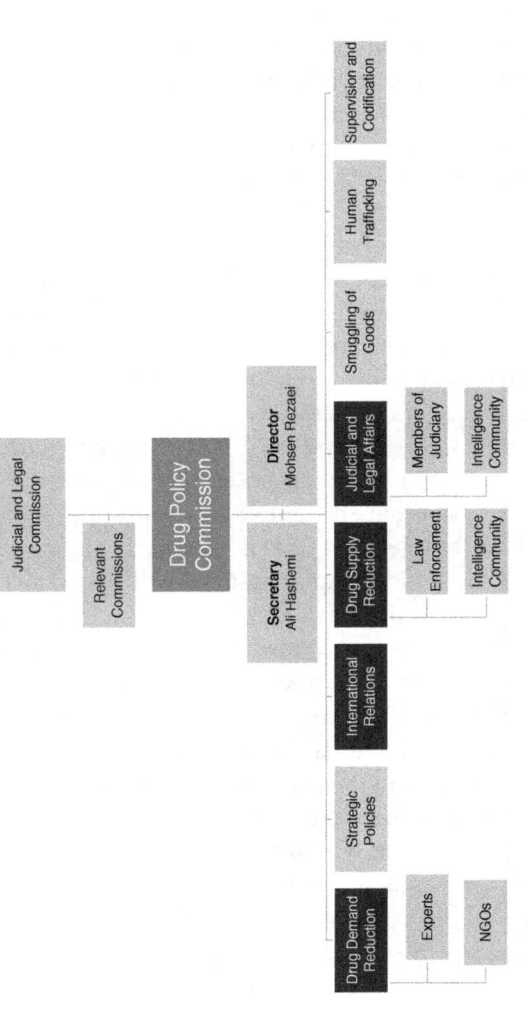

Structure of Drug Policy Commission

- **Council Assembly**
  - **Judicial and Legal Commission**
    - Relevant Commissions
- **Drug Policy Commission**
  - **Director** – Mohsen Rezaei
  - **Secretary** – Ali Hashiemi
  - Drug Demand Reduction
    - Experts
    - NGOs
  - Strategic Policies
  - International Relations
  - Drug Supply Reduction
    - Law Enforcement
    - Intelligence Community
  - Judicial and Legal Affairs
    - Members of Judiciary
    - Intelligence Community
  - Smuggling of Goods
  - Human Trafficking
  - Supervision and Codification

Figure 5.3 Structure of Drug Policy Commission

policies on drug (ab)use, justifying it in terms of social security and risk minimisation, including in national security terms.[43]

First relevant committees discuss changes within drug laws. For issues related to public health, such as prevention and drug (ab)use, discussions take place in the demand reduction section; for issues related to smuggling and trafficking, it is the supply reduction section. Once matured, a proposal or agenda of discussion (*dastur-e kar*) for policy change is sent to the Expediency Council's Judicial and Legal Commission, at the top of which sits the Head of the Judiciary. This is usually the litmus test for any new policy proposal where institutional vetoes play in. Views, according to my interlocutors, are generally security-oriented and punitive with regard to drugs policy, although important changes have taken place over the course of the last decade. The participation of expert panels, practitioners, scholars and civil society groups is standard practice of the evaluation process. For issues related to drug policy, well-known personalities from the medical community are generally invited to present on specific topics of interest to the sub-committees or the council. Prominent epidemiologists within Iranian universities and leading members of NGOs provide their accounts and analyses at this level, with a focus on tangibility of results and experiences rather than political readings and intellectual deconstructions. There is a general predilection for numerical reports and econometric results, which often facilitate the committees' making the case for or against a policy proposal. It is established practice to have the participation of experts known for their opposing views; although this could be complex to apply at all times, it is the norm in debates about drug law reform. Collaboration with research centres is instrumental to the policy debate within the Council. Evidence gathered from the 'field' of drug policy is mediated by researchers and put at the disposal of the bureaucratic apparatus to be prepared for the Council's debates. One research centre playing an important role in this is the Iranian National Center for Addiction Studies (INCAS). Created in 2004, amid the controversies around harm reduction practices, INCAS is a venue for research *and* implementation/design of drug policy. It had a central role in the pilot methadone programme in the early 2000s providing a scientific language and policy evidence for its

---

[43] Interview with Said Sefatian, Tehran, September 2014. See Hashemi's CV retrieved from http://maslahat.ir/Commissions/AntiDrug/Documents.pdf.

scaling up.⁴⁴ Based on its status as a policy and research centre, INCAS has contributed to policy design in the field of addiction not only in Iran, but also in Afghanistan and Pakistan.⁴⁵ Similarly, INCAS initiated Iran's (counterintuitive) programme for treatment of alcohol dependency, receiving final approval from the Ministry of Health on the advice of the Council.⁴⁶ The use of such a medical research centre hints at the traditional acceptance of medical expediency in Shi'ite religious jurisprudence, where substances and/or actions deemed *haram* (forbidden) can be reputed licit if they are proved beneficial to the believer's health.⁴⁷ The clergy's approach to birth control, research on stem cells and the right to use narcotic drugs for medical purposes are examples of this medicalised rationale at the base of jurisprudential arguments and policymaking.⁴⁸

Studies of the economic cost of drug (ab)use and the benefits of a reformed approach – such as decriminalisation of drugs – have also been submitted to the Council by independent researchers or affiliates to INCAS. For instance, a number of studies were provided in favour of harm reduction practices in reducing both costs and harms of drug (ab) use. Among these, Hooman Narenjiha and Roya Noori, two independent researchers, produced an influential comparative study on the pilot experiment programmes in Kermanshah and Tehran, where they argued that by introducing harm reduction, Iran could potentially save 400 billion *tuman*, equivalent to eight budgets of the DCHQ.⁴⁹ The proposals and reports sent to the Council can be accepted, rejected or sent back for revision – similarly to an academic peer-review process, although the Council's timescale might take fewer months. After this

---

⁴⁴ Interview with Hamid-Reza Tahernokhost, September 2012.
⁴⁵ MENAHRA website, retrieved from www.menahra.org/en/short-term-fund ings/menahra-knowledge-hubs/incas/incas-about.
⁴⁶ See INCAS website, retrieved from http://incas.tums.ac.ir/page.php?slct_pg_id=309&sid=1&slc_lang=fa.
⁴⁷ Maziyar Ghiabi et al., 'Islam and Cannabis: Legalisation and Religious Debate in Iran'. *International Journal of Drug Policy* 56 (2018).
⁴⁸ I develop this aspect of contemporary polity in Iran in a side project, titled 'The Medical Republic of Iran', presented at the *International Conference of Iranian Studies*, Vienna, August 2016. For a journalistic account, see Maziar Bahari, 'Quarks and the Koran', *Newsweek* May 23, 2009, retrieved from http://europe.newsweek.com/quarks-and-koran-irans-islamic-embrace-science-80063?rm=eu.
⁴⁹ Hooman Narenjiha and Noori Roya, 'Methadone maintenance therapy outcomes in Iran [Farsi]' (2006), provided by the authors in a printed copy.

step, the proposal can be reviewed by other relevant commissions if it pertains to their field of intervention. The Expediency Council eventually puts the question to a vote. Given that members of the Council also sit on lower-level committees, proposals that arrive at Council level tend to be approved without major impediments and are sent for final endorsement to the Supreme Leader. The adoption and expansion of the harm reduction policy (*kahesh asib/zayan*) on a nationwide scale represented a first major instance of drug policy reform. The adoption of these measures, beside their phenomenological rationale and social root, casts light also on the practicalities of the policymaking process through which this institution formulates drug policy. Inputs from NGO workers, medical researchers and international experts, coupled with the perception and materialisation of a critical situation, engendered a reformulation process that also occurred within the Expediency Council.

The Council also promoted the inclusion of the harm reduction policy within the text of the Major Policies of the Islamic Republic, consolidating the legitimacy of this notion within Iran's legislation. Similarly, the 6th Development Plan, which for the first time was drafted by the Council, includes a reference to drug policy in Article 22. This article states that the target of the Islamic Republic within the next five years is to reduce the national rate of addiction by 25 per cent. The article also adds that, in furtherance of this objective, the government should seek 'the management of drug use in the country', a statement that could be a prelude to shifts towards depenalisation and regulation of certain types of drugs.[50] Indeed, there have been informal discussions within the Expediency Council, about 'heroin shooting rooms', regulation of opium and cannabis production, depenalisation of drug use and abolition of the death penalty for drug crimes, the latter having been approved in 2018.[51] These debates are at times preceded by informal meetings in conference venues where

[50] 'Kahesh-e 25 Dar Sad-E E'tiyad Dar Keshvar Ta Payan-E Barnam-e Shishom-e Touse', Government of the Islamic Republic of Iran, retrieved from www.dolat.ir/NSite/FullStory/News/?Serv=0&Id=266177.
[51] Interview with Said Sefatian, September 18, 2015. On the abolition of the death penalty, see Conclusions of this book. And *Sharq*, September 10, 2016. For an overview of the larger question of drug policy reform, see Ghiabi, 'Islam and Cannabis'.

leading members of the drug policy community meet and discuss together with representatives of the Expediency Council.[52]

From a legislative viewpoint, the Council's strategy affects the rest of the political machinery. The Council has become the arena for confrontation and synthesis of different governmentalities with regard to crisis. In this, the logics of the Iranian state resides within this institution more than other specific agents that have traditionally been identified as 'the regime'.

Conclusions

The Expediency Council has been historically regarded as a conservative institution.[53] Yet, the debates within the Expediency Council reveal an underlying secular logic governing crisis, which often produces what, in the context of the Islamic Republic, can be described as profane politics with oxymoronic outcomes. Profane politics is a form of governance that steps outside its ideological and religious cadre in order to engage with worldly matters. Outside the temple, the *fanum*, the profane is concerned with a politics of the phenomena and with the time governing them (the *seculum* of secular). This oxymoronic dimension is empirically discussed in Part Two of the book, which dwells on the ethnography of policies about drugs. This *interregnum*, on the other hand, explored the genealogical origin and historical developments of crisis politics and its effect on an Iranian form of secularity, which is made of a cumulative effect of expertise, science, technology, security and governmental calculi – one could say *expedients*. The considerations proposed here are not exclusive to drug policy; they are part and parcel of the post-revolutionary process of state reformation at large, as evidenced in the intrusion of the Council in ever more numerous fields of public concern.

This proverbial secularity and holistic engagement is best captured by a paragraph in one of the Expediency Council's publications on the

---

[52] It is sufficient to say that more than thirty leading figures of Iran's drug policy argued, albeit in confrontational terms, for plans for reforms.
See *Mehr*, December 12, 2015, retrieved from www.mehrnews.com/news/2995003.

[53] See, for instance, Farhad Khosrokhavar, 'The New Conservatives Take a Turn', *Middle East Report* 233 (2004), 24–7.

effects of subsidy reform on Iran's drug problem. The author of the paragraph is a leading administrator of the Islamic Republic on matters of illicit drugs. He says:

> If one considers major drug traffickers and dealers, *from a Foucauldian analytical perspective*, their presence in the sphere of trafficking is motivated by the acquisition of a *power* which lies behind the veil of trafficking itself (as long as we see power as an expression of its three faces: capital, status and politics).[54]

The normative limits that apply to politics and political rhetoric, dictated by religious, moral and political constraints, are set within the Expediency Council, as shown in the adoption of post-modernist language and the reference to harm reduction ethics. In Part Two this logic of power – this *governmentality* – is interpreted as an art of governing crisis and managing disorder, providing a new analytical lens to the politics of the Islamic Republic. This art has given way to oxymoronic conditions in which the state adopts *modi operandi* that would otherwise be inconsistent, incompatible and disconnected with each other. Drugs politics is an especial instance of the way this art works, for drugs and drug (ab)use have become a permanent crisis – in ethics, politics, and public health – following the Islamic Revolution.

The establishment of the Expediency Council institutionalises crisis within the Islamic Republic governmental machinery. The rule of emergency, used in the years of the war (1980–8), was constrained in its temporal application and dependent on a large majority in the Parliament. The Council, instead, stands at the highest core of legislative power, immune to the vicissitudes of electoral politics as well as unchained by the nuances of Islamic law: it intervenes in conditions judged – autonomously – exceptional and of crisis. This signature of power signified not only a reification of secular elements, such as the inviolability of the state and primacy of political acumen in place of revolutionary and spiritual leadership, as Khomeini himself had envisioned. It also meant that, in terms of political praxis, not the Supreme Leader, but the Expediency Council has had ultimate governmental

---

[54] Expediency Council, 'Asar-e Ejrai-ye Qanun-e Hadafmandi-ye Yaraneh-ha bar Eqtesad-e Mavadd-e Mokhadder' (Tehran: Expediency Council, undated). Emphasis added. Cf. with what Hajjarian names Iran's infatuation with supermodernism', in *Jomhuriyat*.

power. To paraphrase Foucault's *bons mots*: the Supreme Leader reigns, but the Expediency Council governs.[55]

---

[55] In 1978, Foucault cited Adolphe Thiers in an article on Mohammad Reza Pahlavi, the last Shah of Iran, while he visited Tehran on behalf of the Italian newspaper *Corriere della Sera*. The original French version says: *que le roi règne, mais il ne gouverne pas*. In *Corriere della sera*, vol. 103, no. 230, 1 octobre 1978, p. 1.

Part Two

6 | *The Anthropological Mutation of Methamphetamines*

All drug use, fundamentally, has to do with speed, modification of speed . . . the times that become superhuman or subhuman.

Gilles Deleuze, *Deux régimes des fous*, 138.

After all, the world is industrial and we have to come to terms with it . . . Gone are the old good days of opium, heroin, gone are the young *bangi,* gone is *hashish*, marijuana, and *geraas* [weed, grass]! Now it is all about *shisheh, blour* and *kristal* and *nakh*. The modern people have become postmodern. And this latter, we know, it is industrial and poetical, like the *God's tear* or *Satan's deceit*.[1]

'The *Bangi* of the postmodern time', *Iran* (government newspaper), November 4, 2009.

Introduction

The election of Mahmud Ahmadinejad to the ninth presidency of the Islamic Republic asserted an anomaly within the political process of postrevolutionary, post-war Iran. After the heydays of reformist government, with its inconclusive and juxtaposing political outcomes, the 2005 elections had seen the rise of a political figure considered, up to then, as marginal, secondary, if not eclectic and obscure. Accompanied by his rhetoric, which tapped into both a bygone revolutionary era and a populist internationalist fervour, Ahmadinejad brought onto the scene of Iranian – and arguably international – politics, an energy and a mannerism, which were unfamiliar to Islamist and Western political cadres.

Considering his apparent idiosyncrasies, much of the attention of scholars and media went into discerning the man, his ideas and his

---

[1] *Bangi* is a term that refers to *hashish* smokers in Iran. *Blour, kristal* and *nakh* are slang names for stimulants, such as *shisheh* and ecstasy. *God's tear* and *Satan's deceit* are two names for chemical drugs.

human circles, with symptomatic attention to foreign policy.[2] His impact on the domestic politics of the Islamic Republic, too, has been interpreted as a consequence of his personalising style of government; his messianic passion about Shi'a revival and religious eschatology clashed with his apparent infatuation with Iran's ancient Zoroastrian heritage;[3] and, significantly, his confrontational attitude *vis-à-vis* political adversaries manifested an unprecedented tone in the political script. Ahmadinejad himself contributed greatly to his caricature: his public appearances (and 'disappearances'[4]) as well as speeches, amounting to thousands in just a few years.[5] His interventions in international settings regularly prompted great upheaval and controversy, if not a tragicomic allure prompted by his many detractors. His accusations and attacks against the politico-economic elites were numerous and unusually explicit for the style of national leaders, even when compared to European and American populist leaders, such as Jair Bolsonaro, Donald J. Trump and Matteo Salvini, all of whom remain conformist on economic matters. Ultimately, his remarks about the Holocaust and Israel, albeit inconsistent and exaggerated by foreign detractors, made all the more convenient the making of Ahmadinejad into a controversial character both domestically and globally, while provided him some legitimacy gains and political latitude among hard-liners, domestically, and Islamist circles abroad. Philosopher Jahanbegloo, in his essay 'Two Sovereignties and the Legitimacy Crisis', describes this period 'as the final step in a progressive shift in the Iranian revolution from popular republicanism to absolute sovereignty'.[6] Conversely, in this volume, Part Two and its three Chapters give voice and substance to this period and its new

---

[2] Similarly to what is occurring among political scientists working on US president Donald J. Trump and his way of doing politics, 'Trumpism'.
[3] *Payvand*, August 19, 2010, retrieved from www.payvand.com/news/10/aug/11 84.html.
[4] The president avoided any public appearance for more than a week and refused to fulfil his duties in the spring of 2011, after Supreme Leader Khamenei reinstated Heydar Moslehi. The latter was dismissed from his post as Minister of Intelligence by Ahmadinejad. See *BBC*, May 1, 2011, retrieved from www.bbc.com/news/world-middle-east-13250309.
[5] Ahmadinejad toured inside Iran during his two mandates. He also held cabinet meetings in different Iranian cities so that the people could be closer to government.
[6] Ramin Jahanbegloo, 'The Two Sovereignties and the Legitimacy Crisis in Iran', *Constellations* 17, 1 (2010), 28.

form of profane politics as they emerged after 2005. In its unholy practices, it did not produce enhanced theocracy, nor absolute sovereignty. Instead it made Iranian politics and society visibly profane, with its drug policy being the case *par excellence*. Jahanbegloo's take, and that of other scholars following this line, has shed a dim light on the epochal dynamics shaping the post-reformist years (2005–13).[7] It is over this period that an 'anthropological mutation' took shape in terms of lifestyle, political participation, consumption and cultural order.[8] This anthropological mutation produced new social identities, which were no longer in continuity with neither the historical past nor with ways of being modern in Iran. This new situation, determined by ruptures in cultural idioms and social performances, blurred the lines between social class, rural and urban life, and cultural references among people. Italian poet, film director and essayist Pier Paolo Pasolini described the transformations of the Italian people during the post-war period – especially in the 1970s – as determined by global consumerism and not, as one would have expected, by the *Weltanschauung* of the conservative Christian Democratic party, which ruled Italy since the liberation from Benito Mussolini's fascist regime in 1945. Not the cautious and regressive politics of the Catholic Church, but the unstoppable force of hedonistic consumerism represented the historical force behind the way Italians experienced life and, for that matter, politics. Taking Pasolini's insight into historical, anthropological transformation, I use the term *anthropological mutation* – or, as Pasolini himself suggested, 'revolution' – to understand the epochal fluidity of Iranian society by the time Mahmud Ahmadinejad was elected president in 2005. It was not the reformist government alone that brought profound change in Iranian society. Reform and transformation were key traits of Ahmadinejad's time in government. That is also

---

[7] Mehdi Khalaji, 'Iran's Regime of Religion', *Journal of International Affairs* (2011).

[8] I borrow the expression 'anthropological revolution' from Pier Paolo Pasolini's essay on 1970s Italian society. *Scritti Corsari* (Milano: Garzanti, 1975). These transformations have been described through the frame of 'resistance' from different angles in Mahdavi, *Passionate Uprisings*; Afary, *Sexual Politics*: Section Three; Annabelle Sreberny and Massoumeh Torfeh, *Cultural Revolution in Iran: Contemporary Popular Culture in the Islamic Republic* (IB Tauris, 2013); Khosravi, *Young and Defiant*, and *Precarious Lives: Waiting and Hope in Iran* (University of Pennsylvania Press, 2017).

why the period following Khatami's presidency is better understood as *post-reformism* rather than *anti-reformism*.

Over this period, the Islamic Republic and Iranians all lived through the greatest political upheaval following the 1979 revolution: political mobilisation ahead of the June 2009 elections, especially with the rise of the Green Movement (*jonbesh-e sabz*); then state-led repression against protesters and the movement's leaders, Mir Hossein Musavi and Mehdi Karroubi. The events following the presidential elections in June 2009 exacerbated the already tense conditions under which politics had unfolded in the new millennium. Allegations of irregularities, widely circulated in international and social media, led to popular mobilisation against what was perceived as a *coup d'état* by the incumbent government presided over by Ahmadinejad; then, the seclusion of presidential candidates Mir Hossein Musavi and Mehdi Karrubi, *inter alios*, changed the parameters and stakes of domestic politics irremediably. For the first time since the victory of the revolution in 1979, massive popular demonstrations took place against the state authorities. Meanwhile, the security apparatuses arrested and defused the network of reformist politicians, many of whom had, up to then, been highly influential members of the Islamic Republic. Echoing the words of president Ahmadinejad himself, he had brought 'the revolution in the government'.[9]

In this Chapter, I dwell on a set of sociocultural trends that unfolded during this period, progressively transforming Iranian society into a (post)modern, globalised terrain. It is important to situate these dynamics as they play effectively both in the phenomenon of drug (ab)use and the narrative of state interventions, the latter discussed in the next two Chapters. In particular, the 'epidemic' of methamphetamine use (*shisheh*), I argue, altered the previously accepted boundaries of intervention, compelling the government to opt for strategies of management of the crisis. The following three Chapters explore the period after 2005 through a three-dimensional approach constituted of social, medical and political layers. The objective is to examine and re-enact the micro/macro political game that animated drugs politics over this period. In this setting, drugs become a prism to observe these larger human, societal and political changes.

---

[9] *Asia Times*, August 7, 2007, retrieved from www.atimes.com/atimes/Middle_East/IH07Ak04.html.

Table 6.1 *Rates of Divorce in 2004–5*[11]

	Iran	Tehran
Divorce during in 1393 [2004–5]	163569	37976
Marriage during in 1393	724324	87145
Ratio of divorce per marriage	22.6%	37.8%

Addictions, Social Change, and Globalisation

With the rise of 'neo-conservatives' within the landscape of Iranian institutions, it is normatively assumed that groups linked to the IRGC security and logistics apparatuses, as well as individuals linked to intelligence services, gained substantial ground in influencing politics. The overall political atmosphere witnessed an upturning: religious dialogue and progressive policies were replaced by devotional zeal and 'principalist' (*osulgar*) legislations. Similarly, the social context witnessed epochal changes. These changes can be attributed in part to the deep and far-reaching impact that the reformist discourse had had over the early 2000s, in spite of its clamorous political failures. The seeds that the reformists had sowed before 2005, were bearing fruit while the anathema of Mahmud Ahmadinejad was in power. Longer-term processes were also at work, along lines common to the rest of the world. Larger strata of the population were thus exposed to the light and dark edges of a consumeristic society.[10] The emergence of individual values and global cultural trends, in spite of their apparent insolubility within the austerity of the Islamic Republic, signalled the changing nature of life and the public.

Family structure underwent a radical transformation during the 2000s. With rates of divorce hitting their highest levels globally and with a birth rate shrinking to levels comparable to, if not lower than, Western industrialised countries, the place of family and the individual was overhauled, together with many of the social norms associated with them (Table 6.1). The average child per woman ratio fell from seven in the 1980s to less than two in the new millennium, a datum comparable

---

[10] Adelkhah, *Being Modern*.
[11] Data provided by Welfare Organisation's Centre for Social Urgencies. See also Kashani-Sabet, *Conceiving Citizens*.

to that of the United States.¹² The (mono)nuclearisation of the family and the atomisation of individuals brought a new mode of life within the ecology of ever-growing urban centres. Likewise, the quest for better professional careers, more prestigious education (including in private schools), and hedonistic lifestyles, did not exclusively apply, as it had historically, to bourgeois families residing in the northern part of the capital Tehran. Along with Mahmud Ahmadinejad's coming to power, rural, working class, 'villain' (*dahati*) Iranians entered the secular world of the upper-middle class, at least in their cultural referents.¹³ More than ever before, different social classes shared a similar horizon of life, education being the 'launch pad' for a brighter career, made of the acquisition of modern and sophisticated products, such as luxury cars, expensive clothes, cosmetic surgeries, technological devices and exotic travels (e.g. Thailand, Dubai).¹⁴ These elements entered surreptitiously but firmly into the daily lexicon and imagination of working class Iranians, against the tide of economic troubles and the increasing visibility of social inequality.¹⁵ A decade later, in the late 2010s, consumerism has become a prime force, manifested in the Instagram accounts of most people.

Coterminous to this new popular imagery, the lack of adequate employment opportunities resulted from a combination of haphazard industrial policy, international sanctions and lack of investments, inducing large numbers of people to seek a better lot abroad. With its highly educated population, Iran topped the ominous list of university-level émigrés. According to the IMF report, more than 150,000 people have left the country every year since the 1990s with a loss of approximately 50 billion dollars.¹⁶ After the clampdown on the 2009 protestors, many of them students and young people, this trend was

---

12 *Reuters*, October 22, 2014, retrieved from www.reuters.com/article/2014/10/2 2/us-iran-divorce-idUSKCN0IB0GQ20141022.
13 Zuzanna Olszewska, 'Classy Kids and Down-at-Heel Intellectuals: Status Aspiration and Blind Spots in the Contemporary Ethnography of Iran', *Iranian Studies* 46, 6 (2013).
14 Cf. Fariba Adelkhah, *Les Mille et Une Frontières de L'iran: Quand Les Voyages Forment la Nation* (Paris: Karthala, 2012).
15 Djavad Salehi-Esfehani, 'Tyranny of Numbers. Rising Inequality in Iran: Who Is to Blame?', retrieved from http://djavadsalehi.com/2009/05/25/whos-to-bla me-for-rising-inequality/.
16 *Bloomberg*, May 8, 2014, retrieved from www.bloomberg.com/bw/articles/20 14-05-08/irans-best-engineering-science-grads-take-skills-abroad.

exacerbated to the point of being acknowledged as the 'brain-drain crisis' (*bohran-e farar-e maghz-ha*).[17] A report published in the newspaper *Sharq* indicated that between 1993 and 2007, 225 Iranian students participated in world Olympiads in mathematics, physics, chemistry and computer science.[18] Of these 225, 140 are currently studying at top US and Canadian universities.[19] The case of the mathematician Maryam Mirzakhani, who, in 2014, was the first woman ever to win the Fields Medal (the equivalent of the Nobel Prize in mathematics), is exemplary of this trend.[20] In the words of sociologist Hamid Reza Jalaipour, 'many left the country, and those who remained in Iran had to travel within themselves',[21] by using drugs.

The presence of young people in the public space had become dominant and, in the teeth of the moral police (*gasht-e ershad*) and the reactionary elements within the clergy, exuberantly active. The fields of music, cinema, arts and sports boomed during the late 2000s and physically encroached into the walls and undergrounds of Iran's main cities. The examples provided by Bahman Ghobadi's *No one knows about Persian cats* (winner of the *Un Certain Regard* at Cannes) and the graffiti artist 'Black Hand' – Iran's *Banksy* – are two meaningful cases in an ocean of artistic production of globalised resonance.[22]

Considering the sharpening of social conditions, both material and imagined, there was a steady rise in reported cases of depression (*dépréshion, afsordegi*). Indicative of the growing mental health issue is a report published by the Aria Strategic Research Centre, which claims 'that 30 percent of Tehran residents suffer from severe depression, while another 28 percent suffer from mild depression'.[23]

---

[17] 'After Years of Denial: The Iranian Government Recognises the Brain Drain Crisis', February 27, 2014, retrieved from http://humanities.tau.ac.il/iranian/en/previous-reviews/10-iran-pulse-en/284-iran-pulse-no-65
[18] *Iran Daily*, August 20, 2014, retrieved from www.iran-daily.com/News/640.html.
[19] *Sharq*, May 5, 2012.
[20] *The Guardian*, August 13, 2014, retrieved from www.theguardian.com/commentisfree/2014/aug/13/woman-wins-fields-medal-odds-maryam-mirzakhani.
[21] *Sharq*, September 5, 2006.
[22] See Sreberny, *Cultural Revolution*; and *Urban Iran* (Mark Betty Publisher, 2008). Nahid Siamdoust, *Soundtrack of the Revolution: The Politics of Music in Iran* (Stanford University Press, 2017).
[23] *Payvand*, January 7, 2010, retrieved from www.payvand.com/news/10/jul/1007.html. Also Orkideh Behrouzan, 'Writing Prozāk Diaries in Tehran: Generational Anomie and Psychiatric Subjectivities', *Culture, Medicine, and Psychiatry* 39, 3 (2015).

Obviously, the increased relevance of depression can be attributed to a variation in the diagnostic capacity of the medical community, as well as to changes and redefinition of the symptoms within the medical doctrine.[24] Yet, the fact that depression progressively came to occupy the landscape of reference and human imagery of this period is a meaningful sign of changing perception of the self and the self's place within broader social situations.

The lack of entertainment in the public space has been a hallmark of post-revolutionary society, but its burden became all the more intolerable for a young globalised generation, with expectations of a sophisticated lifestyle, and cultural norms which have shifted in drastic ways compared to their parents. If part of it had been expressed in the materialisation of an Iranized counterculture (seen in the fields of arts and new media), the other remained trapped in chronic dysphoria, apathy and anomie, to which drug use was often the response. The prevalence of depression nationwide, according to reports published in 2014, reaches 26.5 per cent among women and 15.8 per cent among men, with divorced couples and unemployed people being more at risk.[25] In a post-conflict context, characterised by recurrent threats of war (Israeli, US military intervention), the emergence of depressive symptoms is not an anomaly. However, as Orkideh Behrouzan argues, in Iran there is a conscious reference to depression as a political *datum*, manifested, for instance, in the popular expression 'the 1360s (1980s) generation,' (*daheh shasti*) as the 'khamushi or silenced generation' (*nasl-e khamushi*).[26] The 1980s generation lived their childhood through the war, experienced the post-war reconstruction period and the by-products of the cultural revolution, while at the same time gained extensive access – thanks to the unintended effects of the Islamic Republic's social policies – to social media, internet and globalised cultural products.

An event that may have had profound effects on the understanding of depression among Iranian youth is the failure of achieving tangible

[24] Orkideh Behrouzan, *Prozāk Diaries: Psychiatry and Generational Memory in Iran* (Stanford University Press, 2016).
[25] *Iran Daily*, October 15, 2014, retrieved from www.iran-daily.com/News/13436.html.
[26] Orkideh Behrouzan and Michael Fischer, '"Behaves Like a Rooster and Cries Like a (Four-Eyed) Canine": The Politics and Poetics of Depression and Psychiatry in Iran' in *Genocide and Mass Violence Memory, Symptom, and Recovery: Health and Clinical Psychology* (2014), 105.

political reforms following the window of reformism and, crucially, in the wake of the protests of the 2009 Green Movement. The large-scale mobilisation among the urban youth raised the bar of expectations, which clashed with the state's heavy-handed security response, silencing of opponents and refusal to take in legitimate demands. In this, the reformists' debacle of 2009 was a sign of a collective failure justifying the self-diagnosis of depression by the many expecting their actions to bear results.

In 2009, Abbas Mohtaj, advisor to the Ministry of Interior in security and military affairs said, 'joy engineering [*mohandesi-ye shadi*] must be designed in the Islamic Republic of Iran, so that the people and the officials who live in the country can appreciate real happiness'. He then carefully added that 'of course, this plan has nothing to do with the Western idea of joy'.[27] His call was soon echoed by the head of the *Seda va Sima* (Islamic Republic of Iran Broadcasting) Ezatollah Zarghami, who remarked about the urgency of these measures for the youth.[28] The government had since then relaxed the codes of expression in the radio, allowing satirical programmes (*tanz*), perhaps unaware of the fact that political jokes and satire had already been circulating via SMS, social media and the internet, in massive amounts. More extravagantly, the government called for the establishment of 'laughter workshops' (*kargah-e khandeh*), somehow reminful of the already widespread classes of Laughter Yoga in Tehran's parks and hiking routes.

'People should have real joy [*shadi-ye vaqe'i*]', specified an official, 'and not artificial joy [*masnu'i*] as in the West'.[29] Yet, more than ever before, Iranians ventured to trigger joy *artificially*, notably by using drugs, medical or illegal ones. Auto-diagnosis, self-care and self-prescription had become the norm among the population, preluding to a general discourse towards medicalisation of depression and medicalised lifestyles. With antidepressants being the most prescribed drugs and 40 per cent of Iranians self-prescribing,[30] one can infer the

---

[27] *Radio Farda*, August 21, 2010 retrieved from www.radiofarda.com/content/F 12_Happiness_engineering_in_Islamic_Republic/2133969.html.
[28] *Radio Zamaneh*, March 7, 2010, retrieved from http://zamaaneh.com/news/ 2009/03/post_8216.html.
[29] *Radio Farda*, August 21, 2010.
[30] Orkideh Behrouzan, 'Life in the Aftermath of Loss: Lessons for Theory, Pedagogy and Practice', presentation at the University of Oxford, March 2, 2015.

scope of this phenomenon and, particularly, its relevance on drug policy. The appearance of dysphoria and apathy, regardless of generational divide, is also manifested in the spectacular expansion of the professional activities of mental health workers, specifically, psychotherapists, whose services are sought by ever-larger numbers of people, although mostly belonging to the middle and upper classes.[31] Examples of depressive behaviour have often been connected to drug (ab)use. The expansion of *Narcotics Anonymous* (*mo'tadan-e gomnam*, aka *NA*, 'en-ay'), and its resonance with the larger public, exemplified the transition that social life, individuality and governmentality were undergoing.

Other manifestations of this new 'spirit of the time' encompassed addictive behaviours more broadly. For instance, groups such the *Anjoman-e Porkhoran-e Gomnam* (Overeaters Anonymous Society), which appear as a meeting point for people suffering from compulsive food disorders, are on the rise with more than eighteen cities operating self-help groups.[32] Similarly, sex addiction surfaced as another emblematic phenomenon. In the prudish public morality of Ahmadinejad's Islamic Republic, there were already medical clinics treating this type of disorder.[33] A Shiraz-based psychiatrist during the 2013 MENA Harm Reduction Conference in Beirut surprised me when he said that a large number of people had been seeking his help for their sex addiction and compulsive sex, both in Shiraz and Tehran. This, he argued, was in part caused by the increasing use of amphetamine-type stimulants, which *artificially* arouse sexual desire, but was also a sign for the displacement of values in favour of new models of life, often inspired by commercialised products, such as films, pornography, advertisements and social media.[34]

Alcoholism, too, has been acknowledged by the government as a social problem. Today there are branches of *Alcoholics Anonymous* (AA) in Iran and rehab centres for alcoholism, despite alcohol remaining an illegal substance, the consumption of which is punished severely.

---

[31] Gohar Homayounpour, *Doing Psychoanalysis in Tehran* (MIT Press, 2012).

[32] *Hamshahri*, January 16, 2009, retrieved from http://hamshahrionline.ir/details/41920.

[33] That said, issues of sex have been largely discussed by the clergy in manners that are far from puritanical; See Karim Sadjadpour, *Foreign Policy*, April 23, 2012, retrieved from http://foreignpolicy.com/2012/04/23/the-ayatollah-under-the-bedsheets/.

[34] *Sharq*, September 5, 2006.

Beyond the diagnostic reality of these claims, it is undeniable that these changes occurred particularly during the years when president Ahmadinejad and his entourage were in government. Indeed, many of the policies and laws in relation to controversial issues, such as on transsexuality and alcoholism, took form during the post-reformist years.[35] These transformations occurred not as a consequence of the government's performance and vision, but rather as a rooting and continuation of secular, global trends, many of which began during the reformist momentum, to which, awkwardly but effectively, the populist government concurred. This was a new mode of political and social change, one that could be called *reforms after reformism*. Once again, a counter-intuitive phenomenon was at play.

The 'Crisis' of *Shisheh* and Its Narratives

If one combines the widespread use of antidepressant drugs with the impressive rise in psychoactive, stimulant and energizing drugs, most notably *shisheh*, the picture inevitably suggests a deep-seated transformation in the societal fabric and cultural order during the post-reformist era.[36]

In early 2006, officials started to refer to the widespread availability of psychoactive, industrial drugs (*san'ati*) through different channels, including satellite TVs and the internet.[37] They said they had little evidence about where these substances originated from and how they were acquired.[38] Although ecstasy – and generally ATSs – had been available in Iran for almost a decade, its spread had been limited to party scenes in the urban, wealthy capital.[39] The appearance of methamphetamines (under the name of *ice, crystal*, and most notably, *shisheh*, meaning 'glass' in reference to the glass-like look of meth) proved that the taste

---

[35] *Al-Monitor*, October 25, 2013, retrieved from www.al-monitor.com/pulse/originals/2013/10/iran-alcohol-permit-rehab-center.html.
[36] Indeed, one can hardly distinguish the use of prescription drugs, such as *Tramadol*, *Prozac* or *morphine*, with those of illicit drugs such as methamphetamines and heroin, as both are abused by overlapping categories and often through the informal market in Iran. See *Hamshahri*, September 17, 2008.
[37] *Hamshahri*, June 12, 2006.   [38] *Sharq*, June 12, 2006.
[39] UNODC, 'A brief review of ATS in Iran' (unpublished report, November 2010 [pdf]).

for drugs among the public was undergoing exceptional changes, with far-reaching implications for policy and politics.[40]

The most common way to use meth is to smoke it in a glass pipe in short sessions of few inhalations. It is an odourless, colourless smoke, which can be consumed in a matter of a few seconds with very little preparation needed (Figure 6.1). In one of the first articles published about *shisheh* in the media, a public official warned that people should be careful about those offering *shisheh* as a *daru*, a medical remedy, for lack of energy, apathy, depression and, ironically, addiction.[41] By stimulating the user with an extraordinary boost of energy and positive feelings, *shisheh* provided a rapid and, seemingly, unproblematic solution to people's problems of joy, motivation and mood. Its status as a new drug prevented it from being the object of anti-narcotics confiscation under the harsh drug laws for trafficking. After all, the official list of illicit substances did not include *shisheh* before 2010, when the drug laws were updated. Until then the crimes related to its production and distribution were referred to the court of medical crimes, with undistressing penalties.[42]

The limited availability of *shisheh* initially made it too expensive for the ordinary drug user, while it also engendered a sense of classist desire for a product that was considered 'high class [*kelas-bala*]'.[43] As such, *shisheh* was initially the drug of choice among professionals in Tehran, who in the words of a recovered *shisheh* user, was used 'to work more, to make more money'.[44] Yet after its price decreased sensitively (Figure 6.2), *shisheh* became popular among all social strata, including students and women, as well as the rural population. By 2010, it was claimed that 70 per cent of drug users were (also) using *shisheh* and that the price of it had dropped by roughly 400 per cent compared to its first appearance in the domestic market.[45] It was a 'tsunami' of *shisheh* use which took both state officials and the medical community unprepared, prompting some of the people in the field to call for 'the creation of a national headquarters for the *crisis of shisheh*', very much along the lines of the 'headquartisation' mentality described in the early post-war period.[46] This new crisis within the field of

[40] *Shisheh* in Persian does not refer to Arab *narghilah* or *shishah*, which in Iran is generally named *ghaliyun*.
[41] *Hamshahri*, June 10, 2006. [42] *Etemad-e Melli*, April 14, 2009.
[43] Ethnographic notes in Tehran and Arak, 2012–15.
[44] *Hamshahri*, June 25, 2006. [45] *Jam-e Jam*, October 27, 2009.
[46] *Aftab-e Yazd*, June 28, 2010; *Salamat News*, August 28, 2011, retrieved from www.salamatnews.com/news/32808/.

Figure 6.1 Meanwhile in the Metro: Man Smoking *Shisheh*.
Spring 2016. Photo colours have been modified to anonymise the subject.
Telegraph App group, 'Challenges of Addiction', see Chapter Two. I used this
picture in Maziyar Ghiabi, 'Drogues illégales et gestion de l'espace dans l'Iran
moderne', *Hérodote*, 2 (2018).

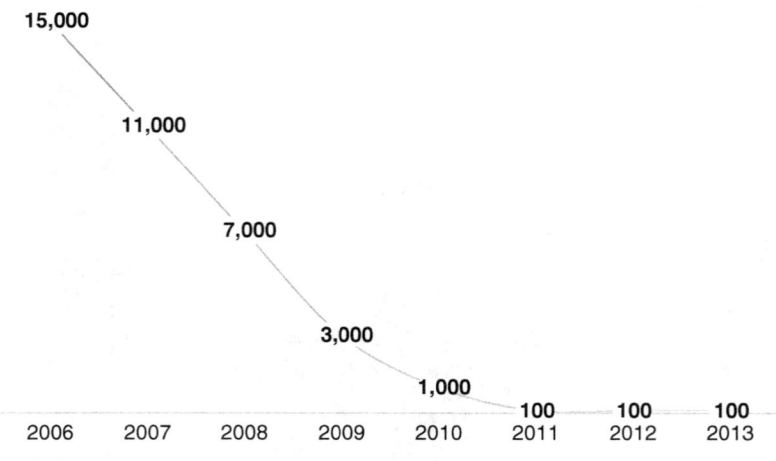

Figure 6.2 Price of One Sut (1/10 of gram) of *Shisheh*. Data extrapolated from several newspaper articles between 2005 and 2013. The price is indicative of a trend rather than a precise estimate. See, *Jam-e Jam*, February 7, 2010, retrieved from www1.jamejamonline.ir/newstext2.aspx?news num=100835179647; *Khabaronline*, April 29, 2011, retrieved from www.khabaronline.ir/detail/147408/society/social-damage; *Fars*, July 7, 2014, retrieved from www.farsnews.com/media.php?nn=13920412001602.

drug (ab)use was the outcome of a series of overlapping trends that materialised in the narratives, both official and among ordinary people, about *shisheh*. The narrative of crisis persisted after 2005 in similar, or perhaps more emphatic, tones.

This new substance differed significantly from previously known and used drugs in Iran. In contrast to opium and heroin, which tended 'to break the spell of time' and diminish anxiety, stress and pain, making users ultimately nod in their chair or lie on the carpet, methamphetamines generally boost people's activities and motivate them to move and work, eliminating the need for sleep and food.[47] In a spectrum inclusive of all mind-altering substances, to put it crudely, opiates and meth would be at the antipodes. All drugs and drug use, wrote the French philosopher Gilles Deleuze, have to do with 'speed, modification of speed ... the times that become superhuman or subhuman'.[48]

---

[47] See Ann Marlowe, *How to Stop Time: Heroin from A to Z* (Basic Books, 1999). Michael W. Clune, *White Out: The Secret Life of Heroin* (Hazelden Publishing, 2013).
[48] Deleuze, *Deux régimes*, 138.

Shisheh had to do with time, people's perception of time's flow; it was the new wonder drug of the century, with its mind-altering speed and physical rush as distinctive emblems of (post)modern consumption.

Opiates derive from an agricultural crop, the poppy, whereas methamphetamines are synthetized chemically in laboratories and therefore do not need agricultural land to crop in. Between 2007 and 2010, Iran topped the international table of pseudoephedrine and ephedrine legitimate imports, with quantities far above expected levels according to the International Narcotics Control Board (INCB).[49] Pseudoephedrine and ephedrine are both key precursors for meth production, the rest of the chemical elements being readily available in regular stores and supermarkets. With Iran's anti-narcotic strategy heavily imbalanced towards its borders with Afghanistan and Pakistan, the production of *shisheh* could occur, with few expedients and precautions, 'at home'. In fact, it did not take long before small-scale laboratories – *ante tempore* versions of Walter White's one in *Breaking Bad* – appeared within borders, inducing the head of the anti-narcotic police to declare, 'today, a master student in chemistry can easily set up a laboratory and, by using the formula and a few pharmaceutical products, he can obtain and produce *shisheh*'.[50] In 2010, the anti-narcotic police discovered 166 labs, with the number increasing to 416 labs in 2014.[51] The supply reduction operations could not target domestic, private production of meth, because this new industry was organised differently from previous illicit drug businesses and could physically take place everywhere.

The high demand for meth and the grim status of the job market guaranteed employment in the '*shisheh* industry'.[52] A 'kitchen' owner who ran four producing units in Southern Tehran revealed that the prices of *shisheh* had shrunk steadily because of the high potential of production in Iran. In his rather conventional words, 'young chemical engineers, who cannot find a job ... work for the kitchen owner at low prices', and, he adds, 'precursors and equipment are readily available in

---

[49] Iraq had the second highest data, part of which can be seen as integrated with meth production in Iran, given historical smuggling connections. See INCB, 'Precursors' (2011), retrieved from www.incb.org.
[50] *Jam-e Jam*, October 27, 2009.
[51] *Daily Mail*, February 12, 2015, retrieved from www.dailymail.co.uk/wires/ap/article-2950946/Drug-abuse-Iran-rising-despite-executions-police-raids.html.
[52] *Sharq*, August 5, 2006.

the capital's main pharmaceutical market at affordable prices'.⁵³ The *shisheh* that is produced is sold domestically or in countries such as Thailand under the local name of *yaa baa*, or Malaysia and Indonesia, where there is high demand for meth. The number of Iranian nationals arrested in international airports in Asia hints clearly at this phenomenon.⁵⁴

Logically, shisheh and the shisheh economy appealed particularly young people, who exploited the initial confusion and lack of legislative norms. At the same time, while opium and heroin had largely remained 'drugs for men' (although increasing numbers of women were using them in the early 2000s), *shisheh* was very popular among women. For instance, the use of *shisheh* was often reported in beauty salons and hairdressers, allegedly because of its 'slimming' virtue. In similar fashion, its consumption was popular among sportsmen, both professional (e.g. football players and wrestlers) and traditional/folkloric (e.g. *zurkhaneh*).⁵⁵ Its consumption appealed to categories of people enchanted with an idea of life as an hedonistic enterprise often governed by the laws of social competition, something that differed ontologically and phenomenologically from Islamising principles.

Reports emerged also about the use of *shisheh* among students to boost academic performance. By making it easy to spend entire nights studying and reviewing, especially among those preparing for the tough university entry examination (*konkur*), *shisheh* had gained popularity in high schools and universities. The shrinking age of drug use, too, has been factual testimony of this trend.⁵⁶ In an editorial published in the state-run newspaper, a satirist announced that, in Iran, 'the modern people have become post-modern. And this latter, we know, is industrial and poetical' and he longed for 'the old good days of the *bangis*

---

⁵³ UNODC, 'A brief review'.
⁵⁴ See Pierre-Arnaud Chouvy and Joël Meissonnier, *Yaa baa: Production, Traffic, and Consumption of Methamphetamine in Mainland Southeast Asia* (NUS Press, 2004). *Middle East Eye*, February 13, 2015, retrieved from www.middleeasteye.net/fr/in-depth/features/iranians-abroad-prison-life-terms-and-execution-925520961; *Asia Times*, June 5, 2011, retrieved from www.atimes.com/atimes/Middle_East/MA05Ak01.html.
⁵⁵ *Jam-e Jam*, May 18, 2008; *Jam-e Jam*, January 12, 2010; *Jam-e Jam*, April 16, 2009. An anecdote: while in Yazd in 2012, I attended a session in a *zurkhaneh* where one of the attendants approached me (unaware of the fact that I was a drug researcher), and offered me a pill, which he said was 'Mercedes' [sic!], a high-quality brand of ecstasy.
⁵⁶ *Sharq*, June 11, 2014.

[the hashish smoker]'.[57] *Shisheh* epitomised the entry into the postmodern world, an epochal, perhaps irreversible, anthropological mutation. In view of this changing pattern of drug (ab)use, the authorities realised, slowly and half-heartedly, that the policies in place with regard to treatment of injecting drug users – harm reduction as implemented up until then – had no effect on reducing the harm of *shisheh*. Harm reduction could not target the 'crisis' of *shisheh*, which unwrapped in a publicly visible and intergenerational manner different from previous drug crises. Its blend, in addition, with changing sexual mannerisms among the youth, aggravated the impotence of the state.[58]

Sex, Sex Workers and HIV

With drug use growing more common among young people and adolescents, people acknowledged *shisheh* for its powerful sexually disinhibiting effects, which, in their confessions during my ethnographic fieldwork, 'made sex [*seks*] more fun [*ba hal*] and good [*khoob*]'. Equally, the quest for sex with multiple partners sounded appealing to those using *shisheh*, engendering the preoccupation (when not the legal prosecution) of the state. With moral codes shifting rapidly and the age of marriage rising to 40 and 35 respectively for men and women, pre-marital unprotected sex became a *de facto* phenomenon.[59]

The combination of sex and drugs resonated as a most critical duo to the ears of policymakers, one that made Iran look more like a land of counterculture than an Islamic republic. Yet, because premarital sex was deemed unlawful under the Islamic law, the issue of sex remained a much-contested and problematic field of intervention for the state.

---

[57] *Iran*, November 4, 2009.
[58] A well-known treatment for methamphetamine addiction goes under the name of MATRIX. See www.drugabuse.gov/publications/principles-drug-addiction-treatment-research-based-guide-third-edition/evidence-based-approaches-to-dr ug-addiction-treatment/behavioral-3.
[59] See Mahdavi, *Passionate Uprising*, chap. 6. Also, *Aftab Online*, October 28, 2012, retrieved from www.aftabir.com/news/view/2012/apr/28/c4_13355915 99.php. The national youth organisation published a report indicating that 'one in four men aged 19 to 29 had experienced sex before marriage', in *The Guardian*, December 9, 2008, retrieved from www.theguardian.com/world/ 2008/dec/29/iran-gender.

Despite the repeated calls of leading researchers, the state institutions seemed incapable, if not unprepared, to inform and to tackle the risk of pre-marital unprotected sex. This attitude accounted, in part, for the ten-fold increase in sexually transmitted diseases in the country during the post-reformist period.[60]

Many believed that while harm reduction policies were capable of tackling the risk of an HIV epidemic caused by shared needles, these measures were not addressing the larger part of the population experiencing sexual intercourse outside marriage (or even within it), with multiple partners, and without any valuable education or information about sexually transmitted diseases. The director of the Health Office of the city of Tehran put it in this statement during a conference, 'we are witnessing the increase in sexual behaviour among students and other young people; one day, the *nadideh-ha* [unseen people] of today will be argument of debate in future conferences'.[61] The rate of contagion was expected to increase significantly in the years ahead, a hypothesis that was indeed confirmed by later studies.

As for the risk of HIV epidemics emerging from Iran's unseen, but growing population of female sex workers, the question was even more controversial. Sex workers, in the eye of the Islamic Republic, embodied the failure of a decadent society, one which the Islamic Revolution had eradicated in 1979, when the revolutionary government bulldozed the red-light districts of Tehran's *Shahr-e Nou* to the ground and cleansed it – perhaps superficially – of prostitutes and street walkers.[62] Government officials had remained silent about the existence of this category, with the surprising exception of Ahmadinejad's only female minister Marzieh Vahid-Dastjerdi. The Minister of Health and Medical Education broke the taboo publicly stating in front of a large crowd of (male) state officials, 'every sex worker [*tan forush*, literally 'body seller'] can infect five to ten people every year to AIDS'.[63] The breaking of the taboo was a part of the attempt to acknowledge those

---

[60] *Hamshahri*, July 24, 2009. Also retrieved from http://hamshahrionline.ir/print/86098. The increase, once again, could be the effect of improved means of diagnosis of STD and people's accessibility to healthcare.
[61] *Etemad*, February 13, 2007.
[62] For a photographic account of sex workers in Iran, see 'Photos: Tehran's brothel district Shahr-e-No 1975-77 by Kaveh Golestan', *Peyvand*, retrieved from http://payvand.com/blog/blog/2010/12/10/photos-tehrans-brothel-district-shahr-e-no-1975-77-by-kaveh-golestan/.
[63] *Sharq*, August 5, 2010.

widespread behaviours that exist and that should be addressed with specific policies, instead of maintaining them in a state of denial.[64] The framing of the phenomenon rested upon the notion of 'risk', 'emergency' and crisis. The opening of drop-in centres for women was a step in this direction, albeit initially very contested by reactionary elements in government. In 2010, the number of these centres (for female users) increased to twelve, the move being justified by the higher risk which women posed to the general population: 'a man who suffers from hepatitis or AIDS can infect five or six persons, while a woman who injects drugs and makes ends meet through prostitution may infect more persons'.[65]

The government, however, remained unresponsive to this call. Mas'ud Pezeshkian – former Minister of Health under the reformist government (2001–5) – commented that 'until the profession [of sex worker] is unlawful and against the religious law [*shar'*] there should be no provision of help to these groups'.[66] The result of this contention was a lack of decision and coherence about the risk of an HIV epidemic. According to an official report, the majority of groups at risk of sexual contagion (e.g. sex workers, homeless drug users) were still out of reach of harm reduction services.[67] If drug users in prison embodied the main threat (or crisis) during the reformist period, the post-reformist era had been characterised by the subterfuge of commercial sex and unprotected sexual behaviour, with the incitement of stimulant drugs such as *shisheh*.

A study published by Iran's National AIDS Committee within the Ministry of Health and Medical Studies – with the support of numerous international and national organisations – revealed that only a small percentage (20 per cent) of the population between fifteen and twenty-four years old could respond correctly to questions on modes of transmission, prevention methods and HIV.[68] The crisis of this era was propelled, one could say, through sex, but also based on a certain ignorance of safe sexual practices, because of unbroken moral taboos.[69]

---

[64] Reference to prostitution was usually 'clothed' (*aba dasht*) by state representatives with the expression *zanan-e asib-dideh* (harmed women).
[65] *Iran Daily*, May 4, 2010.   [66] Ibid.
[67] *Sharq*, October 13, 2010. See also http://en.trend.az/iran/society/2446081.html.
[68] MHME, 'Islamic Republic of Iran AIDS Progress Report: On Monitoring of the United Nations General Assembly Special Session on HIV and AIDS', UNODC (unpublished report, March 2014 [pdf]).
[69] The closest European case of existing barriers to sexual education is Italy; see *Politico*, November 30, 2011, retrieved from www.politico.eu/article/no-sex-education-please-were-italian/.

The Disease of the Psyche

The changing nature of drug (ab)use and sexual norms – in the light of what I referred to as the broad societal trends of the post-reformist years – rendered piecemeal and outdated the important policy reforms achieved under the reformist mandates. In fact, *shisheh* could not be addressed with the same kind of medical treatment used for heroin, opium and other narcotics. Treatment of *shisheh* 'addiction' required psychological and/or psychiatric intervention, with follow-up processes in order to guarantee the patient a stable process of recovery.[70] This implied a high cost and the provision of medical expertise in psychotherapy that was lacking, and already overloaded by the demand of the middle/upper classes. Besides, methadone use among drug (ab)users under treatment engendered a negative side effect in the guise of dysphoria and depression, which could only partially be solved through prescription of antidepressants. The recurrence to *shisheh* smoking among methadone users in treatment became manifest, ironically and paradoxically, as a side effect of methadone treatment and a strategy for chemical pleasure.[71]

The mental hospitals were largely populated by drug (ab)users, the majority of whom with a history of 'industrial drugs' use, a general reference to *shisheh*.[72] The rise in referrals for schizophrenia, bipolar disorder, suicidal depression and other serious mental health issues needed to be contextualised along these trends. Suicide, too, remained a problematic datum for the government as it revealed the scope of social distress and mental problems emerging publicly.[73] But the increase of *shisheh* use markedly brought the question of drugs into the public space, with narratives of violence, family disintegration, abuse and alienation becoming associated with it. Although drug scares have always circulated in Iran (as elsewhere), they have mostly regarded stories of decadence, overdose, and physical impairment. They rarely concerned schizoid and violent behaviour in the public. With *shisheh*, drug use itself became secondary, while the issue of concern became the presence of highly intoxicated people, with unpredictable behaviours, in the public space.[74] As a law enforcement agent

---

[70] *Hamshahri*, August 8, 2009.
[71] Interviews with Hasan Solhi, Arak, September 2014.
[72] *Sepideh*, July 26, 2012. [73] *Sharq*, July 26, 2010.
[74] This reflects the historical precedents that had emerged in 19th and early 20th century Mexico when, Isaac Campos recalls, many would be described as *running amok* after marijuana use. Campos, *Home Grown*.

The Disease of the Psyche 185

in the city of Arak confessed, 'the *heroini* shoots his dose and stays at his place, he nods and sleeps; these people, *shishehi-ha* ['shisheh smokers'], instead, go crazy, they jump on a car and drive fast, like *Need 4 Speed*,[75] they do strange things [*ajib-o gharib*] in the streets, talk a lot, get excited for nothing, or they get paranoid and violent'.[76] With this picture in mind, it does not surprise that Iran has had the world's highest rate of road accidents and bad driving habits.[77] The trend of road accidents became also an issue of concern to the public (and the state), in view of investigations revealing, for instance, that '20 per cent of trucks' drivers are addicted', or that '10 per cent of bus drivers smoke *shisheh* with risks of hallucination and panic' while behind the wheel.[78] Stories emerged also about violent crimes being committed by people on *shisheh*, establishing a worrying association between this substance, violent crimes (often while in a paranoid state) and, ultimately, long-term depression and mental instability.[79] More than being a sign of a material increase in violence, these stories are telling about the framing of this new substance under the category of crisis and emergency.

At the same time, *shisheh* became a cure for depression and lack of energy, also overcoming the urban–rural divide. I had confirmation of this more than once during my time spent in a small village in central Iran between 2012 and 2015. The shepherd known to my family since his adolescence, one night arrived in his small room, prepared some tea and warmed up his *sikh* (short skewer) to smoke some opium residue (*shireh*) which he had diligently prepared in the preceding weeks. One of the workers from a nearby farm, a young man of around twenty, came in and after the usual cordial exchanges, sat down, took his small glass pipe and smoked one *sut* of *shisheh*.[80] After their dialogue about the drop in sheep meat price in the market, the shepherd asked for some

---

[75] A well-known racing videogame.
[76] Ethnographic notes in Arak, March 2013.
[77] Reza Banakar and Shahrad Nasrolahi Fard, 'Driving Dangerously: Law, Culture and Driving Habits in Iran', *British Journal of Middle Eastern Studies* 39, 2 (2012).
[78] See *Aftab-e Yazd*, August 30, 2008.
[79] For stories about *shisheh*, which went viral in Iran, see *Mehr*, December 22, 2012, retrieved from www.mehrnews.com/news/1770270/; and *Sharq*, November 3, 2013, retrieved from http://sharghdaily.ir/1392/08/14/Files/PDF/13920814-1874-22-12.pdf.
[80] A *sut* is one dose of *shisheh*, equivalent, roughly, to 1/10 gram.

advice, 'you see, it has been a while I wanted to give up opium, because you know it's hard, I have smoked for thirty years now, and I feel down, without energy [*bi hal am*] all the time. Do you think I should put this away [indicating the opium *sikh*] and instead try *shisheh*?'.[81]

In this vignette, the use of *shisheh* represents a response to the search for adrenaline, libido and energy in the imaginatively sorrowful and melancholic timing of rural life. Many others, unlike my shepherd friend, had already turned to *shisheh* in the villages, whether because of its lower price, its higher purity or opium's adulterated state.[82] The government invoked the help of the Village Councils – a state institution overseeing local administration – in an attempt to gain control over Iran's vast and scattered villages, but with no tangible results, apart from sporadic anti-narcotics campaigns.[83] By the late 2000s, drug adulteration (especially opium) increased substantially, encouraging drug users to shift to less adulterated substances – for example, domestically produced *shisheh* – or to adopt polydrug use. This caused a spike in the number of drug-related deaths, up to 2012, due principally to rising impurity (Figure 6.3).[84] The cost of using traditional drugs like opium and heroin was becoming prohibitive and less rewarding in terms of pleasure. Inevitably, many shifted to *shisheh*.

Conclusions

The phenomenon of drug use intersected over this period with long-term transformations that had bubbled below the surface of the governmental rhetoric and imagery of the Islamic Republic. Changing patterns of drug consumption, hence, was not the simple, consequential effect of new drug imports and lucrative drug networks, although these played their role in facilitating the emergence of new drug cultures. From the late 2000s onwards, drugs affected, and were affected by, broader trends in society, such as changing sexual norms, consumption patterns, social imagination, economic setting and ethical values. This represented a fundamental 'anthropological mutation', for it changed the way individuals experienced their existences in society

---

[81] Ethnographic notes in the Markazi region.
[82] *Hamshahri*, December 12, 2007.   [83] *Hamshahri*, May 1, 2007.
[84] *Rooz*, September 4, 2006.

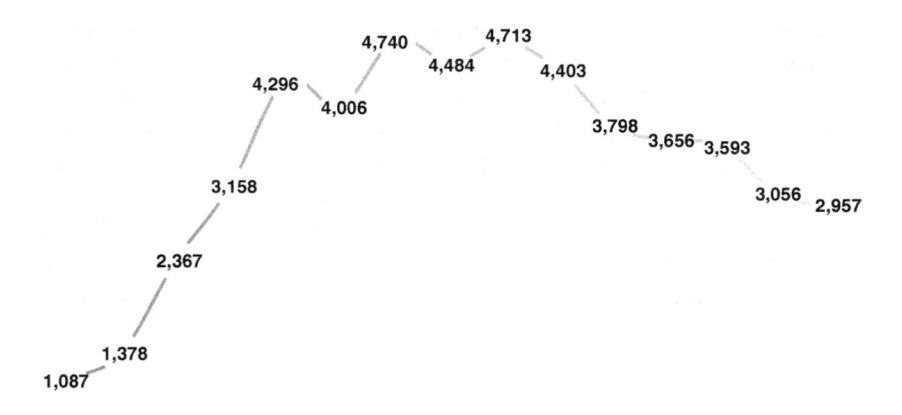

```
       4,740   4,713
             4,484
  4,296           4,403
       4,006
                     3,798
                         3,656 3,593
    3,158
                              3,056
                                   2,957
 2,367

1,378
1,087
```

1999 2000 2001 2002 2003 2004 2005 2006 2007 2008 2009 2010 2011 2012 2013

Figure 6.3 Drug-Use-Related Deaths Data collected and assembled from public declarations by the Iranian Legal Medicine Organisation and unpublished UNODC reports, including in DCHQ, 'Statistics' (UNODC, unpublished, undated [Excel file]). Cf. ISNA, December 6, 2010, retrieved from http://isna.ir/fa/print/8909-09724/.

and shaped their relation to the surrounding world. By this time, new cultural, ethical values gained traction, relegating to the past the family-centric, publicly straight-laced way of being in the world. The pursuit of sensorial pleasure, personal recognition and aesthetic renewal became totalizing – and totalitarian – in more rooted and uncompromising ways than the clerical ideology preached by the ruling class in the Islamic Republic. Not the ideology of the clergy, but the driving force of post-modern consumerism was the totalitarian drive of social change. To this epochal moment, the state responded haphazardly and incongruently, mostly unaware or unconcerned of what this transformation signified and in what ways it manifested new societal conditions where the old politics and rhetoric had effect. Rather than attempting a reconfiguration of the new cultural, social and ethical situation, the political order coexisted with the coming of age of new subjectivities, without recognizing them effectively.

Drugs, and *shisheh* in particular, were a manifestation of the profound changes taking place over this period to which the state reacted with hesitation and through indirect means. This chapter focused on social, cultural and human (trans)formations from the mid 2000s onwards, with an especial attention to the rise of *shisheh* consumption and its contextual psychological, sexual and economic dimensions. The next two Chapters dwell on how the state countered this changing drug/addiction phenomenon. An emblem of the anthropological mutation in lifestyle, imagery, values and flow of time, *shisheh* contributed to the change in political paradigm with regard the public place. It also brought about a shift in drug (ab)use and in the governance of drug disorder. *Shisheh*, hence, is both cause and effect of these transformations.

7 | The Art of Managing Disorder

I call the camp if someone calls me!
Police Officer in Arak, September 2014.

Introduction

One hot morning of early September 2014, Tehran's University of Medical Sciences hosted the Eighth International Congress on Addiction Science. The venue was that of important scholarly events – the Razi (Rhazes) Conference Hall – located near the symbol of modern Tehran, the Milad Tower. A lively movement of people, mostly young students, male and female, animated the premises of the building, where the registration procedures and distribution of materials of various kinds, including breakfast, was taking place. One could tell, *prima facie*, that the schedule was expected to be dictated by some high-ranking, prominent participation, particularly among government officials.

The conference, an attendant involved in the organisation revealed to me, was meant to be 'a new start' for Iran's drug policy and the academic community, especially in its engagement with its Western counterparts. The conference panels narrated the underlying dynamics within the policy community, in the wake of the eclipse of the post-reformist government. As such, the conference was a telling vignette of the features and apparent paradoxes of post-reformist drug policy.

At 8AM, I had successfully snuck into a panel on 'Women and Addiction', which occurred behind closed doors; if truth be told, I had to use my network in the UNODC to get access to the room where a female ministerial advisor did not want her statements to be reported publicly. The audience was almost entirely composed of women whose stricter type of *hijab* was telling of their employment post in state institutions. Despite the novelty of the issues debated in the panel, with off-the-records data being revealed, after the second presentation my attention drifted to a concomitant panel in Hall 3, titled 'Harm Reduction among Drug Users'.

Since this panel included influential officials in the policy community and well-known advocates of harm reduction, it seemed a (political) manifestation not to be missed. I left the panel on Women and Addiction and moved to the opposite room where the panel on Harm Reduction was taking place. On this panel were prominent members of the policy community from different ministries and the DCHQ, plus a number of high-ranking officials in the audience. The presenters were Dr Ahmad Hajebi, Director of Mental Health Office at the Ministry of Health; Dr Mehdi Guya, Director of the Centre of Infectious Diseases at the Ministry of Health; and Farid Barrati-Sadeh, Director of Treatment at the DCHQ.

Despite the friendly tone of the exchanges, one could sense the latent animosity between the participants. As the panel contemplated a Q&A session, the comments remained mostly cursory, provocative and colourful. But the last speaker, Farid Barrati-Sadeh, an outspoken official with regular presence in the media, opted to use the time allocated for his presentation in order to, as he said, 'clarify and point out some of the contradictions in the exposition of our friends'. From the very outset of his presentation, the speaker remarked that the current implementation of drug laws was not only haphazard and fragmentary, but also contradictory in itself. This, he argued, was due to the lack of interest of his 'friends' in the Ministry of Health, who were 'unwilling to engage with harm reduction and keep on criticising the *setad* [i.e. DCHQ] for every problem in this country'. Raising the tone of his voice, he accused the other speakers who preceded him, Dr Mehdi Guya and Dr Ahmad Hajebi, 'of refusing to adopt new protocols for the new treatment camps under the 2010 law', a law approved by the 'organs of the Islamic Republic and has the authoritative support of the Leader of the Revolution', that is to say Ayatollah Khamenei. Comments of disapproval could be heard from the front line of the conference hall, where the other speakers sat. The presentation of the DCHQ official extended in a *quid pro quo* with the other speakers, with mutual accusations of incoherence, hypocrisy and managerial unwillingness/incapacity. It then terminated when Minoo Mohraz, Iran's internationally prominent HIV/AIDS scholar, intervened on the panel floor, taking the microphone away from one of the speakers and, with severity, reprimanding all the panellists about their rowdy behaviour and 'their inconclusive messiness'.[1] She then remarked that

> as a person who is not *ejrai* [executive, i.e. a public official] – I am a scientist [*adam-e 'elmi*] – I have duties towards the people, whatever you want to say and discuss about, I ask you to sit together and discuss. People cannot bear this anymore ... I ask you to solve this and to support harm reduction; ... use the budget to promote useful programmes, not to establish compulsory treatment camps [*kamp-e darman-e ejbari*].

For an external viewer, the contest might appear one centred around budgetary allocations between different state institutions entrusted with harm-reduction duties. It soon became explicit, however, that budgetary discussions were only a side note on the more equivocal and vexed page of 'compulsory treatment' and the 'camps' in general.

The 2010 Drug Law Reform

The roots of the diatribe among the panellists went back to the text of the 2010 drug law reform. This reform, approved after long and complex negotiations within the Expediency Council, emblematised the developments with regard to drug (ab)use under the presidency of Mahmud Ahmadinejad. The conference debates, although taking place after the demise of Ahmadinejad, actually concentrated on the experiences of the last government. In a way, the debate itself was taking place so overtly – and loudly – because of the political change represented by the election of Hassan Rouhani in 2014, which had resulted in a lost grip on the institutional line of command within the policymaking institutions. Criticism was accordingly welcomed as a sign of renewal, even when the people in charge at a bureaucratic level remained, largely, the same.

The 2010 law reform materialised the inherent idiosyncrasies of the politics of drugs in the twenty-first century. The law itself provides a localised example of the paradigm of government with regard to the crises that the post-reformist governments had faced. Post-reformism reflects the scenario left by the demise of governmental reformism following Khatami's last presidential term and its unsuccessful efforts

---

[1] For a brief biography, see under Dramatis Personae in the Bibliography.

at triggering political reform. Under the umbrella of post-reformism, I indicate those attempts at governance which fall short of calling overt reforms, but which produce diffused changes within political practice. It encompasses ideologically strong administrations calling for a revolution in government while instilling a grassroots form of management of social and political conflicts (i.e. Ahmadinejad); as well as centrist, business-oriented administrations pledging moderate, slow and timidly progressive civic change (i.e. Rouhani).

The year 2010 was momentous in formulating a new approach, called post-reformism, regarding illicit drugs. Discussions of the new anti-narcotic laws were ongoing and, as the country had already built the infrastructure for large-scale interventions, the new political formula had the potential to be ground-breaking. Instead, the text of the 2010 reform of the anti-narcotic law reproduced the multiple ambiguities of harm reduction (and public policy generally) in Iran, the law itself becoming the contested ground between different governmentalities towards what was defined 'addiction', as partly manifested in the diatribe reported at the beginning of this Chapter. It was an oxymoronic law producing oxymoronic governance.

Apart from updating the list of narcotic drugs with the insertion of new synthetic, industrial drugs, notably *shisheh*, the key changes in the new texts concerned Article 15 and Article 16.

Abstract from the 2010 Drug Law Reform
Article 15 – The addict is required to refer to legitimate state [*dowlati*], non-state [*gheyr-e dowlati*], or private [*khosusi*] centres, or to treatment and harm reduction grassroots organisations [*sazman-ha-ye mardom-nahad*], so to apply to addiction recovery. The addict who enrols in one of the above-mentioned centres for his/her treatment and has obtained an identification [*gavahi*] of treatment and harm reduction, as long as he/she does not publicly manifest addiction [*tajahor be e'tyad*], is *suspended* [*mo'af*] from criminal sanctions. The addict, who does not seek treatment of addiction, is a criminal.

Note 2 – The Ministry of Welfare and Social Security is responsible ... to cover the entire expenses of addiction treatment of destitute [*bi-beza'at*] addicts. The government is required to include this in the yearly sections of the budget, and to secure the necessary financial credits.

Article 16 – Addicts to narcotic drugs and psychoactive substances, included in Articles 4 and 8, who do not have the identification mentioned in Article

15 and who are overtly addicted, must be maintained, according to the decision of the judicial authority, for a period of one to three months in a state centre licenced with treatment and harm reduction. The extension of the maintenance period is permitted for a further three months. According to the report of the mentioned centre and based on the opinion of the judicial authority, if the addict is ready to continue treatment according to Article 15, he/she is permitted to do so according to the aforementioned article.

Note 2 – The judicial authority, for one time, can suspend the sanction against the addict for a six-month period, given appropriate guarantees and the allocation of an identification document mentioned in Article 15, and can refer the addict to a centre as enunciated in this aforementioned article. The aforementioned centres are responsible to send a monthly report on the trend of treatment of the addict to the judicial authority, or to his representative ...

Note 3 – Those contravening the duties enunciated in Note 2 of this article can be condemned to incarceration from one day to six months.[2]

Several issues emerge from analysing these two articles. First, the 2010 reformed law legitimised harm-reduction practices applied since the early 2000s, including them in an institutional legal order. The law explicitly mentions the legitimacy of 'harm reduction', although it does not specify what falls under this label. Second, the law institutes centres for the implementation of harm reduction; these centres, it is spelled out, include both state centres and private clinics, as well as charitable and grassroots organisations. In other words, Article 15 of the 2010 law legitimises those agents already active in the field of drug (ab)use, explicating their social role with regard to addiction. It enshrines their function according to what I define in the Chapter 8, the governmentalisation of addiction. More crucially, the 2010 law establishes a distinction between those drug (ab)users who are willing to seek treatment and refer to a recognised institution (e.g. clinic, camp), as contemplated in Article 15, and those who do not seek treatment, who therefore become subject to Article 16. This has two main effects: on the one hand, the new law protects registered addicts since it provides them an identification card, allowing them to carry limited quantities of methadone with them – in the case of MMT patients – or to seek harm reduction treatment – in the guise of clean syringes and

[2] 'Text of the 2010 drug law reform', retrieved from www.1vakil.com/component/content/article/29–1389-05–29-12-10-49/104–89.html. Emphasis added.

needles – without the risk of police arrest. On the other hand, those addicts who do not register for treatment in a recognised institution, are still liable of a crime – the everlasting crime of addiction – and could be forcibly sent to state-run compulsory camps (*kamp-e maddeh-ye 16*). Their crime is that of being intoxicated in a visible manner, publicly (*tajahor*).

Concomitant to the new law, governance of drug consumers adopted new analytical frames, which follow the logic of what I define oxymoronic governance. Drug (ab)users were now described and treated as 'patient criminal [*mojrem-e bimar*]' who, if not under treatment, 'will be object a court ruling on compulsory treatment, to which the police will enforce a police-based treatment [*darman-e polis-madar*]'.[3] What was formerly a criminal – and perhaps the emblem of a criminal – the 'addict', is now a patient whose crime resides in his condition, his dependency to an illegal substance. This new subjectivity is the object of institutional care, not through the expertise of medical professionals alone, as would be for other patient types, and not through the whip of policemen, as would occur for simple criminals. Dealing with the drug (ab)user produces a new figure within state law and order, that of the therapeutic police, a force which treats disorder of an ambivalent kind. This enmeshment of criminalisation and medicalisation provides a cursory glance at the new governmentality under post-reformism. By adopting a medical lens, through a law-and-order approach, the therapeutic police is where policing encounters addiction. Its means are, from a practical point of view, in continuity with orthodox policing. 'Quarantine', used during the 1980s, came back into vogue when officials addressed the need to isolate risky groups, such as IDUs and HIV-positive individuals.[4] Quarantine, a quintessential medical practice with mandatory enforcement, was not a metaphorical hint, but an actual practical disposition. Police and medicine needed cooperation, at close range, on the matter of drugs. This new mode of intervention was rooted in the framing of the addict as a *mojrem-e bimar*, a 'patient-criminal', who needed to be countered by a 'therapeutic police'.

In line with the post-reformist vision based on the 'therapeutic police' and governmentalisation of addiction, the new law contemplated direct intervention in tackling addiction, by forcing into

---

[3] *Iran*, May 12, 2007. Emphasis added. [4] *Hamshahri*, May 1, 2007.

treatment those who were reluctant, or unable, to do so. If, at the level of political discourse, the new drug law was characterised by the concomitance of insoluble traits (i.e. assistance and punishment), it did not mean that its practical effects were totally unintended. While addiction was publicly recognised as a 'disease' and medical interventions were legitimated nationwide through public and private clinics, the figure of the drug (ab)user remained inherently deviant and stigmatised among the official state cadre, especially when connoted with the disorderly – and dysfunctional – features of poverty and social marginalisation. The law intended to *manage disorder* instead of bring about order; to *govern crisis* instead of re-establishing normalcy, whatever the content of the latter proved to be.

The provisions of the law seem to respond, among other things, to the necessities dictated by the expanding crisis of *shisheh* in the public space as described in Chapter 6. Public officials during the late 2000s seemed to agree that people abusing methamphetamines could not be cured, or that a cure for them was either unavailable or too expensive to be provided on a large scale.[5] This persuaded cadres of the state to seek mechanisms of intervention that were not necessarily coherent with each other, but which, from a public authority perspective, responded to the imperatives of public order. In other words, they adopted an oxymoronic form of politics, the adoption of otherwise incompatible means.

The text of Article 16 stresses the need to intervene against 'those addicted publicly'. It envisions public intervention *vis-à-vis* the manifest effects of drug use, materialised by disorderly presence in the streets, noisy gatherings of drug users, vagrancy and mendicancy.[6] This interpretation of the *shisheh* 'crisis' was rooted on a law enforcement model, updated with a new medical persuasion – that of the incurability of *shisheh* addiction.[7] Since methadone substitution programmes and classical harm-reduction practices (i.e. needle exchange) were inadequate to respond to the treatment of *shisheh* users, the state resorted to a practice of isolation and confinement, this time, however, not through incarceration in state prisons. Instead, it gave birth to a new model, that of the compulsory state-run camps, a paradigm of

[5] Interview with Tahernokhost, September 2012; and Razzaghi, September 2012.
[6] Based on my ethnographic observations, it is usually recycling of garbage and informal economic exchanges, *sensu lato*. See Ghiabi, 'Under the Bridge'.
[7] Interview with Razzaghi, Tehran, September 2012.

government of the drug crisis that exemplified, *in nuce*, the post-reformist govern*mentality* on crisis.

Therapeutic Police: Compulsory Treatment Camps

Part of the diatribe portrayed in the conference vignette opening this chapter reflected the opposing views existing on the role of the therapeutic police and the status of compulsory treatment camps. Since the implementation of the 2010 reform – but to a minor degree since Ahmadinejad's election in 2005 – the state regularly intervened to collect homeless drug users and confine them to compulsory camps, much to the astonishment of those who had worked towards the legitimation of harm reduction.[8] In reality, part of the medical community and NGO sector – notably the NGO *Rebirth* (*Tavalod-e Dobareh*) – had supported the text of the 2010 law on the basis that it recognised the legitimacy of treatment and harm reduction, as a prelude towards decriminalisation of addiction. Compulsory treatment camps, supporters of the 2010 law argued, were the necessary venue to medicalise addiction among those who could not be persuaded to seek treatment. It would be, they added, *the safest and fastest way to introduce the addict into the cycle of treatment*, facilitating recovery.[9] Yet, therapeutic policing relied on a system which paid little attention to recovery. Centres managed by law enforcers often unveiled situations of degradation and abuse, which prompted several officials to publicly express their opposition to this model, on the grounds that it neither brought results, nor offered humanitarian support.[10]

Operating since the late 2000s, compulsory treatment camps have been active in sixteen regions. Although the media and officials refer to them as 'camps', the official name for them, hitherto, has been *ordugah*, which translates in English as 'military camp'. One official lambasted the use of this term as 'unappreciative' of the government's effort to treat drug addicts.[11] The origins of this institutional model can be

---

[8] These operations are usually called *nejat*, 'salvation' and, prior to 2010, they contemplated incarceration for short periods and physical punishment for the arrested (lashes).
[9] *Mehr*, September 26, 2012, retrieved from www.mehrnews.com/news/1608510/.
[10] The reason for this degradation of standards in state-run camps can putatively be identified in the mismanagement of funds and the lack of interest in establishing well-functioning infrastructures.
[11] *IRNA*, July 21, 2011.

traced back to the early years of the Ahmadinejad government.[12] Their purpose, however, became antithetical to the original idea. In 2007, the new head of the DCHQ, C-in-C Ahmadi-Moghaddam, already announced that 'the addict must be considered a patient-criminal [*mo'tad-e mojrem*] who, if he is not under treatment, the court will rule for him compulsory treatment [*darman-e ejbari*] and the police will be the executor of a police-based treatment'. He then added, 'we have to build maintenance camps [*ordugah-e negahdari*]; the NAJA has already built camps for the homeless and vagrants, which in the opinion of treatment officials can be used as maintenance camps for addicts for a certain period'.[13] This announcement is an *ante tempore* elucidation of the 2010 law model. It coincided with the appointment of the head of the police as director of the DCHQ. The fact that, genealogically, the compulsory treatment camps were formerly camps for the internment of vagrants and homeless people, unveiled the primary concern of the state regarding the management of public order.[14]

Much like the 1980s, the officials adopted a language that underlined the need to 'quarantine' problematic drug (ab)users.[15] Yet, this rhetoric did not prelude to a return to past forms of intervention; the post-reformist 'quarantine' envisaged the presence and 'supervision of doctors, psychologists, psychiatrists and infection experts as well as social workers' and the referral, after the period of mandatory treatment, to 'the non-state sector, NGOs and treatment camps'.[16] The rationale, it was argued, was to introduce so-called dangerous addicts and risky groups into the cycle of treatment, the first of which was managed by the state, through the therapeutic police, while afterwards it was outsourced to non-state agents, through charities, NGOs and civil society organisations.

The government made large budgetary allocations to the NAJA in furtherance of the construction of compulsory camps. In 2011, 81 billion *tuman* (equivalent to ca. USD 8 million), were allocated to

---

[12] Their genealogical root, beyond Iran's borders, is the therapeutic model envisaged by Italian psychiatrist Franco Basaglia in the 1960s and 70s for the closure of mental asylums. John Foot, *La 'Republica dei matti': Franco Basaglia e la psichiatria radicale in Italia 1961–1978* (Feltrinelli, 2015), chapter 7.
[13] *Iran*, May 12, 2007.
[14] A similarity that is reminiscent of the 1980s approach; see Ghiabi, 'Drugs and Revolution'.
[15] *Hamshahri*, April 30, 2008.   [16] Ibid.

the Ministry of Interior, to build a major compulsory treatment camp in Fashapuyieh, in the southern area of the capital.[17] This first camp was designed to inter around 4,000 addicts in the first phase (with no clear criteria of inclusion), with the number going up to 40,000 once the entire camp had been completed.[18] Other camps were expected to be operating in major regions, including Khorasan, Markazi, Fars and Mazandaran.[19] A gargantuan project resulted from the implementation of Article 16 of the 2010 law. The deputy director of the DCHQ, Tah Taheri, announced that 'about 250,000 people needed to be sent to the compulsory treatment camps by the end of the year' as part of the governmental effort to curb the new dynamics of addiction.[20] The ambitious plan had the objective of unburdening the prison organisation from the mounting number of drug offenders, a move likely to also benefit the finances of the Judiciary and the NAJA, always overwhelmed by drug dossiers and structurally incapable of proceeding with the drug files.

The nature of the compulsory treatment camps resembled more that of the prison than anything else. Legislation on illicit drugs mandated the separation of drug-related criminals from the rest of the prison population. Authorities failed to implement the plan on a large scale, leaving the prisons filled with drug offenders.[21] Up to 2010, the prison population had increased to 250,000 inmates, a number that, given the state's commitment *not to incarcerate drug addicts*, was symptomatic of an underlying duplicity, or ambivalence, in state intervention.[22] Mostafa Purmohammadi, a prominent prosecutor, identified 'addicted prisoners' as one of the main concerns of the prisons and he advised the implementation of mandatory treatment camps to alleviate the dangers and troubles of the prison system.[23] Consequently, for the first time in many decades, the prison population decreased by some 40,000 people in 2012, reaching the still cumbersome number of 210,000 inmates. This datum, heralded as evidence of success by the post-reformist

---

[17] After 2009, incidentally, the head of the DCHQ was Mostafa Najjar, then Ministry of Interior.
[18] *Jam-e Jam*, February 28, 2011, retrieved from www1.jamejamonline.ir/paper text.aspx?newsnum=100836959206.
[19] Ibid. [20] *Jam-e Jam*, May 16, 2011. [21] *Salamat News*, May 8, 2012.
[22] *Tabnak*, February 8, 2013, retrieved from www.tabnak.ir/fa/news/301709.
[23] Purmohammadi was Minister of Interior between 2005 and 2008, as well as Minister of Justice in Rouhani's first government since 2013. *Ruzegar-e Ma*, August 27, 2011.

government, could be actually traced back to the introduction, on a massive scale, of the compulsory camps for drug (ab)users, managed by the therapeutic police. The actual population confined in state institutions for charges of criminal behaviour (including public addiction), had actually mounted to almost double the size of prisons prior to the 2010s.

Since the establishment of the Islamic Republic, the overall number of prisoners had increased by six times, and the number of those incarcerated for drug-related charges by fourteen times, with one in three court cases allegedly being drug-related in 2009.[24] If, during the reformist period, the introduction of harm reduction had been prompted, among other things, by the HIV epidemic in prisons, the post-reformist government under Ahmadinejad reacted with outrage against the waste of money that the incarceration of drug offenders represented. An official from the Prison Organisation in 2010 outlined that 'the maintenance of every prisoner costs 3,000 *tuman* per day ... which is equivalent to a waste of public capital of around 450,000,000 *tuman* per day'.[25] Researchers from state institutions demonstrated that treating drug (ab)users would cost an average of fifteen times less than incarcerating them. In view of the ratio of drug (ab)users in prison – an astonishing 70 per cent – the creation of the compulsory treatment camps provided an alternative device for the management of a costly population.[26] The head of the Judiciary, Ayatollah Sadeq Ardeshir Amoli Larijani, leading member of the conservative faction and brother to the Parliament speaker Ali Larijani, echoed these results, asking for a swift re-settling of 'addicted prisoners' in the compulsory camps for the sake of treatment. Compulsory camps, rather than being under the supervision of the Prison Organisation, are managed by the DCHQ.[27]

Out of the conviction that the drug (ab)user population would be relegated to the camps, the Ahmadinejad government suspended the needle exchange programmes in prisons, affirming that 'the situation [of HIV/AIDS] was under control'.[28] The assumption among officials

---

[24] *Hamshahri*, January 22, 2009.
[25] *Jam-e Jam*, April 11, 2010. The equivalent of ca. USD 150,000 per day.
[26] *Hamshahri*, April 30, 2009. *Sharq*, August 8, 2010.
[27] *Aftab News*, June 16, 2011, retrieved from http://aftabnews.ir/prtb89b8wrh b5fp.uiur.html.
[28] *Hamshahri*, November 1, 2009.

became that since drug (ab)users are now referred to compulsory camps, needle exchange has become irrelevant in prisons. At the same time, the government proceeded towards a significant expansion of methadone treatment, bringing more than 40,000 prisoners under treatment by 2014. Methadone, in this regard, represented an acceptable solution, as it was produced domestically, it was readily available through private and public clinics and, last but not least, facilitated greatly – by virtue of its pharmacological effects – the management of unruly subjects, such as drug users, in the problematic contexts of prisons.[29] In the account of several former drug offenders in prison, the authorities tended to encourage methadone treatment with high doses, without much scrutiny of either the side effects of excessive methadone use, or the internal economy of methadone within the prison.[30]

Inspired by the relative success of its methadone programmes (in prisons, as much as outside), the DCHQ agreed to pilot methadone treatment programmes inside some of the compulsory treatment camps supervised by the NAJA. This, it seems, was identified as a productive way to introduce the highest number of drug addicts into the cycle of treatment, via less harmful drugs such as methadone. By familiarising arrested drug (ab)users to methadone, the authorities sought to maintain them off, allegedly more dangerous drugs, such as heroin. But because the number of methamphetamine users had increased significantly, methadone proved ineffective, and the authorities sought alternatives in the model of the compulsory camps. Based on forced detoxification, these camps treated all drug (ab)use without distinction. Shafaq camp embodied the new model of treatment of drug (ab)use.

In 2010, the government inaugurated the mandatory treatment camp of Shafaq in the village of Shurabad, south of Tehran. The location of this centre sounded familiar to those acquainted with Iran's history of drugs: during the 1980s, Shurabad had been one of the major collective rehabilitation centres for drug (ab)users, one that was often given focus in media reports. In the 1990s, it was transformed into a female prison, before eventually being abandoned. Its revivification synchronised well

---

[29] In the context of the prison, an addict in need of heroin, crack or opium would reasonably accept the distribution of methadone in order to avoid withdrawal symptoms. *Naloxone*, the 'anti-overdose' medication is legal but not distributed in prison as part of the harm reduction programmes.

[30] Ethnographic notes in Arak with drug (ab)users in a camp, April 2014.

with the post-reformist government's call to bring back the revolutionary principles of the Islamic Revolution, in the spirit of Sadegh Khalkhali and his onslaught against drugs. However, the Shafaq centre did not resemble the old, obsolete structure of the 1980s. It was rebuilt with the objective of instituting a model for other compulsory camps as well as for other non-state rehab camps.

The target population of this camp consisted of marginal drug (ab)users, a fluid category made of poor or pauperised homeless or with instable housing, people visiting or living around the *patoqs* in Tehran. Shafaq's management was initially entrusted to retired Colonel Khalil Hariri, a leading commander of Anti-Narcotic Police who had been stationed in the Sistan and Baluchistan region for nine years with the primary duty of fighting drug traffickers.[31] His appointment revealed the government's priorities on treatment: a top security official in anti-narcotics acting as director of an addiction treatment centre. In Shafaq, the government allocated ca. 100,000 tuman (ca. USD 8) per treated addict, which officials said would cover the employment of medical and social cadres to supervise recovery, which they expected to last for a three-month period.[32]

The camp of Shafaq operated from early 2010 to late 2012, when a huge scandal broke out bringing its closure. Fifty-three people, rounded up by the police because of their status as 'public addicts', had died of chronic dysentery after having spent a few weeks in the camp. Media reported the deaths and several journalists managed to contact people who had previously been inside the camp, unearthing dramatic accounts. The picture that emerged from the reports was gruesome: a single silo with no windows, composed of fourteen rooms on two lines, each occupying fifty beds, with no heating system installed, inadequate sanitary services and insufficient alimentary provisions, the centre soon became the symbol of the state's inhumane treatment of drug (ab)users.[33]

Overcrowded rooms and the lack of medical personnel added to the ordinary accounts of beatings, mistreatment and abuse by the personnel, including physical violence against elderly individuals.[34] The use of

---

[31] *Hamshahri*, April 5, 2010, retrieved from http://hamshahrionline.ir/details/10 4358/Society/vulnerabilities.
[32] *Keyhan*, June 13, 2011. Heavy currency fluctuation over this period.
[33] Interviews with drug users who were confined in the camp or had friends confined there; Tehran, September 2013 and March 2014.
[34] *Tabnak*, December 25, 2013, retrieved from www.tabnak.ir/fa/news/366881.

cages, bars and handcuffs, constant police surveillance, disciplining rules and physical violence exposed, on the one hand, the contrast with the humanitarian and medicalised precepts of harm reduction (Article 15) and, on the other hand, embodied a coercive and securitising strategy based on the management of the margins, perceived as disorderly and chaotic. Dozens of people I encountered in the drug-using hotspots – the *patoq* – mentioned their experience, or that of their cohorts, in the camp, remarking, not without some pride, the fact they were still alive despite what they had gone through.[35] Whether their accounts were effectively experienced or empathically imagined, scarcely mattered. In fact, the narratives of Shafaq established a shocking precedent among the population of homeless, pauperised drug (ab)users, which delegitimised governmental interventions on the *problematique* of addiction, while unwrapping the inconsistencies behind the state's framing of 'addiction' as a medical problem.

Even the work of harm reduction organisations, which had stepped up in supporting the needs of homeless drug users, was negatively affected by the public outcry against Shafaq. Social workers operating in the *patoq*s had to reassure the drug-user community of their non-involvement in 'compulsory camps'. In several *patoq*s, the outreach programmes had to be stopped because of the threat of violence by the *patoq*'s thugs [*gardan-koloft*, literally 'thick-necks'], who feared that strategic information was gathered by the NGOs and sent to the police (an allegation that had some factual evidence, in fact). One man from the Farahzad *Chehel pelleh* (literally '40-steps') *patoq* explained me that 'Shafaq is a place that even the bottom line people [*tah-e khatti-ha*] cannot bear! And these guys [indicating the outreach team], we don't trust them, one day they give us syringes, the other day they stare at us when the police comes and brings us to hell!' Anathema of the homeless drug-using community in Tehran, a young interlocutor of mine would use the metaphor of *barzakh* to describe Shafaq: the Islamic purgatory, or limbo, whereby one could spend the eternity before the judgement at the end of times.[36] Intellectually, this image connected with the theological, eschatological meaning of 'crisis' as

---

[35] Ethnographic notes in the Farahzad *patoq*, Tehran, March–April 2014.
[36] Interview with Hamid, former street addict now active in an NGO, Tehran, April 2014.

the moment of the ultimate judgment, the moment that decisions take shape regardless of established conventions.

Beside Shafaq, the compulsory treatment camps became sites of risk themselves, with the spread of HIV and other venereal diseases being reported on a number of occasions. For instance, Majid Rezazadeh, the Welfare Organisation's head of prevention, recounted that 'a budget for harm reduction is allocated to the compulsory camps, but these [camps] are not only unsuccessful in decreasing the rate of addiction, but they have become actual locations for the spread of the virus of AIDS in the country'.[37] Indeed, the debate about the status of these camps proceeded up to the post-Ahmadinejad period. One of the conference presenters mentioned earlier in this chapter, Ahmad Hajebi, invited the DCHQ, to pledge publicly to the definitive closure of the compulsory treatment camps, because 'they are not places for human beings'.[38]

Nonetheless, compulsory camps have been part of the political economy of addiction in the Islamic Republic: the police identified this model as an easy source of governmental funds, based on a regulation that ensured state bonuses to the NAJA for every drug offender referred to state-run camps. By collecting homeless drug users from across the cities' hotspots on a regular basis, the police benefit from a substantial financial flow, justified by the expenses that it putatively incurs managing the camps. Given that most of the state-run camps are known for their Spartan and down-to-earth conditions, it is implied that considerable amounts of money are filling the coffers of the NAJA through addiction recovery subsidies. This also implies that the NAJA has a stake in the continuation *and* proliferation of the activities of the compulsory camps.[39] Although incidental to the case of compulsory camps, the rumours and accusations about the expensive cars and unchecked revenues of police officials might be a collateral effect of the compulsory camp model.[40] According to a member of the DCHQ, the municipality of Tehran spends around 400 million *tuman* per month on taking care of the city's addicts, or rather for the provision

---

[37] *Jam-e Jam*, December 1, 2011.   [38] *Qatreh*, December 20, 2013.
[39] *Mardomsalari*, September 22, 2012.
[40] A number of interviewees referred to the fact that these camps are becoming a steady source of personal revenue for people, a fact, they all claimed, demonstrated by the luxury cars, watches, suits and other amenities that police officials, even lower-ranking ones, possessed. I could not verify these claims.

of services to them.[41] Thus, the police becomes the ultimate power-broker in drug (ab)use, especially when higher numbers of arrests contribute to a boost in budgetary allocation.

The existence of the compulsory camp model testifies to the endurance of a securitisation approach, based on law enforcement techniques, which coexists with a medicalised and managerial approach to drug (ab)use.[42] But the camps, paradigmatically, embody a new mode of law enforcement – one that, instead of contesting harm reduction, uses its rhetoric for a new purpose. Security rather than humanitarian concerns govern this model foregrounded in a management of disorderly population – one could name them the 'downtrodden' to use Iran's revolutionary lexicology – through coercive mechanisms, while leaving drug (ab)users, from middle class backgrounds, unmolested.[43] While reports about Shafaq in the newspapers prompted a political reaction, bringing about the closure of the camp (and its reopening under a new management in 2014), other centres have continued to operate with similar modalities, even though with less outrageous conditions. In 2014, the director of *Rebirth* provocatively asked the authorities, 'to take the addicts to prisons' instead of the treatment camps, because at least as a prisoner the addict would have minimal support from medical and social workers.[44]

Private Recovery Camps

Private rehabilitation centres have been operating legally or informally since the mid 1980s, although their veritably extra-ordinary expansion can be traced back to the early 2000s and the new politico-medical atmosphere brought in by the reformists. In particular, the coming of

---

[41] *Tabnak*, December 30, 2013, retrieved from www.tabnak.ir/fa/news/366881. For the first time in decades, Rouhani's Minister of Interior, Abdol-Reza Rahmani-Fazli, acknowledged that drug money could have potentially affected political trends in Iran, including during elections and in the police forces; see *IRNA*, February 21, 2015, retrieved from www.irna.ir/fa/News/81514008/.

[42] Interview with Razzaghi, Tehran, September 2012.

[43] In the Islamist Koranic lexicon 'downtrodden', *mostaʻzafin*, refers to the poorest section of society, antithesis of the arrogant, *mostakbarin*. The term was in vogue in the years preceding the 1979 Revolution, among Islamist Marxists and the Left, and then it was adopted in the official state ideology under Khomeini. By early 2010s, it was de facto abandoned in the state rhetoric.

[44] *Khabaronline*, May 11, 2015, retrieved from www.khabaronline.ir/detail/415509.

age of the NGO *Rebirth* laid the ground for a mushrooming of charitable, private rehab centres, popularly known as *camps*. The word *camp* in Persian, rather than recalling the heinous reference to the Nazi concentration camps, hints at the *camp-e tabestani*, 'summer camps', 'holiday camps' that had become very much *à la mode* among middle-class Iranians in the 1990s.[45]

Born of the philosophy of *Narcotics Anonymous*, the equivalent of *Alcoholics Anonymous* for illicit drugs, and the idea of communitarian recovery, the camps are based on a detoxification process, usually based on twenty-one- to twenty-eight-day sessions, and on the self-management of daily duties by those interned.[46] As charitable institutions, they are under the supervision of the Welfare Organisation, but their most immediate relationship with the state is with the police. Regularly contacted by the police in order 'to accommodate' arrested drug users for rehab programmes whenever the state-run compulsory camps are overwhelmed, the camps operate on the frontier between public order and private service.[47] While people referred by the police to the compulsory camps are treated free of charge, those referred to the rehab camps are expected to pay the fees, at least partially. The camp owners admit that only in rare cases, they demand full amount and that they accept any monetary contribution the drug (ab)user, or his family, is capable of making. Most of the time, however, people referred to the private camps by the police refuse to pay and, *par consequence*, as a camp owner explained, 'addicts are arrested by the police on Monday, and released by us [the camp owners] on Tuesday, because they don't have money [to pay the fees]'.[48] This has triggered criticism of the police, especially in view of the 2010 law reform that puts emphasis on 'the judicial supervision of the arrest, treatment and release process', which would require a judicial dossier to be opened for every referral. The conservative newspaper *Keyhan* reminded the NAJA that 'the [private] camps have no right to maintain the addicts without a ruling of the Judiciary; similarly they cannot let the addict

---

[45] I am grateful to Fariba Adelkhah for pointing out this aspect.
[46] The average length of presence in these camps is hard to infer, but referrals generally tend to spend at least two sessions in the camps.
[47] Interview with camp managers, including in the village of Hasanabad (Arak) April 2014; Fatemiyyeh (Arak) July 2014; Shahr-e Ray, February 2014; Tehran, September 2015.
[48] Interview with camp manager, Hasanabad (Arak).

leave the camp without approval of the judicial authorities'.[49] Both practices, as blatantly obvious from fieldwork observation, are the rule rather than the exception.

Despite the promise of monetary subsidies from the state, most of the camps exist within an economy of subsistence based on donations from local communities, recovered addicts, the mosques and a few governmental vouchers. However, the landscape of treatment camps includes also sophisticated examples, such as *Rebirth's* camps of Verdij and Lavisan. Both located geographically at the north-east and north-west of Tehran, these camps are a different model of recovery, one that drastically differs from that of Shafaq and other camps.[50] In reference to these camps, several interlocutors pointed out that these places are not *mardomi*, popular, in the sense that ordinary, working class citizens cannot access them. They have gained credit among wealthier strata of the populace seeking recovery. In 2014, the monthly fee for a twenty-one-day period of rehab in the centre was 6,875,000 *tuman* [ca. USD 170], an amount the popular classes can hardly afford, although demand for access to the centres has been steady. Media reports have called these camps – somehow advertising them – as 'a golden exile'.[51] Inside Verdij, in particular, there is a trendy coffeeshop, with a thrilling view of the forest; the people residing there can be identified as typical northern Tehranis. Some of them, it is reported by the NGO, spend up to a year in the centre, trying to find psychological tranquillity before going back to their lives.

With crippling sanctions hitting the economy in the early 2010s, however, popular classes have been unable to devote resources to sophisticated forms of treatment. Ordinary people opt for less costly options that promise better results than a twenty-one-day session in a camp. So, the panorama of private treatment camps is vast, with services that respond to middle class expectations as well as to the necessities of the popular classes. Accordingly, the conditions of the camps vary along with the costs of treatment, as for other health services.

---

[49] *Keyhan*, June 10, 2012.
[50] Northern Tehran is known for its cleaner and fresh air – as opposed to the polluted and arid villages of southern Tehran.
[51] *Iran*, February 21, 2009, retrieved from www.aftabir.com/news/view/2009/feb/21/c4c1235195499_social_psychopathology_addiction.php.

Women in the Private Camps

Official statistics reported in newspapers in the last decade reveal that one in ten drug (ab)users in Iran is female.[52] Yet, there are also strong indications that a growing number of women are using *shisheh*, which would logically imply that the percentage of female users has increased in the last decade. Women represent only 5 per cent of all referrals to state institutions providing service for drug dependency, but a much higher presence is unveiled in formal and informal treatment camps.[53] The stigma for women is also more resilient and, in several cases, female treatment camps have been set on fire because they deemed these camps as immoral and a 'nest of sexual vice', the equivalent of a brothel in public parlance.[54]

In 2011, the government approved the construction of one compulsory treatment camp for female addicts, to be located in the Persian Gulf region of Hormozgan. The site would host a multifarious category whose common feature could be identified in relation to the street (and the moral order): runaway girls trapped in drug (ab)use, streetwalkers, sex workers, female mendicants and petty drug dealers and users. All these categories blur into each other, at least if one *sees like a state*.[55] The location itself indicated that the site of this camp had to be peripheral; south along the coast of Hormozgan, the camp would work half as an exile and half as a refuge from the public gaze. Hormozgan itself, however, had historically been characterised by heavy drug (ab)use, including among women, a fact that perhaps further justified the location of the camp there. The particularity of this project was also its joint-venture nature between the state and a private organisation expected to manage the centre, an exception both to the 2010 law and to the practice in other camps.[56] Given the sensitivity of a female treatment camp, the authorities partly disengaged from its routine administration and partly took advantage of the existing expertise and activism of NGOs dedicated to subaltern women's affairs. But a single female camp, located at the very periphery of Iran, could not comply with the necessities dictated by the expanding

---

[52] In a decade, the number of female drug 'addicts' has almost doubled, according to the DCHQ; see *Fararu*, August 2, 2016, retrieved from http://fararu.com/fa/news/283802/.
[53] *Hamshahri*, June 24, 2009.   [54] *Sharq*, July 24, 2012.
[55] Scott, *Seeing like a State*.
[56] *Khabaronline*, June 10, 2011, retrieved from www.khabaronline.ir/print/156388/.

shisheh use among women. This void had been already filled by the establishment of female treatment camps, managed by private individuals or charities. I shall refer to one of them to which I was given repeated access over the course of my fieldwork in 2014. The women's camp, situated in the city of Arak, operated under the charity organisation *Wings of Freedom*.[57]

Operating as a sister branch of a male treatment camp, the female camp could hardly be described as a camp. It was an apartment inside a four-storey building in a formerly middle-class area (mostly inhabited by public employees), today referred generally as *payin-shahr*, 'downtown' (in Persian, it indicates 'a popular periphery'). As I entered the gate of the apartment, I was greeted by a young woman in her twenties, who immediately mocked me because – in the scholarly enthusiasm of accessing a place otherwise forbidden to men and, even more, to male researchers – I had forgotten to take off my shoes, a gaffe which is indefensible in Iranian culture. The woman, Samira from Khorramabad, said, 'You people go abroad for two weeks and this is the result'; I nodded, as privately I agreed with her, and I proceeded inside, not without awkwardness.

The apartment had three rooms and a small kitchen, with a long corridor used by the women as a lounge to watch satellite TV (which is formally banned according to national laws). The room where I met the director, a woman in her late thirties, was imbued with a powerful smell of cigarettes, an indication that the women, while recovering, smoked heavily. I took out my *Bahman Kucik* (a popular brand of cigarettes) and offered them to my interlocutors, a move that instigated another amused reaction by everyone in the room. 'They do not smoke', glossed the director; as I stared at her, she realised that I had understood and elaborated, 'They cannot smoke *in front of you*, doctor!' I then lit my cigarette, apologised to my interlocutors and started the conversation.

The management of the camp can indeed be problematic. In the past, the director had been assaulted by an interned woman who had threatened her with a knife while trying to escape. After having regained control of the situation, the director reacted by beating the woman who had threatened her. The director was later condemned by a judge for her violent behaviour against the patient in the camp. The camp was

---

[57] The name has been changed to guarantee anonymity.

Private Recovery Camps

shut down for few months, before obtaining another licence under her husband's organisation, which, I came to discover, is also a rehab camp for male drug (ab)users.[58] The director had access to several CCTV cameras in the apartment and she could watch the video on her laptop; she could also control the three rooms of 'the camp' from the desk of her office, or when she was at home, via an online application to which the CCTV camera were connected. 'In this way', she explained, 'I can check on the girls when I am not here'. She argued that the camp was self-managed by the women themselves, who cook, clean and take care of the daily management of the place. They have a friendly, intimate relationship, she held, and she would like the place to be as comfortable and welcoming as possible. The door at the entrance of the apartment, nonetheless, has to remain locked at all times when she is not in, 'otherwise the girls might run away and might go back to use drugs'. When I asked her what would happen if a person inside the apartment felt sick or needed urgent help, she justified it by saying that she could be reached at any time via mobile phone and that she checked on them regularly via the CCTV. She also relied on one of the women, Samira, who helped her doing the grocery shopping and kept an eye on the other women while she is away. Samira had been in the camp for one year and a half, since she was referred there by the women's Prison Organisation. She had spent time in prison on several occasions for *shisheh* possession, aggression, armed robbery and 'moral crimes' (euphemism for alleged sex work). Whether institutionalisation in this private camp had produced positive effects on her life is hard to say. Certainly, I and Samira herself had the perception that her existence was suspended and that, despite having stopped using drugs, addiction was still very much present in her life. In a way, nothing extraordinary: 'I do not smoke anymore' or 'I do not drink anymore' are part of the experience of people with a dependency, of the eternally 'recovering addict'.[59]

The fee for a twenty-one-day period is of 450,000 *tuman* (ca. USD 110). The people coming to the camp do not live in Arak, rather, they usually come from other cities, since they want to avoid being recognised by their communities. This small apartment had

---

[58] I later came to know that this story was also widely reported in the news. See *Sharq*, September 24, 2012.

[59] On this oxymoronic figure, see the 'detoxified addicted' in Deleuze, *Deux régimes*.

two women from Khorramabad, a Kurdish woman from the Kermanshah region who did not speak Farsi, and another from northern Khuzestan. The police had sent three of the women as part of a compulsory treatment programme. Since there is just one compulsory camp for women – located approximately 120 km from Arak – the authorities rely on private camps to accommodate these women, in which case, they also pay the fees for their treatment. Generally, the director explains, the women referred by the police are more problematic, some manifesting serious health issues, while others have several criminal charges pending in their dossiers. It is not rare for these camps to refuse to take over people referred by the police, out of fear of health contagion or in order to preserve their reputation.

Most of the female treatment camps, naturally, operate at the margins of the city, or inside apartments in popular neighbourhoods, in order to pay lower rent and avoid being recognised as recovery camps. There is no overt indication outside as to the nature of the apartment and no explicit address is provided, and the referrals occur through the state line of enquiry – e.g. the police – or through informal connections. The female treatment camps operate along those margins in which state intervention is rendered more problematic by the sensibility of the gender issue, while popular resentment and stigma against them menaces their presence in public. The state, for that matter, is reticent to allocate sufficient licences for the female camps, out of concern that the mushrooming of these institutions – once they are formally recognised by the state – would stipulate a less ambiguous datum of female drug (ab)use, one which might refute the unchanging official version to which the government has hitherto pledged. In this way, it also secures flexibility in its cooperation with civil society.

This condition more evidently marks female drug (ab)users, but it does effect the phenomenon of treatment as a whole. It is no coincidence that, according to several surveys, 90 per cent of rehab camps, both male and female, are unlicensed, and operate in a starkly different environment than the examples of fancy treatment camps of Verdij and Lavisan in the North of Tehran. Indeed, to locate the political dimension of the camp, one has to investigate the phenomenon of the illicit treatment camps (*kamp-ha-ye gheyr-e mojaz*).

Illegal Treatment: 'The Hand that Captures the Snake'

The phenomenon of camps suggests that these institutions, regardless of their public/private, legal/illegal status, exist on a continuum. It constitutes, *in toto*, a primary means of intervention – or mode of government – of addiction. It has become common knowledge – if not a joke! – that contemporary Iranian society offers a wide range of informal, illegal centres for the provision of services (e.g. retirement houses, pharmacies, education centres) and that, despite the government's repeated calls for their closure, these enterprises continue a lucrative existence.[60] But the sheer quantitative dimension of the illegal recovery camps – nine out ten rehab camps – signifies that this category effects more largely and, perhaps categorically, the phenomenon itself. Indeed, one could say that legal treatment camps are marginalia within the pages of addiction recovery and treatment.

Already in 2007, the government warned against the mushrooming of illegal treatment camps and gave an ultimatum of three months to all camp managers to register for a licence at the Welfare Organisation.[61] The DCHQ announced that 'by the end of the year, the problem of the camps will be solved', yet in 2014, the number of these institutions was higher than ever, with a veritable burgeoning across the country.[62] In Tehran alone, there were more than four hundred illegal camps, while in Isfahan, out of three hundred camps, only sixteen had a licence.[63] In the city of Arak, where I conducted part of the fieldwork, there were about fifty illegal camps, located in nearby villages, main routes or in private houses.[64] These camps, *prima facie*, provide treatment for underprivileged people, and their families. With the burden of economic sanctions trickling down to the popular strata, treatment in these institutions represented a more affordable and realistic solution. Given the rootedness of the illegal camps, officials in the DCHQ have started to change their approach, describing the camps as 'a positive sign, because it implies that many people in Iran seek treatment'.[65] The officials hold that, as the country's [official] treatment capacity

---

[60] See *Hamshahri*, May 4, 2008.
[61] *Hamshahri*, March 9, 2010. The Welfare Organisation has an ad hoc office for drug addiction, which issues these licences.
[62] Ibid. [63] Ibid. Interview with Tahernokhost, Tehran September 2012.
[64] Interview with Hasan Solhi, Arak, March 2014.
[65] *Jam-e Jam*, May 16, 2011.

could not meet the demand for treatment, the camps are instrumental in this endeavour, even when they operate illegally.⁶⁶

In the management of addiction, however, their role bypasses the logic of treatment and service provision. Hamid-Reza Tahernokhost, UNODC expert, defines the illegal camps as 'the hand that captures the snake [*dast-e mar-gir*]'.⁶⁷ In post-reformist governance, exclusively legal, bureaucratic or administrative means are insufficient and ineffective. To deal with crisis – and drug crisis – the state exploits the extra-legal function of the camps in areas from which the state itself had progressively disengaged, or has dissimulated its presence. In this regard, the illegal camps operate in a grey area, which qualify as Agamben's 'state of exception', as I elaborate later.

The workings of the illegal camps can be sketched thus: In a situation where someone acts violently and volatilely, usually under the influence of *shisheh*, the family of the subject usually opts for the intervention of the camps' personnel. This is regarded as a preferable option to the intervention of the police. By calling the illegal camp, the family avoids criminal charges, which could produce incarceration and time-consuming lawsuits, all of which cause greater economic burden to the family itself. Similarly, the intervention of the camp 'thugs' – the *gardan-koloft* – maintains a lower profile for the family than that of the police, which, especially in popular neighbourhoods, can cause rumours and *aberurizi* (reputation damage). Saving one's face remains a top priority for the family as much as for the individual drug user.⁶⁸

The police, too, seems to support the illegal camp system and, at times, informs the personnel of the camps about the location of the complaint (*shekayat*). In this way, the camps take on the duties of the police (NAJA), with regard to drug (ab)use. A police officer confirms this informally during a conversation,

> I am really happy that these camps exist; if a family calls us, instead of sending a soldier or a policeman, we call one of the people from the camps. So, if someone gets beaten, that's the camp people, which also means that, if someone has to beat someone else, it's always the camp people [and not the police]. Instead of taking the addict here to the police station, where he might

---

⁶⁶ *Hamshahri*, January 25, 2010.
⁶⁷ *Dast-e margir*: a Persian expression indicating doing something dangerous – like capturing a snake – by using someone – a proxy.
⁶⁸ Ethnographic notes in popular, poor neighbourhoods of Shush, Dowlatabad in Tehran; and *Futbal, Cheshm-e Mushak* in Arak. See also *Jam-e Jam*, April 16, 2012.

vomit, feel sick and make the entire place dirty, he goes to the camp. Instead of coming here to shout and beat up people, or to bring diseases, HIV, he goes there. I call the camp if someone calls me.[69]

The camps are an apparatus of management of social crises, in the guise of drugs addiction. De facto, most of the illegal treatment camps operate as compulsory treatment camps, because the people who are interned, for periods which vary between twenty-one days and one year, have been forced into the camps. They have not been forced by the police, but by their local communities, usually their family members. The police plays the part of the observer or the informant. It instructs the camps, in some occasions, of the location and situation of the complaint, but no formal undertaking is enacted. The camp operates in an economy of punishment and recovery of their own, autonomous but not independent from the state.

The illegal camps have become rapidly part of a mechanism of intervention, which goes beyond treatment, per se. Inside them – several personal stories disclose – the managers of the camps can adopt 'alternative techniques' for the treatment of addiction, the most infamous ones being *kotak-darmani* ('beating-treatment'), *ab-darmani* ('water-treatment'), *sag-darmani* ('dog-treatment') and *zangir-darmani* ('chain-treatment').[70] Each of these options suggest the use of an element – water, dogs, chains or punches – to inflict violence on the recovering drug (ab)user. It indicates the use of force and violence and constriction in preventing interned people from wanting to use drugs again. That occurs generally regardless of whether the person seeks to use drugs in the camp or not. It is a form of preventive measure of dissuasion and – how to say this? – a punishment for having used drugs in the first place. Although there is generally a propensity towards sensationalising these accounts – as most newspapers do on topics related to illicit drugs – the deaths of interned people are the public signature of the camps' practice in the collective narrative.

Conversely to the state-run camps, the liability of the crime remains exclusively with the camp managers, as noted in the statement of the

---

[69] Interview with a former police officer in Arak, September 2014. Similar accounts emerged with people active in the management of rehab camps.
[70] *Andisheh-ye Nou*, October 12, 2009; *Salamat* News, October 22, 2013, retrieved from www.salamatnews.com/news/85137/.

police officer mentioned above. The authorities severely punish casualties within the illegal camps. According to Islamic law, the judge applies *qesas*, retributive justice ('an eye for an eye'). That implies the death penalty for those who are responsible for the camps where the death had occurred and was proven to be the result of the personnel's mismanagement. (More precisely, the capital sentence is meted in cases where the family of the victim refuses to accept the *diyeh*, the 'blood money'.) Although there are no clear data on the rate of deaths within the illegal camps, the reports in the newspapers suggest that the events are not sporadic.[71] Among impoverished drug (ab)users, the narratives of the camp gained solid ground and instil vivid fear, a sentiment that is somehow reminiscent of a persecution. In this way, the camps fulfil a double promise: they intervene along the problematic margins of society (its uncivil society), through the creation of extra-legal, unaccountable and, in view of their quantitative dimension, omnipresent institutions. They represent an apparatus in the management of disorderly groups and, more generally, the drug crisis. As such, they decrease the work of the police, while receiving nothing in exchange. At the same time, the camps are managed by former drug (ab)users, whose place within normative society remains unsettled. These individuals struggle to find employment in regular businesses, their housing status endures as uncertain, often relying on temporary family accommodation. The camp, hence, becomes the only stable unit in their life, functioning both as occupation and residence.[72] The heads or managers of the camps are usually also those who make the initial investment to pay the rent of the location, whether a house with garden, a flat, a silo or an abandoned compound. Two or more people, friends or family, set up the camp and employ a number of handymen who are often former 'patients' of the camps, now willing to help out for a small stipend or to pay their debt. In this regard, there is no substantial difference between legal and illegal camps. In this peculiar way, post-reformist governance of crisis succeeded in its quest 'to socialise the war on drugs' and 'to mobilise (*basij kardan*)', by other means, civil society for statist ends.[73]

---

[71] *Etemad-e Melli*, June 11, 2009. Death is often caused not by physical violence, but by medical inaccuracy (e.g. interruption of anti-depressant drugs).
[72] Ethnographic observation in six rehab camps in Tehran, Arak and Qom provinces, 2012–15.
[73] Comments on the need 'to socialise the war on drugs' were made at the 'ASCongress 2014', intervention by DCHQ official Hamid Sarrami.

A public clinic manager, who also serves as a psychiatrist in a compulsory camp, explains that 'the [illegal] camp system has successfully managed to keep the antisocial elements of society within itself: a group of antisocial people is represented by the owners of the camps, and the other group is represented by the patients, those interned in the camps'.[74] Regardless of whether the camps are constituted by antisocial groups – whatever this category signifies – the camp system functions as 'safety valve' for recovered drug (ab)users, whose psychological and social status is in need of a stable occupation, which would otherwise be unachievable. With the camps providing motivation and an ecosystem in which to find their place within society, the camp owners practise a system in which the phenomenon of drug (ab) use dissolves into the machinery of treatment – under the rationale of harm reduction. This system seemingly replicates itself. Former patients are employed in addiction treatment and, whether willingly or involuntarily, mistreat other drug (ab)users, perpetuating previous securitising policies.[75]

This phenomenon unwraps a form of grassroots authoritarianism, whereby social elements belonging to diverse societal milieux, partake in mechanisms of control, discipline and treatment. Its relationship with the state remains, peremptorily, ambiguous, based on rhetorical condemnation, haphazard prosecution and clandestine connections, for instance, in the referral of complaints by the police to the illegal camps. Despite almost a decade of reiterated calls to close the doors of the illegal treatment camps, these institutions maintain solid roots and operate, *qua* rhizomes, across the margins of rural and urban Iran. Their ubiquity has given rise to the phenomenon of *kamp-gardi*, 'camp-touring', which refers to the unending journey of the drug (ab)users from camp to camp, a circumnavigation that rarely offers a way out and often leads to the individual becoming either destitute or incorporated into the activities of a particular camp.[76] Those whose experiences have been more telling are often called by the rest of the community as the 'Marco Polo', because they have visited as many

---

[74] Interview with Solhi. The camps, as such, qualify as the fourth sector of Iran's economy – the informal yet accepted. See Adelkhah, *Les Mille et Une*, 470.
[75] Iran is no exception in this regard; see Garcia, *The Pastoral Clinic*.
[76] Observation on the accounts of people's lives in/out the camps. See also *Jam-e Jam*, December 19, 2010.

camps as the Venetian traveller had done during his travels of the *Milione*.[77]

An odyssey similar to that through camps, clinics and prisons goes also through other venues, such as public parks and the street where the state manages disorder differently.

A Site of Disorder: Harandi Park

In the southern district of Tehran's Bazaar, between Moulavi Street and Shoosh Street, there are four public gardens. The biggest and most popular of these is Harandi Park, which stands at the heart of the old neighbourhood of Darvazeh Ghar. Between 2014 and 2017, Harandi Park and, to a similar extent, the other parks as well, saw large groups of drug users who camped there with tents, sleeping bags, bonfires and piles of cardboard on the ground. Over the warm seasons – between March and November – the number of street drug users residing within the perimeter of the parks and the connecting alleys reached over three to four thousand, with additional visitors towards the evening.[78]

While on a stroll across the lawn in a late morning, I encountered waste collectors and gardeners working their way between groups of drug users, chatting or just passing through their circles. Every now and then, a police motorbike would ride on the main road circumscribing the park or in the middle of it, with neither the people or the police officers taking much notice. The entrance of a larger tent, close to a smelly empty pool that operated as an open-air loo, was animated by the bustling of a dozen of people. I was told later that the tent was where the main distribution of heroin (*gart*) and *shisheh* in the Harandi area takes place and that it is the centre of gravity of the park.

This is not an underground, hidden site of criminality and a marginal zone of crisis/disorder, as often described in the public imagery. The park stands in the middle of one of Tehran's working class and poorer neighbourhoods, with a symbiotic relation to its great bazaar, located close to the main metro line (Line 1) connecting the wealthy north with the city's southern poorer districts. In contrast to the everlasting declarations of the 'War on Drugs' and the ever-increasing

---

[77] Ethnographic notes in Shahr-e Rey, September 2012-2015.
[78] Accounts of Shush and Harandi Parks also appeared in newspapers. See *Iran*, October 5, 2015.

number of drug arrests, the situation in Harandi casts light on a different approach based on limited tolerance of public drug use and the tacit acceptance of street hustling.

Activism among civil society groups and NGOs has attracted public attention to this place, which, by 2015, had become a leitmotif of debate around drug policy and harm reduction in Tehran. The city municipality and the mayor of the district denied their acceptance of the situation and reiterated that there is no plan to transform Harandi in a social experiment of de facto drug decriminalisation. In discussions with people in the drug policy community, the 'Harandi model' referred to an experience and experiment of alternative management of street drug use. An alternative to the collection plans of drug (ab)users, it refrained from incarceration or forced treatment in the compulsory camps. Instead, by having large gatherings of so-called 'risky' drug (ab)users concentrated in specific areas, such as Harandi Park, social workers and medical personnel could proceed to intervene with welfare services while familiarising local drug (ab)users to the options of recovery and the cycle of addiction treatment, notably methadone. The 'dispersion of risk' is reduced, according to public officials, who imply that, without Harandi, the whole of Tehran would be a scene of open-air drug use and drug hustling, with the spectre of HIV epidemics looming all-too-large over the populace. It would be *uncontrollable*.[79]

That is why the neighbourhoods of this area have been provided with automatic syringe distributors, located within the reach of support centres managed by NGOs (Figure 7.1). The presence of civil society groups had, in fact, become central in this area and public attention reached its azimuth when, in autumn 2015, several groups of volunteers, humanitarian associations and philanthropic citizens started to bring cooked meals and clothes to the park and distributed them among the drug (ab)users. The provision of food had been a matter of satire amid detractors of this tolerant approach, who hold that 'the drug addicts are no longer satisfied by bread and egg or bread and cheese, but they expect sophisticated food and are spoiled for choice'.[80] Others claimed that public attention is driven by a sentimental piety not grounded in a real understanding of

---

[79] From a historical angle, Harandi may be equivalent, in terms of drugs, to *Shahr-e Nou*, the pre-revolutionary red-light districts of Tehran. Ghiabi, 'Drogues Illégales'

[80] *Sharq*, November 16, 2015 retrieved from www.sharghdaily.ir/News/78788.

Figure 7.1 Automatic Syringe, Condom Distributor, Harandi Park

the complex situation of drug addiction in this area. Philanthropic endeavours practiced, in the words reported by a piece on *Sharq*, 'addict-nurturing [*mo'tadparvari*]'.[81] A public official cynically suggested that

[81] Ibid.

the provision of food might well be a stratagem used by providers of addiction treatment (e.g. Article 15 camps) to attract people towards their facilities and, incidentally, attract public funding towards their organisations.

Although complaints against insecurity and unsafety were rife among residents of this neighbourhood, Harandi Park had by then become a spotlight for national drug policy and a site of confrontation of competing governmentalities regarding illicit drugs. On October 9, 2015, I was invited to attend the 'First Marathon of Recovered Female Drug Addicts' organised by the House of Sun (*khaneh-ye khorshid*), an event which would take place, deliberately, across the four parks of Harandi, Razi, Baharan and Shush. On the edge of Harandi Park's southern corner, the House of Sun has been active for over two decades in providing free-of-charge services and support to female drug (ab) users and those women seeking refuge. A large crowd of women (and some men) attended the opening ceremony of the marathon and waited for the start of this seemingly sporting event. Two female players of the Iranian national football team led a collective session of gymnastic activities, a way to symbolically recover the body of the park from the sight of widespread drug consumption and destitution. Truth be told, the event revealed itself to be not a marathon – not even close – but rather a public demonstration that brought more than a thousand women and their sympathetic supporters to march inside the park and in the middle of the gathering of mostly male drug users (Figure 7.2). The term 'marathon', I thought, was probably used to get around the politicisation of the event in the eye of the municipality then led by Mohammad Baqer Qalibaf, which could have regarded a women-led march against drugs as too sensitive a topic (Figure 7.3).

Many of the women who took part in leading this manifestation had previous experience of life in the park and were acquaintanted with people who were still living and using there. 'Our Iran is paradise! Don't smoke, it's not nice! [*Iran-e ma beheshté, dud nakonid ke zeshté*]', was among the slogans that were chanted; prayers for the souls of the drug addicts were interludes between the chants and on the sides of the march, many of these women would approach people laying on the grass trying to connect with them and dissuade them from using drugs. A man, I witnessed, approached an older women and pathetically begged her to stop chanting against drug users, 'because

Figure 7.2 'Every day 8 addict die in Iran'
A man says, 'I don't know why we have always to be near-extinction so that they decide to do something.' Received via Telegram App, 'The Challenges of Addiction.'

we are feeling ashamed and embarrassed in front of you'; others would cover their face or shout aggressively against the voyeuristic lens of the many photographers attending the event (Figures 7.4 and 7.5).

The event resonated loudly within the drug policy community, but it also manifested some of the profound changes that Iranian society had

A Site of Disorder: Harandi Park 221

Figure 7.3 Members of the National Football Team

experienced over the course of the 2010s. Women who had a history of drug abuse openly participated in the event, without hiding their immoral past and marched in the parks where they once spent their drug habit. In doing so, they also addressed drug users in the park

Figure 7.4 Marathon March, Tehran

directly and invited them to give up. The associations that participated in this manifestation were not the traditional anti-drug campaigners, but an array of harm reduction groups, users-led organisations and groups of people who had a history of drug use and were open about discussing addiction as a social dilemma. Some public officials attended the event, but, overall, it was mostly associations, grassroots groups, a few members of international organisations and social workers and activists. Leila Arshad (aka Lily), the main organiser of the event and

A Site of Disorder: Harandi Park 223

Figure 7.5 'Give Me Your Hands, so We Can Walk in the Path of Purity'

director of the House of Sun, had long been working in this neighbourhood.⁸² While those attending the marathon had gathered in the courtyard of the NGO, she held the microphone and said, 'one of our objectives is to catch the attention of the public officials and people towards your problems [recovered female drug abusers]: lack of employment, absent housing, insurance and treatment, respect and social inclusion'.⁸³ Some of the volunteers catering the event were employees and volunteers of *Doctor without Borders* (MSF), which runs, among other things, a mobile clinic with outreach services in the area.

A few weeks following the marathon, a group of thirty or forty men raided the informal camping in Harandi Park, set fire to several tents and attacked a number of street drug users with sticks and clubs. The municipality declared that the attack was perpetrated 'by the

---

[82] She has also worked with award-winning Iranian film director Rakhshan Bani Etemad.
[83] I recorded the speech, which was also retrieved from www.entekhab.ir/fa/news/229385.

people', denying any state responsibility of the authorities. Others hinted at the lack of responsiveness of the police.[84] Harandi Park, for that matter, embodied a most explicit case of the art of managing disorder in the Islamic Republic. In 2018, the municipality opted to develop the camp into a sporting area and fenced all its surroundings.

Conclusions: The Art of Managing Disorder

There is no fundamental rupture, or watershed, between the state-run compulsory camps (*kamp-e maddeh-ye 16*) and the informal, illegal camps (*kamp-e gheyr-e mojar*), or the 'Harandi model'. Both fulfil an ultimately political prerogative in reaction to a phenomenon that has permanently been framed as a crisis. Because of that, the camps enter a field of interest to the state – one could say an expediency (*Interregum*) – in which the underlying rule is political management of risk, emergency, disorder and crisis. It is not, as one would expect in the Islamic Republic, a matter of moral evaluation, religious justification or variation in (post)Islamist change.

The art of managing disorder defines the governmental approach to the (drug) crisis. This art operates at the level of fabrication, make-believe and of practice, confuting the notional existence of law and the state, as seen in the case of the camps. In intervening on the phenomenon of drug (ab)use, the post-reformist state defined its *modus operandi* as one based on secular pillars of management. It did not thwart harm reduction practices, per se, or out of religious, moral opposition. It actually adopted the language of harm reduction, it scaled up its less contentious services (i.e. methadone and rehab camps) and, at the same time, it brought about institutionalisation of the agents under the umbrella of the state. While the state financed a significant bulk of harm reduction programmes, through the DHCQ, the police proceeded towards a securitisation of disorderly groups, based on a form of imprisonment, by other means. These means were constituted by the compulsory treatment camps, whose objective has been not to treat or reduce the harm of drug use as such, but of managing the disorderly presence of risky groups – i.e. homeless, vagrant, poorer drug users – in the public space. This process,

[84] See *Etemad-e Melli*, November 11, 2015, retrieved from http://etemadmelli.com/?p=2121.

Conclusions: The Art of Managing Disorder 225

on the one hand, secured a key role for the state under the guise of the 'therapeutic police', while, on the other, allowed a drastic intervention on those categories perceived as disorderly and, indeed, pathological.

The multitude of illegal treatment camps hints, instead, at another statist rationale. The state provides licences for these camps through the Welfare Organisation, but in order to do so, the government needs to guarantee minimum financial support, which, given the large number of these centres, would drain the budget from other treatment programmes, notably the compulsory treatment camps. 'The closure of the illegal treatment camps is not part of the main policy of the state', declared a public official in a conference, adding that 'the existence of these camps is better than their non-existence, because their closure would mean disorder [*bi-samani*, also 'instability', 'chaos'] among the dangerous addicts'.[85] In view of their indirect connection to the police, which sees them as a useful complement *vis-à-vis* problematic drug users, these institutions are part of the state effect. Despite their private and unrecognised status, they perform a public, state-sanctioned role (Table 7.1).

In doing so, camp owners and managers do not benefit, at least in most cases, from a particularly lucrative business. As confirmed both by ethnographic data and by interviews, they do not display middle class lifestyles and they mostly belong to the working class, underprivileged strata of the populace. Their income, as their status, is unstable, insecure, and exposed to several risks, including that of being closed down abruptly, or facing criminal charges for mistreatment or torture. Hence, the camps operate in an 'in-between zone', where they neither have actual leverage on the political mechanism of drug policy, nor do they profit from economic returns. Instead, they parallel the market of drugs with a market – which is equally illegal, yet tolerated – of treatment and recovery.

'The condition of crime *is suspended* for the addicts who seek help from recognised institutions' reads Article 15 of the 2010 drug law. This sentence is ambiguous under many points. First, what does 'seeking help' mean? In the Iranian legislation, it seems to signify either detoxification ('cold turkey') in private camps or registration to a methadone programme. Seeking help in the form of clean syringes or medical and psychological assistance of various kinds does not guarantee the *suspension of the law*, even in sites of disorder like

---

[85] *Jam-e Jam*, December 19, 2010

Table 7.1 *Public, Private and Illegal Camps*

	State-run	Private	Illegal
Legal status	Legislated under Article 16 of the 2010 drug law.	Legislated under Article 15 of the 2010 drug law.	Illegal.
Management	Managed by the NAJA, with support from Welfare Organisation, Ministry of Health.	Manage by private organisations, charities, associations, etc.	Managed by private individuals, or group of people.
Funding	Receive direct state funding, through DCHQ.	No direct funding from the state. Fees are applied for treatment periods of ca. 21 days. Donations from families. Subsidies from DCHQ per treated addict.	No subsidies or governmental funding. Fees apply per person, mostly in the form of donations and contributions.
Personnel	Social workers, policemen, medical professionals (e.g. psychologist, psychiatrist, epidemiologist). *De facto*, limited specialist support.	Former drug users; *NA* members; social workers and volunteers.	Former drug users and, allegedly, current users.
Methods	Detoxification; in some facilities, methadone substitution is provided. *NA* support is usually available.	Detoxification, mostly based on *NA* twelve steps; some organisations adopt specific therapies, e.g. music-therapy, meditation.	Detoxification Use of physical force and violence to deter people from using drugs is reported.

Target group	Street drug users; homeless drug users; poor, marginal people. *Patoqs*. Polydrug users.	Depends on the organisation; mostly, lower-middle class drug users, both urban and rural. In specific cases, upper-class people. All drugs.	Poor drug users, young people, men under psychotic attacks; mostly *shisheh* and polydrug users.
Means of referral	Arrests. Police operations, drug addicts collection plans (*tarh-e jam'avari*). Coercive.	Voluntary referral, through advertisement and word of mouth.	Family referral, community referral; police referral. Mostly coercive.
Fees	Free.	Set fees, often negotiated.	Flexible fees, based on individual status, negotiation, need.

Harandi Park, where the suspension is aleatory. Therefore, drug users who do not want to substitute their drug of choice with a legal substitute, e.g. methadone, or do not agree – or cannot afford – to go through rehabilitation in a private camp, are not protected by the law. They are relegated, ultimately, to an institutionalised exception exemplified by a state-run compulsory camp, an illegal camp or the public space. This 'suspension' lands the addict in a zone of 'exception'. The exception is a paradigm of government of the drug crisis, which allows the coexistence of otherwise inconsistent and incompatible visions and interventions, as exemplified by the idiosyncrasies of Article 15 and Article 16 of the 2010 law. This cacophony within a single law and between the text of the law and its execution, lays, on the one hand, in the formal, *de jure*, insolubility of different *governmentality* within the state, while, on the other hand, it embodies an instrumental approach in the establishment of multiple, discontinuous responses under the art of governing crisis and managing disorder.

As in Giorgio Agamben's *State of Exception*, this condition produces a 'no-man's land between public law and political fact, and between juridical order and life' and it 'appears as the legal form of what cannot have legal form'.[86] It is, in other words, an oxymoronic form of politics. To corroborate this analysis, Agamben adds:

> the state of exception proceeds by establishing within the body of the law a series of caesurae and divisions whose ends do not quite meet, but which, by means of their articulation and opposition, allow the machine of law to function.[87]

While categorising as criminal the multitude of drug (ab)users who do not agree to intern in a camp or substitute their drug of choice with methadone, the governmental machine has preserved its ability to 'manage the disorder', or to politically employ the crisis posed by massive drug (ab) use. The result is a paradigm of government – *the art of managing disorder* – that deals with the crisis without solving it, and therefore reconfigures the *locus* of harm reduction, in this case, by incorporating it in a grey area of state control/repression. Thus, the 'caesurae' and 'divisions' of the 2010 law, instead of undermining the machinery of drug laws, make it actually function, as demonstrated in the coterminous

---

[86] Agamben, *State of Exception* (University of Chicago Press, 2005), 1.
[87] Ibid., 35.

Conclusions: The Art of Managing Disorder

implementation of Article 15 and Article 16. This mixture of policies allows the machine of the Iranian state to function.

The role of the police is absolute in this frame; whereas one can locate the text of the law and the policies with regard to drug (ab)use, the function of the police is indeterminable and discretionary. The police is the governmental machine that enacts and reproduces the drug control in praxis and, because decisions on the political dimension of the 'problem' belong to the sphere of government and justice, the police acts only and exclusively on the effects of the drug problem, for instance, in the identification of temporary risky groups, or in the clearing of disorderly presences from the public space. This coexistence between insoluble, albeit instrumental to each other, ideological traits, justifies the praxis of the law – the political machinery operating on the ground. Being the administrative and enforcement tool of the politico-judicial machine, the police works on the contentious ground between what is formalised de jure and what materialises de facto. This ground is the grey zone where the rights of the drug (ab) user are at the same time enounced and violated, therefore entering the realm of an institutionalised exception, for instance, in the compulsory treatment camps, or that of a state of exception, in the illegal camps.

In this context, the status of the addict – the individual who can be object of welfare support and at the same time of criminalisation, i.e. the *mojrem-e bimar* ('patient criminal') – is exemplified by the paradigm of Agamben's *homo sacer* – the person whose right to life cannot be legitimately taken, but who is contemporaneously excluded from ordinary law.[88] The legal status of the addict, within the current regime of drug control, is one of naked life, whose civil/political dimension is questioned and relegated to a grey area. Naked life is life stripped of rights. The denouement of the addicts' rights produces political control over their life, making them a subject at the mercy of politico-juridical control, and an element in the political economy of treatment (e.g. state-run camps). Protection and punishment are two overlapping ends in the social body of the addict. A manager of a state-run clinic uses these apt words to corroborate this argument:

---

[88] *Homo Sacer: Il Potere Sovrano E La Nuda Vita* (1995), 114–15. Here Agamben refers to the notion of *homo sacer* as the figure that blurs the demarcation between biological life (*bios*) and naked life (*zoë*).

Those who are in the camps are in the middle between criminal and patient. They have not been accused of any crime. From a legal point of view, they have not committed a crime, ... there is no legal judgement [*mahkumiyat*], usually there is a complaint [*shekayat*] about bad behaviour [*bad raftari*].[89]

The informal nature of the 'complaint' produces the informal response of the illegal camps or, more rarely, that of the state-run camps. In both cases, the person who is being 'treated' enters a field of informality and ambiguity, as neither bureaucratic nor juridical procedures are in place. Indeed, despite the law envisioning a criminal charge against an addict who is re-arrested after a period in a compulsory camp, the police regularly refer people to the camps who had paid dozens of visit to these centres, amazingly without having a criminal record.[90] The dossier, *alas!*, is missing.

In the conference that opened this chapter, a presenter, much to the astonishment of the audience, remarked:

I have the feeling *we are crying on a grave which is empty*.[91] How many people, arrested for drug addiction and sent to compulsory camps, have actually been in front of a judge? And [if this has happened] had the judge said anything to them about treatment? I doubt that we can find ten people in the whole country who have met a judge before going to a camp, so I think the question here is something else and it is not related to compulsory treatment ... The problem, it seems to me, is that the question is not medical and therapeutic, but one of social and political control.

The lack of judicial supervision and bureaucratic mechanisms is inherent to the state's management of disorder and crisis. It is not a by-product of a lack of administrative capacity or clashing institutional interests. This coexistence of criminalisation of drug use and tolerance of the crime stems from a discretionary practice of the law. It epitomises the 'force of the law' in conditions otherwise unlawful. In practical terms, this makes the agenda of police officers and their immediate superiors the 'single most important element' in the application of the drug laws.[92]

[89] Interview with Solhi, February 2014.
[90] Ethnographic notes in the *patoq* of Farahzad, March-April 2014. See also *Jam-e Jam*, December 19, 2010.
[91] A Persian proverb meaning: *don't count your chickens before are they hatched.*
[92] A situation similar to the 'British Compromise'. See Mills, *Cannabis Nation*, 185.

Conclusions: The Art of Managing Disorder

The force of the law applies materially against those more exposed in the ecology of the police: the street, parks and the public place. In this regard, the art of managing disorder applies more blatantly to the poor, the homeless, the street addict, the sex worker, while those who preserve their drug use in the private sphere do not face the force of the law. Public addiction becomes being addicted in public: homeless people are badly dressed, dirty, in other words, are living at a *street level*, exposed to the public gaze of the police. At this point, drugs are not the real problem. The addict in the guise of social marginalisation, moral unsettledness and class subordination incarnates the problem.

To conclude, one can infer that the framing among many public officials that addiction is a problem without solution – especially in the case of *shisheh* for which a substitute drug had not been viable – compelled the authorities to intervene through new techniques of political management. The compulsory state camps, *in tandem* with the illegal camps, have produced this governmentality. Emran Razzaghi defines the camps the number i of Iran's drug policy equation: 'an imaginary number that we bring in and take away later; ... they don't have a meaning in themselves but they contribute to the change of the equation'.[93] In this, they represent a primary means in the art of managing disorder of the drug phenomenon. They also confirm, together with Agamben, that 'the true problem, the central mystery [*arcano*] of politics is not sovereignty, but government; it is not God, but the angel; it is not the King, but the minister; it is not the law, but the police – that is, the governmental machinery that they form and keep moving'.[94]

Instead of the God-like state of the Islamic Republic, with its, *prima facie*, religiously inspired laws, I attempted to study the minister, the practices of the laws as much as the rhizomes of the state, all of which, I realise, form the governmental machinery of the Iranian republic.

---

[93] Interview with Razzaghi, September 2012.   [94] Agamben, *Il Regno*, 303.

8 | *Drugs and Populism: Ahmadinejad and Grassroots Authoritarianism*

> The Ahmadinejad government has nine crises every day of government.
>
> *Fararu*, August 1, 2009.

Introduction

If the reformist period was one of 'one crisis every nine days of government', the post-reformist years characterised themselves for a permanent state of crisis, a status well captured by the expression 'nine crises every day of government'.[1] Crisis was critical to the formation of Mahmud Ahmadinejad's vision of governance in policy and polity. Crisis remained central after Ahmadinejad, too, reigning over Hassan Rouhani's period in power. Among these multiple crises, one can mention the following, in escalating order: the football, wrestling and judo federation crises (2012–17); the aviation maintenance crisis (2006–18); the automobile manufacturing crisis (2011); the House of Cinema crisis (2014–15); the housing bubble crisis (2010s); the market recession crisis; the inflation crisis (*passim*); the hydrogeological crisis (in the example of Lake Urmia, 2010–19); the Kahrizak prison crisis (2009); the 2009 election crisis; and, *ça va sans dire*, the nuclear crisis (2006–?).[2]

---

[1] *Fararu*, August 1, 2009, retrieved from http://fararu.com/fa/news/28972.
[2] *The Guardian*, July 15, 2009, available at www.theguardian.com/world/2009/jul/15/iran-plane-crash; *Al-Monitor*, May 3, 2014, retrieved from www.al-monitor.com/pulse/originals/2014/05/iran-water-crisis.html; *The Guardian*, July 2, 2010, retrieved from www.theguardian.com/commentisfree/2010/jul/02/iran-kahrizak-detention-centre; *RFERL*, January 4, 2012, retrieved from www.rferl.org/content/iran_shuts_down_house_of_cinema/24442278.html; *Washington Post*, October 5, 2012, retrieved from www.washingtonpost.com/world/national-security/food-prices-inflation-rise-sharply-in-iran/2012/10/04/44521436-0e69-11e2-bb5e-492c0d30bff6_story.html.

Introduction

The sanction regime imposed on Iran added pressure on a situation that was already deemed critical, contributing to the perception among Iranians and their political leaders, of a permanent crisis haunting the country. The first round of nuclear-related sanctions took place in 2006, when the United Nations Security Council (UNSC-1696) agreed to impose restrictive measures on Iran's nuclear enrichment programmes. In 2010 and 2012, a second and third round of sanctions began with UNSC-1929 and was further tightened with the sanction regime imposed by the United States under Barack Obama, closely followed by the European Union. Following Donal Trump's election, the United States withdrew from the Joint Comprehensive Plan of Action (JCPOA, aka in Iran as *BARJAM*) and in 2018 implemented a set of sanctions against the Iranian economy. The Islamic Republic's isolation caused by unilateral US sanctions coupled the crises ongoing at the domestic level.

On top of all these, the drug phenomenon entered into a new dimension, one that the state had not foreseen and found difficult to deal with. The changing nature of drug (ab)use – the phenomenon of *shisheh* – buttressed the formation of a crisis that had been a feature of the reformist period, as described in Chapters 4 and 6.

The dynamics of post-reformist society characterised by the use of new stimulant drugs and non-traditional sexual norms, situated the post-reformist government in a paradoxical situation. The outcome of this situation was expected to be a reaction based on normativity and condemnation of new societal trends, followed by a reversal of the progressive policies, such as the controversial harm reduction legislation. Contrary to expectations, however, the Ahmadinejad government did not reverse the trend in favour of harm reduction and it generally continued the process of expansion of civil engagement in the field of drug policy. It scaled up progressive policies on addiction into a nationwide project. In view of the threat of *shisheh*, state representatives stressed the need to make distinctions between different substances, pointing out that the institutions should encourage shifting to less harmful drugs, such as opium.[3] High-ranking officials reiterated that 'the management of the drug market has to be in control of the *nezam* [political order]', and that the destruction of the poppy farms – successfully implemented in the 1980s – had been a strategic mistake.[4] From the second half of the 2000s onwards, officials included in their public agenda the reintroduction of poppy cultivation and other

---

[3] *Iran*, May 12, 2007.   [4] *Aftab-e Yazd*, September 4, 2006.

drastic reforms in the field of illicit drugs, including regulation of drug consumption.

Under Ahmadinejad, drug consumption underwent further changes. The average age of drug use dangerously decreased; more women were using hard drugs than ever before; traditional drugs were supplanted by domestically produced synthetic drugs, while the government spent considerable financial resources on drug control programmes. By 2012, according to a public survey, only 7 per cent of Iranians believed the government have been effective in dealing with the drug problem, which for 87 per cent represented the country's main social problem.[5] Surveys revealed that people considered the police the worst-performing institutions in the 'War on Drugs'.[6] This was despite the LEAs having arrested, over the course of three decades, more than 3.9 million people for drug crimes.[7] The compound effect of these data and the public impact of *shisheh* narratives (re)produced a crisis, similar to the one which characterised the initial years of the reformist government at the end of 1990s, with the HIV 'epidemic'. However, the response of the Ahmadinejad government differed substantially from that of Khatami's reformism, highlighting their diverging paradigms of government as illustrated in the previous chapter. In line with the style of president Ahmadinejad, the government maintained a populist approach towards drug policy, often circumscribed by an aura of secrecy and bombastic promises. In the occasion of a drug-burning ceremony, president Ahmadinejad declared 'the problem of drugs is not only a cultural, social and economic, but it is an important political problem', adding that only 'the reform [*eslah*] of the governance system of the world [*nezam-e hakem bar jahan*]' could uproot the drug problem.[8] Unlike his reformist predecessor, Ahmadinejad engaged in individual and collective meetings with recovered drug addicts, listening to their requests and recriminations. During a gathering in Tehran's Azadi Stadium, Ahmadinejad, in front of 20,000 former drug users, said, 'Ahmadinejad [referring to himself], like your younger brother, stands beside you in trying to solve your problems; the government is honoured to be on your side and on the side of your recovery'.[9] Significantly, the president's reference to himself (and the government) as the younger brother was symptomatic of the vision that the post-

---

[5] *Sharq*, September 24, 2012. *Mardomsalari*, September 16, 2010.
[6] *Etemad*, April 12, 2010.   [7] *Aftab-e Yazd*, September 4, 2006.
[8] *Keyhan*, June 27, 2007.   [9] *Jam-e Jam*, June 27, 2011.

reformist state had with regard to its role in addiction recovery and treatment. While many of the promises remained unfulfilled (e.g. priority for recovered addicts in employment), his call to adopt 'new strategies and approaches of fighting drugs', was the prelude to the rise of a new mode of governance, one that defied both harm reduction and prohibition alike.[10] The government played the role of the younger brother, who seeks advise from its civilian counterpart, civil society, the older brother. It acted through a modality of indirect government of the crisis. As seen in the previous Chapter, the principle modality of intervention in the post-reformist time was embodied by the art of managing disorder.

This chapter elucidates the practices born of the post-reformist moment. While in the previous chapter I discussed the on-the-ground mechanisms of management made up of informal and clandestine elements, in this section I engage with the way government and civil society cooperate in drugs politics. Here, I systematically consider the strategies of intervention within the broader scheme of the government's approach to illicit drugs. This is produced by the institutionalisation of methadone clinics and the governmentalisation of NGOs operating in the field of addiction. Neither belong to the institutional realm of the state, but function through state subsidies, supervision and collaboration, hence materialising 'twilight institutions' and parastate formations. The aim is not only to illustrate how the reformist-supported policy of harm reduction metamorphosed under post-reformism, but also to connect the daily operations of public and private institutions within the broader framework of state formation and interactions between state and social phenomena.

'A National Question, Not a Governmental Duty'

Withdrawal from formerly state-prerogative fields and the appeal for massive privatisation of non-key public assets were two key features of this era. The Constitution of the Islamic Republic, under article 44, allows privatisation of public assets, a plan that had occurred in several instances in the post-war period. Iran's highest juridical and executive authority, Ali Khamenei, decreed in 2006 that '80 per cent of the public sector should be privatized'.[11] Under Ahmadinejad, about 90.5 per cent

---

[10] Ibid. *Keyhan*, June 27, 2007.
[11] Kevan Harris, 'The Rise of the Subcontractor State: Politics of Pseudo-Privatization in the Islamic Republic of Iran', *International Journal of Middle East Studies* 45, 1 (2013), 46.

■ Public ■ Private

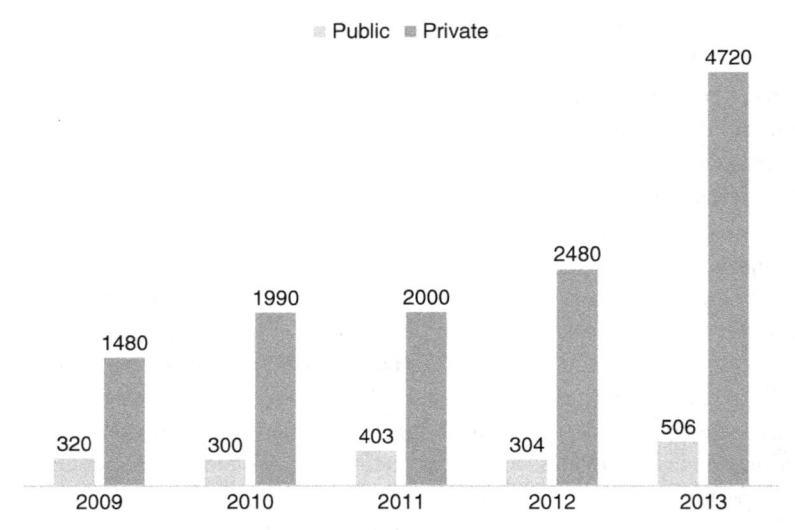

Year	Public	Private
2009	320	1480
2010	300	1990
2011	403	2000
2012	304	2480
2013	506	4720

Figure 8.1 Methadone Clinics (2009–13)
DCHQ, 'Drug control in 2013'.

of the total value of transfers of state enterprise in the post-war period took place, a fact that is revelatory of the extent to which his government sought the lightening of state governmental duties, while promising to bring the oil money to the dining table of the populace.[12] This trend applied even more drastically to those areas of governmental action reputed burdensome and socially problematic, such as drug consumption and drug (ab)use. With the approval of harm reduction policies, the state authorised the creation of private methadone clinics (MMT), where people seeking treatment could initiate a treatment process. Methadone clinics soon became a vibrant phenomenon in the market of medical services, providing a steady source of revenue for medical practitioners, often GPs with no specialisation in addiction recovery (Figure 8.1).[13]

In 2009, there were about 160,000 people registered in private clinics for methadone; in 2014, the number had gone up to almost 570,000 people.[14] This astonishing increase in just a matter of five years explained the high demand for methadone among the population, but spoke also of

---

[12] 'Justice share' (*sahm-e edalat*) is a case.
[13] GPs had to undergo a training session at INCAS.
[14] DCHQ, 'Drug Control in 2009'; and DCHQ, 'Drug Control in 2014'.

a fundamental medicalisation of drug use among the users themselves.[15] Of the country's 5,300 clinics, around 4,900 (95.3 per cent) belong to the private sector (Figures 8.1 and 8.2). More interestingly, while the number of public clinics has remained stable, that of private clinics has multiplied constantly up to 2014, when they allegedly reached saturation level.[16] By 2014, almost 800,000 people were registered under MMT, a figure that ranks among the highest worldwide. Drug (ab)users unable to register in private clinics, were supported through a network of state-run clinics, where the cost of methadone was heavily subsidised. These were usually connected to state-run compulsory camps under the management of the therapeutic police.

The post-reformist state admitted that it needed the private sector to fulfil its governmental duties. In an interview, the deputy director of the DCHQ, Tah Taheri, stated that 'because the government is unable to treat all the people, we rely also on the private sector. In the case of addicts who do not have enough money, we [the state] provide subsidies for them, but if their family, as usual, intervenes, the family pays for the treatment'.[17] The statement confirms that the reliance on the private sector for medical provision in the field of addiction recovery was (and is) a deliberate strategy of the state, complemented by the development of domestic methadone production. Today, Iran is self-sufficient in methadone production (Figures 8.2 and 8.3).[18]

The government's reluctance to expand public treatment was a question of economic calculation. The diatribe about 'addiction insurance' (*bimeh-ye e'tiyad*) elucidates this aspect well. Following approval of harm reduction, public pressure mounted on the provision of insurance on addiction recovery. Often recovering in psychiatric hospitals and clinics, drug (ab)users seeking addiction recovery could not benefit from insurance coverage. Families paid the fees for those patients recovering in mental service centres, despite 'addiction' being acknowledged as a medical condition, 'a pathology', a 'disease'. In response of this situation, the DCHQ director for treatment and social support explained

---

[15] Mohammad Keyvan Ara, Mas'ud Kianush and Mehdi Jianpour, 'Addicts' Experiences about the Medicalisation of Addiction [*Tajarob-e mo'tadan az pezeshki shodan-e'tiyad*]', *Rafah-e Ejtema'i*, 29 (2010).
[16] Interview with Hamid Reza Tahernokhost, March 2013.
[17] *Jam-e Jam*, May 16, 2011.
[18] *Jam-e Jam*, June 30, 2010, retrieved from www1.jamejamonline.ir/newstext2.aspx?newsnum=100942401191.

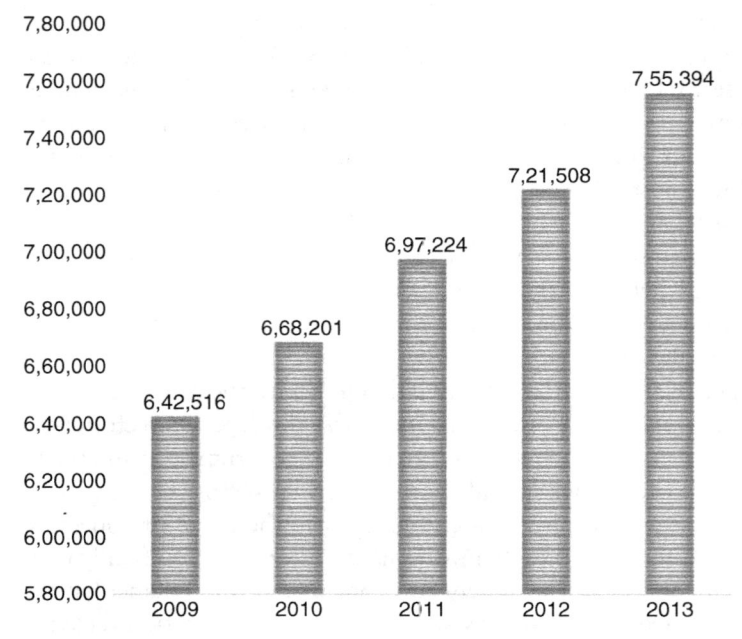

Figure 8.2 Methadone Maintenance Treatment Patients (2009–13) DCHQ, 'Drug control in 2013'.

that medical insurance did not cover addiction, as it involved consumption of illicit substances, and therefore fees could not be covered by public funds. Addiction remained an ambiguous pathology in the state vision; tactically, this implied that the state was not responsible for the financial coverage of costly psychiatric treatment. Given the rising numbers of *shisheh* users, drug policy officials scrupulously considered the likelihood of future 'epidemics' of mental disorder and the rising demand for psychiatric assistance. By 2015, approximately 400,000 people were known to consume methamphetamine, with polydrug use – the combination of different illicit substances – being on the rise.[19] Were the state to insure all drug (ab)users, the real number of Iranian people on drugs would be publicly visible and politically legible. This legibility risked

---

[19] *Jam-e Jam*, May 12, 2013. Again, one has also to bear in mind that the data are not transparent. Despite the *shisheh* 'epidemics', the total number of drug users in Iran remained unchanged according to the government. See *Serat News*, April 20, 2015, retrieved from www.seratnews.ir/fa/news/238533/.

'A National Question, not a Governmental Duty' 239

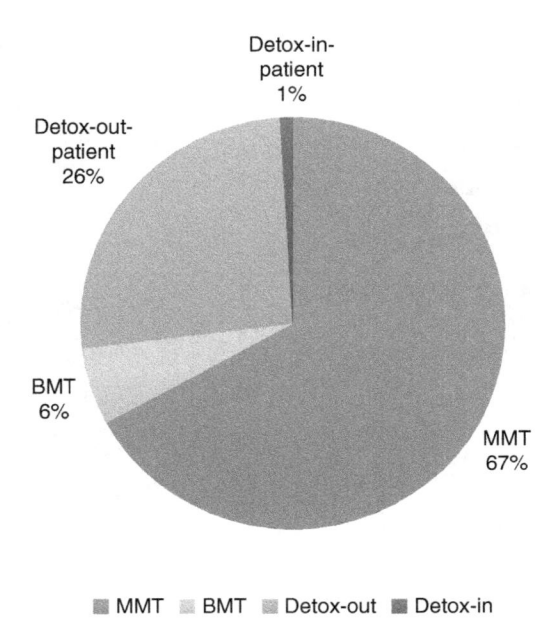

Detox-in-patient 1%
Detox-out-patient 26%
BMT 6%
MMT 67%

■ MMT ■ BMT ■ Detox-out ■ Detox-in

Figure 8.3 Patients in Medical Facilities for 'Drug Abuse' (2013) DCHQ, 'Drug control in 2013'.

undermining the political order and its decade-long attempt at moralising to the public. Covering the data by a thick veil of ambiguity guaranteed economic saving and political gains (Figure 8.4).[20]

One could sum up the post-reformist approach to the issue of drug (ab)use with the words of an Iranian parliament member – and staunch Ahmadinejad supporter – who said, 'the fight against drugs and addiction is not a governmental duty, but a national question [*matalebeh melli*]'.[21] To be successful in the treatment of drug (ab)users, Iran needed 'a social movement [*harekat-e ejtemai*, sic!]', with the government having a 'supervisory duty [*nezarati*]'.[22] The national question regarded *all*: public as well as private, civil society as well as institutions and agents of the state. This was a prelude, it might be argued, to the outsourcing of governmental duties to the private, or pseudo-private, sector. I shall now introduce how the machine of government reacted and what techniques of government unfolded in response to the fluid drug phenomena of the 2010s.

[20] *Aftab-e Yazd*, June 13, 2010.   [21] *Aftab-e Yazd*, June 29, 2010.
[22] *Aftab-e Yazd*, August 13, 2008.

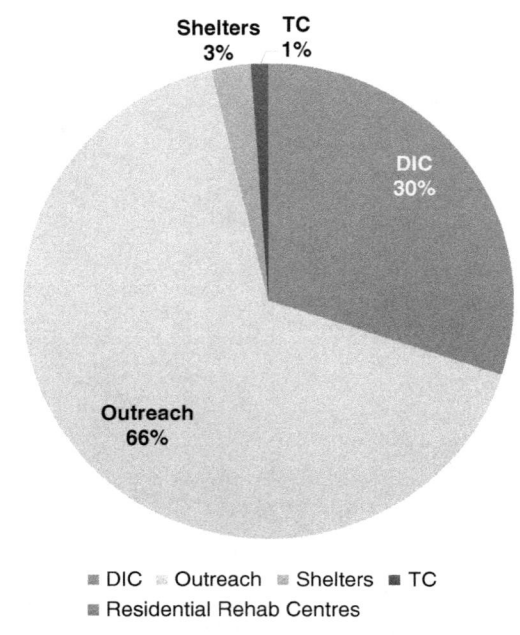

Figure 8.4 Number of People Admitted to Rehab Centres DCHQ, 'Drug control in 2014'.

Harm Reduction Revisited

With the political backing for reform fading away, the new government moved towards a securitisation of social activism, especially those groups supporting reforms on civic issues. In a matter of a few years, most of the key social agents that had supported harm reduction were defused of their reformist clout. In June 2008, Iranian authorities arrested Kamiar and Arash Alaei, the two brothers who piloted the successful Triangular Clinics, on charges against the security of the state. They were accused of cooperating with foreign government to destabilise the Islamic Republic. Bijan Nasirimanesh, who operated the first DICs in Shiraz and Tehran, left the country in early 2009, while the NGO he founded continued to provide services inside Iran. In 2011, Said Madani, author of one of the first books about drug addiction in Iran, was arrested and sentenced to six years in prison and ten years of exile in Bandar Abbas for his political activities related to the Nationalist-Religious

Movement.²³ Thus, the personalities and networks behind the reform were prevented from carrying on their reformist-minded plan in the field of drug policy. Besides, the post-reformist government targeted, systematically, reform-oriented academics and members of the scientific community, when in 2006 it reportedly forced numerous scientists and professors to resign from their post or to accept early retirement. By weakening the academic profile which had been behind the push for innovation and change, the government enhanced its political control and centralisation over drug policy institutions. This did not mean a setback for civil society participation in addiction recovery and drug policy. Although observers considered the coming to power of Ahmadinejad as a direct threat to the progressive harm reduction system, practices of support to drug (ab)users continued and effectively widened their quantitative scope following his election in 2005. By 2007, there were 51 government facilities, 457 private outpatient centres and an additional 26 transition centres.²⁴ By 2009, there were already 1,569 treatment centres, 337 government centres and 1,232 non-government centres, which have been operational throughout the country, providing services to 642,516 persons.²⁵ The fact that harm reduction and addiction recovery had been included in the 2010 text of the General Policies of the Islamic Republic of Iran [*siyasat-ha-ye kolli-ye nezam*], emanated by the Expediency Council and approved directly by the Supreme Leader, surely contributed to this process.²⁶

Drugs politics pursued a discontinuous, unsettled path. During his eight years of government, Ahmadinejad appointed three different directors to the highest post at the DCHQ. First, he selected Fada Hossein Maleki (2005–7), who then moved to occupy the post of special ambassador to Afghanistan, a key anti-narcotics role.²⁷ From 2007 to 2010, the caretaker of the DCHQ was the Commander-in-Chief of the National Police Esma'il Ahmadi-Moghaddam, who also maintained his post as head of the police. After 2010 and up to the end of Ahmadinejad's second mandate, the president appointed his Defence and then Interior Minister Mostafa Najjar (2010–13), who also remained in charge of the ministry during his

---

[23] *BBC Persian*, February 19, 2014, retrieved from www.bbc.co.uk/persian/iran/2014/02/140219_l57_saeed_madani.
[24] Calabrese, 'Iran's War on Drugs'. [25] DCHQ, 'Drug Control in 2009'.
[26] The text of the General Policies is retrieved from http://maslahat.ir/DocLib2/Approved%20Policies/Offered%20General%20Policies.aspx.
[27] Fada Hossein Maleki's official website, retrieved from http://fh-maleki.ir/fa/2015-01-16-17-08-19.html?showall=1&limitstart.

mandate at the DCHQ. Apart from the change in the directorship of the organisation, this period was characterised by a lack of direct political management in the DCHQ. The overlapping duties – as ministers and head of anti-narcotics – of the DCHQ directors meant that the DCHQ suffered from the lack of an independent strategy and scrupulous management. Internal sources to the DCHQ confirm that both the president and DCHQ directors rarely participated in the weekly meetings, leaving the organisation mostly in a state of disarray and decisional confusion.[28] Different officials brought forth conflicting policies, often resulting in an inconsistent puzzle. Loosely speaking, however, Ahmadinejad designed the post-reformist priorities in countering drug and drug (ab)use. Maleki was the exception, but both Ahmadi-Moghaddam and Najjar represented the security-oriented and policing side of drug policy. The former was Mohammad Baqer Qalibaf's successor as NAJA commander; logically, he followed a 'tough on crime' line. Once appointed, Ahmadi-Moghaddam went on reassuring that the entry of the police at the head of the DCHQ did not imply that all prevention programmes will be stopped. His compromise with the medical side of the problem was taken into account, in his view, by appointing as a caretaker of the DCHQ his deputy in the NAJA, who had a previous career as a medical professional.[29]

Another aspect that characterised this period is the attempt at centralisation and de-bureaucratisation of drug policy. With the involvement of the police in the daily affairs (and, hence business) of treatment, the DCHQ tended also to centralise both budget and strategic decision-making in Tehran. The charging of NAJA as supervisor of the DCHQ preluded to a process of centralisation, which was meant to quicken state response to changing drug consumption patterns, while also ensuring implementation of agreed policies. At the same time, there was a general call among state cadres to 'de-bureaucratise' drug policy, as institutional obstacles were considered detrimental to effective policymaking. This approach was positively attuned with Ahmadinejad's management of governmental affairs, exemplifying a political oxymoron. Centralisation meant that the government had the authority to change direction in drug policy – as much as in other fields of interest. It helped the rise of groups and agents aligned with the vision of the ruling cadres. That also enabled

---

[28] *Fars*, August 21, 2013, retrieved from www.farsnews.com/newstext.php?nn=13920529000532.
[29] *Etemad-e Melli*, May 6, 2007.

a faster and controlled privatisation of welfare and social services, outsourcing them to groups that reproduced the ideology of those in power, or those holding political capital. The oxymoron of centralisation and de-bureaucratisation fine-tuned this game.

Soon after his election, the president issued the order to dismantle the highly efficient and reputable Planning and Management Organisation (MPO), and to transfer its duty to the president's office. The move was allegedly justified by the president's call for new thinking about the economy and the budget, a reckless inspiration that left deep traces in the economy and that established a paradigm for other sectors of public policymaking. This was Ahmadinejad's 'revolution in government' moment. Similarly, the DCHQ made clear that 'the fight against drugs, at a regional and provincial level, must proceed regardless of bureaucratic administration'.[30] This statement occurred on May 2007, while Ahmadinejad's decision to dismantle the MPO was finalised in October of that same year, a coincidence implying that centralisation and de-bureaucratisation were two mutual processes during this era. Victims of this trend were scientific and expert groups in matters of drug policy (as well as economic policymaking). The government gained greater room for manoeuvre in budgetary allocation and management, much to the advantage of the NAJA and the DCHQ. The targeting of the scientific community and the 'experts' was part and parcel of Ahmadinejad's government overall anti-intellectualism and mistrust towards transnational academic networks. It also suggests that the politics of drugs went hand in hand with wider political confrontations, usually categorised under the register of *factionalism*.[31] While the reformist government encountered lines of opposition in its push for policy change, the Ahmadinejad government did not face serious institutional challenges, as the Parliament, the Guardian Council and the Supreme Leader's Office expressed sympathy and alignment with the ideology and political persuasion of the new government. Instead, it was intergovernmental infighting that characterised policy implementation during this period. This is evidenced by a set of different issues, such as the contrasting statistics and data that different ministries provided on the number of drug users, the existence, or not, of drug (ab)use among students, the

---

[30] *Iran*, May 12, 2007.
[31] See Mehdi Moslem, *Factional Politics in Post-Khomeini Iran* (Syracuse University Press, 2002).

supervisory authority with regard to rehab camps and, most problematically, the allocation of the budget.[32] With oil prices at unprecedented heights, the budget of the DCHQ had benefitted from state largesse. In 2008, the budget allocated to the DCHQ by the Majles totalled 77,386,200 USD – with a 40 per cent increase compared to 2007 – 45 per cent of which was allocated to supply reduction activities (i.e. policing, intelligence and anti-trafficking).[33] By 2013, the budget had shrunk to 6,768,000,000 tuman (ca. 4.5 million USD) due to a combination of low oil prices and the fall of the Iranian currency.[34] With lower budgetary allocation, internecine criticism surfaced as a trait of the post-reformist period, with NGOs lamenting the lack of governmental funds for their activities.[35]

During the bountiful years, the DCHQ expanded its activities to such different fields as filmmaking, cultural events, sport training and musicotherapy, without much supervision and control, despite the reiterated calls for centralisation. In line with the short-termism of Ahmadinejad's policymaking, the budget was used to renew infrastructures, buy new cars, refurnish the buildings and invest in any sort of social activity, without coherence and objectives. Part of it was dedicated to research projects and the creation of doctoral degrees focused on drug phenomena. While research and scientific investigation were sought to support policy interventions, the content of a considerable number of these academic programmes was limited in scope and methodology, and bounded to a framing of drug issues as exclusively epidemiological or, for that matter, moralising. Abundance of research into aspects of religious exegesis and drug use is one evidence of this; endless epidemiological publications is the other side of the coin.[36] Most of it is listed under the budget of the Ministry of Education that sponsors PhD grants and other types of university research programmes (Table 8.1). By 2014, however, only 3 per cent of all research on drugs and addiction could be said to belong to the social sciences, *sensu lato*, most of which lacked fieldwork engagement and critical analysis.[37] No serious historical,

---

[32] *Aftab-e Yazd*, August 20, 2011; *Etemad-e Melli*, October 2, 2009.
[33] DCHQ, 'Drug Control in 2009'. [34] DCHQ, 'Drug Control in 2014'.
[35] The account is a recurrent theme of my interviews with managers of therapeutic communities and rehab camps.
[36] *Jam-e Jam*, January 5, 2009.
[37] Fieldwork notes 'ASCongress', September 10, 2014. Declaration by head of the DCHQ.

Table 8.1 *Budgetary Allocation (2014)*

INSTITUTIONS	BUDGET (IN MILLION RIALS)
MIN OF HEALTH, TREATMENT, MEDICAL EDUCATION	7,000
WELFARE ORGANISATION	45,000
PRISON ORG	5,000
MIN OF EDUCATION	70,000
MIN OF SCIENCE, AND RESEARCH AND TECH	25,000
MIN OF CULTURE	5,000
BASIJ ORG	13,000
OTHERS	22,000

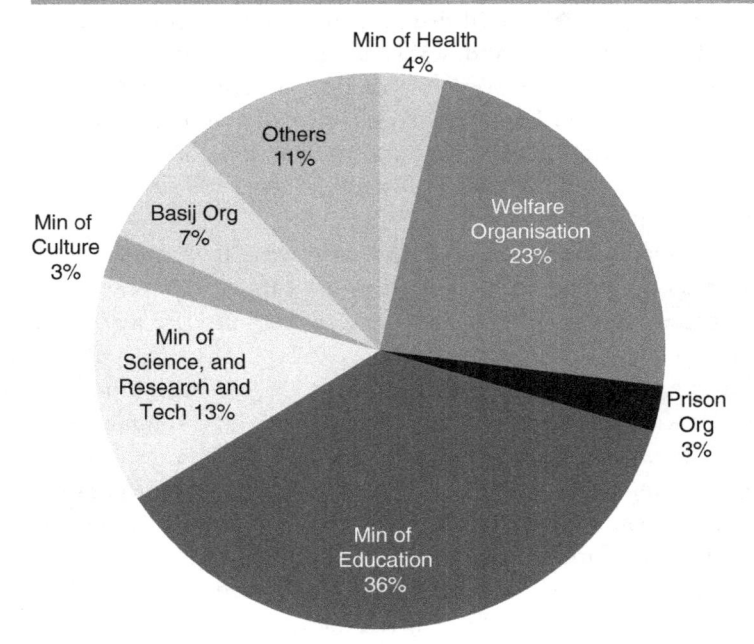

Figure 8.5 Percentage of Drug Control Budget in 2014 (in millions of rials)

sociological and anthropological approach was encouraged over these years.

A case in point about the lack of practical results from investments in research is given by the murky and secretive nature of drug statistics (Figure 8.5). Reiterated calls for transparent numbers about drug use led to the creation of a national committee on addiction data in 2006.[38] Although the authorities had regularly published data on drug confiscation, arrests, people under treatment and numbers of clinics, other categories have been vaguely referred to or left ambiguous. Notably, statistics with regard to drug use among students have been systematically denied by the Ministry of Physical Education and Training, while researchers have referred to this phenomenon on several occasions, prompting a journalist to publish an editorial asking, 'In the end, are there or not addicted students?'[39] Ultimately, the DCHQ clarified that the government had data on youth addiction, but that these data were secret (*mahramane*) and were only available to high-ranking officials. This prompted other officials to argue that up to 30 per cent of the 3.3 million students in Iran were addicted (where 'addicted' meant, vaguely, hard-drug consumption).[40] *Ipso facto*, the creation of research units and statistics taskforces did not lead to significant development of legibility and of in-depth knowledge of the phenomenon. One reason for this is provided by the fact that the DCHQ has only disclosed fragmentary information about its epidemiological studies of drug abuse, allegedly, due to the weak methodology of the study.[41]

When not spent in research, DCHQ money was often mismanaged. In the words of a public official, 'in previous years, in some cases, the money for researches in the field of drugs was even spent for aviculture and fish farming'.[42] Another official explains that 'the Prison Organisation and the Welfare Organisation ... used the money to build services which were not for addicts, but, for example, were used to build other prisons and centres of support, so we decided this time to take control of this budget'.[43] Public criticism and accusation of mismanagement and corruption were in tune with those against the rest of the post-reformist government. New cars, expensive mobile phones, unnecessary gadgets and travels, compelled the director of the DCHQ, in 2007, to make a disclaimer, refuting the idea that many had established about the DCHQ as a 'generous charity organisation'.[44]

[38] *Hamshahri*, June 24, 2006.   [39] *Jam-e Jam*, June 5, 2008.
[40] *Etemad*, August 16, 2009.
[41] Interview with public official in the field of drugs policy, September 2015.
[42] *Mardomsalari*, December 21, 2009.   [43] *Jam-e Jam*, May 16, 2011.
[44] *Aftab-e Yazd*, May 12, 2007.

The Plateau of Ten Thousands NGOs

The lack of a supervisory budgetary system and the negligence of bureaucratic procedures made governmental action in the field of drugs, to say the least, adventurous and haphazard. This does not signify, however, that a strategy did not exist during this period. On the contrary, the strategy for intervention occurred, even systematically, through indirect channels, intermediaries of the state and outsourcing mechanisms. Within few years into Ahmadinejad's presidency, Iranian civil society counted more than ten thousand different NGOs/charities in the field of drug abuse and harm reduction alone.[45] Evidently, the number needs to be anatomised, as its quantitative and face value does not often match its qualitative contribution in practical terms.

The mushrooming of NGOs during this period stemmed from the same logics that determined the privatisation of addiction recovery, notably the methadone clinics. In the same way as medical practitioners opted to run methadone clinics, often with only rudimentary knowledge of drug abuse problems, charities and support groups for addiction recovery were being registered by former drug users and laypeople out of philanthropic, personal or familiar interest in the field of rehabilitation. Many also realised, perspicaciously, that the field of addiction treatment was lucrative. In Iran, most NGOs operating in the field of addiction benefit from some kind of governmental support, however limited it may be. Especially during the first years of the post-reformist government, NGOs benefited from the largesse of the DCHQ; once the generous financial support came to an end following the drop in oil prices in the early 2010s, there were considerable recriminations against the paucity of support and consequent budgetary tightening.[46] Ahmadinejad himself referred to the question of non-state organisations, pledging the government's plan to strengthening the role of NGOs working on addiction recovery, by providing specialised public support.[47] The range of organisations covered anything from public awareness initiatives to needle exchange programmes, family support, post-incarceration assistance and other activities. The methods and philosophy of action among these NGOs differed

---

[45] *BBC Persian*, October 1, 2010, retrieved from www.bbc.co.uk/persian/iran/2010/10/100923_l07_iran89_drugs_addiction.shtml.
[46] *Jam-e Jam*, April 10, 2010.   [47] *Hamshahri*, June 26, 2006.

Figure 8.6 *Congress 60* weekly gathering in Park-e Taleqani

significantly and, in some cases, rivalry between different organisations reached the point of conflict. A rather hilarious case was represented by the banner exposed by a leading NGO, *Congress 60* (Figure 8.6). Out of one of the windows in its central building, which overlooked on the court of a detoxification centre of another NGO, the banner said, 'the addict was not beaten by a snake, so you don't need to detoxify him ['de-poison', *samzodai*]'.[48]

As the number of these organisations does not allow adequate and thoughtful consideration of all, or even some, of them, I shall pay heed to those more paradigmatic (Table 8.2). A unique case is represented by *Narcotics Anonymous* (*Moʻtadan-e Gomnam*, aka NA), whose appearance and spectacular expansion encapsulates the multifaceted trends of post-reformist civil society and governance of addiction.

Narcotics Anonymous: Recovering Spirituality

Based on the frame of its mother organisation in the United States, *Narcotics Anonymous* is an Iranian NGO with numerous centres across all cities and villages of the country, which operates as

---

[48] Interview with Mohsenifar, September 2014.

Table 8.2 *Comparison of Drug Addiction NGOs*

NGO	Activity	Type of Organisation	Main location
Tavalod-e Dobareh (Rebirth)	Detoxification based on 12-steps (NA); prevention; management of treatment facilities; outreach programmes; research publication.	Hierarchical; centralised; pressure group; umbrella organisation.	HQ in Tehran, nationwide.
Congress 60	Drug cessation: based on founder's philosophy. Special process of progressively decreasing drug intake. Cultural, artistic activities and methods.	Centralised; spiritual programmes.	Tehran and main provincial towns.
Narcotics Anonymous	Detoxification; spiritual methods; gatherings; information dissemination.	Grassroots; decentralised; spiritual programmes.	Countrywide; international.
Khaneh-ye Khorshid (The House of Sun)	Women's treatment and harm reduction; support for sex workers, runaway girls, women with drug (ab)use.	Grassroots; first-aid; workshop and capacity building.	Darvaz-e Ghar, South of Tehran.
Aftab Society	Detoxification; information dissemination.	n/a.	Tehran.
Iran Life Quality Improvement Association (ILQIA)	Prevention and education.	n/a.	Tehran, Shahr-e Rey.
Jami'at Hamyaran-e Salamat-e Ravan-e Ejtemaii	Prevention and mental health awareness.	n/a.	Tehran

a self-help group following the philosophy of the twelve-step programme (common also to *Alcoholics Anonymous*). These are accompanied by '12 Traditions', which provide general guideline for the management of NA as a whole and its self-care groups. With its emphasis on God's ultimate power over the individual and its spiritualising commitment to sincerity and mutual support, the group soon found sympathetic minds among the population. By the early 2010s, arguably, every city and many villages had at least one NA group within their districts. Although it is problematic to quantify the membership, NA followers exceeded half a million, and its self-help groups regularly met in prisons, treatment and rehab camps, and often within the meetings and spaces of other NGOs. In 2014, there were about 18,195 weekly NA meetings in Iran, with the capital Tehran also offering English-language meetings.[49] If Iranian society had among the highest numbers of drug (ab)users worldwide, it also had the highest ratio of NA members.[50]

The sheer size of *Narcotics Anonymous* during the post-reformist period endowed it with an especial status *vis-à-vis* the state. At the time of its first appearance in 1994, many regarded the organisation with suspicion. Its founder Foruhar Tashvigi had come in contact with the NA system while living in the USA and, once back in Tehran, faced with friends and family members seeking support for their drug (ab) use, decided to start self-help groups in the capital.[51] These meetings soon developed into larger networks of people and became publicly prominent throughout the country. Despite NA's adamantly non-political nature, the organisation faced backlash from the state. The conservative clergy soon prompted ideological opposition to the rituals and activities of these groups, because of the reference, typical of NA gatherings, to unorthodox spirituality, which was inconsistent with traditional Shi'a theology and eschatology. The accusation of proselytising and staging confessions – a practice which is alien to Islamic practices and may be a derivation of Catholic rituality – were moved against the NGO, which stopped its activities for the public in

---

[49] 'The Needle and the Crescent: The remarkable rise of NA in Iran', *The Fix*, retrieved from www.thefix.com/content/Iran-Narcotics-Anonymous-phonemoneon-Lavitt2099.

[50] This phenomenon alone would deserve ample space, which falls beyond the study presented here. One wonders to what extent NA is part of what, in the Chapter 6, I defined as Iran's 'anthropological mutation'.

[51] Christensen, *Drugs, Deviancy*, 189.

1995. During the early 2000s, *NA* meetings were again permitted; Christensen holds that they 'were modified and were Iranized' to make them more acceptable to the authorities.[52] With its persuasion for pluralistic interpretations of religion, the reformist government facilitated the expansion of *NA* activities, acknowledging their humanistic contribution for those seeking support. The meetings were also a steady relief for recovered drug users to whom the state could hardly provide help.

The Ahmadinejad government did not hamper *NA* activities either. With its priority on prayer, responsibility and aggregation, *Narcotics Anonymous* chartered in friendly waters with the populist, yet highly spiritualising, religiosity of the post-reformist president. Although Ahmadinejad's rhetoric was imbued with Shi'a messianic ecstasy, it was also deliberately folkloric and anti-intellectual in its spontaneity. Alike the prayers of *NA* meetings and the devotion of its members, it defied, ambiguously, the schemes of religious orthodoxy and the clergy. The accusation of proselytising, the use of Catholic-inspired confessions and admissions of guilt – all of which are alien to Islamic doctrine – did not prevent popular and traditional strata of society from joining *NA* meetings, much as Ahmadinejad's religious heterodoxy was not perceived as alien or misplaced by the urban poor and the plebeian masses.[53] All of this had the potential to challenge the clerical authority over divine mediation and spiritual healing.

Personal encounters with *NA* members confirmed the consonance of this organisation with the broader post-reformist (govern)mentality. On several occasions, *NA* members asked me *what I believed in*. To my scepticism and temporising, one member, a fifty-year-old taxi driver, anxiously told me, 'I believe in this *one entity*, which is God [*khoda*], no matter what God; it is *energy* [in English], light and it gives me the strength to be responsible of my work [*mas'ul be karam*]'.[54] Another

---

[52] Ibid.
[53] The most paradigmatic example of this period's religious heterodoxy is represented by Ahmadinejad's cult of the 'Jamkaran well', where allegedly the 'Hidden Imam', Mahdi – the Shi'ite Messiah who will appear at the end of times – had fallen. After the president's example, people had gathered in Jamkaran and dropped their letters inside the well as a way to communicate with the 'Hidden Imam', in disrespect of clerical authority (including Khomeini who never visited the site), which had traditionally been opposed to this cult. Today the site is also popular with Afghan *hazara* visiting or residing in Iran.
[54] A taxi driver, *NA* member, while heading to Tehran Imam Khomeini Airport, September 2014.

explained to a journalist about the steps of his recovery: 'the second step was when I found hope [*omid*] in the only and superior force of the Universe that could help me, which is God ... for the third step, now, I need to be ready to entrust my will to live to this compassionate God'.[55] One element that recurred during my meetings with NA members – whose milieux included working class people such as business holders, women and men alike – was typified by the reference to the philosophy of NA as a comparative advantage in the job market. A rehab camp manager, proud of his NA membership, lamented that 'unlike in the US, where employers prefer *AA* or *NA* members, because they are more reliable and disciplined', Iranian employers 'think that if you are an addict you are helpless'.[56] Self-discipline and group membership were two distinctive traits of NA to which members referred to legitimise their reliability as workers, employees and, ultimately, citizens. There are also episodes in which the NA system, through the personal network that it establishes, facilitates the life of its members, for instance, in finding a job, an accommodation or even a partner. The application of the twelve-step philosophy in the context of the Islamic Republic has given birth to a *melange* of universalising spiritualism with Islamic reference. By teaching, in NA words, 'the spiritual ways [*osul-e ma'navi*] of sincerity [*sedaqat*], optimism [*roushan-bini*], faith [*iman*], positive tendency [*tamayol*] and humility [*forutani*]', it also propagated the proper ethical lines of the post-reformist presidency, in which optimism, faith and humility have been key traits.[57] By the early 2010s, NA meetings were held in sporting centres, *hosseiniyeh* and locations often used for official religious gatherings.[58] None of these has precedents in Iran's history and the language of NA spirituality is highly globalised, with its references bypassing Iran's traditional syncretism. Ist NA nothing but a secular expression of a religious sentiment? Or is it a spiritual profession of Iranian

[55] *Hamshahri*, June 25, 2006.
[56] In a rehab camp belonging to *Tavalod-e Dobareh*, Shahr-e Rey, August 2012.
[57] *Hamshahri*, June 23, 2009.
[58] *Hosseiniyeh* is a traditional gathering site for collective prayers, usually in memory of martyrdom of the third Shi'a Imam, Hossein. An example can be found in the advertisement by the West Azerbaijan regional office of the Prison Organisation, retrieved from www.west-azarprisons.ir/index.php?Module=SMMNewsAgency&SMMOp=View&SMM_CMD=&PageId=2273.

secularity after the demise of the modernist dream, embodied in its fight against addiction?

When the *Narcotics Anonymous* world service in the United States was invited to visit the Iranian branch of *NA*, the amalgam of religious enthusiasm with mass participation astonished the US visitors. During a visit in Qom, Iran's religious capital, a man approached the representative from the US branch and, looking into his eyes, said 'you are my belief'![59] The fact that this vignette occurred in Qom and during a period of high tension in US–Iran relations makes this all the more significant and illustrates the dimension and intensity of the *NA* phenomenon in Iran, one that truly deserves research, the scope of which bypasses this book.

From a governmental perspective, *NA* amalgamated, spontaneously, with the post-reformist push for entrusting social and health programmes to the drug (ab)users themselves, minimising, in one move, both financial expenditure and moral involvement in the pernicious affair of addiction. As a senior member of *NA* recalls, '[since 2005] with the spiritual help of the government, we have been active also outside rehab centres, through our meetings' in parks, buildings, theatres and town halls. The organisation benefited from the reformist government's *spiritual support*, but, based on the *NA* constitution, it could not accept financial aid from outside entities. The entire organisation runs with money from the members and donations from those who benefit from its meetings, a principal reason it is considered less politicised. *NA* distributed 1.7 million information pamphlets about drugs and addiction yearly,[60] a datum that explains the governmental role with which this NGO has been progressively entrusted. In 2013, *Narcotics Anonymous* was voted the top NGO by the government. Based on its status as a non-governmental entity, the prize was received by its sister NGO, *Rebirth* (*Tavalod-e Dobareh*). *NA* representatives take part in meetings of the DCHQ and other policy circles, but not as members of *Narcotics Anonymous*. Their policy branch within the civil society world is *Tavalod-e Dobareh*, 'Rebirth'.

[59] *NA Today*, 'Special edition: The Iranian updates' [aka *The Iran Diaries*], February 2007, retrieved from www.na.org.au/content/natoday/2007/natoday200702.pdf.
[60] Ibid.

Rebirth: Grassroots Authoritarianism and Twilight Institutions

In order to strengthen therapeutic support for drug users, the founder of *NA* Iran created *Tavalod-e Dobareh* in 1999. Since then, *Tavalod-e Dobareh* has provided support to drug (ab)users in the guise of rehab centres, shelters for homeless drug users and counselling services. *Tavalod-e Dobareh* was initially conceived as a sister organisation of *NA*, which followed the twelve-steps philosophy. It did not seek external support and operated through a strictly non-profit vision.[61] With the approval of the harm reduction policy and its scaling up during the post-reformist period, *Tavalod-e Dobareh* progressively established itself as a 'super-NGO', with broad governmental duties and an active presence in the policymaking debate. It became a major beneficiary of public funds in the field of addiction recovery and, for that matter, drug policy. As an NGO, *Tavalod-e Dobareh* has a permanent seat in the Civic Participation Programme of the DCHQ, often providing on-the-ground knowledge about the state of addiction in the country, while also cooperating (and criticising), very much off-the-records, with the NAJA in its programmes of 'therapeutic policing' and 'collection of dangerous addicts' (*tarh-e jam'avari*). Recently, it has also started a vast, long-term programme on addiction studies, which is meant to establish the NGO as a research hub on drug abuse in the MENA region.[62]

In his own words 'a former drug addict with seventeen years of cleanness', Abbas Deylamizadeh is the outspoken and charismatic director of *Tavalod-e Dobareh*, whose appearances on the national TV and interviews with local and foreign newspapers have gained him notoriety in the field and a reputation in policy circles.[63] Abbas, as most colleagues call him, stresses the importance that he gave to 'the organisation's academic output', 'collaboration with joint researches with

---

[61] Christensen, *Drugs, Deviancy*, 189.
[62] *ISNA*, April 27, 2014, retrieved from http://isna.ir/fa/news/93020704452/. *Tavalod-e Dobareh* participated actively in the 8th and 9th International Conference on Addiction Studies in Tehran, presenting several poster studies and research material.
[63] *Sharq*, June 28, 2012 and *Etemad-e Melli*, August 9, 2009. Deylamizadeh was elected Executive Director of the Asian Regional Network on Harm Reduction, retrieved from www.menahra.org/en/menahra-resources/external-publications/437-asian-regional-network-elected-its-chairperson-and-executive-committee-members.

national and foreign academic institutions', 'publishing in reputable and well-known journals'.[64] In one of our meetings, I had the impression, for once, of being in front of a career service panel, or a demanding supervisor, drafting the strategic vision of a research institution. Yet, this drive towards academic production does not simply concern an attempt to build public awareness or to integrate the world of policy with that of research – a mirage called also evidence-based policymaking. Infatuation with the academic world – the director read for a PhD degree in Economic Management in the island of Kish – is a common trait of policy circles where status is buttressed by titles and degrees. Research prestige goes hand in hand with the imperative of securing funding for the NGO and being competitive against other organisations. An academic profile would secure *Tavalod-e Dobareh* a competitive edge over other organisations, given Iran's PhD-obsessed mentality.[65]

What distinguishes this NGO from the multitude of other organisations is not its research drive, but its nationwide structure of intervention with regard to addiction recovery and its complementarity with the post-reformist governmental strategy. With this is mind, *Tavalod-e Dobareh* provides insight into the post-reformist management of the drug phenomenon, highlighting its 'twilight' nature: not a state institution, *Tavalod-e Dobareh* exercises both public authority and governmental duties.[66] The twilight nature of the NGO, however, does not hint at an inherent weakness of the state, as it does for twilight institutions discussed in other regional contexts (e.g. Africa by Christian Lund or the Middle East by Nora Stel). Instead, the twilight nature of *Tavalod-e Dobareh* unfolds how the state retreats from those spaces and situations posing a threat or challenge, or where its interference is unproductive and cumbersome.

'With regard to the economic side of the problem of addiction', Deylamizadeh claimed during a public speech, 'we have to remind one point. Unfortunately our approach is that in order to deal with addiction

---

[64] Interview with Abbas Deylamizadeh, Tehran, March 2014.
[65] *The Guardian*, November 5, 2008, retrieved from www.theguardian.com/world/2008/nov/05/ali-kordan-fake-oxford-degree.
[66] Cf. Christian Lund, 'Twilight Institutions: An Introduction'. *Development and Change* 37, no. 4 (2006); Stel, Nora, 'Languages of Stateness in South Lebanon's Palestinian Gatherings: The PLO's Popular Committees as Twilight Institutions'. *Development and Change* 47, no. 3 (2016): 446–71.

we spend [*hazineh*], while we should invest [*sarmayegozari*]'.⁶⁷ His call for investment into treatment was a timely one. *Tavalod-e Dobareh* manages a large number of rehab camps and has been charged by the government with the provision of services, through DICs and shelters for homeless people. The fact that the director of this organisation speaks a language that policymakers understand – notably the language of numbers and of capital [*sarmaye* in Persian] – has helped *Tavalod-e Dobareh* gain further legitimacy. As quantitative, econometric analysis had helped the acceptance of harm reduction, the use of numbers is instrumental to justify funding requests or to point out an emerging crisis:

> We have a 43% rate of success; it means that during these years, 43% of those who came to our [rehab] camps at the time of dismissal, and after, have preserved their 'cleanness', between two months and six months ... Today 1,825,000 tuman [ca. USD 2400] is spent for one addict per year, and we don't know if this bears results.⁶⁸

Through a mathematical calculation, the director of the NGO attempts to demonstrate that he can provide a successful method to cure a large number of people, while spending less. Where these numbers came from, I must admit, remained vague. Moreover, *Tavalod-e Dobareh* follows the NA philosophy and therefore its treatment facilities do not provide pharmaceutical cures, like methadone, which alone require higher expenditure. In addition, the organisation maniacally keeps track of the number of syringes that it distributes and collects, of condoms it provides during outreach programmes, of leaflets and brochures and meetings.⁶⁹ The effect is startling and enables the NGO to present itself as a highly reliable, technically sound and professionally engaged entity. Another key aspect of the rehab centres managed by the NGO is that these services, per se, function as employment venues for many former drug users. Given the difficulty for many recovering addicts to find a job in Iran's already problematic market, the NGO plays an important part in involving former service-seekers into the management of the facilities, basically 'keeping them busy'.⁷⁰ The creation of employment has been a long overdue task for the

---

⁶⁷ *Hamshahri*, May 20, 2007.   ⁶⁸ Ibid.
⁶⁹ Outreach interventions in Farahzad and Dowlatabad *patoqs*, March and April 2013, September and October 2014, September 2015.
⁷⁰ *Hamshahri*, January 4, 2009.

government, which is conscious of the fact that, without the complex network of NGO centres, many former drug users would remain unemployed, which potentially increases the risk of relapse. Yet, this form of occupation is not faultless. While visiting different centres of *Tavalod-e Dobareh* in Tehran, several lower-ranking members expressed their disaffection with the management as well as payment of stipends. A thirty-year-old female social worker, graduate and mother of two, who was in charge of psychological counselling, criticised the central office, pointing out that NGOs – including *Tavalod-e Dobareh* – have become a mechanism 'for money making [*pulsazi*]'. She also added, 'I am paid 400,000 Tuman [ca. 140$] per month and they don't even want to cover my medical insurance ... After I leave work here, I go and work in a [private] methadone clinic in another part of town, because I need to survive in this city'.[71] Another employee in charge of the kitchen of a DIC in southern Tehran confessed, 'I earn 170,000 tuman [ca. 60$] per month and I spend every single day of the week here in the DIC. I like my kitchen and I like cooking for people, even though I can prepare only *adasi* [lentil soup] with the few things that are left in the cupboard'.[72]

Because resources and support from the central office of *Tavalod-e Dobareh* are limited, the local DICs and rehab camps demand support from the community or from the families of the service-seekers, an endeavour which is made more difficult given the marginal location of these centres and the lack of family relationships among most of the people frequenting them. Indeed, few of the people who help running these centres stay longer than a few months, because the stipends they receive are too meagre. The organisation counts on the fact that many recovered addicts want to take part in the management of the activities and tend to accept little or no pay. Among the three volunteers that I met during a week spent in the Farahzad Shelter, none of them received financial support from the NGO. The shelter, located in one of the so-called risky zones of Tehran, hosted up to fifty homeless drug users every night, most of whom hung out in the nearby *patoq* ('drug den') (Figures 8.7 and 8.8). The three-man team would fulfil multiple duties, including that of outreach team providing clean needles and condoms, collecting used needles, nursing infections and scars and

---

[71] Interview, Southern Tehran, April 2014.
[72] Interview with the cook of a DIC in Southern Tehran, April 2014.

Figure 8.7 Gathering of Drug Users, Farahzad's 'Chehel Pelleh'

referring drug users to rehab and clinics.[73] Apart from physiological cigarette breaks, their work required high alert and great motivation and temper all day long, plus a set of skills in medical intervention that was beyond rudimentary (Figure 8.9).

Working with no money was probably a consequence of the *NA* ecosystem to which *Tavalod-e Dobareh* belonged initially. Having said that, the volunteers' uneasiness with this system was profound, especially when faced with the sophisticated status of the *Tavalod-e Dobareh*'s central office. There, the personnel, most of whom had a history of drug abuse and went through the *NA* path, were given relatively good stipends, vouchers for lunch and transportation, and could benefit from other amenities that are part of the NGO assets.[74] By creating this model of recovery through the work of the NGO itself, *Tavalod-e Dobareh* promotes a vision of life in society aligned with the idea of a careerist individual, who is responsible and, hence, can ascend to professional success. This spirit was very much at the heart of the

---

[73] In Farahzad *patoq*, March 2014.
[74] Discussions with *Tavalod-e Dobareh* employees in Tehran, March 2014.

Grassroots Authoritarianism and Twilight Institutions 259

Figure 8.8 Sanitary Intervention by Outreach Programme

director's solidarity to drug abusers *and* his desire for academic output. But it also unwrapped the ways in which the marketization of drug treatment (even when charitable and non-profit) had materialised during post-reformism. Once again, the drug market engendered a pathological marketization.

The vision behind the expansion of *Tavalod-e Dobareh* is that 'every addict, regardless of his history of use and type of drugs, should enter a camp [*ordugah*] for addiction. Then, we call him/her a path-seeker [*rahju*] ... But if he uses drugs while there, he is immediately sent

Figure 8.9 Outreach Team in Farahzad's '*Chehel Pelleh*'

out!'[75] This vision overlapped with the strategy that the post-reformist government had envisioned about harm reduction. In a way, the rehab camps that this NGO operated complemented the state-run camps, supplementing their organisational and logistical incapacity to address the multitude of drug (ab)users. In order to implement this strategy, *Tavalod-e Dobareh* had formulated a system based on 'half-way houses' (*khane-ha-ye nime-rah*).[76] In these 'houses', the 'path-seekers' find a place to stay after the twenty-eight days of mandatory recovery in the camp; they stay there for up to one year, with other people, making it 'very similar to a student house'. The main objective of these 'houses' is 'to preserve the public space from the recovering addict', who 'cannot get out of the house for the first three months'.[77]

These plans have received support from the government of Mahmud Ahmadinejad, who identified in *Tavalod-e Dobareh*, a model of civil society responsive to (un)civil phenomena. Already in 2004, Ayatollah Khaz'ali, a top cleric sitting in the Assembly of Experts, met with the

---

[75] *Hamshahri*, May 20, 2007.
[76] Its vision is in tune with North American *halfway houses*.
[77] *Hamshahri*, May 20, 2007.

founder of *Tavalod-e Dobareh* to congratulate his efforts, echoing the Khomeinist proverb, 'saving one addict is saving a generation'. In the years that followed, the organisation met and lobbied among a number of prominent clerics, including Khomeini's grandson Hasan, with the intent to gain legitimacy and support within the implementing machinery of drug policy.[78] The creation of a news agency, managed by *Tavalod-e Dobareh,* focused on drugs and addiction also came to play an instrumental role in the public pressure campaign of the NGO. From the late 2013 onwards, the *Addiction News Agency* (ADNA) became the centre of gravity of most information related to public statements and debates around drug policy reform and, although it presented conflicted opinions and different policy perspectives, it operated in order to put pressure on policymakers. In *ADNA*, the drug policy community displays its public face and struggle.[79]

With its nationwide network of centres and a multitude of people willing to engage in its activities, *Tavalod-e Dobareh* had the infrastructure and means to complement the state in an area of intervention which had become troublesome ethically (e.g. harm reduction during post-reformism), and cumbersome economically (e.g. the cost of 'free treatment' for a multitude of people). The NGO covers also harm reduction practices across Tehran and other major cities, providing shelter facilities, mobile clinic centres in Southern Tehran, DICs as well as in-patient and detox venues of all kinds, including for younger people. It operates twelve major centres (both DICs and rehab centres) in Tehran, ten in the province of Shiraz and a dozen more across other regions. Some minor NGOs, which operate at local levels, associate themselves with this umbrella NGO, often with the purpose of increasing their chance to acquire funding, visibility and legitimacy.

But the contribution of *Tavalod-e Dobareh* has gone beyond these calculations. By proposing a vision based on hierarchy, self-management, quantitative results and individual responsibility, without tackling deep-seated political shortcomings, the NGO embodies an authoritarian model at a grassroots level. This model does not necessarily require adherence to 'law and order'. Indeed, this has been opposed by *Tavalod-e Dobareh* rather vehemently. Instead, this model enacts strict rules of inclusion in the community – which is the NGO itself – for

---

[78] Website of *Rebirth*, see www.rebirth.ir.
[79] *Addiction News Agency*, see http://adna.ir/.

those individuals who wish to recover, by redeploying former drug (ab) users as working elements in the daily operations of the NGO. Without providing a path to 'return to normal life', recovered addicts become a self-perpetuating machine in the management of the drug crisis, by supervising rehab camps, participating in outreach programmes, taking care of administrative affairs or cooking meals in a DIC. As a confirmation of this mechanism, the director explained in a letter to the state authorities, that the weakening of harm reduction services in the DICs is problematic because these centres provide employment to the recovered addicts and involve them in social activities.[80]

That *Tavalod-e Dobareh* acquired a governmental role within drugs politics is also confirmed by its collaboration, on a regular basis, with law enforcement units. The 'drug addicts' collection plans' had been a sphere of action in which the expertise and knowledge of the NGO proved critical for the NAJA. *Tavalod-e Dobareh*'s access to the *patoq* (hotspots) gained the NGO the status of especial interlocutor. In fact, one could argue that with its involvement in arrests and referrals to compulsory camps, the NGO has defied the fundamental ethics of harm reduction, which is rooted in the absence of judgement on drug use and opposition to policing methods. Instead, it has operated as a mechanism of grassroots control, with the task of legibility, management of critical phenomenon and facilitator of state intervention. The NGO operates as a rhizome (from the Greek, *mass of roots*) of the state, which, instead of reproducing vertical lines of control and power relations, becomes diffused and horizontal – similar to the roots (rhizomes) of a plant. When societal control is practiced, this is cropped out through the rhizomes that stem from the horizontal roots of the state itself, camouflaged as other forms of intervention, i.e. civil society. For those arguing that post-reformist Iran witnessed increased top-down security, the metaphor of the rhizome is a reminder that power and authority operate through diffused and grassroots lines of production. This form of governance is what I define as the *art of managing disorder* (Figure 8.10).

Among the instances of *Tavalod-e Dobareh*'s collaboration with LEAs, one in particular had resonance among street drug users and the public. In the wake of the important Non-Aligned Movement

---

[80] *Hamshahri*, January 4, 2009.

Figure 8.10 Rhizomes and Grassroots Authoritarianism
Drawing courtesy of Italian artist, Federica di Violante, aka *Fruk*.

Summit (NAM) of Tehran in August 2012, the authorities requested those NGOs operating in the *patoqs* and having knowledge about 'street addicts', to facilitate their collection – i.e. arrests – for the period of the meeting. A week ahead of the event thousands of street drug users, as well as large numbers of homeless vagrants, were gathered and sent to state-run rehab camps to, allegedly, be treated for addiction.[81] The obvious rationale was the cleansing of the city in view of the international meeting, which was expected to rejuvenate the NAM in the post-Arab Spring context, and show the spotless beauty of the capital.

The collaboration with the police goes beyond material support. *Tavalod-e Dobareh* has been discussing the possibility of taking over the management of compulsory camps – currently under the supervision of the NAJA. The NGO pledged to rehabilitate around 60 per cent of the drug abusers if given the chance to operate the facilities, a numerical data which is exponentially higher than the current official 'rate of success'.[82] In this regard, too, the NGO is reminiscent of Ahmadinejad's style of government, both bombastic, fictional and retracing a fundamentally populist governmentality with authoritarian overtones . One can interpret the nature of this super-NGO, through the ambiguous combination of welfare activities with a securitising persuasion. The outcome, it seems, blurs and contaminates the confines and boundaries of what is normatively regarded as the

---

[81] Summer 2012; discussions with drug users in several *patoqs*; confirmed also by *Aftab-e Yazd*, September 19, 2012.
[82] Interview with Deylamizadeh, Tehran, March 2014.

Iranian state, described as a top-down project with grassroots participation, and what is numbered under the constellation of civil society, which is hereby re-enacted as a grassroots model of authoritarianism, and not a panacea enabling democratic transition.

Conclusions

'If we make our drug policy based only on one approach', a state official confessed, 'it is as if we had an economy based only on one product, which means there is a high risk of failing and ending up badly, for which there is no cure or treatment. From this point of view, the duty of the government is to support indirectly the self-help groups and the NGOs'.[83] The post-reformist language of the state has tendentiously emphasised national commitment, as opposed to governmental duty, to fight drugs and to prevent addiction – not in line with the Islamist motto: *'amr bil-ma'ruf wa nahi 'an-il monker*, 'commanding good and forbidding evil'. What materialised, instead, in the field of state intervention was more consonant with practices of neoliberal governance in times of crisis. The coexistence of a moralising rhetoric and securitising gaze, with a push for privatisation and outsourcing, went hand in hand as the post-reformist government sought to ease the burden of a publicly visible and financially cumbersome drug phenomenon. The field of addiction, over this period, increasingly became the turf of private clinics and, along its margins and more problematic populations, of NGOs. In this, it produced a rupture with the past.

The maintenance of a security-oriented approach was deemed necessary but not prevalent in countering drug (ab)use. The security approach (*nezami*), in the words of a prominent drug policy official, was required because 'otherwise addicts are not pressured to give up'. This method, added the official, 'has the objective of building the will [*raghebsazi*] of the addict ... through targeted pressures'.[84] With policing methods overlapping with treatment imperatives and, as in the case of *Tavalod-e Dobareh*, harm reduction practices, the state pressured the marginal groups of drug (ab)users, with the prospect of institutional rehabilitation, or incarceration. While adopting a language of quantification of social phenomena, cost-and-benefit analysis and epidemiological surveys – neglecting societal and politological introspection – the state and prominent NGOs, such as *NA* and

[83] *Qods*, May 4, 2011.   [84] Ibid.

Tavalod-e Dobareh, worked along compatible, intertwining lines. These differed substantially from the ways civil society had engaged with the state – and vice versa – during the reformist period. At that time, mentioning critical phenomena, such as HIV epidemics, played a constructive role in formulating new approaches to drugs and drug (ab)use. Later, in the post-reformist era, the lines of enquiry insisted, on the one hand, on the return to religious-revolutionary orthodoxy as a solution to the multiple, oft-denied, crises. On the other hand, this zeal denoted a variant of neoliberalism, *à la iranienne*, with marketization of private treatment, governmentalisation of (un)civil society and policing of disorderly margins. The contours of state imperatives were drawn, consequently but unsystematically, by the economisation of political interventions, through a combination of medicalisation (through methadone) and harm reduction securitisation, one via clinics, the other via NGOs and charities, managing addiction recovery in the camps.

This art of governing crisis and managing disorder was distinctive to the post-reformist state, whose mechanisms of power did not arise from either strict ideological rules, nor monolith interest groups, but evolved from the confluence of multiple lines of interventions, which had the ultimate objective of containing, dispersing (also topographically) the crises. The performance of this strategy was diffused and propelled through grassroots elements, via rhizomes of authority, which operated in the twilight zone of state/society. In this example, one can find new empirical material for understanding governance under post-reformism. Thus, populism managed the crisis.

Epilogue

Power, Crisis, Drugs

An old man [*shaykh*] said to a prostitute: 'You're drunk!
At every moment you're caught in [a man's] trap'.
She said, 'Oh old man, I am all the things you say;
Are you all the things you show?'

Omar Khayyam cited by Supreme Leader
Ali Khamenei during a public meeting
in Khorasan (October 14, 2012)[1]

At the end, when worst comes to worst, the hypocrite who pretends to be good does less harm than the one who publicly behaves as a sinner.

Don Quijote de la Mancha, *caballero andante*.

Over the course of the last decade, the question around illegal substances and their use and abuse has become central to contemporary politics. It is sufficient to observe the recurrent attempts of parliaments and civil society groups to reform domestic cannabis laws in the Western hemisphere. In June 2018, Canada, following an electoral promise by the liberal-oriented Prime Minister Justin Trudeau, introduced a bill legalising cannabis for consumption and marketization. It is the first instance of a G7 country adopting such regulation nationwide, but there are antecedents on a different scale. Several states in the United States of America had already introduced plans of marketization of cannabis products, while Uruguay, under the government of radical maverick Pepe Mujica, enshrined a historically progressive approach to illegal drugs by establishing a state-led monopoly over cannabis, following decriminalisation of all drug use. European states, too, are discussing – although timidly – the potential for drug policy reform, including the United Kingdom, France and Italy.

---

[1] Khamenei cited the last two verses of Khayyam's poem. His speech explored the importance of responding to social participation and deviance with careful methods rather than hard discipline. See ISNA, October 14, 2012, retrieved from www.isna.ir/news/91072314939.

It is a sign of the times that the debates and the proposals turn around calculation of economic benefits, cannabis embodying in the view of many a bonanza for the ailing, austerity-prone economies of Western capitalist states. With the exception of Uruguay, whose governance of illicit drugs runs against the risks of marketization, most policy models being brought to the table hold the primacy of economic return as a justification. Questions around health, development, rights, and consumption remain contentious, as evidenced by the lack of interest in regulations going beyond cannabis. Heroin, amphetamine-type stimulants (ATS), methamphetamine, and cocaine are excluded from governments' considerations for reform as they represent thornier issues in terms of public ethics, with less appealing economic returns in terms of taxation and marketization. Substances other than cannabis have less appeal among the urban middle class, which, all in all, is only touched by the criminalising force of prohibition in a limited way.

That said, one would expect reformist debates to be the turf of Western, liberal governments. And yet, these same debates have taken place also in the Islamic Republic, a partial demonstration that the Iranian state is in tune with global policy developments (and policy impediments). Not only have reforms of the illicit drug laws been regularly discussed in policy circles, they have also given way to proposals that are more radical and innovative than those currently discussed in the Western hemisphere. Iran having a larger and diverse drug-consuming population, means that reforms of the drug laws have bypassed the question of cannabis. Public officials have openly addressed the need to reform the drug laws in such a way so as to address the multi-layered dimensions of the drug phenomenon. In 2016, an official of the Expediency Council, the body responsible for updating drug laws (as discussed in the *Interregnum*, Chapter 5), provided an outline of reform based on the text of the General Policies of the State (*siasat-ha-ye kolli-ye nezam*), this latter being a text approved directly by Iran's highest political authority, the Supreme Leader. His proposal proposed a holistic approach to the drug phenomena. According to this plan, drastic reforms needed to be carried out if public institutions intended to comply with the disposition of the General Policies of the State, which seek to decrease the number of drug abusers ('addicts') by 25 per cent over the following five years. Given that successive governments have struggled with raising levels of drug consumption since the outset of the 1979 revolution, the policy plan required a structural as well as a discursive shift. Thus, the proposal called for multi-layered governance of illicit drugs, centred around the imperative of *managing drugs* rather than simply *prohibiting them*.

When it reached the Expediency Council, the issue was framed as the necessity to adopt the 'management of all strata of the drug problem'. It highlighted four fields in which management needed to become the governing principle on drugs: managing cultivation, managing production, managing distribution (supply), and managing consumption (demand). Such a plan signifies state-led regulation and control of all matters related to intoxicant drugs. In other words, the state should intervene in the entire cycle of the drug market, from cultivation of crops in the case of the poppy and cannabis; production as in the case for opium and opiates; to distribution through forms of regulation of drug access; to consumption by intervening in the public health dimension of drug use, through already established forms of harm reduction and substitution. Evidently, the implications of the proposal are several: decriminalisation, depenalisation or legalisation of illicit drugs, according to the different circumstances of drug consumption and/or production. That entails a new governance of the drug phenomenon which runs against Iran's four-decade-long (or, rather, century-long) War on Drugs. It would also mean that by changing the legal status of drug consumption, rates of addiction – which often overlap with drug use – would decrease significantly, fulfilling the objectives of the General Polices of the State. A discursive shift would parallel a policy/legal reassessment.

This plan hints at a comprehensive regulation of narcotic and psychoactive drugs, based on laws that set the line of legality and conditions for the use of certain substances. It would represent, in part, the formalisation of current practices of government, such as the limited tolerance of cannabis and opium, and, in part, the instantiation of a new political model for narcotic and psychoactive drugs, based on the historical experience gained in the last hundred years. Conscious of indigenous aspects of drugs history, the proposal is also aware of its agricultural relevance with cannabis and the poppy being established ecotype plants. Connected to the proposal are also the pilot programmes being discussed by municipal authorities in Tehran with regard to the establishment of safe injection rooms (*otagh-e tazrigh*) and the expansion of currently available harm reduction programmes, such as needle and syringe distribution; opiate maintenance and substitution in the form of methadone, buprenorphine and opium syrup out-patient programmes; and the vast ecosystem of addiction recovery, treatment and rehabilitation.

The proposal was publicly addressed in the conference on Addiction Studies in Tehran and was further discussed in semi-public venues connected to the Expediency Council and the Parliament. It was also widely circulated in the media and newspapers, receiving, as one would expect, harsh criticism from different scholars, officials and politicians. Not based on disrupting drug consumption and trafficking through the threat of the law, moralisation, indoctrination and/or forced public health measures, the proposal is among the boldest reforms ever put forth in Iran's already experimental history of drugs policy. Were the plan to enter into force in the near future, it would imply a systemic change in the state–society relations of the Islamic Republic, one that would go further than the drug phenomenon. It would also have far-reaching impact on the regional and international drug environment. Cultivation and production of narcotics would signify a diversion of huge financial resources to the state budget, diverted from the illegal networks from Afghanistan and Pakistan as well as inside Iran. Resources spent for law enforcement and border control would be available for development programmes, especially for those regions where the drug economy has historically represented among the few viable economic activities for the local population, especially in Sistan and Baluchistan. With softer drugs available (e.g. cannabis, hashish and opium), with milder or no adulteration, harder drugs and modes of consumption (e.g. heroin injection, meth smoking) could be curtailed and managed through the public health system. That would effect a redirection of the current health budget towards recovery and health promotion among those affected by the criminalising policies run by former governments. Such policy would touch upon the way the state intervenes on key aspects of everyday citizenship, such as consumption, public intoxication, self-care and pleasure.

Although the approval of the proposal is not imminent, steps have been taken in the direction of drug law reform, starting from one of the thorniest issue, that of the death penalty for drug traffickers. Iran allegedly leads the ranking of death sentence per capita. The great majority (60–75 per cent) of these sentences are based on charges related to large-scale drug trafficking, especially along the borders with Afghanistan and Pakistan.² The international community has mounted pressures against the death penalty for drug offences for decades now; however, officials in Tehran were reluctant to consider a change of terms in national drug laws regarding this matter. Rather than international pressures, it was a domestic debate that propped up changes in the law. With levels of incarceration increasing and drug trafficking prosperous as ever, a cross-cutting agreement emerged among public officials on the need to reform the application of the death penalty. A key discriminating factor in Iran's international standing in human rights, an internal auditing process on the death penalty began by mid 2014, as part of the larger discussion about reform of the drug laws. With the death penalty being discussed as a subfield of drug laws, the debate could take place within the Expediency Council and not, as in other ordinary situations, in the Parliament. The Council, as discussed in this book, has the power to approve laws that go beyond the remit of Islamic Law; its deliberations are not vetoed by the Guardian Council and, therefore, could be in contrast both with Islamic jurisprudence (and the Constitution of the Islamic Republic). The death penalty is, after all, an explicit provision included in the *shari'ah*.

In 2015, Javad Larijani, advisor on human rights to the Judiciary, expressed regret that 'the skyrocketing number of executions for drug charges is bringing some people to question the validity of *qesas* [retributive] law'.³ *Qesas*, which could be translated as 'retaliation in kind' – 'an eye for an eye' – is the retributive law that is used in cases of major crimes as defined by religious jurisprudence. According to *shari'ah* – the Islamic religious law – crimes that qualify for *qesas* are usually considered as a dispute between believers – citizens – but in the case of drug trafficking, it is the state that takes over the role of prosecutor, applying retribution to offenders who are caught dealing drugs multiple times. It is implied that the state accuses the traffickers of 'sowing death' in the social body and that is why repetitive felonies are deemed a capital offence.⁴

Because the death sentence for drug offences is based on *maslahat*, 'expediency', its use is subject to interpretation and if deemed 'not

---

² BBC, July 23, 2015, retrieved from www.bbc.com/news/world-middle-east-33635260.
³ And brother to both the former Head of the Judiciary and current President of the Expediency Council, Sadegh, and Speaker of Parliament, Ali.
⁴ This shift in the application of a traditional category of the Islamic law speaks also about the modernisation of the means of prosecution in the Iranian context.

useful', it can be substituted with other forms of punishment. This echoes the declaration of the former Head of the Judiciary and current President of the Assembly of Experts, Ayatollah Shaikh Mohammad Yazdi, who declared that 'the death penalty for drug crimes is the product of states [*hokumat-ha*], not of religious law [*shar'*]'.[5] The declaration substantiated the way drugs and drugs policy have gone from being a highly moralised and ideological field – as described in this book's narrative on the Islamic Revolution in Chapter 3 – to a secular field of intervention to which, according to the Head of the Expediency Council, religious law should not apply. This transition from the religious terrain to that of political rationales – governed primarily by the state and its social agents – is the underlying narrative that runs along this text.

The question of the death penalty opens up other venues which are relevant in these concluding pages. Acceptance that most of those punished for drug trafficking belong to the poorer, marginalised classes whose economic opportunities are limited to the illegal drug economy has triggered sociological considerations among law makers and enforcers. Drugs being a commodity that increases in value by moving across geographical space and specifically borders, implies that border populations such as the Baluchi minority and the Afghan migrant population have been among the immediate targets of national anti-narcotic strategy. This has kept at bay the top rings of criminal organisations, often based outside Iran (in Afghanistan and Pakistan, or much farther), while exposing individuals and families residing within the remit of Iranian law enforcers to systematic structural violence. Contrary to drug laws in the United States and other Western countries (e.g. France) where drug laws target, for instance, the Afro-American, Latino or Arab population, the Iranian strategy has not identified ethnic and religious minorities as preferred objects of its anti-narcotic strategy. Instead it results from the overlapping of geographic determinism – in the spatial presence of impoverished minorities close to borderlands – and political determinism towards underdeveloped communities over several decades. That has resulted in what seems a selective implementation of the anti-narcotic strategy, with its burden being disproportionally imposed on the social and geographical margins of the Iranian plateau. This claim also holds water in the case of

---

[5] *Sharq*, October 11, 2015, retrieved from http://sharghdaily.ir/News/75647.

those arrested for minor drug offences. It is pauperised, plebeian and proletarian communities residing in the large metropoles that face the criminalising means of drugs laws. Part Two of this book made a case of how drugs politics affects recovery and punishment among impoverished communities.

All these overriding concerns have materialised in the later part of the 2010s and have fuelled what is a vibrant drug policy debate, with repercussions branching throughout political and social life. The revision of the law, however, has encountered obstacles along its way and it is still pending review. It is not Islamic jurisprudence that impedes policy update. One important element in this process is the unpopularity of softening punishment. As elsewhere, the 'tough on crime' and, more so, the 'tough on drugs' is hard to break after decades of anti-narcotic propaganda. Policymakers are aware of this and do not want to be associated with a softer stance on drug trafficking, even though their harsher stance has brought a halt to international funding for anti-narcotics since 2011, after the success of human rights campaigners.[6] Lack of popular support for drug law reform is another facet of what I described in Chapters 7 and 8 as grassroots authoritarianism. The idealised version of civil society leading to a reformist society or to the adoption of an open society, with inherently liberal values, remains a dream with little substance (and that is why it is the dream of scholars who study politics without engaged, ethnographic means). It is grassroots groups, charities and civil society organisations that often adopt and implement drugs prohibition and application of punitive measures against drug (ab)users. Addiction recovery in the treatment camps is a quantitatively important case for this assertion, whereas the ideology and practice of NGOs and charities is another example of how capitalist (or so-called neoliberalism; i.e. marketization, competition, hierarchism) processes work at the heart of society. They do so autonomously from the state policies, but they reproduce lines of interests that are statist, including in the maintenance of tough drug laws and the inclusion of the death penalty for drug offenders. That does not imply that all grassroots groups are authoritarian and regressive; indeed, many organizations lobby for humanitarian and compassionate reforms in drug policy as well as other fields. Yet, they don't necessarily represent the entire picture of what we call 'civil society'.

[6] See Christensen, 'Human Rights and Wrongs'.

The issue of the death penalty has received overwhelming coverage in discussions about Iranian politics and, more selectively, Iran's drug policy. That is right and proper, but the analysis of the drug situation should go far beyond that. For that matter, the issue of the death penalty itself needs a more sophisticated portrayal, which can take into account the global and local dimensions of the drug trade and its geopolitics, including the fact that 80 per cent of the global opium supply travels through Iran towards European countries. Compared to other geographical spaces, such as the Mexican–American border where the cocaine supply is at its most blatant, levels of violence in Iran, including state violence, remain exceptionally low (in Mexico more than 260000 people died in drug violence since Felipe Calderon's election in 2006). Rather than representing an apologia of the anti-narcotic strategy of the Islamic Republic, this datum suggests that scholars and analysts of global drugs politics should open up their interpretative frames. To start with, they should ask one simple question: Why has drug violence, and anti-narcotic violence especially, been much lower in the context of Iran, compared to Mexico, Colombia, Brazil or Afghanistan? A response to the question could open up the comparative dimension of drugs politics, one embedded in geopolitics, state-society and drugs history. It would also help positioning the Iranian case within the global debate on drugs politics, beyond exceptionalist framing focusing on Islamic culture, or authoritarian politics.

Although one should not be over-optimistic about the prospect of smooth and unhindered change in drug laws, the very existence of public debates and the tabling of new proposals signals a historical shift in the multifaceted realities of illicit drugs. Increasingly, those intervening in this terrain agree in dismissing the *war machine* of prison, police and punishment for a *management machine* which operates through an assemblage of health, welfare and consumption. Paradigmatic of this shift could be the onset of safe drug injection rooms in Tehran, a proposal that is being currently examined by governmental officials and for which there are potential prospects of success.

If only for it being a history of great human and political experimentation, drugs politics in Iran is a history of salience. This book tracked this journey from the outset in the early 1900s up to its changing regimes in the 2010s. There is probably no other country in the world with such a fluid and counterintuitive history of drugs as Iran. Yet, the Iranian story is an untold one. Figures E.2 and E.3 sketch the transformation(s) of drug phenomena and the effect of the state on them – *state effect* – in the last century. Long-term processes of modernisation, secularisation, reaction

Power, Crisis, Drugs 277

Figure E.1 Caricature of the Safe Injection Room Proposal
'The Head of the Working Group on Decreasing Addiction [DCHQ]: "Society does not have the capacity of accepting the safe injection room for addicts"'; below, a man, 'Actually the capacity of society is very high. The capacity of this room is low'. Sent by Telegram App, 'Challenges of Addiction', February 2016.

and revolution, combined with the Brechtian 'historical incidents', the politics of drugs can only be understood in light of history and of ethnographic engagement.

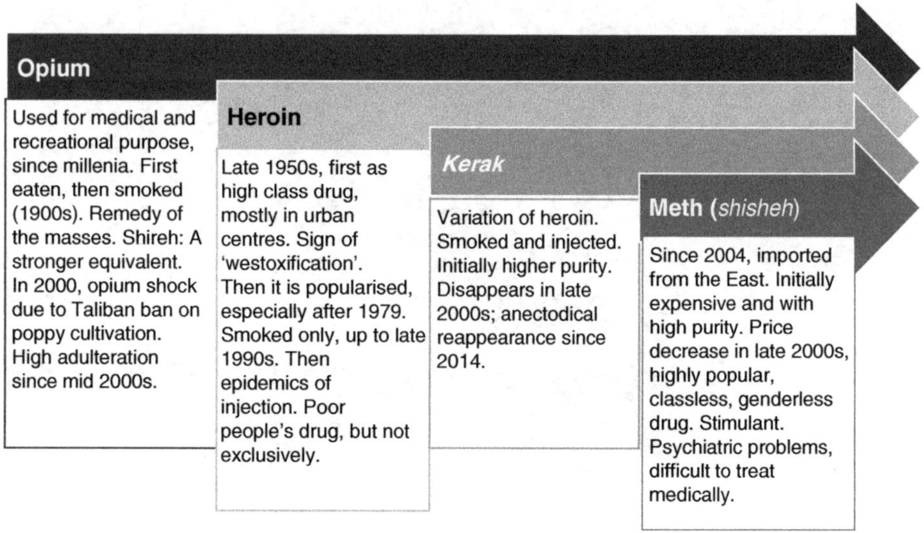

Opium

Used for medical and recreational purpose, since millenia. First eaten, then smoked (1900s). Remedy of the masses. Shireh: A stronger equivalent. In 2000, opium shock due to Taliban ban on poppy cultivation. High adulteration since mid 2000s.

Heroin

Late 1950s, first as high class drug, mostly in urban centres. Sign of 'westoxification'. Then it is popularised, especially after 1979. Smoked only, up to late 1990s. Then epidemics of injection. Poor people's drug, but not exclusively.

Kerak

Variation of heroin. Smoked and injected. Initially higher purity. Disappears in late 2000s; anectodical reappearance since 2014.

Meth (*shisheh*)

Since 2004, imported from the East. Initially expensive and with high purity. Price decrease in late 2000s, highly popular, classless, genderless drug. Stimulant. Psychiatric problems, difficult to treat medically.

Figure E.2 Changes in Drug Phenomenon in Iran (1800–2015)

Power, Crisis, Drugs

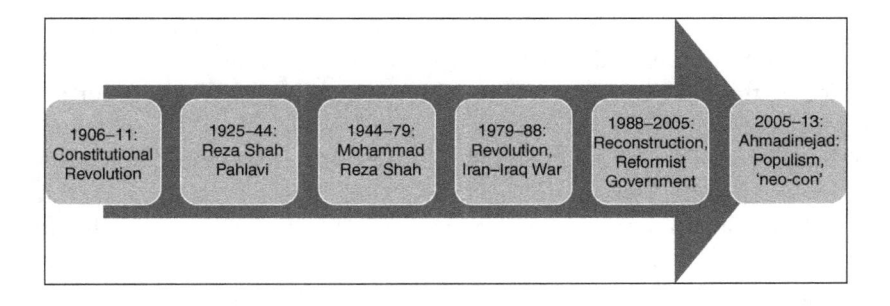

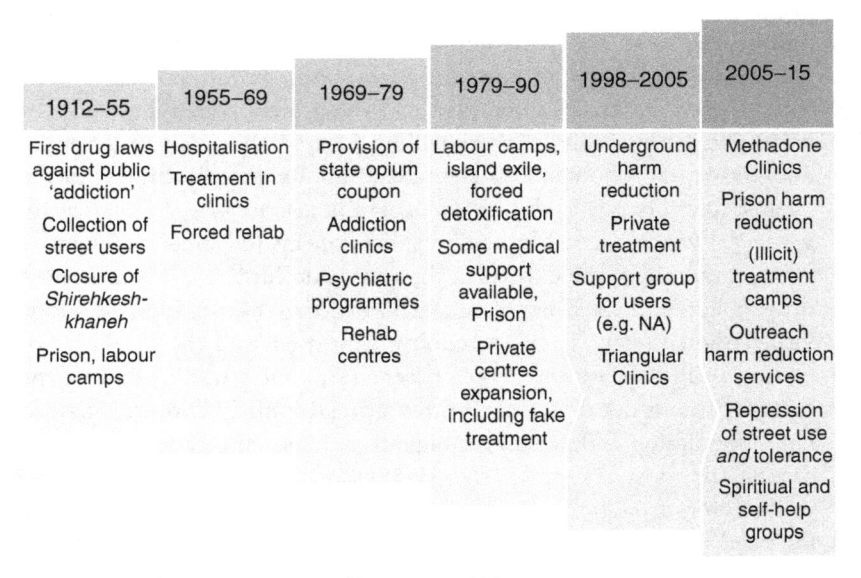

1906–11: Constitutional Revolution	1925–44: Reza Shah Pahlavi	1944–79: Mohammad Reza Shah	1979–88: Revolution, Iran–Iraq War	1988–2005: Reconstruction, Reformist Government	2005–13: Ahmadinejad: Populism, 'neo-con'

1912–55	1955–69	1969–79	1979–90	1998–2005	2005–15
First drug laws against public 'addiction'	Hospitalisation	Provision of state opium coupon	Labour camps, island exile, forced detoxification	Underground harm reduction	Methadone Clinics
Collection of street users	Treatment in clinics	Addiction clinics	Some medical support available.	Private treatment	Prison harm reduction
Closure of *Shirehkesh-khaneh*	Forced rehab	Psychiatric programmes	Prison	Support group for users (e.g. NA)	(Illicit) treatment camps
Prison, labour camps		Rehab centres	Private centres expansion, including fake treatment	Triangular Clinics	Outreach harm reduction services
					Repression of street use *and* tolerance
					Spiritiual and self-help groups

Figure E.3 Changing Regimes of Power and Treatment

Over the decades, the Iranian people and governments have gone through several realities in drug politics, compromising of a *zero tolerance* for traffickers, *limited tolerance* for cannabis and opium, *tolerance* in special zones of drug use, *acceptance* of harm reduction and even *provision* of certain drugs, as in the case of methadone and opium tincture. That paralleled the epochal shifts from traditional opium consumption in the first part of the twenty century to chemical calibration as exemplified with meth and polydrug use, together with the rise of LSD and other psychedelics.

Despite drugs' historical roots in the plateau and the history of policy experimentation, Iran remained an insular and hidden case study within the global debate on illegal drugs and, for that matter, among historians and social scientists working on modern Iran. I have tested this on several occasions, the most telling of which occurred during a drug policy roundtable organised by LSE-Ideas 'International Drug Policy Project' in London. While listening to the presentation of an invitee from the Tehran bureau at the UNODC, the person sitting on my left, an international drug policy expert and harm reductionist, shook her head in disapproval of what was being presented. The Iranian presenter was illustrating the data about the scaling up of harm reduction programmes, listing statistics on treatment facility and services since the mid 2000s. Once the presentation was over, the woman on my side whispered in my ear (not knowing that I worked on Iran's drug policy too), 'these data are all false, how can she present something like that here? She is not credible. It's ridiculous!' Later, she was comforted by another expert who shared her disbelief about the truthfulness of the Islamic Republic's harm reduction programmes, *because it was so exaggerated*. I was surprised by the harshness of this judgement, given that most, if not all, of the experts in the room had little clue about Iranian drug policy and have never engaged with the case of Iran, let alone visited the country. Their incredulity expressed well the insularity of Iranian drug policy in mainstream debates about drugs, in spite of the fact that Iran is not only a main international trafficking route, but also has a population with one of the highest number of illicit drug users and among the most comprehensive systems of medical intervention and welfare for drug (ab)users in the Global South. Iran needed to be included in the frame of reference of international drug policy, but it was distrusted even by drug policy reformers.

Given this, the primary objective of this book is to open up a field of investigation on drugs politics in Iran as embedded in global currents on the theme. Instead of looking at drugs as a standalone object that can be analysed and narrated in isolation, the book provides an understanding of drug phenomena as part of historical movements in society and politics. Drugs, in this way, fall at the interstices of power, knowledge and change, an entryway into the transformation of institutions, policies, ideologies and human agency. In Part One, the book's narrative dwelt on historical disruptions and continuity in illicit drug governance, from the first pushes of Constitutionalists on opium control to the authoritarian and revolutionary attempts at reforming the social body. Crisis drove the spirit of government on narcotics throughout the twentieth century. Governments, civil society and international drug controllers inter-played with the spectre of crisis embodied in drug addiction, its moral falls and health epidemics. In this way, crisis becomes a genealogical tool in situating drugs in Iran's modern history; it is also a paradigm of governance on the disorder associated with drug consumption.

Drug governance is a form of crisis politics. In Iran, this governance has given birth to political venues charged with the duty to govern the crisis. To do so, the Expediency Council acquired overriding powers on legislating and reforming laws on illicit drugs, as part of its prerogative in crisis politics. The origins of drugs politics, and the permanent crisis to which it gives way, has found an institutional home in the Expediency Council. This genealogical root is manifest in a new form of governance of illicit drugs and addiction disorder with the rise of the post-reformist state.

In the new millennium, the Iranian state demonstrated a profound capacity for reforms in the field of drugs, often with idiosyncratic outcomes. Most of these reforms took place during Mahmud Ahmadinejad's governments (2005–13). The short-decade of Ahmadinejad's rule resulted in the most impenetrable (especially for social scientists) and contorted era of post-revolutionary politics. Under the populist presidency, the state introduced deep-seated reforms in governance and society. Instead of adopting the established position arguing that governance during this period (2005–13) was top-down and authoritarian, I use ethnographic observation and fieldwork material to demonstrate quite the contrary. The state adopted multiple tactics towards the drug crisis, and relied on competing agents, most of whom belonged not to the realm of public institutions or of traditional security or disciplinary forces, but to that of civil society, exemplified in the activities of addiction recovery charities and NGOs. This is the way grassroots authoritarianism worked under (and beyond) the post-reformist state. Grassroots authoritarianism is a form of power operating in the face of crisis. It is autonomous of the state, but its goals are not independent of it. The metaphor of the rhizome describes the grassroots nature of crisis governance. Rhizomes, in political parlance, represent a form of power that does not flow from the vertical hierarchy, but rather pops up from the ground, the grassroots, the social milieu made of ordinary people. Because they operate autonomously from public policy, their actions and social presence is seen as independent of state power and public authority. In that, they belong to the sphere of civil society; and yet they reproduce state prerogatives on the management of social margins and public (dis)order. Beyond the realm of illicit drugs, this approach speaks about forms of politics and governance that defy binary schemes of state versus society, authoritarianism versus resistance, structure versus agency. Instead, it outlines an assemblage in which competing forms of governance coexist.

Crisis has transmuted into the central engine of contemporary politics (or perhaps it has always been so?), amid the decline and disappearance of systemic, ideological referents, including in the ideologically strong Islamic Republic. Governments justify change, reforms and political undertakings in crises – material or imagined – whereby the present lives amidst the *most serious crisis*, prosaically and ordinarily. In Europe, this has taken shape with increasingly visibility following the economic crisis of 2008, where the dictum of austerity has brought deep constitutional reforms that render ordinary politics divested of popular input. A clear example is given by the way public spending, labour laws, and other fields of public policy have become dependent on the European Union's financial, banking legitimation, especially in countries such as Greece, Italy and Spain. The crisis of public debt is permanent and it is transformed in a form of governance with indefinite power. Beyond economic policymaking, crisis is also key in other fields: security is a privileged terrain when one looks at how the threat of terrorism in France and the United Kingdom – but discursively throughout the West starting from the United States – has reformed domestic laws and civil rights in favour of ever-narrower, authoritarian readings. That has also worked in fields unrelated semantically as much as phenomenologically to terrorism, such as the refugee crisis.[7] Rulers in the Middle East and North Africa, following the revolts in the Arab world, which went under the unhappy name of 'Arab Spring', adopted a similar form of governance.[8] The threat of

---

[7] France's extension of the 'state of emergency' for over more than twelve months after the Paris terrorist attacks is one such example; Italy's request for the EU budget approval in the wake of the earthquake and refugee crises is another; similarly, Recep Erdogan's use of emergency laws following the failed coup in Turkey. See *BBC*, November 13, 2016, retrieved from www.bbc.co.uk/news/world-europe- 37965708; *Politico*, October 26, 2016, retrieved from www.politico.eu/article/italy-matteo-renzi-pledges-to-veto-eu-budget-over-refugee-crisis/.

[8] Bronwlee & Ghiabi, 'Passive, Silent and Revolutionary'.

Islamist radicalism legitimised the counterrevolution in Egypt and Syria, militarising the question of public order and rendering the demands for political participation devoid of value. The Islamic State in Iraq and Syria (ISIS, aka *daesh*) contributed to turning the discourse of crisis into a paradigm of governance throughout the Mediterranean. The election of Donald J. Trump to the White House in Washington DC reified crisis as a discourse in power, starting with the escalating confrontation with North Korea (and *détente)*, the looming war with Iran, the anti-migrant wall crisis, up to indifference to climate change, with its dooming effects, to mention just a few examples from international affairs.

The Islamic Republic is no exception to this rule of global politics. In 2012, *The Economist* argued that 'one reason for the Islamic Republic's durability against what many would regard as overwhelming odds is the dogged but subtle *crisis management* of Ayatollah Ali Khamenei'.[9] Yet, how could the management of crisis be the turf of one man, be it even the Supreme Leader? While crises are addressed collectively and politically in so-called liberal democracies, they are expected to be managed and controlled individually in the Islamic Republic. The argument in this book has run counter to this type of framing. There are underlying governmentalities and political machineries – even beyond the state itself – that partake in the management and government of crises. In light of this, one can understand how crisis has become an idiom of reform and management in the Islamic Republic, bearing in mind that politics globally has progressively adopted similar processes of formation.

'Crisis' is not an exceptional condition in post-revolutionary Iran. In fact, crisis has been perpetual ever since the establishment of the modernising state in the early twentieth century, intensifying sharply in the aftermath of the 1979 Revolution. With the establishment of a revolutionary regime, the public discourse on politics has been reproduced – not only by Iranian officials, but also among international observers – through recurrent allusion to the notion of crisis: 'the hostage crisis' which lasted 444 days between 1980 and 1981 and contributed to the election of Ronald Regan; 'the oil crisis' that has had its ups and downs from the 1973, 1979, to the 1980s embargo up to the crippling sanction regime in the 2010s; 'the post-war crisis' of the

---

[9] *The Economist*, May 5, 2012, retrieved from www.economist.com/node/21554242.

1990s when reconstruction of Iran's domestic infrastructure and ailing economy challenged the very political order of the republic; 'the water crisis' which became manifest in the case of Lake Orumiyeh in 2015 and it is today the most serious environmental challenge for the state; 'the corruption crisis' that first brought Ahmadinejad to power in 2005 and later escalated in internecine struggle among members of the establishment, with the revelation of an embezzlement case worth up to one billion dollars in 2011; and, ultimately, 'the nuclear crisis' which, despite the successful negotiations of 2013 and the signing of the Joint Comprehensive Plan of Action (JCPOA) between Iran and world powers, is the heart of crisis politics, following Donald Trump's aggressive and destabilising strategy against Tehran.

There are theoretical implications for the perpetuation of crisis in politics. The intensification of a discourse of crisis proceeds over the blurring of boundaries between what is legitimately policy (and the state) and what is performed at the level of political intervention. In other words, what takes place in the realm of theory of governance, of laws, regulations, and agreed conventions and in the rhetoric of politicians, and what takes place in the political practice of the time, in the on-the-ground workings of political machines. As Janet Roitman argues, the reference in modern politics to crisis is a blind spot, which is claimed constantly in the political rhetoric, but 'remains a latency'.[10] The Iranian state, in this respect, has mastered, often maliciously and sometimes progressively, the arts of governing crisis and managing disorder, establishing itself closer to modes of governance of contemporary Western states. Indeed, crisis as an interpretative frame and as a governmental tool brings Iranian and global politics closer.

Crisis, its Greek etymology (*krisis*) reminds us, takes effect in the domains of theology, law and medicine, the moment when a religious minister, a physician, or a jurist *decides* upon matters of life and death. The encounter of religion, law and medicine is at the heart of the Islamic Republic's state formation and governance, whereby politics, not only in the field of drugs, operates through the logics of management and control. In situations of risk, 'plagues' and crisis, states and private entities often form partnerships, in which quantified evaluation and self-supervision are set as the norm. The medical community, when a plague, epidemic or health crisis is declared, assumes a potent political

---

[10] Roitman, *Anti-Crisis*, 39.

role, which underpins state legitimacy, sovereignty and interventions. Through the expansion of political technologies, modern societies also witness the economisation of intervention, shifting their imperative from disciplining the subject to economically managing unruly subjects or crisis/disorder. By transforming people into numbers, this form of governance proceeds to a broader shift in the framing of state and society, one which has been usually explained only in terms of Western liberal societies, and which, as this book demonstrates, operate in specular ways in the Islamic Republic. Beyond this similarity – that could be an (un)fortunate exception – the investigation of drugs politics and the technologies of management of crisis in the Islamic Republic are exploratory of deeper, fundamental paradigms of government of this state, and society, in the larger context of global politics.

Decentralised, societal and multifarious rhizomes, analogous to the root structure of a plant, partake in the state formation that characterised revolutionary Iran. Crisis and, more specifically, the drugs phenomenon had a productive effect on this process. So far, the study of Iranian politics has been strongly embedded in statist, centralising and personality-obsessed perspectives, with some notable exceptions.[11] To a certain degree, this obsession with *the regime* is the side effect of the place the Islamic Republic has come to occupy in the scholarship of global politics. Discussion of contemporary Iran risks being at the mercy of the production of think-tank knowledge, with its focus on security and leadership apparatuses, driven by anti-Islamic Republic ideology, which is currently being given unprecedented momentum sustained by Trump's alignment with Saudi and Israeli interests. Knowledge produced through these networks assumes that government and the state in Iran are inherently obstructive and regressive whereas social agents are bearers of positive change, or that change cannot result from indigenous inputs. They also proselytize an idea of post-revolutionary Iran as dominated by the idea of obscurantist Islam, totalitarian in its scope. This argument does not merit careful discussion, as I believe the preceding chapters demonstrated how politics takes form in Iran and, indirectly, what is (or is not?) the place and influence of Islam or, for that matter, obscurantism in the Islamic Republic.

Running counter to this framing, the book reasserted the centrality of the state in the study of political and social phenomena by adopting

---

[11] Harris, *A Social Revolution*; Bayat, *Street Politics*; Keshavarzian, *Bazaar and the State*; Christensen, *Drugs, Deviancy and Democracy*.

a grassroots lens, attentive to political practice. Without transforming the political order into a *deus ex machina* of the present, the state represented in this book is the bearer of meaning in the study of power and its effects inasmuch it makes itself insular, invisible and masked. In the case of Iran (but also elsewhere), this camouflage happens through privatisation of its means of intervention, such as treatment, rehabilitation, coercion and surveillance medicine, but it is not a prelude to its disappearance or irrelevance. More importantly, this condition of the state is not revelatory of multiple sovereignties within its structure, as has been regularly argued for the Islamic Republic.[12] The state unfolds forms of 'indirect government' entangled in the incoherent tactics and competing strategies that public and private agents co-produce. That often signifies more state intervention and a capacity of consolidation greater than that of direct state action.

The other major study of Iranian drug policy concludes by asking the question 'how can the Iranian state sustain itself in the midst of these political contradictions?'[13] The answer, Christensen holds, is in 'continuous political disagreements as to which form of Islamic order and means of governance should be employed and, in effect, what kind of state the Islamic Republic should become'.[14] This tension, however, is a fundamental rationale of modern politics everywhere, of which we are reminded by Foucault when he writes that 'the state is at once that which exists, but which does not yet exist enough'.[15] The contentious nature of Iranian drug policy could be interpreted too, as a quest beyond the not yet enough *Islamic* Republic; but we need agreement that the Islamic nature of the political order remains marginal in the making of its polices, especially in its crisis politics. Governance drives the engine of state formation, a birthright anointing the establishment of the Islamic Republic, to which Ayatollah Khomeini gave paramount importance, and to which his successor Ayatollah Ali Khamenei has been faithful. Less crucial is the intellectual diatribe around how Islamic the Republic should be, or through which means this Islamic identity should be

---

[12] Christensen, *Drugs, Deviancy*, 225–32; Ramin Jahanbegloo, 'The Cultural Turn in New Democratic Theory' in *Democratic Theorists in Conversation* (Palgrave Macmillan, London, 2014), 56–71; Naser Ghobadzadeh, and Lily Zubaidah Rahim, 'Electoral theocracy and hybrid sovereignty in Iran', *Contemporary Politics* 22, 4 (2016), 450–68.
[13] Christensen, *Drugs, Deviancy*, 225.   [14] Ibid., 226.
[15] Dean and Villadsen, *State Phobia*, 113.

achieved, or the many shades of reforming Islamic politics. The latter questions exist in the agenda of politicians and a number of public institutions, but they are not the driving force, the political engine, behind the art of government in the new millennium.[16] Rather, they are what they claim to be: intellectual discussions around ways of thinking about the political order rather than ways of interpreting politics and political practice.

At no time has the distance between intellectual analysis and political practice been greater than during Mahmud Ahmadinejad's presidency, from 2005 to 2013. This was a key moment in the state formation process of the Islamic Republic. With scant non-ideological scholarly research, Ahmadinejad's period in government corresponded to a major transformation of politics. The high hopes of reformism under Mohammad Khatami turned into a straightforward populist demand of economic equality and revolutionary policymaking. Privatisation reconfigured the very infrastructure of the economy, with lasting effects up until the Rouhani administration. A new nationalist, anti-imperialist discourse, combined with religious allure, reasserted Iran's foreign policy amidst the growing conflict in the Middle East, first in Iraq and Afghanistan, then in Syria and beyond. Instead, deep-seated secular trends animated social changes, with the rooting of global consumer culture, new civic dynamics in gender and sexuality, and individual subjectivities animated by competition, appearance and self-care. By 2013, when Iranians elected Hassan Rouhani president of the Republic, Iranian society had gone through a decade of transformation in every existing field of state–society relations, of which, obviously, drugs politics – its assemblage of consumption, treatment and punishment – were epiphenomenal.

Scholarship on this period was mostly informed by studies 'at distance', with little or no on-the-ground engagement. Most contributions analysed governmental discourses, foreign policy or security matters, or, when they addressed societal aspects, they did so either through studies of digital media – a key aspect of this era's social and political life, but not to be regarded as one existing in isolation, rather as in symbiosis with 'lived life' – or by riding the wave of social movements (e.g. Green Movement in 2009). Conscious of this limitation, this book addressed questions of power and politics through an on-the-ground

---

[16] For some reason, these discussions have been object of interminable scholarly productions on post-revolutionary Iran.

approach, following phenomenological lines of enquiry. Extensive ethnographic observation, interviews with public officials, experts, activists, professionals, and drug consumers informed the book with first-hand information on the history and current state of drugs politics.

Throughout this book, I referred to Iranian politics as bearing an inherent oxymoronic value. I did this not so much to distinguish it from other forms of politics, but rather on the assumption that modern politics is fundamentally contradictory, even dialectical. These contradictions cannot be dissected from a distance; they must be embraced from an engaged point of view. For too long, protracted debates have been waged over whether Iran is an Islamic Republic, whether the Republic is Islamic or Islam can be republican.[17] This book's theoretical contribution stands in that politics needs to be understood in its governmental processes, in its becoming and in the ramifications of its contradictions, in the built-in inconsistencies that drive the political machine in its perpetual and multidirectional transformation, a fact that makes Iran a privileged case for the study of state formation in contemporary times. Indeed, the political order does not stand domineering above society, determining its shape, its means, its political culture. And civil society is not simply the panacea for reform and for a renewal in politics; often, it adopts means of intervention and ideas that are more restrictive and less participatory than the state itself.

Through this approach, the books shows that, with regard to 'crisis' and at the governmental level, politics works along secular (i.e. worldly), profane (unreligious, 'outside the temple') lines. The Islamic Republic works as a modern, secularised political machine; Islam is not its primary fuel.

---

[17] A sound discussion of this topic is by Bayart, *L'islam Républicain*.

Select Bibliography

This bibliography contains sources used in writing this book and those which had a substantial influence on this work. It should not be regarded as a record of all the material that I have consulted over the period of research. Its objective is to provide a clear list of the sources cited in the text, as well as a selection of the intellectual, scientific material that has inspired it. As such, it should also work as a reference for those interested in pursuing further research on drug and crisis politics in Iran.

It is divided into two major sections: primary sources and secondary sources. In the first section, I have included interviews, reports and newspapers in Persian. In the second section, I listed the books, articles and non-Persian newspapers. There is also a list of the interviews with public officials, UN representatives, NGO workers, medical practitioners and activists carried out during my fieldwork between 2012 and 2016. It indicates only those interviews that had a formal setting and that were pre-organised and agreed upon with the interviewee. It is not a list of the discussions, debates and chats that I had with people in the drug policy community or drug using community. (For the biographies of the interviewees, see Appendix One *Dramatis Personae*).

The newspapers in Persian are cited without reference to the title and authors of the articles. I opted to do so to be consistent throughout the text, as many of the articles published in these newspapers did not have an explicit author and/or a specific title. For those articles accessed online, I provide the online address. The dates of publication have been converted from the Iranian calendar to the Gregorian calendar. The bibliography and the footnotes follow the guidelines of the *Chicago Manual of Style* 16th Edition.

Appendix 1 *Dramatis Personae*

Ahmadi-Moghaddam Esma'il (PhD), Chief of the Police (NAJA) between 2005 and 2015; he directed the DCHQ between 2007 and 2010.
Ahmadinejad Mahmud (PhD), President of the Republic (2005–2013).

Alaei Kamran, together with Arash Alaei (his brother) established the first Triangular Clinics in Kermanshah. He was sentenced to a five-year prison sentence in 2008 and sentenced to three years incarceration, allegedly for 'conspiracy to overthrow the government'. Arash, his brother, was sentenced to five years.

Arlacchi Pino (PhD), Italian sociologist working on the Mafia, he was appointed Executive Director of the UNODC in 1997, known for his commitment to a 'drug-free world'.

Bahari Maziar is an Iranian/Canadian journalist and filmmaker, incarcerated for espionage in 2009. He worked for *Newsweek* from 1997 to 2011.

Costa Antonio Maria (PhD), Italian economist appointed Executive Director of the UNODC between 2002 and 2008. Supporter of zero-tolerance approach to drugs.

De Leo Antonino, UNODC representative in Tehran (2009–2013), currently head of UNODC in Bogotá, Bolivia.

Deylamizadeh Abbas (Babak), director of *Tavalod-e Dobareh* (Rebirth NGO). A recovered addict since 2002, he is an influential public speaker on issues related to addiction.

Fellah Mohammad, former director of the DCHQ from 1993 to 2002, had previously been working in the Prison.

Hashemi Ali, former head of the DCHQ. A high-ranking bureaucrat who has acted over the course of the last decades as advisor to President Mohammad Khatami (1997–2005), member of the National Security Council (1986–1997) and member of the IRGC (1979–1986).

Hashemi Shahrudi Mahmud (*ayatollah*), Iraqi-born head of judiciary between 1999 and 2009. He passed away in 2018.

Hashemi-Rafsanjani Akbar (ayatollah), former president of the Republic (1989–1997) and long-term head of the Expediency Council (1989–2017).

Khamenei Ali (*ayatollah*), Supreme Leader of the Islamic Revolution and head of state of the Islamic Republic (1989–).

Khatami Mohammad (*hojjatol-eslam*), former president of the Republic (1997–2005). Reformist.

Larijani Ardeshir Sadeq (*hojjatol-eslam*), head of the judiciary (2009–) and head of the Expediency Council (2019–), one of the four Larijani brothers. Conservative.

Larijani Ali (PhD), Speaker of the Parliament (2008–); philosopher and former Supreme Leader representative to National Security Council.

Maleki Fada Hossein, director of the DCHQ (2005–2007) and Iran's former ambassador to Afghanistan.

Mazzittelli Antonio Luigi, first UNODC representative in Tehran (1999–2004). UNODC representative in Mexico City, Mexico.
Mohraz Minoo (PhD), professor of infectious diseases, scholar of medical sciences and long-term HIV expert. She is also a long-time member of Iran's Committee to Fight AIDS.
Mohsenifar Setareh, former official at the Ministry of Health, has been working at the UNODC and UNAIDS in Tehran since the mid-2000s.
Mostashahri Gelareh, former official at the Ministry of Health, has been working at the UNODC, in the capacity of drug demand reduction expert.
Najjar Mostafà Mohammad, Minister of Interior (2005–2009) and Minister of Defence (2009–2013) under Ahmadinejad, he also acted as director of the DCHQ between 2010 and 2013.
Narenjiha Hooman (PhD), former TV presenter in the state-run Channel 2, doctor in addiction treatment and advisor at the DCHQ in matters of drug prevention.
Nasirimanesh Bijan, founder of the NGO *Persepolis* for Harm Reduction, allegedly the first civil society organisation to run harm reduction programmes.
Qalibaf Mohammad Baqer (PhD), current mayor of Tehran and former presidential candidate in 2005 and 2013. Already Head of the Police (NAJA) and General of the IRGC during the Iran–Iraq War.
Razzaghi Emran (PhD), professor of psychiatry at Tehran University of Medical Sciences since 1991, former director of the Iranian government Bureau of Youth Health, founder of the Iranian National Center for Addiction Studies (INCAS) and co-founder of the Middle East and North Africa Harm Reduction Association (MENAHRA).
Roberto Arbitrio, UNODC representative in Tehran (2004–2009), currently UNODC Technical Operation Section Chief.
Rouhani Hasan (*hojjatol-eslam*, PhD), President of the Republic (2013–) and former director of the National Security Council and Centre for Strategic Research. He obtained his PhD at Glasgow Caledonian University in 1999.
Sefatian Said, former Director General of the Treatment, Rehabilitation and Vocational Training Department at the DCHQ. He is advisor to the judiciary and the Expediency Council about matters of drug addiction and HIV.
Shirazi Bahram, director of the NGO *Ayin-e Mehr* in Tehran, which runs methadone maintenance programmes, outreach teams, low-threshold shelters and therapeutic support for addicts.

Soltani Fariba, first DDR expert at the UNODC, Tehran. She left the Tehran office in 2005.
Yazdi Mohammad, former head of the judiciary (1989–99) and temporary head of the Assembly of Experts (2015–).
Wisse Ernst, Representative of *Medicines Sans Frontiers* (Doctors without Borders) bureau in Tehran between 2013 and 2016.

Primary sources

Interviews

(See Appendix One for biographical details of the interviewees)

Head of clinic. Interview/Discussions. Arak: February 10 to March 1, 2014.
Head of clinic. Interview. Arak: March 27, 2014.
Camp manager. Interview/Discussions. Arak: April 23–25, 2014.
Female camp manager. Interview/Discussions. Arak: March 30, 2014.
Camp manager. Interview/Discussions. Shahr-e Rey: April 13 and 16, 2014.
NGO director. Interview/Discussions. Tehran: April 20, 2014. Manager of Drop-in Center. Interview. Tehran: April 9, 2015.
De Leo, Antonino. Interview. Tehran: September 2, 2012.
Deylamizadeh, Abbas [aka Babak]. Interview. Tehran: March 16, 2014.
Elham [social worker in MMT clinic]. Interview/Discussions. Arak: February 10 to March 1, 2014.
Kamiar, Alaei. Interview. Via Skype: October 20, 2014.
Mazittelli, Antonio. Interview. Via Skype: October 29, 2014.
Mohsenifar, Setareh. Interview. Tehran: August 4, 2012.
   Interview. Tehran: March 12, 2014. Follow up via email.
Mostashari, Gelareh. Interview. Tehran: July 5, 2012.
   Interview. Tehran: April 4, 2014. Follow up via email.
   Interview. Tehran: September 17, 2015.
Narenjiha, Hooman. Interview. Tehran: April 4, 2014.
   Interview. Tehran: September 14, 2015.
Nasirimanesh, Bijan. Interview. Via Skype: November 3, 2014. Follow up via email.
Noori, Roya [Researcher, head of MMT clinic]. Interview. Tehran: April 4, 2014.
Razzaghi, Emran. Interview. Tehran: August 28, 2012.
   Interview. Tehran: March 15, 2014.

Sefatian, Said. Interview. Tehran: April 9, 2014.
    Interview. Tehran: September 20, 2015.
Shirazi, Bahram. Interview. Tehran: April 10, 2014.
    Interview. Tehran: April 8, 2015.
    Discussions in the field. Tehran (Chehel Pelleh *patoq*): September 20, 2015.
Soheil [Shelter manager]. Interviews/Discussions. Tehran: March 1–15, 2014.
    Interview. Tehran: March 19, 2014.
Solhi, Hasan. Interview. Arak: March 2, 2014.
    Interview. Arak: March 4, 2014.
Soltani, Fariba. Interview. Via Skype: July 11, 2014.
Tahernokhost, Hamid-Reza. Interview. Tehran: July 25, 2012.
    Interview. Tehran: March 5, 2013.
    Interview. Tehran: April 8, 2014.
Wisse Ernst, Interviews. Tehran: September 12–13, 2014.
    Discussions. Paris: April 20, 2016.

Conferences and Workshops

Seventh International Society for the Study of Drug Policy Conference, Bogotá: May 15–17, 2013. Retrieved from www.issdp.org/.
Second Middle East and North Africa Harm Reduction Conference. Beirut: November 12–15, 2013. Retrieved from www.menahra.org/en/.
Eighth International Society for the Study of Drug Policy Conference. Rome: May 21–23, 2014. Retrieved from www.issdp.org/.
Eighth International Conference on Addiction Science. Tehran: September 8–10, 2014. Retrieved from http://ascongress.ir/en_Default.aspx.
Ninth International Conference on Addiction Science. Tehran: September 9–11, 2015. Retrieved from http://ascongress.ir/en_Default.aspx.
Ruzbeh Hospital Roundtable. With Dr Emran Razzaghi. Tehran: October 1, 2015.
LSE Ideas Expert Group Workshop. London: February 15, 2016.

Reports, Laws, Regulations (Persian)

'Decriminalisation Bill in the Drug and Treatment of Drug Abusers Law'. Government of the Islamic Republic of Iran. Dated July 24, 2006 [scanned file].

'Law Bill on Permission to Buy Opium for Legitimate Addicts in the Country'. Governmental Paper. Dated June 9, 1980 [scanned document].

'*Kahesh-e 25 darsad-e E'tiyad dar Keshvar ta Payan-e Barnam-e Shishom-e Touse*' [Decrease by 25% in addiction rate in the country expected by the end of the 6th Development Programme]'. Government of the Islamic Republiuc of Iran. Dated September 14, 2015. Retrieved from www.dolat.ir/NSite/FullStory/News/?Serv=0&Id=266177.

'Text of the 2010 drug law reform'. Retrieved from www.1vakil.com/com ponent/content/article/29–1389-05–29-12–10-49/104–89.html.

Expediency Council. '*Dabirkhane-Ye Majma'e* [Directory of the Council]'. Retrieved from http://maslahat.ir/DocLib2/Irec%20Pillars/Irec%20Se cretariate.aspx.

Majmu'e Mosavabat-E Majma'e Tashkhis-E Maslahat-E Nezam [Collection of Decrees of the Expediency Council]. Edited by the Directory of the Expediency Council. Tehran: Expediency Council, 1388 [2009].

'*Asar-e Ejrai-Ye Qanun-e Hadafmandi-ye Yaraneh-ha bar Eqtesad-e Mavadd-e Mokhadder* [Effects of the Subsidy Reform on the Economy of Narcotic Drugs]'. Tehran: Expediency Council, undated.

'*Pishineh* [Records]'. Retrieved from http://maslahat.ir/Commissions/Ant iDrug/DocLib/History.aspx.

'*Shura-ye Majma'e* [Council's Assembly]'. Retrieved from http://maslahat. ir/DocLib2/Irec%20Pillars/Irec%20council.aspx.

'*Siasat-ha-ye Kolli-ye Pishnahadi* [Proposed General Policies]'. Retrieved from http://maslahat.ir/DocLib2/Approved%20Policies/Offered%20G eneral%20Policies.aspx.

'*Siasat-ha-ye Kolli* [General Policies]'. Tehran: Expediency Council, 2009 [1388].

Khosh Soluk and Mehran. *Dokhtaran-e Farari, E'tiyad va AIDS*. Tehran: Barhman, 2004 [1383].

Lam'i, Dariush and 'abdollah Amiri. Sazman-e gheyr-e Doulati NGO) dar rastay-e Mobarez-e ba Mavadd-e Mokhadder va E'tiyad. Kermanshah: Kousar, 2001 [1380].

Madani, Qahrfarkhi, Said. Bar-resi-ye Tajarob-e Modiriyyat-e Kahesh-e Taqaza-ye Suye Masraf-e Mavvad-e tey-ye Dou Daheh-ye Akhir (1358–1380). UNODC: 2004, unpublished [pdf copy].

Ministry of Health and Medical Education. 'Islamic Republic of Iran AIDS Progress Report: On Monitoring of the United Nations General Assembly Special Session on HIV and AIDS'. UNODC: March 2014, unpublished [pdf copy].

NAJA. *Tarikhcheh* [History]'. Retrieved from http://police.ir/Portal/Home/Default.aspx?CategoryID=1e3abacf-2e74-46da-ae12-f3f7511572cf.
UN. 'Twenty-Sixth Special Session of the UNGA on HIV/AIDS'. Retrieved from www.un.org/ga/aids/statements/docs/iranE.htm.
Vosuqi, Mansur. *Arziyabi Vaziyat-e Moujud dar Marakez-e Bazparvari-ye Mo'tadan*. Tehran: University of Welfare and Rehabilitation, 1997 [1376].
Welfare Organisation. *Arziyabi Vaziyat-e Moujud dar Marakez-e Bazparvari-ye Mo'tadan*. Tehran: 1998 [1378], Unpublished report [pdf copy].
West Azerbaijan Regional Office of the Prison Organisation. Retrieved from www.west-azarprisons.ir/index.php?Module=SMMNewsAgency&SMMOp=View&SMM_CMD=&PageId=2273.

Reports, Conventions, Regulations, Declarations (English)

'2015 Afghan Drug Report'. Islamic Republic of Afghanistan, Minister of Counter Narcotic (2015). Retrieved from www.unodc.org/documents/afghanistan/UNODC-DRUG-REPORT15-Full-081215.pdf.
'Methadone and Buprenorphine and International Drug Control Conventions'. *NIDA* (2009). Retrieved from www.ncbi.nlm.nih.gov/books/NBK143176/.
'Twenty-Sixth Special Session of the UNGA on HIV/AIDS'. United Nations. Retrieved from www.un.org/ga/aids/statements/docs/iranE.htm.
'Memorandum for the CIA heroin coordinator'. US State Department: July 1, 1971. Retrieved from http://2001–2009.state.gov/documents/organization/70647.pdf.
Barroso, Manuel. 'A Europe for All Weathers'. Meeting with EU Heads of Delegation. Brussels: November 30, 2011. Retrieved from http://europa.eu/rapid/press-release_SPEECH-11-838_en.htm.
Bulletin on Narcotics. 1958, 2 (5).
    1960, 4 (4).
    1976, 3 (3).
Central Treaty Organisation (CENTO). *'Seminar on Public Health and Medical Problems Involved in Narcotics Drug Addiction'*. Tehran: CENTO, April 8–12 (1972): 25–26.
DCHQ. 'Drug Police in 2009'. Retrieved from www.dchq.ir.
    'Drug Police in 2010'. Retrieved from www.dchq.ir.
    'Drug Police in 2011'. Retrieved from www.dchq.ir.

'Drug Police in 2012'. Retrieved from www.dchq.ir.
'Drug Police in 2013'. Retrieved from www.dchq.ir.
'Drug Police in 2014'. Retrieved from www.dchq.ir.
'Drug Police in 2015'. Retrieved from www.dchq.ir.
INCB. 'Precursors'. 2011. Retrieved from www.incb.org.
League of Nations. 'First Opium Conference – Minutes and Annexed'. Geneva: November 3rd, 1924 – February 11th, 1925.
  'Records of the Second Opium Conference'. Vol. I. Geneva: November 17th, 1924 – February 19th, 1925.
  'Commission of Enquiry into the Production of Opium in Persia'. Geneva: September 16th, 1927.
Khajehkazemi, Razieh, Mehdi Osooli, Leily Sajadi, Mohammad Karamouzian, Abbas Sedaghat, Noushin Fahimfar, Afshin Safaie, Ehsan Mostafavi, and Ali-Akbar Haghdoost. 'HIV prevalence and risk behaviours among people who inject drugs in Iran: the 2010 National Surveillance Survey'. *Sexually Transmitted Infections* (2013): sextrans-2013.
Nissaramanesh, Bijan, Mike Trace, and Marcus Roberts. 'The rise of harm reduction in the Islamic Republic of Iran'. *Beckley Foundation Drug Policy Programme, Briefing Paper* 8 (2005).
Saidi, Hossein, Mohammad Ghadiri, Saeed Abbasi, and Seyed-Foad Ahmadi. 'Efficacy and safety of naloxone in the management of postseizure complaints of tramadol intoxicated patients: a self-controlled study'. *Emergency Medicine Journal* 27, no. 12 (2010): 928–930.
Saleh, Jehan S. 'Iran suppresses opium production'. *Bulletin on Narcotics* 8, no. 3 (1956): 1–2.
UNODC. *Global Illicit Drug Trends*. 1999. Retrieved from www.unodc.org/wdr2014/en/previous-reports.html.
  World Drug Report. 2004.
  World Drug Report. 2005.
  World Drug Report. 2006.
  World Drug Report. 2007.
  World Drug Report. 2009
  World Drug Report. 2011.
  World Drug Report. 2012.
  World Drug Report. 2015.
  'A brief review of ATS in Iran', unpublished report [pdf copy], November 2010.

'Commentary on the Single Convention (1961)'. Retrieved from www.u nodc.org/documents/treaties/organized_crime/Drug%20Convention/Commentary_on_the_single_convention_1961.pdf.

Participatory workshop with the NGOs to identify joint strategies on Drug Demand Reduction. Unpublished report [pdf copy], November 2004.

Vazirian, Mohsen, Bijan Nassirimanesh, Saman Zamani, Masako Ono-Kihara, Masahiro Kihara, Shahrzad Mortazavi Ravari, and Mohammad Mehdi Gouya. 'Needle and syringe sharing practices of injecting drug users participating in an outreach HIV prevention program in Tehran, Iran: a cross-sectional study'. *Harm Reduction Journal* 2, no. 1 (2005): 1.

World Health Organization. 'Atlas on substance use (2010): resources for the prevention and treatment of substance use disorders' (2010). Retrieved from https://scholar.google.co.uk/scholar?q=ATLAS+of+Substance+Use+Disorders&btnG=&hl=en&as_sdt=0%2C5.

Wright, A. E. 'The Battle against Opium in Iran: A Record of Progress'. *Bulletin on Narcotics* 10, no. 2 (1958): 8–11.

Zamani, Saman, Masahiro Kihara, Mohammad Mehdi Gouya, Mohsen Vazirian, Masako Ono-Kihara, Emran Mohammad Razzaghi, and Seiichi Ichikawa. 'Prevalence of and factors associated with HIV-1 infection among drug users visiting treatment centers in Tehran, Iran'. *Aids* 19, no. 7 (2005): 709–716.

Newspapers, Magazines and Other Media (Persian)

Aftab-e Yazd. September 4, 2006
  May 12, 2007
  August 13, 2008
  August 30, 2008
  February 21, 2009. Retrieved from www.aftabir.com/news/view/2009/feb/21/c4c1235195499_social_psychopathology_addiction.php.
  June 13, 2010
  June 28, 2010
  June 29, 2010
  June 16, 2011. Retrieved from http://aftabnews.ir/prtb89b8wrhb5fp.uiur.html.
  August 20, 2011
  September 19, 2012
Andisheh-ye Nou. October 12, 2009

Enqelab-e Eslami. May 11, 1980
   May 15, 1980
   October 30, 1980
   April 14, 1985
   October 16, 2001
Etela'at. May 8, 1980
   May 10, 1980
   January 7, 1981
   April 24, 1983
   January 27, 1986
   August 28, 1986
   January 10, 1988
   January 23, 1988
   January 19, 1989
   July 24, 1989
   July 12, 1995
E'temad-e Melli. February 13, 2007
   May 6, 2007
   April 14, 2009
   June 11, 2009
   August 9, 2009
   August 16, 2009
   October 2, 2009
   April 12, 2010
   November 11, 2015
E'tiyad-e Pajuheshi [Addiction Research]. Vol. 29. Tehran: DCHQ, January 2013. Retrieved from http://publisher.dchq.ir.
   Vol. 32. Tehran: DCHQ, July 2013. Retrieved from http://publisher.dchq.ir.
   Vol. 33. Tehran: DCHQ, January 2014. Retrieved from http://publisher.dchq.ir.
   Vol. 35. Tehran: DCHQ, July 2014. Retrieved from http://publisher.dchq.ir.
   Vol. 36. Tehran: DCHQ, October 2015. Retrieved from http://publisher.dchq.ir.

Fararu. August 1, 2009. Retrieved from http://fararu.com/fa/news/28972.
   August 2, 2016. Retrieved from http://fararu.com/fa/news/283802/.
Farhang News. June 30, 2015. Retrieved from www.farhangnews.ir/content/130464.

Fars. August 21, 2013. Retrieved from www.farsnews.com/newstext.php?nn=13920529000532.
 July 7, 2014. Retrieved from www.farsnews.com/media.php?nn=13920412001602.
Hamshahri. October 22, 2003. Retrieved from www.hamshahrionline.ir/hamnews/1382/820730/news/_ejtem.htm.
 June 10, 2006
 June 24, 2006
 June 25, 2006
 June 26, 2006
 May 1, 2007
 May 20, 2007
 December 12, 2007
 April 30, 2008
 May 4, 2008
 September 17, 2008
 January 4, 2009
 January 16, 2009. Retrieved from http://hamshahrionline.ir/details/41920.
 January 22, 2009
 April 30, 2009
 June 23, 2009
 July 24, 2009. Also Retrieved from http://hamshahrionline.ir/print/86098.
 November 1, 2009
 January 25, 2010
 March 9, 2010
 April 5, 2010. Retrieved from http://hamshahrionline.ir/details/104358/Society/vulnerabilities.
Iran. November 4, 2009
 May 12, 2007
 August 4, 2012. Retrieved from www.magiran.com/npview.asp?ID=2555859.
 October 5, 2015
IRNA. February 21, 2015. Retrieved from www.irna.ir/fa/News/81514008/.
ISNA. December 6, 2010. Retrieved from http://isna.ir/fa/print/8909-09724/.
 April 27, 2014. Retrieved from http://isna.ir/fa/news/93020704452/.
Jam-e Jam, May 18, 2008
 June 5, 2008

January 5, 2009
April 16, 2009
October 27, 2009
January 12, 2010
February 7, 2010. Retrieved from www1.jamejamonline.ir/newstext2.aspx?newsnum=100835179647.
April 10, 2010
April 11, 2010
June 30, 2010. Retrieved from www1.jamejamonline.ir/newstext2.aspx?newsnum=100942401191.
December 19, 2010
February 28, 2011. Retrieved from www1.jamejamonline.ir/papertext.aspx?newsnum=100836959206.
May 16, 2011
May 27, 2011
June 27, 2011
December 1, 2011
April 16, 2012
May 12, 2013

Jomhuri-ye Eslami. June 27, 1979
October 25, 1979
May 13, 1980
April 17, 1983
August 5, 1986
January 11, 1988
August 5, 1988
November 6, 1988
January 23, 1989

Kayhan. July 6, 1980
January 5, 1981
May 21, 1981
January 8, 1982
June 14, 1998
September 30, 1999
February 13, 2001
May 27, 2007
June 27, 2007
June 13, 2011
June 10, 2012

Khabaronline. April 29, 2011. Retrieved from www.khabaronline.ir/detail/147408/society/social-damage.
  June 10, 2011. Retrieved from www.khabaronline.ir/print/156388/.
  May 11, 2015. Retrieved from www.khabaronline.ir/detail/415509.
Ma'vi. May 10, 2006
Mardomsalari. December 21, 2009
  September 16, 2010
  September 22, 2012
Mehr. September 26, 2012-. Retrieved from www.mehrnews.com/news/1608510/.
  December 22, 2012. Retrieved from www.mehrnews.com/news/1770270/.
  December 12 2015. Retrieved from www.mehrnews.com/news/2995003.
Iran. July 21, 2011
Nouruz. October 11, 2000
Payvand. April 18, 2004. Retrieved from www.payvand.com/news/04/apr/1120.html.
  January 7, 2010. Retrieved from www.payvand.com/news/10/jul/1007.html.
  August 19, 2010. Retrieved from www.payvand.com/news/10/aug/1184.html.
Qatreh. December 20, 2013
Qods. May 4, 2011
Radio Zamaneh. March 7, 2010. Retrieved from http://zamaaneh.com/news/2009/03/post_8216.html.
Resala. October 20, 2000
Rooyesh. June 09, 2007. Retrieved from http://rooyesh.blog.com/2007/06/09/inside-iran-increasing-aids-awareness/.
Rooz. September 4, 2006
Ruzegar-e Ma. August 27, 2011
Salamt-e Ejtema'. Vol. 5. Tehran: DCHQ, March 2015. Retrieved from http://publisher.dchq.ir.
  Vol. 6. Tehran: DCHQ, July 2015. Retrieved from http://publisher.dchq.ir.
  Vol. 7. Tehran: DCHQ, March 2016. Retrieved from http://publisher.dchq.ir.
Salamat News. August 28, 2011. Retrieved from www.salamatnews.com/news/32808/.

  May 8, 2012
  October 22, 2013. Retrieved from www.salamatnews.com/news/85137/.
Sepideh. July 26, 2012

Sharq. June 12, 2006
August 5, 2006
September 5, 2006
July 26, 2010
August 5, 2010
August 8, 2010
October 13, 2010
May 5, 2012
June 28, 2012
July 24, 2012
September 24, 2012
November 3, 2013. Retrieved from http://sharghdaily.ir/1392/08/14/Files/PDF/13920814-1874-22-12.pdf.
June 11, 2014
October 11, 2015. Retrieved from http://sharghdaily.ir/News/75647.
November 16, 2015. Retrieved from www.sharghdaily.ir/News/78788.
Sobh-e Emruz. January 31, 2000
Tabnak. February 8, 2013. Retrieved from www.tabnak.ir/fa/news/301709.
December 30, 2013. Retrieved from www.tabnak.ir/fa/news/366881.
December 21, 2015. Retrieved from www.tabnak.ir/fa/news/555470.
Yas-e-no Daily. December 21, 2003

Secondary Sources (English and Persian)

Books and Journal Articles

Abrahamian, Ervand. *Iran between Two Revolutions.* Princeton University Press, 1982.
  Khomeinism: Essays on the Islamic Republic. University of California Press, 1993.
  Tortured Confessions: Prisons and Public Recantations in Modern Iran. University of California Press, 1999.
  The Coup: 1953, the CIA, and the Roots of Modern US–Iranian Relations. The New Press, 2013.
Abrams, Philip. 'Notes on the Difficulty of Studying the State (1977)'. *Journal of Historical Sociology* 1, no. 1 (1988): 58–89.
Adelkhah, Fariba. *Being Modern in Iran.* Columbia University Press, 2000.
  Les Mille et une Frontières de L'Iran: Quand les Voyages Forment la Nation. Karthala Editions, 2012.

Adelkhah, Fariba, and Zuzanna, Olszewska. 'The Iranian Afghans'. *Iranian Studies* 40, 2 (2007): 137–65.
Afary, Janet. *The Iranian Constitutional Revolution, 1906–1911: Grassroots Democracy, Social Democracy, & the Origins of Feminism*. Columbia University Press, 1996.
Sexual Politics in Modern Iran. Cambridge University Press, 2009.
Afkhami, Amir. 'Compromised Constitutions: The Iranian Experience with the 1918 Influenza Pandemic'. *Bulletin of the History of Medicine* 77, no. 2 (2003): 367–92.
'From Punishment to Harm Reduction: Resecularization of Addiction in Contemporary Iran'. *Contemporary Iran: Economy, Society, Politics* (2009): 194–210.
Agamben, Giorgio. *Homo Sacer: Il Potere Sovrano e La Nuda Vita*. Bollati Boringhieri, 1995.
Means without End: Notes on Politics. Vol. 20. University of Minnesota Press, 2000.
'Security and Terror'. *Theory & Event* 5, no. 4 (2001).
Stato Di Eccezione. Bollati Boringhieri, 2003.
'Comment l'Obsession Sécuritaire fait Muter le Monde'. *Le Monde Diplomatique*. January 2004. Retrieved from www.monde-diplomatique.fr/2014/01/AGAMBEN/49997.
'Elogio della profanazione' in *Profanazioni*. Roma: Nottetempo (2005).
Il sacramento del Linguaggio: Archeologia del Giuramento (Homo sacer II, 3). Vol. 164. Laterza, 2008.
Signatura Rerum: Sul Metodo. Bollati Boringhieri, 2008.
Il Regno e la Gloria: Per una Genealogia Teologica del l'Economia e del Governo (Homo Sacer, II, 2). Bollati Boringhieri, 2009.
'From the State of Control to the Praxis of Destituent Power'. Public Lecture in Athens, November 16 (2013).
'For a Theory of Destituent Power'. *Kronos* (2013).
Ahmad, Jalal Al-e. *Occidentosis: A Plague from the West*. Mizan Press, 1983. *Safar be velayat-e Ezra'il [A journey to the land of Israel]*. (Majid, 1373 [1995]).
Alavi, Nasreen. *We Are Iran*. Raincoast Books, 2005.
Alemi, AA, and MM Naraghi. 'The Iceberg of Opium Addiction an Epidemiological Survey of Opium Addiction in a Rural Community'. *Drug and Alcohol Dependence* 3, no. 2 (1978): 107–12.
Alexander, Bruce. *The Globalization of Addiction: A Study in Poverty of the Spirit*. Oxford University Press, 2010.
Alimardani, Ali Akbar. 'Mavadd-e Mokhadder va Rezhim-e Pahlavi'. *Faslnameh-ye Motale'at-e Tarikh* 25 (2008 [1388]): 112–147.

Ansari, Ali M. *Islam, Iran and Democracy: The Politics of Managing Change*. Royal Institute of International Affairs, 2006.

Arjomand, Said Amir, and Nathan J. Brown, eds. *The Rule of Law, Islam, and Constitutional Politics in Egypt and Iran*. SUNY Press, 2013.

Asad, Talal. 'Where Are the Margins of the State?' *Anthropology in the Margins of the State* (2004): 279–88.

Assari, Shervin, Mosaieb Yarmohamadivasel, Maryam Moghani Lankarani, Mahmood Sehat, Hooman Narenjiha, Hassan Rafiey, Roya Noori, Peymaneh Shirinbayan, and Khodabakhsh Ahmadi. 'Having Multiple Sexual Partners among Iranian Intra-Venous Drug Users'. *Frontiers in Psychiatry* 5 (2014): 125.

Auyero, Javier. 'Introductory Note to Politics under the Microscope: Special Issue on Political Ethnography'. *Qualitative Sociology* 29, no. 3 (2006): 257–9.

Auyero, Javier, Lauren Joseph, and Matthew Mahler. *New Perspectives in Political Ethnography*. Springer, 2007.

Azarkhosh, Jahan-'alì. *Afat-e Zendegi*. Chapp-e Gohar, 1956 [1334].

Bakhash, Shaul. 'Iran's Remarkable Election'. *Journal of Democracy* 9, no. 1 (1998): 80–94.

Banakar, Reza, and Shahrad Nasrolahi Fard. 'Driving Dangerously: Law, Culture and Driving Habits in Iran'. *British Journal of Middle Eastern Studies* 39, no. 2 (2012): 241–57.

Bayart, Jean-François. 'Thermidor en Iran'. *Politique Étrangère* (1991): 701–14.

Le Politique par le bas en Afrique Noire. Karthala Editions, 2008.

L'Islam Républicain: Ankara, Téhéran, Dakar. Albin Michel, 2011.

Bayat, Asef. *Street Politics: Poor People's Movements in Iran*. Columbia University Press, 1997.

'Un-Civil Society: The Politics of the "Informal People"'. *Third World Quarterly* 18, no. 1 (1997): 53–72.

Making Islam Democratic: Social Movements and the Post-Islamist Turn. Stanford University Press, 2007.

Life as Politics: How Ordinary People Change the Middle East. Stanford University Press, 2013.

Bayat, Asef, and Linda Herrera. *Being Young and Muslim: New Cultural Politics in the Global South and North*. Oxford University Press, 2010.

Beck, Lois. *Nomad: A Year in the Life of a Qashqa'i Tribesman in Iran*. University of California Press, 1991.

Behrouzan, Orkideh. 'An Epidemic of Meanings: HIV and AIDS in Iran and the Significance of History, Language and Gender'. In *The Fourth Wave: Violence, Gender, Culture and HIV in the 21st Century*. Paris: UNESCO (2011).

'Writing Prozāk Diaries in Tehran: Generational Anomie and Psychiatric Subjectivities'. *Culture, Medicine, and Psychiatry* 39, no. 3 (2015): 399–426.

Prozak Diaries: Psychiatry and Generational Memory in Iran. Stanford University Press, 2016.

Behrouzan, Orkideh, and Michael MJ Fischer. '"Behaves Like a Rooster and Cries Like a (Four-Eyed) Canine": The Politics and Poetics of Depression and Psychiatry in Iran'. In *Genocide and Mass Violence Memory, Symptom, and Recovery: Health and Clinical Psychology* (2014): 105–36.

Belmonte, M., ed. *Foreign Relations of the United States, 1969–1976, Volume E–4, Documents on Iran and Iraq, 1969–1972*, Washington, DC, 2006.

Berridge, Virginia, and Griffith Edwards. *Opium and the People*. ABC, 1982.

Berridge, Virginia, and Alex Mold. *Concepts of Addictive Substances and Behaviours across Time and Place*. Oxford University Press, 2016.

Borjian, Maryam. 'The Rise and Fall of a Partnership: The British Council and the Islamic Republic of Iran (2001–09)'. *Iranian Studies* 44, no. 4 (2011): 541–62.

Boroujerdi, Mehrzad. 'The Paradoxes of Politics in Postrevolutionary Iran'. In *Iran at the Crossroads*. New York: Palgrave Macmillan, 2001: 1–27.

Bourdieu, Pierre. 'Rethinking the State: Genesis and Structure of the Bureaucratic Field'. In Steinmetz, *State/Culture: State-Formation after the Cultural Turn* (1999): 53–75.

'The Mystery of the Ministry: From Particular Wills to the General Will'. *Constellations* 11, no. 1 (2004): 37–43.

Bourdieu, Pierre, and Loïc Wacquant. *An Invitation to Reflexive Sociology*. University of Chicago Press, 1992.

Bourgois, Philippe. 'Disciplining Addictions: The Bio-Politics of Methadone and Heroin in the United States'. *Culture, Medicine and Psychiatry* 24, no. 2 (2000): 165–95.

'Anthropology and Epidemiology on Drugs: The Challenges of Cross-Methodological and Theoretical Dialogue'. *International Journal of Drug Policy* 13, no. 4 (2002): 259–69.

In Search of Respect: Selling Crack in El Barrio. Vol. 10. Cambridge University Press, 2003.

Bourgois, Philippe, and Jeffrey Schonberg. *Righteous Dopefiend*. Vol. 21. University of California Press, 2009.

Brass, Paul R. 'Foucault Steals Political Science'. *Annual Review of Political Science* 3, no. 1 (2000): 305–30.

Brownlee, Billie Jeanne, and Maziyar Ghiabi. 'Passive, Silent and Revolutionary: The "Arab Spring" revisited'. *Middle East Critique* 25, no. 3 (2016): 1–18.

Burchell, Graham. 'Liberal Government and Techniques of the Self'. In *Foucault and Political Reason: Liberalism, Neo-Liberalism, and Rationalities of Government*. University of Chicago Press, 1996.

Burroughs, William. 'The Limits of Control'. *Semiotext(e): Schizo-Culture* III, no. 2 (1978), 38–42.

Buxton, Julia. 'The political economy of narcotics'. In *Production, Consumption & Global Markets*. Fernwood Publishing & Zed Books, 2006.

Calabrese, John. *'Iran's War on Drugs: Holding the Line'*. The Middle East Institute, 2007.

Campos, Isaac. *Home Grown: Marijuana and the Origins of Mexico's War on Drugs*. University of North Carolina Press, 2012.

Carrier, Neil, and Gernot Klantschnig. *Africa and the War on Drugs*. Zed Books, 2012.

Chouvy, Pierre-Arnaud. *Opium: Uncovering the Politics of the Poppy*. Harvard University Press, 2009.

Chouvy, Pierre-Arnaud, and Joël Meissonnier. *Yaa baa: Production, traffic, and consumption of methamphetamine in mainland Southeast Asia*. NUS Press, 2004.

Christensen, Janne Bjerre. 'Human Rights and Wrongs in Iran's Drug Diplomacy with Europe'. *The Middle East Journal* 71, no. 3 (2017), 403–32.

Drugs, Deviancy and Democracy in Iran: The Interaction of State and Civil Society. Vol. 32. IB Tauris, 2011.

Clark, Janine A. 'Field Research Methods in the Middle East'. *PS: Political Science & Politics* 39, no. 3 (2006): 417–24.

Clune, Michael W. *White Out: The Secret Life of Heroin*. Hazelden Publishing, 2013.

Collins, John, eds. 'Governing the Global Drug Wars' (LSE Ideas, 2012).

'Regulations and Prohibitions: Anglo-American Relations and International Drug Control, 1939–1964'. London School of Economics, PhD Thesis, 2015.

Courtwright, David. *Dark Paradise*. Harvard University Press, 2009.

Forces of Habit: Drugs and the Making of the Modern World. Harvard University Press, 2009.

Courtwright, David T., Herman Joseph, and Don Des Jarlais. *Addicts Who Survived: An Oral History of Narcotic Use in America before 1965*. University of Tennessee Press, 2013.

Cowan, Richard. 'How the Narcs Created Crack'. *National Review* 38 (1986): 26–31.
Cronin, Stephanie. 'Resisting the New State: Peasants and Pastoralists in Iran, 1921–41'. *The Journal of Peasant Studies* 32, no. 1 (2005): 1–47.
  ed. *The Making of Modern Iran: State and Society under Riza Shah, 1921–1941*. Routledge, 2003.
  Tribal Politics in Iran: Rural Conflict and the New State, 1921–1941. Vol. 3. Routledge, 2007.
  Subalterns and Social Protest: History from below in the Middle East and North Africa. Vol. 7. Routledge, 2008.
  Soldiers, Shahs and Subalterns in Iran: Opposition, Protest and Revolt, 1921–1941. Springer, 2010.
Dalvand, Shahin, Cyrus Agahi, and Christopher Spencer. 'Drug Addicts Seeking Treatment after the Iranian Revolution: A Clinic-Based Study'. *Drug and Alcohol Dependence* 14, no. 1 (1984): 87–92.
Das, Veena. 'The Signature of the State: The Paradox of Illegibility'. *Anthropology in the Margins of the State* (2004): 225–52.
Das, Veena, and Deborah Poole. *Anthropology in the Margins*. SAR Press, 2004.
Davis, Mike, and Daniel Bertrand Monk, eds. *Evil Paradises: Dreamworlds of Neoliberalism*. The New Press, 2011.
de Groot, Joanna. 'Kerman in the Late Nineteenth Century: A Regional Study of Society and Social Change'. University of Oxford, DPhil Thesis, 1978.
Dean, Mitchell, and Kaspar Villadsen. *State Phobia and Civil Society: The Political Legacy of Michel Foucault*. Stanford University Press, 2016.
Deleuze, Gilles. *Foucault*. University of Minnesota Press, 1988.
  'Post-scriptum sur les sociétés de contrôle'. In *Pourparlers*. Paris: Les Editions de Minuit, 1990.
  Deux régimes de fous: Textes et entretiens 1975–1995. Minuit, 2003.
  Due Regimi di Folli e Altri Scritti: Testi e Interviste 1975–1995. Einaudi, 2010.
Deleuze, Gilles, and Félix Guattari. '*Mille Plateaux: Capitalisme Et Schizophrénie Ii*'. Minuit, 1980.
Ebrahimnejad, Hormoz. *Medicine, Public Health, and the Qājār State: Patterns of Medical Modernization in Nineteenth-Century Iran*. Vol. 4. Brill, 2004.
Ehteshami, Anoushiravan. *After Khomeini: The Iranian Second Republic*. Routledge, 2002.

Ehteshami, Anoushiravan, and Mahjoob Zweiri. *Iran and the Rise of Its Neoconservatives: The Politics of Tehran's Silent Revolution*. IB Tauris, 2007.
Elling, Rasmus. *Minorities in Iran: Nationalism and Ethnicity after Khomeini*. Springer, 2013.
Encyclopedia Iranica, 'Song in Praise of Opium'. April 27, 1969. Retrieved from www.iranicaonline.org/articles/song-praise-opium.
Erami, Narges, and Arang Keshavarzian. 'When Ties Don't Bind: Smuggling Effects, Bazaars and Regulatory Regimes in Postrevolutionary Iran'. *Economy and Society* 44, no. 1 (2015): 110–39.
Faghihi, Rohollah. 'Rezaei Returns to His Military Roots'. *Al-Monitor* May 13, 2015.
Fardoust, Hossein. *The Rise and Fall of the Pahlavi Dynasty*. Hadis Publishing House, 1995
Farhi, Farideh. 'Constitutionalism and Parliamentary Struggle for Relevance and Independence'. In *The Rule of Law, Islam, and Constitutional Politics in Egypt and Iran*. Edited by Arjomand and Brown, 2013.
Farhoudian, Ali, Mandana Sadeghi, Hamid Reza Khoddami Vishteh, Babak Moazen, Monir Fekri, and Afarin Rahimi Movaghar. 'Component Analysis of Iranian Crack: A Newly Abused Narcotic Substance in Iran'. *Iranian Journal of Pharmaceutical Research* 13, no. 1 (2014): 337–44.
Farrell, Graham, and John Thorne. 'Where Have All the Flowers Gone?: Evaluation of the Taliban Crackdown against Opium Poppy Cultivation in Afghanistan'. *International Journal of Drug Policy* 16, no. 2 (2005): 81–91.
Fasihi, Samin, and Farideh Farzi. 'Mas'aleh-ye Tariyak dar Jame'eh-ye 'asr-e Reza Shah'. *Tarikh-e Eslam va Iran* 25, no. 25 (2015).
Fassin, Didier. *L'espace politique de la santé: essai de généalogie*. Presses universitaires de France, 1996.
  La Force de L'ordre: Une Anthropologie de la Police des Quartiers. Editions du Seuil, 2011.
Feifer, Gregory. *The Great Gamble: The Soviet War in Afghanistan*. Harper New York, 2009.
Feldman, Gregory. 'Illuminating the Apparatus: Steps toward a Nonlocal Ethnography of Global Governance'. In *Policy Worlds: Anthropology and the Analysis of Contemporary Power*. Edited by Cris Shore, Susan Wright, and Davide Pero. Berghahn Books, 2011: 32–49.
Foot, John. *La 'Republica dei matti': Franco Basaglia e la psichiatria radicale in Italia 1961–1978*. Feltrinelli, 2015.
Foucault, Michel. '*Surveiller et Punir*'. Gallimard, 1975.

Discipline and Punish: The Birth of the Prison. Vintage, 1977.
Language, Counter-Memory, Practice: Selected Essays and Interviews. Cornell University Press, 1980.
'Il Faut Défendre La Société'. *Cours Au Collège De France, 1976*' (1997).
Garcia, Angela. *The Pastoral Clinic: Addiction and Dispossession along the Rio Grande*. University of California Press, 2010.
Garland, David. *Punishment and Welfare: A History of Penal Strategies*. Gower, 1985.
Geertz, Clifford. 'Deep Hanging Out'. *The New York Review of Books* 45, no. 16 (1998): 69–72.
Ghiabi, Maziyar. 'Drugs and Revolution in Iran: Islamic Devotion, Revolutionary Zeal and Republican Means'. *Iranian Studies* 48, no. 2 (2015): 139–63.
'Deconstructing the Islamic Bloc: Middle East and North Africa and Pluralistic Drug Policy'. In *Collapse of the Global Order on Drugs? From UNGASS 2016 to the High Level Review 2019*. Edited by Stothard and Klein. Esmerald Publication, 2018.
'Drogues illégales et gestion de l'espace dans l'Iran moderne'. *Hérodote* 2 (2018): 133–51.
'Maintaining Disorder: The Micropolitics of Drugs Policy in Iran'. *Third World Quarterly* 39, no. 2 (2018): 277–97.
'Spirit and Being: Interdisciplinary Reflections on Drugs across History and Politics'. *Third World Quarterly* 39, no. 2 (2018): 207–17.
'Under the Bridge in Tehran: Addiction, Poverty and Capital'. *Ethnography* (2018): 1466138118787534.
Ghiabi, Maziyar, Masoomeh Maarefand, Hamed Bahari, and Zohreh Alavi. 'Islam and cannabis: Legalisation and religious debate in Iran'. *International Journal of Drug Policy* 56 (2018): 121–7.
Ghobadzadeh, Naser. *Religious Secularity: A Theological Challenge to the Islamic State*. Oxford University Press, 2014.
Ghobadzadeh, Naser, and Lily Zubaidah Rahim. 'Electoral Theocracy and Hybrid Sovereignty in Iran', *Contemporary Politics* 22, no. 4 (2016): 450–68.
Gingeras, Ryan. 'Poppy Politics: American Agents, Iranian Addicts and Afghan Opium, 1945–80'. *Iranian Studies* 45, no. 3 (2012): 315–31.
'Istanbul Confidential: Heroin, Espionage, and Politics in Cold War Turkey, 1945–1960'. *Diplomatic History* 37, no. 4 (2013): 779–806.
Godazgar, Hossein. 'Islam Versus Consumerism and Postmodernism in the Context of Iran'. *Social Compass* 54, no. 3 (2007): 389–418.
Gramsci, Antonio. *Quaderni dal Carcere*. Torino: Einaudi, 1977.
Groseclose, Elgin Earl. *Introduction to Iran*. Oxford University Press, 1947.

Gubrium, Jaber, and A. Holstein. 'Active Interviewing'. In *Qualitative Research: Theory, Method and Practice*, second edition. Sage, 1997.
Haghdoost, Ali-Akbar, Ali Mirzadeh, Mostafa Shokoohi, Abbas Sedaghat, and Mohammad Mahdi Gouya. 'Hiv Trend among Iranian Prisoners in 1990s and 2000s; Analysis of Aggregated Data from Hiv Sentinel Sero-Surveys'. *Harm Reduction Journal* 10, no. 1 (2013): 1.
Hajjarian, Saeed. *Jomhuriyat; Afsunzodayi az Qodrat [Republicanism: Demistification of Power]*. Tehran: Tarh-e Nou, 1379.
Hansen, Bradley. 'Learning to Tax: The Political Economy of the Opium Trade in Iran, 1921–1941'. *The Journal of Economic History* 61, no. 1 (2001): 95–113.
Hansen, Thomas Blom, and Finn Stepputat. *States of Imagination: Ethnographic Explorations of the Postcolonial State*. Duke University Press, 2001.
Sovereign Bodies: Citizens, Migrants, and States in the Postcolonial World. Princeton University Press, 2009.
Hari, Johann. *Chasing the Scream: The First and Last Days of the War on Drugs*. Bloomsbury Publishing USA, 2015.
Harris, Kevan. 'A Martyrs' Welfare State and Its Contradictions: Regime Resilience and Limits through the Lens of Social Policy in Iran'. In *Middle East Authoritarianisms: Governance, Contestation, and Regime Resilience in Syria and Iran*, 2013: 61–80.
'The Rise of the Subcontractor State: Politics of Pseudo-Privatization in the Islamic Republic of Iran'. *International Journal of Middle East Studies* 45, no. 1 (2013): 45–70.
Hibou, Béatrice. *Privatizing the State*. Columbia University Press, 2004.
'Economic Crime and Neoliberal Modes of Government: The Example of the Mediterranean'. *Journal of Social History* 45, no. 3 (2012): 642–60.
'Introduction. La Bureaucratisation Néolibérale, Ou La Domination Et Le Redéploiement De L'état Dans Le Monde Contemporain'. In *La Bureaucratisation Néolibérale* 7–20: La Découverte, 2013.
Homayounpour, Gohar. *Doing Psychoanalysis in Tehran*. MIT Press, 2012.
Hourcade, Bernard. 'L'émergence Des Banlieues De Téhéran'. *Cahiers d'études sur la méditerranée orientale et le monde turco-iranien* no. 24 (1997): 165–181.
Hyatt, Susan Brin. 'What Was Neoliberalism and What Comes Next? The Transformation of Citizenship in the Law-and-Order State'. *Policy Worlds: Anthropology and the Analysis of Contemporary Power* 14: 105.
Inda, Jonathan Xavier, ed. *Anthropologies of Modernity: Foucault, Governmentality, and Life Politics*. John Wiley & Sons, 2008.

Ismail, Salwa. *Political Life in Cairo's New Quarters: Encountering the Everyday State*. University of Minnesota Press, 2006.
Jahanbegloo, Ramin. 'The Two Sovereignties and the Legitimacy Crisis in Iran'. *Constellations* 17, no. 1 (2010): 22–30.
'The Cultural Turn in New Democratic Theory' in *Democratic Theorists in Conversation*. Palgrave Macmillan, 2014: 56–71.
Kashani-Sabet, Firoozeh. 'Hallmarks of Humanism: Hygiene and Love of Homeland in Qajar Iran'. *The American Historical Review* 105, no. 4 (2000): 1171–1203.
Conceiving Citizens: Women and the Politics of Motherhood in Iran. Oxford University Press on Demand, 2011.
Katouzian, Homa. *Iranian History and Politics: The Dialectic of State and Society*. Routledge, 2012.
Keane, Helen. 'Critiques of Harm Reduction, Morality and the Promise of Human Rights'. *International Journal of Drug Policy* 14, no. 3 (2003): 227–32.
'Foucault on Methadone: Beyond Biopower'. *International Journal of Drug Policy* 20, no. 5 (2009): 450–2.
Keshavarzian, Arang. *Bazaar and State in Iran: The Politics of the Tehran Marketplace*. Cambridge University Press, 2007.
Keyvan Ara Mohammad, Kianush Mas'ud and Jianpour Mehdi, 'Addicts' experiences about the medicalisation of addiction [Tajarob-e mo'tadan az pezeshki shodan-e'tiyad]'. *Rafah-e Ejtema'i*, 29 (2010).
Khalaji, Mehdi. 'Iran's Regime of Religion'. *Journal of International Affairs* (2011): 131–47.
Khalkhali, Sadegh (ayatollah), *Ayyam-e Enzeva* Vol. I–II. Nashr-e Sayeh, 2010.
Khatam, Azam. 'Struggles Over Defining the Moral City: The Problem Called 'Youth' in Urban Iran'. *Being Young and Muslim: New Cultural Politics in the Global South and North*. 2010.
Khiabany, Gholam. *Iranian Media: The Paradox of Modernity*. Routledge, 2009.
Khomeini, Imam, Ruhollah Khomeini, and Hamid Algar. *Islamic Government: Governance of the Jurist*. Alhoda UK, 2002.
Khosravi, Shahram. *Young and Defiant in Tehran*. University of Pennsylvania Press, 2008.
Precarious Lives: Waiting and Hope in Iran. University of Pennsylvania Press, 2017.
Khosrokhavar, Farhad. 'The New Intellectuals in Iran'. *Social Compass* 51, no. 2 (2004): 191–202.
'The New Conservatives Take a Turn'. *Middle East Report* 233 (2004): 24–27.

Khosrokhavar, Farhad, and Amin Ghaneirad. 'Iran's New Scientific Community 1'. *Iranian Studies* 39, no. 2 (2006): 253–67.
Kian-Thiébaut, Azadeh. 'L'individu dans Le Monde: Paradoxe de L'iran Islamique'. *Cahiers d'Etudes sur la Méditerranée Orientale et le monde Turco-Iranien*, no. 26 (1998).
Kreutzmann, Hermann. 'Afghanistan and the Opium World Market: Poppy Production and Trade'. *Iranian Studies* 40, no. 5 (2007): 605–21.
Krohn-Hansen, Christian. 'Negotiated Dictatorship: The Building of the Trujillo State in the Southwestern Dominican Republic'. In *State Formation: Anthropological Perspectives*. Edited by C. Krohn-Hansen and K. G. Nustad. Pluto Press, 2005: 96–122.
Kubik, Jan. 'Ethnography of Politics: Foundations, Applications, Prospects'. In *Political Ethnography: What Immersion Contributes to the Study of Power*. University of Chicago Press, 2009: 25–52.
Künkler, Mirjam. 'The Special Court of the Clergy and the Repression of Dissident Clergy in Iran'. In *The Rule of Law, Islam, and Constitutional Politics in Egypt and Iran*. Edited by Arjomand and Brown. Suny Press, 2009.
Kurzman, Charles. *The Unthinkable Revolution in Iran*. Harvard University Press, 2009.
Ladier-Fouladi, Marie. '*Iran, un Monde de Paradoxes*'. L'Atlante, 2009.
Landriscina, Mirella. 'Professional Performances on a Well-Constructed Stage: The Case of an Institutionalized Advocacy Organization'. In *New Perspectives in Political Ethnography*, 180–204: Springer, 2007.
Langford, Michelle. 'Allegory and the Aesthetics of Becoming-Woman in Marziyeh Meshkini's *The Day I Became a Woman*'. *Camera Obscura* 22, no. 1 64 (2007): 1–41.
Law, John. *After Method: Mess in Social Science Research*. Routledge, 2004.
Levine, Harry G. 'Global Drug Prohibition: Its Uses and Crises'. *International Journal of Drug Policy* 14, no. 2 (2003): 145–153.
Lund, Christian. 'Twilight Institutions: An Introduction'. *Development and Change* 37, no. 4 (2006): 673–84.
MacCormack, W., Moses Khan, and Muḥammad K. Āmirī. *Memorandum on Persian Opium: Prepared for Dr. Ac Mispaugh, Administrator General of the Finances*. Parliament Press, 1924.
Machiavelli, Niccolò. *Il Principe*. Einaudi, 1961.
Discorsi sopra la prima deca di Tito Livio. Mursia, 1969.
Mahdavi, Pardis. *Passionate Uprisings: Iran's Sexual Revolution*. Stanford University Press, 2009.
'Who Will Catch Me If I Fall? Health and the Infrastructure of Risk for Urban Young Iranians'. *Contemporary Iran: Economy, Society, Politics* (2009).

Mahdavi, Shireen. 'Shahs, Doctors, Diplomats and Missionaries in 19th Century Iran'. *British Journal of Middle Eastern Studies* 32, no. 2 (2005): 169–191.

Majd, Hooman. *The Ayatollah Begs to Differ: The Paradox of Modern Iran*. Anchor Canada, 2009.

Marcus, George E. 'Ethnography in/of the World System: The Emergence of Multi-Sited Ethnography'. *Annual Review of Anthropology* (1995): 95–117.

Marlowe, Ann. *How to Stop Time: Heroin from A to Z*. Basic Books, 1999.

Mars, S. *The Politics of Addiction: Medical Conflict and Drug Dependence in England since the 1960s*. Springer, 2012.

Martin, Vanessa. *Creating an Islamic state: Khomeini and the Making of a New Iran*. Vol. 24. IB Tauris, 2003.

Matthee, Rudolph P. *The Pursuit of Pleasure: Drugs and Stimulants in Iranian History, 1500–1900*. Princeton University Press, 2005.

Mauss, Marcel. 'Essai sur le don forme et raison de l'échange dans les sociétés archaïques.' *L'Année sociologique (1896/1897–1924/1925)* 1 (1923): 30–186.

McAllister, William B. *Drug Diplomacy in the Twentieth Century: An International History*. Psychology Press, 2000.

McCoy, Alfred W. *The Politics of Heroin: Cia Complicity in the Global Drug Trade, Afghanistan, Southeast Asia, Central America*. Lawrence Hill Books, 2003.

McLaughlin, Gerald T, and Thomas M. Quinn. 'Drug Control in Iran: A Legal and Historical Analysis'. *Iowa Law Review* 59 (1973): 469.

Mehrjerdi, Zahra Alam. 'Crystal in Iran: Methamphetamine or Heroin Kerack'. *DARU Journal of Pharmaceutical Sciences* 21, no. 1 (2013): 1.

Mehryar, A. H., and M. R. Moharreri. 'A Study of Authorized Opium Addiction in Shiraz City and Fars Province, Iran'. *British Journal of Addiction to Alcohol & Other Drugs* 73, no. 1 (1978): 93–102.

Messkoub, Mahmood. 'Social Policy in Iran in the Twentieth Century'. *Iranian Studies* 39, no. 02 (2006): 227–52.

Michelstaedter, Carlo. *La Persuasione e La Rettorica*. Adelphi, 1986.

Migdal, Joel S. *State in Society: Studying How States and Societies Transform and Constitute One Another*. Cambridge University Press, 2001.

Migdal, Joel S, and Klaus Schlichte. 'Rethinking the State'. In *The Dynamics of States: The Formation and Crises of State Domination*. Routledge, 2005: 1–40.

Milani, Abbas. 'Three Paradoxes of Islamic Revolution in Iran'. In *The Iranian Revolution at 30* (2010).

Mills, James. 'Decolonising drugs in Asia: the case of cocaine in colonial India'. *Third World Quarterly* 39, no. 2 (2018): 218–231.

Millspaugh, Arthur Chester. *The American Task in Persia, by AC Millspaugh*. Century Company, 1925.

Americans in Persia. Brookings Institution, 1946.

Mitchell, Timothy. 'Society, Economy, and the State Effect'. In Steinmetz, *State/Culture: State-Formation after the Cultural Turn*. Cornell University Press, 1999.

Rule of Experts: Egypt, Techno-Politics, Modernity. University of California Press, 2002.

'Society, Economy, and the State Effect'. In *The Anthropology of the State: A Reader*. Edited by Sharma and Gupta. John Wiley & Sons, 2009: 169–86.

Moinifar, Heshmat Sadat. 'Religious Leaders and Family Planning in Iran'. *Iran and the Caucasus* 11, no. 2 (2007): 299–313.

Mold, Alex. *The Treatment of Addiction on Twentieth Century Britain*. Northern Illinois University Press, 2008.

Monroe, Kristen R. *Perestroika!: The Raucous Rebellion in Political Science*. Yale University Press, 2005.

Moslem, Mehdi. *Factional Politics in Post-Khomeini Iran*. Syracuse University Press, 2002.

Mottahedeh, Negar. *Displaced Allegories: Post-Revolutionary Iranian Cinema*. Duke University Press, 2008.

Musto, F. David. *The American Disease: Origins of Narcotic Control*. New York: Oxford University Press, 1999 [1973].

Mowlana, Hamid. 'The Politics of Opium in Iran: A Social-Psychological Interface'. In *Drugs, Politics, and Diplomacy*. Edited by Simmons and Said (1974): 162–63.

NA Today, 'Special edition: the Iranian updates' [aka The Iran Diaries], February 2007. Retrieved from na.org.au/content/natoday/2007/natoday200702.pdf.

Nadelmann, Ethan A. 'Global Prohibition Regimes: The Evolution of Norms in International Society'. *International Organization* 44, no. 4 (1990): 479–526.

Nader, Laura. *The Life of the Law: Anthropological Projects*. University of California Press, 2002.

Najmabadi, Afsaneh. *Professing Selves: Transsexuality and Same-Sex Desire in Contemporary Iran*. Duke University Press, 2013.

Narenjiha, Hooman, and Noori Roya. 'Methadone Maintenance Therapy Outcomes in Iran [unpublished report, Farsi]' (2006).

Narenjiha, Hooman, Hassan Rafiey, Mohammad Reza Jahani, Shervin Assari, Yashar Moharamzad, and Mohsen Roshanpazooh. 'Substance-

Dependent Professional Drivers in Iran: A Descriptive Study'. *Traffic Injury Prevention* 10, no. 3 (2009): 227–30.
Navaro-Yashin, Yael. *Faces of the State: Secularism and Public Life in Turkey*. Princeton University Press, 2002.
Neligan, Anthony Richard. 'The Opium Question with Special Reference to Persia'. *JSTOR*, 1929.
Nietzsche, Friedrich. *The Gay Science*. Trans. Josefine Nauckhoff. Cambridge University Press, 2001.
Noori, Roya, Homan Narenjiha, Habibollah Aghabakhshi, Gholamreza Habibi, and Babak Khoshkrood Mansoori. 'Methadone Maintenance Therapy Outcomes in Iran'. *Substance Use & Misuse* 47, no. 7 (2012): 767–73.
Okazaki, Shoko. 'The Great Persian Famine of 1870–71'. *Bulletin of the School of Oriental and African Studies* 49, no. 1 (1986): 183–92.
Olszewska, Zuzanna. 'Classy Kids and Down-at-Heel Intellectuals: Status Aspiration and Blind Spots in the Contemporary Ethnography of Iran'. *Iranian Studies* 46, no. 6 (2013): 841–62.
Pasolini, Pier Paolo. *Scritti Corsari*. Garzanti, 1975.
Polsky, Andrew J. *The Rise of the Therapeutic State*. Princeton University Press, 1993.
Poole, Deborah. 'Between Threat and Guarantee: Justice and Community in the Margins of the Peruvian State'. In *Anthropology in the Margins of the State*. James Currey, School of American Research Press, 2004: 35–65.
Qahrfarkhi, Said Madani. *E'tiyad Dar Iran [Addiction in Iran]*. Nashr-e Sales, 2011 [1390].
Rabi'i, Naser. *Ta'rikh-e zindan dar 'asr-e qajar va pahlavi*. Qaqanus, 2011.
Rabinow, Paul. *Reflections on Fieldwork in Morocco*. University of California Press, 2007.
Rafiey, Hassan, Hooman Narenjiha, Peymaneh Shirinbayan, Roya Noori, Morteza Javadipour, Mohsen Roshanpajouh, Mercedeh Samiei, and Shervin Assari. 'Needle and Syringe Sharing among Iranian Drug Injectors'. *Harm Reduction Journal* 6, no. 1 (2009): 1.
Rahimi-Movaghar, Afarin, Masoumeh Amin-Esmaeili, Behrang Shadloo, Alireza Noroozi, and Mohsen Malekinejad. 'Transition to Injecting Drug Use in Iran: A Systematic Review of Qualitative and Quantitative Evidence'. *International Journal of Drug Policy* 26, no. 9 (2015): 808–19.
Rahnema, Ali. *Behind the 1953 Coup in Iran: Thugs, Turncoats, Soldiers, and Spooks*. Cambridge University Press, 2014.

Randeria, Shalini, and Ciara Grunder. 'The (Un) Making of Policy in the Shadow of the World Bank: Infrastructure Development, Urban Resettlement and the Cunning State in India'. *Policy Worlds: Anthropology and the Analysis of Contemporary Power* 14 (2011): 187–204.

Regavim, Ram Baruch. 'The Most Sovereign of Masters: The History of Opium in Modern Iran, 1850–1955'. PhD thesis, University of Pennsylvenia (2012).

Rejali, Darius M. *Torture & Modernity: Self, Society, and State in Modern Iran*. Westview Press, 1994.

Rhodes, Tim, Singer, Philippe Bourgois, Samuel R. Friedman, and Steffanie A. Strathdee. 'The Social Structural Production of HIV Risk among Injecting Drug Users'. *Social Science & Medicine* 61, no. 5 (2005): 1026–44.

Ridgeon, Lloyd. 'Revolution and a High Ranking Sufi: Zahir Al-Dowleh's Contribution to the Constitutional Movement'. In *Iran's Constitutional Revolution: Popular Politics, Cultural Transformations and Transnational Connections*. Edited by H. E. Chehabi, and V. Martin. I.B. Tauris, 2010.

Robins, Philip. *Middle East Drugs Bazaar: Production, Prevention and Consumption*. Oxford University Press, 2016.

Roitman, Janet. *Anti-Crisis*. Duke University Press, 2013.

Rose, Nikolas. *The Politics of Life Itself: Biomedicine, Power, and Subjectivity in the Twenty-First Century*. Princeton University Press, 2009.

Rosenberg, Tina. 'How Iran Derailed a Health Crisis.' *The New York Times* (2010). https://opinionator.blogs.nytimes.com/2010/12/03/how-iran-derailed-a-health-crisis/

Rostami-Povey, Elaheh. *Afghan Women: Identity and Invasion*. Zed Books, 2007.

Salar, Abdoh, and Charlotte Noruzi. *Urban Iran*. Mark Batty Publisher, 2008.

Salehi-Esfehani, Djavad. 'Tyranny of Numbers. Rising Inequality in Iran: Who Is to Blame?' Retrieved from http://djavadsalehi.com/2009/05/25/whos-to-blame-for-rising-inequality/

Sarrami, Seyfollah. *Ahkam-e Hokumati va Maslahat [Governmental Ordinances and Expediency]*. Center of Strategic Studies. Tehran: 'abeir, 2001 [1380].

Schatz, Edward. *Political Ethnography: What Immersion Contributes to the Study of Power*. University of Chicago Press, 2013.

Schayegh, Cyrus. *Who Is Knowledgeable Is Strong: Science, Class, and the Formation of Modern Iranian Society, 1900–1950*. University of California Press, 2009.

Schirazi, Asghar. *The Constitution of Iran: Politics and the State in the Islamic Republic*. IB Tauris, 1998.
Scott, James C. *Seeing like a State: How Certain Schemes to Improve the Human Condition Have Failed*. Yale University Press, 1998.
Seddon, Toby. *A History of Drugs: Drugs and Freedom in the Liberal Age*. Routledge, 2009.
Semati, Mehdi. *Media, Culture and Society in Iran: Living with Globalization and the Islamic State*. Vol. 5. Routledge, 2007.
Shahidi, Mohammad Hossein, *Mavadd-e Mokhadder, Amniyat-e Ejtema'I va Rah-e Sevvom*. Entesharat-e Ettela'at, 2010 [1389].
Shore, Cris, and Susan Wright. *Anthropology of Policy: Perspectives on Governance and Power*. Routledge, 2003.
Shore, Cris, Susan Wright, and Davide Però. *Policy Worlds: Anthropology and the Analysis of Contemporary Power*. Vol. 14. Berghahn Books, 2011.
Siamdoust, Nahid. *Soundtrack of the Revolution: the Politics of Music in Iran*. Stanford University Press, 2017.
Siassi, Iradj, and Bahman Fozouni. 'Dilemmas of Iran's Opium Maintenance Program: An Action Research for Evaluating Goal Conflicts and Policy Changes'. *International Journal of the Addictions* 15, no. 8 (1980): 1127–40.
Singer, Merrill. *Drugging the Poor: Legal and Illegal Drugs and Social Inequality*. Waveland Press, 2007.
Singer, Merrill, and J. Bryan Page. *Social Value of Drug Addicts: Uses of the Useless*. Left Coast Press, 2013.
Sreberny, Annabelle, and Massoumeh Torfeh. *Cultural Revolution in Iran: Contemporary Popular Culture in the Islamic Republic*. IB Tauris, 2013.
Steinmetz, George, ed. *State/Culture: State-Formation after the Cultural Turn*. Cornell University Press, 1999.
Stel, Nora. 'Languages of Stateness in South Lebanon's Palestinian Gatherings: The PLO's Popular Committees as Twilight Institutions'. *Development and Change* 47, no. 3 (2016): 446–71.
Tashviqi, Foruhar. *Tavalod-e Dobareh*, Vol. I–II. Maktab-e Emam-ol-Hadi, 2012.
Tavakoli-Tarqi, Mohammad. 'Tajaddod-e Ruzmarreh va Ampul tadvin'. *Iran Nameh* 34 (2009).
Taussig, Michael. 'Maleficium: State Fetishism'. *The Nervous System* (1992): 111–40.
Tazmini, Ghoncheh. *Khatami's Iran: The Islamic Republic and the Turbulent Path to Reform*. Vol. 12. IB Tauris, 2009.
Tellenbach, Silvia. 'Principle of Legality in the Iranian Constitutional and Criminal Law'. In *The Rule of Law, Islam, and Constitutional Politics in Egypt and Iran*. Edited by Arjomand and Brown. Suny Press, 2013.

Trouillot, Michel Rolph, Chris Hann, and Lszl Krti. 'The Anthropology of the State in the Age of Globalization 1: Close Encounters of the Deceptive Kind'. *Current Anthropology* 42, no. 1 (2001): 125–38.

Tyrrell, Ian. *Reforming the World: The Creation of America's Moral Empire*. Princeton University Press, 2010.

Valentine, Douglas. *The Strength of the Wolf: The Secret History of America's War on Drugs*. Verso, 2004.

Wacquant, Loïc. *Punishing the Poor: The Neoliberal Government of Social Insecurity*. Duke University Press, 2009.

White, Adam. *The Everyday Life of the State: A State-in-Society Approach*. University of Washington Press, 2013.

WHO. 'Best Practice in Hiv/Aids Prevention and Care for Injecting Drug Abusers: The Triangular Clinic in Kermanshah, Islamic Republic of Iran'. *Cairo: Regional Office for the Eastern Mediterranean* (2004): 12.

Windle, James. *Suppressing Illicit Opium Production: Successful Intervention in Asia and the Middle East*. IB Tauris, 2016.

Yanow, Dvora. 'A Policy Ethnographer's Reading of Policy Anthropology'. *Policy Worlds: Anthropology and the Analysis of Contemporary Power* 14 (2011): 300.

Zarghami, Mehran. 'Methamphetamine Has Changed the Profile of Patients Utilizing Psychiatric Emergency Services in Iran'. *Iranian Journal of Psychiatry and Behavioral Sciences* 5, no. 1 (2011): 1–5.

Zheng, Yangwen. *The Social Life of Opium in China*. Cambridge University Press, 2005.

Zhou, Yongming. *Anti-Drug Crusades in Twentieth-Century China: Nationalism, History, and State Building*. Rowman & Littlefield, 1999.

Zibbell, Jon E. 'Can the Lunatics Actually Take over the Asylum?: Reconfiguring Subjectivity and Neo-Liberal Governance in Contemporary British Drug Treatment Policy'. *International Journal of Drug Policy* 15, no. 1 (2004): 56–65.

Zigon, Jarrett. *'HIV Is God's Blessing': Rehabilitating Morality in Neoliberal Russia*. University of California Press, 2010.

'What Is a Situation? An Assemblic Ethnography of the Drug War'. *Cultural Anthropology* 30, no. 3 (2015): 501–24.

Newspapers, Magazines and Other Media (English)

Al-Monitor. October 25, 2013. Retrieved from www.al-monitor.com/pulse/originals/2013/10/iran-alcohol-permit-rehab-center.html.

May 3, 2014. Retrieved from www.al-monitor.com/pulse/originals/2014/05/iran-water-crisis.html.

May 13, 2015. Retrieved from www.al-monitor.com/pulse/ru/contents/articles/originals/2015/05/iran-mohsen-rezaei-irgc-return.html.

Asia Times. August 7, 2007. Retrieved from www.atimes.com/atimes/Middle_East/IH07Ak04.html.

June 5, 2011. Retrieved from www.atimes.com/atimes/Middle_East/MA05Ak01.html.

BBC News. November 27, 1999. Retrieved from http://news.bbc.co.uk/2/hi/middle_east/539470.stm.

February 12, 2015. Retrieved from www.bbc.com/news/technology-31434370.

BBC Persian. August 10, 2005. Retrieved from www.bbc.co.uk/persian/iran/story/2005/08/050801_pm-khatami-presidency.shtml.

October 1, 2010. Retrieved from www.bbc.co.uk/persian/iran/2010/10/100923_l07_iran89_drugs_addiction.shtml.

February 19, 2014. Retrieved from www.bbc.co.uk/persian/iran/2014/02/140219_l57_saeed_madani.

August 10, 2016. Retrieved from www.bbc.com/persian/iran/2016/08/160810_l12_iran_drug_dealer_execution.

BBC. 'Analysis: What Now for Iran?' February 23, 2004. Retrieved from http://news.bbc.co.uk/2/hi/middle_east/3514551.stm.

May 1, 2011. Retrieved from www.bbc.com/news/world-middle-east-13250309.

July 23, 2015. Retrieved from www.bbc.com/news/world-middle-east-33635260.

August 10, 2016. Retrieved from www.bbc.com/news/technology-37012071.

Bloomberg. May 8, 2014. Retrieved from www.bloomberg.com/bw/articles/2014-05-08/irans-best-engineering-science-grads-take-skills-abroad.

Daily Mail. July 1, 2014. Retrieved from www.dailymail.co.uk/news/article-2676733/Hundreds-military-style-boot-camps-set-China-bid-tackle-internet-addiction-teenagers.html.

February 12, 2015. Retrieved from www.dailymail.co.uk/wires/ap/article-2950946/Drug-abuse-Iran-rising-despite-executions-police-raids.html

Dan Baum. 'Legalize it all'. *Harper's Magazine*. April 2016. Retrieved from https://harpers.org/archive/2016/04/legalize-it-all/.

Goffman, Alice. 'The Ethics of Ethnography'. *The Slate*. June 15, 2015. Retrieved from www.slate.com/articles/news_and_politics/crime/2015

/06/alice_goffman_s_on_the_run_is_the_sociologist_to_blame_for_the_inconsistencies.html.
International Harm Reduction Association. 'What Is Harm Reduction?'. Retrieved from www.ihra.net/files/2010/05/31/IHRA_HRStatement.pdf.
Iran Daily. May 4, 2010
    August 20, 2014. Retrieved from www.iran-daily.com/News/640.html.
    October 15, 2014. Retrieved from www.iran-daily.com/News/13436.html.
Middle East Eye. February 13, 2015. Retrieved from www.middleeasteye.net/fr/in-depth/features/iranians-abroad-prison-life-terms-and-execution-925520961.
Jim Muir. 'Analysis: What Now for Iran?' BBC. Retrieved from http://news.bbc.co.uk/2/hi/middle_east/3514551.stm.
New York Times. May 7, 1952
    February 15, 1953
    June 17, 1953
    January 12, 1958
    April 2, 1964
February 11, 1973
Peyvand. 'Tehran's Brothel District'. December 10, 2012. Retrieved from http://payvand.com/blog/blog/2010/12/10/photos-tehrans-brothel-district-shahr-e-no-1975–77-by-kaveh-golestan/.
Politico. 'Matteo Renzi pledges to veto EU budget over refugee crisis'. October 26, 2016. Retrieved from www.politico.eu/article/italy-matteo-renzi-pledges-to-veto-eu-budget-over-refugee-crisis/.
Radio Farda. August 21, 2010. Retrieved from www.radiofarda.com/content/F12_Happiness_engineering_in_Islamic_Republic/2133969.html.
Radio Free Europe/Radio Liberty. April 6, 2006. Retrieved from www.rferl.org/content/article/1067452.html.
    October 3, 2006. Retrieved from www.rferl.org/content/article/1071768.html.
Reuters. October 22, 2014. Retrieved from www.reuters.com/article/2014/10/22/us-iran-divorce-idUSKCN0IB0GQ20141022.
Sadjadpour, Karim. *Foreign Policy.* April 23, 2012. Retrieved from http://foreignpolicy.com/2012/04/23/the-ayatollah-under-the-bedsheets/.
Serat News. April 20, 2015. Retrieved from www.seratnews.ir/fa/news/238533/.

The Daily Star. June 2, 2013. Retrieved from www.dailystar.com.lb/News/Middle-East/2013/Jun-02/219165-iran-court-bans-state-owned-news paper-for-6-months.ashx#axzz2fMW4j9X7.
The Economist. 'The on-demand economy'. Retrieved from www.economist.com/news/leaders/21637393-rise-demand-economy-poses-difficult-questions-workers-companies-and;
  'Ever-resilient but maybe more malleable'. May 5, 2012. Retrieved from www.economist.com/node/21554242.
  'Schumpeter: Getting Hooked'. January 3, 2015.
The Fix. 'The Needle and the Crescent: the remarkable rise of NA in Iran'. Retrieved from www.thefix.com/content/Iran-Narcotics-Anonymous-phonemoneon-Lavitt2099.
The Guardian. November 5, 2008. Retrieved from www.theguardian.com/world/2008/nov/05/ali-kordan-fake-oxford-degree.
  December 9, 2008. Retrieved from www.theguardian.com/world/2008/dec/29/iran-gender.
  July 15, 2009. Retrieved from www.theguardian.com/world/2009/jul/15/iran-plane-crash.
  August 13, 2014. Retrieved from www.theguardian.com/commentisfree/2014/aug/13/woman-wins-fields-medal-odds-maryam-mirzakhani.
  October 29, 2014. Retrieved from www.theguardian.com/global-development/2014/oct/29/sao-paulo-brazil-crack-addicts-drugs.
  February 15, 2015. Retrieved from www.theguardian.com/society/2015/feb/15/students-smart-drugs-higher-grades-adderall-modafinil.
The Independent. December 2, 2012. Retrieved from www.independent.co.uk/life-style/health-and-families/health-news/sex-addiction-the-truth-about-a-modern-phenomenon-8373873.html.
The Telegraph. January 12, 2012. Retrieved from www.telegraph.co.uk/technology/internet/9009125/Internet-addiction-affects-the-brain-like-a-drink-or-drug-problem.html.
Washington Post. April 23, 2015. Retrieved from www.washingtonpost.com/blogs/monkey-cage/wp/2015/04/23/irans-political-economy-under-and-after-the-sanctions/.
Websites
Addiction News Agency, www.adna.ir.
Al-Monitor, www.al-monitor.com.
BBC, www.bbc.com/persian.
Council for the Discernment of the Expediency of the State, www.maslahat.ir.
DCHQ, www.dchq.ir.

Encyclopedia Iranica, www.iranicaonline.org.
Fars News Agency, www.fars.ir.
Harm Reduction International, www.hri.global.
Head of the Judiciary, www.dadiran.ir.
Islamic Republic News Agency, www.irna.ir.
Jam-e Jam, www.jamejamonline.ir.
Mehr News Agency, www.mehr.ir.
Office of the President of the Islamic Republic of Iran: www.president.ir.
Sharq, www.sharghdaily.ir.
UNAID, www.unaids.org.
UNDP, www.undp.org.
UNODC, www.unodc.org.
WHO, www.who.org.

Index

(ab)use
    definition and theory, 22, *See* addiction
(dis)order, 32, 96
'addiction insurance' (*bimeh-ye e'tiyad*), 237
'attari, 38
1360s (1980s) generation, 172
1906–11 Constitutional Revolution. *See* Constitutional Revolution
1909 Shanghai Conference, 40
1911 The Hague Convention on Opium, 41
1925 Geneva Convention on Opium, 45
1941 Pahlavi, Reza in exile, 47
1941–1946 Allied occupation, 48
1953 *coup d'etat* against Mossadeq, 51
1955 Opium Prohibition, 53
1963 White Revolution, 57
1969 Opium Regulation, 63–72
1979 revolution, 8, 27, 168, 270. *See* Islamic Revolution
2009 elections, 168, 170
2nd *Khordad* movement (*jonbesh-e dovvom-e Khordad*), 98
6th Development Plan, 158

Abelabad prison, 109
aberurizi (reputation damage), 212
addiction
    and depression, 176
    and HIV, 203
    and modernity, 37–43
    and NGOs, 245–64, 247, 248, 275, 281
    and spirituality, 253
    and the police, 194–204, 230
    and women, 207–10
    as a crime, 79, 94, 123, 126, 192, 194, 199
    as a disease. *See* medicalisation of
    as a governmental category, 239
    as apparatus, 194–204, 212, 213
    as backwardness, 43
    as crisis, 281
    as disability, 68
    as governmental category, 22, 193, 194, 211, 281
    as invented concept, 37
    conference on, 28, 67, 189, 272
    decriminalisation, 115, 196
    definition, 22
    discussed in the media, 125–6
    etymology, 37
    first case of heroin addiction in Iran, 58
    governmental effect of, 70
    islands for confinement of drug offenders, 81, 128
    Khalkhali's understanding of, 77
    legislation on, 191–6, 233, 241
    linked to ancien regime, 71
    methamphetamine (meth). *See shisheh*
    orientalism, 36
    rates of, 11, 49, 67, 158, 203, 246, 246n, 271
    research on, 240, 244, 254
    shift towards medicalisation, 93, 128, 194, 195, 196, 238
    shisheh, 195
    to sex, 174
Addiction News Agency (ADNA), 261
addiction para-medicine, 97
addicts. *See* drug users *or* addiction
Adelkhah, Fariba, 158, 205
Afghanistan
    criminal networks, 274

323

Afghanistan (cont.)
  illicit drugs as means of survival, 83
  Iran's anti-narcotic strategy, 179
  Iranian ambassador in Kabul, 241
  Iranian foreign policy, 287
  lack of anti-drug cooperation, 83
  Northern Alliance (Afghanistan), 102
  opium production under the Taliban, 101
  opium trafficking, 60, 65, 84, 101, 272
  record opium production, 101
  refusal to end poppy cultivation, 64, 65
  Soviet occupation, 79
  US-led invasion in 2001, 135
  violence related to illicit drugs, 89, 276
Afghans, 84, 274
Agamben, Giorgio, 10
  emergency as permanetn technology of government, 20
  homo sacer, 229
  state of exception, 212, 228
  the true problem of politics, 3, 231
Ahmadinejad, Mahmud
  election in 2005, 165
  new style of government, 232
  on drugs, 232–65
  on harm reduction, 233, 235, 260
  reforms in drug policy, 281
  relations with intellectuals, 287
  representing a new class in power, 170
  second election in 2009, 3
  vision for civil society, 260
  with drug addicts, 234
Ahmadi-Moghaddam, Esma'il, 197, 241, 242
AIDS hospital, 117
Alaei brothers, 117, 118, 124
  arrested on charges of national security, 240
  collaboration with Mohraz, Minoo, 120
  coordination with UNODC, 132
  Triangular clinics in prisons, 120
alcohol (spirit), 49, 50, 51, 125
alcohol dependency, 157
alcohol, ban on, 51, 54, 74

Alcoholics Anonymous, 174, 205, 250
alcoholism, 174, 175
Al-e Ahmad, Jalal, 3, 58
allegory, 27, 29, 30
  in cinema, 28
amphetamine-type stimulants (ATS), 22, 175, 270
Anslinger, Harry J., 52, 55
anthropological mutation, 13, 167, 181, 186, 188
anthropology, 18
anti-imperialism, 287
anti-narcotic police, 179, 201
Anti-Narcotics Bureau (1980s), 71
anti-opium campaigns, 41
Arab Spring, 263, 282
Arak, 185, 189, 208, 209, 210, 211
Arendt, Hannah, 18
Aria Strategic Research Centre, 171
Arlacchi, Pino, 129
art of managing disorder, 14, 15, 235, 262
  as analytical category, 15
  definition, 28
  empirical case, 224
  paradigm of government, 140, 224, 228, 231
ashrar (evils), 83
assemblage
  harm reduction, 114, 125, 135
  methods, 27, 31, 282
Assembly of Experts, 260, 274
authoritarianism, 14, 264
  grassroots, 14, 215, 262, 275, 281
Auyero, Javier, 27
Axis of Evil, 134
Azadi Stadium, 234

baba karam, 60
Bahari, Maziar, 119
Bahman Kucik, 208
Baluch, 84
Baluchistan, 9, 67, 81, 84, 201, 272
banderole (opium), 70
bangi, 165, 180
Bani Etemad, Rakhshan, 223
Bani Sadr, Abolhassan, 74, 77, 79
Barrati-Sadeh, Farid, 190
barzakh, 202

basij, 85, 214
Bazaar (Tehran), 216
bazaar agents, 44
Bazargan, Mehdi, 73
Behrouzan, Orkideh, 109, 172
Beirut, 28, 174
Bimarestan-e Mo'tadan (Addicts' Hospital), 66
birth control, 157
bi-samani (disorder), 225
Black Hand, 171
bonyad, 76, 91
bonyad-e mo'tadan (addicts' foundation), 76
border control, 83, 179, 272
borders
 and the value of illicit drugs, 87
 minority population, 84, 274
 US-Mexico in the War on Drugs, 276
 void of security in the East, 78
Bourgois, Philippe, 24
brain drain, 171
Brass, Paul, 17
Breaking Bad (TV series), 179
British Council, 130
budget
 benefits of drug regulation/legalisation, 272
 benefits of harm reduction, 157
 centralisation during Ahmadinejad's government, 242
 construction of addiction recovery camps, 197, 203
 cost of War on Drugs, 63
 division within public institutions, 245
 funds allocated for drug policy during Ahmadinejad's government, 243, 244
 funds for the police, 203
 number of drug arrests, 204
 greater room for manouvre during Ahmadinejad's period, 243
 impact of oil price, 247
 in the 2010 Drug Law Reform, 192
 misuse, 191, 244
 Pahlavi government spending on anti-narcotics, 56
 research in drug policy, 244
 subsidies for recovery camps, 225, 244

bureaucracy
 under Ahmadinejad, Mahmud, 242–5
Bush, George W., 134
Bushire, 44

camps (addiction recovery)
 apparatus, 199, 213, 231, 265
 compulsory
 for vagrants, 197
 compulsory model, 96, 191, 194, 196–204, 213, 217, 225, 260, 263
 controversies, 190
 employment among recovering drug abusers, 262
 illegal, 211–31
 personnel, 215
 origins, 25
 origins in Iran, 89
 private, 204–10, 219, 225
 relation with police, 212, *See* police: relation with addiction camps
 role of *Rebirth NGO*, 256, 257
 spectrum of models, 224, 226
 use of violence in the camps, 275
 women's camps, 30, 207–10
camps, concentration (Nazi), 205
Canada, 11, 21, 269
cannabis
 agricultural relevance in Iran, 271
 benefits of legalisation, 270
 discussed in the Expediency Council, 158
 in the drug laws of the Islamic Republic, 152
 legalisation in Iran, 270, 272
 legalisation in Uruguay, 11, 269
 origins of global prohibition, 11
 potential for global reform, 21, 269
 thereapeutic use, 10
 tolerance of use in Iran, 271, 279
 US approach towards, 55
Caspian region, 53, 67
CCTV, 209
cheragh khamush, 122
cheshmandaz (long-term policy of the state), 148
China, 31, 52
Christian Orthodoxy, 32

CIA, 4, 52, 56, 61, 68, 79
civic, groups, 89, 118, 121, 124, 125, 134
civic, issues, 240, 254, 287
civic, venues, 113
civil society
   and relation with UNODC, 133
   as device of crisis management, 128
   as *government in practice*, 127
   as governmental instrument, 99, 110, 115–21, 123, 197, 210, 262
   as grassroots authoritarianism, 264, 281
   as partner of the government, 14
   as rhizome, 262
   as surrogate party, 127
   charitable and humanitarian plans, 217
   co-regulation and pilotage with the state, 134, 281
   device of crisis management, 265
   during Ahmadinejad, 235, 241, 247
   during post-reformism, 235, 241
   during reformism, 115–21, 135
   engagement from below, 13, 114, 115–21, 122
   for statist ends, 214, 282
   idealised version of, 275
   in addiction recovery, 23, 204–31, 247–65
   in cannabis law reforms, 269
   in drug policy reform, 114, 269
   in favour of prohibition, 275
   in harm reduction, 115–21, 122
   in meetings on drug policy, 132
   in support of Khatami's election, 98, 99
   in the methodology, 30
   in UN development plans, 129
   participation in Additction Science Conference, 156
   public activism, 217
   responsable for uncivil phenomena, 260
class (social), 91
   bourgeois, 38, 66, 77, 90, 95, 170, 174, 184, 204, 205, 225, 270
      drug consumption, 59, 66, 78
      treatment, 96
   capitalist, 44

   clergy, 74
   dangerous, 17
   desire, 176
   deviant, 77
   marginal, 274
   plebian (village), 66, 82, 170
   subordination, 231
   technocratic, 97
   working, 39, 47, 82, 170, 206, 252
      drug consumption, 47, 66
clergy
   bast in Isfahan (1923), 44
   during Mossadeq, Mohammad, 51
   on drugs, 125
   on governance, 125
   on innovation, 157
   policy, 9
   on Narcotics Anonymous, 251
   opposition to the Shah (Pahlavi, Mohammad Reza), 57
   reactionary elements, 171, 250
Cold War, 52, 63
Colombia, 89, 276
Committee to Combat AIDS, 109, 120, 123
communism, 49
communism (anti-), 55
Congress 60, 248, 249
constitution (Islamic Republic), 90, 141, 142, 145, 147, 149, 235, 273, 282
Constitutional Revolution, 37, 39, 42, 43, 69, 71
Constitutionalists, 40, 41, 74, 280
Construction Jihad (*jahad-e sazandegi*), 89
consumerism, 167, 170
   consumeristic society, 169
consumerism, hedonistic. *See hedonism*
corruption
   accusations of, 87, 152, 246
   among public officials in the Islamic Republic, 77
   Khalkhali's onslaught, 73
   mofsed fil-'arz, 74
   Western moral, 119
Costa, Antonio Maria, 130
Council for the Revision of the Constitution, 142
courts, revolutionary, 74, 75, 85, 153

Index 327

crises
 theoretical implicantions, 19
crisis
 as a central engine of politics, 282
 as discourse, 282
 as idiom of reform, 31, 110, 113, 124, 135, 283
 as narrative device, 20
 as opportunity, 123, 128, 153, 228, 256
 as ordinary event, 79, 98, 135, 232
 caused by HIV epidemic, 121–2
 caused by increase in *shisheh* use, 168, 176, 181, 195, 233, 234
 definition, 19–20, 202
 during Ahmadinejad's government, 232
 enabling public-private partnership, 284
 ethymology, 284
 theoretical implications, 284
 used in neoliberal governance, 264
crisis management
 and the role of apparatuses, 20
 and the role of civil society, 128
 in the 2000s, 125
 in the Expediency Council, 13, 125
 in the HIV epidemic, 118
 in the opiate crisis, 107
 Iran–Iraq War, 95
 Khamenei's skills of, 283
 through lack of judicial supervision, 230
crisis, art of governing, 160, 228, 265, 284
crisis, spaces of, 216
criticism for management of drug policy budget, 246
Cronin, Stephanie, 45

DARIUS Institute, 132
dar-ol-'alaj (opium dens), 47
daru ('medicine', slang for heroin), 176
Darvazeh Ghar, 117, 128, 216
dast-e mar-gir (hand that captures the snake), 212
Davvalu, Hushang, 62
DCHQ
 announcement of new addiction data, 26

civic participation programme, 254
criticism for budget management, 244
criticism from other public institutions, 190
in mediation between opponents and supporters of harm reduction, 128
in the 1988 law, 92, 93, 152
internal structure, 93
international policy, 103
involved in corruption case, 87
lack of adequate research tools, 246
management of compulosry addiction recovery camps, 203
management of compulsory addiction recovery camps, 211, 237
management of drug policy budget, 244
on methadone programme, 200
on the feasibility of medical insurance, 237
role in harm reduction reform, 122, 123, 126, 127, 132
role in national drug policy, 93
supervisng compulsory addiction recovery camps, 199
under the Ahmadinejad government, 198, 241
dead-end law making (*qanungozari-ye bon-bast*), 153
dealers, 59, 86, 152, 160, 207
death penalty
 a provision based on *maslahat*, 273
 against drug traffickers, 9, 12, 272
 against public officials guilty of drug corruption, 87
 as part of Islamic jurisprudence, 273
 coverage in international media, 276
 for addiction camps personnel guilty of patients' death, 214
 for recedivist drug offenders, 152
 in the 1988 anti-narcotics law, 80
 reform of the law, 273
 support among the general population, 275
 suspension approved by the Expediency Council, 158

decrees
    informal, 72
Deleuze, Gilles, 10, 165
    on drugs, 165–178
depression, 184–8
dervishes, 45
desire (sexual), 7, 174
desire (social), 176, 259
Deylamizadeh, Abbas, 254, 255
Dialogue among Civilisations, 130, 133
DIC, 116, 128, 257
disease
    addiction as chronic disease, 22, 68, 213, 237
    addiction not considered a disease, 123
    addiction recognised as a disease, 195
    infectious, 24, 105, 203
    sexually transmitted, 182
    Westoxification, 58
disorder. *See* art of managing disorder
    as category of analysis, 111
disorder (medicine)
    bipolar, 184
    food, 174
    sexual, 174
disorder, maintenance of, 14
disorderly groups, 116, 195, 202, 204, 214, 224, 229, 265
divorce, rates of, 169, 172
diyeh (blood money), 214
Dizelabad prison, 109
Doctor without Borders (MSF), 223
doreh (circle), 38
Driving with the lights off, 123
drug (ab)users. *See* addict
drug assemblage, 12, 14, 23, 24, 26, 56, 134, 276, 287
drug control machinery, 57, 69
drug control, international. *See* international drug control
drug ecosystem, 135
drug laws, 190–6
    approved by the Expediency Council, 151–61
drug market, 86, 102, 259, 271
drug of choice, 176, 228
drug policy
    Ahmadinejad, Mahmud, 232–65
    budget, 246, *See* budget

community, 190
Expediency Council, 140, 148, 150
international cooperation, 129, 130, 133
    Europe, 130
international diplomacy, 133
reform, 132, 158, 234, 270, 272, 273, 275
Drug Policy Commission, 154, 155
drug politics
    deconstruction of, 31
    definition, 6
    genealogy, 17, 36
    governance, 27
drug production, 57, 69
drug traffickers, 61, 62, 63, 83, 201, 272
    lexicon used in the Islamic Republic, 83
drug trafficking, 11, 57, 59, 67, 68, 72, 129, 134
    criminal cartels, 87
    using camels across borders, 87
drug tsar, 74
drug users
    death rate, 103
    female, 210
    homeless, 213, 214, 216–31, 257, 262
    in prison, 110, 112
    injecting, 24, 103, 106, 119, 121, 181
    recovering, 215
drug-free world, 76, 129
drugs. *See* opiates, heroin, opium, meth or *shisheh*
    adulteration, 186
    age of use, 180
    among women, 207, 209
    as a question of *raison d'etat*, 152
    as ideological objects, 18
    as part of a global conspiracy, 83
    changing patterns of consumption, 82, 181, 186
    condemnation by the clergy, 74, 85
    death penalty.*See* death penalty
    decriminalisation, 157
    definition, 21–6
    depression, 172, 184–8
    eradication, 69, 72, 78, 101

hotspots of consumption, 116, 117, 202, 203, 262
in Islam, 9
increase in value across borders, 87
legalisation, 68, 158
medicalisation. *See* addiction: medicalisation
number of consumers, 67, *See* addiction: rates of
propaganda, 85, 253
quest of happiness, 173
regulation, 158
statistics, 84, 176, 185, 207, 234, 238, 270
synthetic, 23, 175, 184, *See* meth *or shisheh*, methadone
with sex, 181–8, 233
drugs (anti)
campaigns, 74
drugs (anti-)
campaigns, 77, 86
drugs (anti-depressant), 175
drugs (prescription), 173, 175
Dubai, 170

E'temad-e Melli (newspaper), 29
e'tiyad. *See* addiction
economy
informal, 45, 116
ecstasy, 22, 107, 165, 175, 180, 251
Ehteshami, Anoushirvan, 98
elites
connected to the Pahlavi regime, 77
in modernisation, 36
in the Society for the Fight against Alcohol and Opium, 49
in transnational networks, 69
under Ahmadinejad, 166
elites, modernist, 54
emergency, 20, 122, 125, 143, 144, 160, 183, 185, 224
emergency, rule of. *See* emergency
eslahat, 99, 234
estekbar-e jahani (global arrogance), 82
Etela'at (newspaper), 29, 76
ethnography. *See* fieldwork: ethnography
immersion, 30
interdisciplinary, 15, 31
mimesis, 30

observation, 10
of policy/politics, 159, 189
vignette, 30
vignettes, 194–204
Europe
allied with Saddam Hussein, 83
as destination for illicit drugs, 78
as destination for illicit drugs, 276
cooperation on drug policy with Iran, 134
drug trafficking, 87
financial crisis, 3
first harm reduction experiments, 25
funding support for UNODC in Iran, 130
heroin culture in the 1960s, 59
high demand for heroin, 101
HIV epidemic, 25
origins of the idea of addiction, 37
Pahlavi court suspected of smuggling heroin into Europe, 62
potential for drug policy reform, 269
sanctions against Islamic Republic, 233
using the politics of crisis, 282
Evin Prison, 4
Expediency Council
and the Supreme Leader, 142–5, 147
as sovereign, 161
criticism, 151
governmentality, 140, 159, 160, 274
in theory, 140
on crisis, 13, 125, 160
on drug laws, 13, 91, 94, 124
on drug policy, 151–61, 191, 241, 271
on expediency, 125
origins, 141–6
powers, 149, 150, 153, 273, 281
structure, 146–7, 153, 158
expertise (*karshenasi*), 149
experts, 131, 280

Facebook, 27
Fadayan-e Khalq, 74
family
atomisation process, 170
avoiding shame of drug use, 250
challenged by generational change, 7

family (cont.)
    deciding on blood money, 214
    paying addiction recovery fees, 237
    seeking help through illegal addiction recovery camps, 212, 213
    support for impoverished drug users, 214
    threatened by opium, 50
    threatened by *shisheh*, 184
Farahzad shelter, 257
Farahzad Valley, 202, 258, 260
    Chehel Pelleh, 202
Fardoust, Hossein, 61
Farmand, Hassan Ali, 51
Fars, 198
Fashapuyieh, 198
Fellah, Mohammad, 93, 94, 108, 126, 127
fieldwork
    access, 30, 31
    engagement, 244
    ethnography, 29, 30, 181, 206, 208, 211, 281
    puzzle, 27
    qualitative, 6, 12
    risks, 4
Foucault, Michel, 161
    genealogy, 69, See genealogy
    in politics, 17
    methodology, 17
    on crime, 75
    on power, 16
    on the state, 17, 55, 286
    quoted by Iranian official, 160
Friday Prayer, xviii

gardan-koloft (thugs), 202, 212
gart (dust, slang for heroin), 216
Gendarmerie
    during the Islamic Republic, 75, 78, 95
    during the Pahlavis, 61
gender
    and state ethics, 210
    considered by revolutionary courts, 112
    methods, 30
    trends during Ahmadinejad's period, 287

gender code, 85
gender politics, 14, 129
gender reassignment surgery, 7–9
genealogy, 17, 69
General Policies of the State, 147, 151, 251, 270
Germany, 23, 131
gharbzadegi. *see* Westoxification
Ghobadi, Bahman, 171
Gilan, 67
Gingeras, Ryan, 52
Global North, 15
Global South, 15, 280
Godfrey's Cordial (poppy syrup in the UK), 39
Gorgan, 53
governmental ordinances (*ahkam-e hokumati*), 142
governmentality, 31, 113, 174, 194, 228, 231, 263
    on crisis, 135, 140, 159, 160, 196
gowd, 86, 111
Goya, Francisco, 16
Greece, 282
Green Movement, 168, 173, 287
Guardian Council, of the Revolution, 143
    interpreting the Constitution, 142
    members partaking in Expediency Council meetings, 146
    sidelined by the Expediency Council, 144, 145
    sympathetic to Ahmadinejad's government, 243
    unable to discuss laws approved by Expediency Council, 149, 273
    veto powers, 100, 141
Guya, Mehdi, 190

Hajebi, Ahmad, 190, 203
Hajjarian, Saeed, 127, 144, 160
hakem-e shar' (leading state prosecutor post-1979), 73, 76
hallucination, 185
Hamadan, 51, 118
Harandi, 216, 217, 219, 223, 228
harbeh-ye este'mari (colonial weapon), 83
Hariri, Khalil, 201
harm reduction

Index   331

and the use of media, 124
approval by the Judiciary, 114
as apparatus, 25, 31, 135, 204, 265
conference on, 174, 190
controversies, 202, 203, 215, 217
definition, 24
ethics, 160, 261, 262
existing in a paradox, 27, 228
first experiments, 115, 117
genealogy, 111
implemented underground, 117, 121, 122
in prison, 111
in the laws, 115, 158, 192, 193, 195, 202, 236
international dimension, 12
opposed by the UNODC in Vienna, 130
opposition to, 119, 121, 124, 127, 128
safe injection rooms, 158, 271, 276
scaling up, 158, 254
spectrum of different models, 25
supporters, 100, 123, 132, 133, 191
harm reduction system, 106, 114, 135, 241
harm reduction, research on, 157
harm reductionists, 122, 126, 127, 222, 280
Hashemi Shahrudi, Mahmud (ayatollah), 114, 148
Hashemi, Ali, 154
hashish. *See* cannabis
 as a soft drug, 272
 condemned as heterodox by clergy, 55
 confiscation during revolutionary period, 74
hashish smoker. *See bangi*
Headquarters (Supreme Leader), 147
Hedayat, Sadegh, 39
hedonism, 170, 180
heroin
 adulteration, 102, 108, 186
 and the flow of time, 178
 as a plot by the enemies of the revolution, 82
 centre of distribution, 216
 chemists, 60

confiscation, 64, 83, 103
 in the revolutionary period, 74
criminalisation in the US, 64
demand in Europe, 101
democratisation of consumption, 78
diffusion, 59, 81, 82, 105, 106, 180, 216
discussed by Khomeini, 57
embodying global consumption models, 58
excluded from legal reform, 270
fall in price, 79–83
first case of overdose, 58
international trafficking, 61, 62, 68, 79
maintenance programme, 64, 68
prouction of, 60
shape and colour, 107
shift to injection, 103, 119
heroin culture
 in Europe, 59
heroin-e hamid-reza (Pahlavi), 62
Hibou, Beatrice, 18
historical incidents (Breachtian), 277
HIV
 epidemic, 13, 24, 25, 108, 110, 113, 117, 118, 199, 213, 217, 234, 265
 in prison, 109, 110, 111, 117, 199
 risk of contagion, 105, 106, 213
 stigma, 118
HIV, crisis of. *See* crisis: HIV
HIV-positive people, 110, 119, 194
homelessness, 117
Hormozgan, 85, 110, 207
hosseiniyeh, 252
hotspots (*patoq*), 202, 203, 262
House of Sun (*khaneh-ye khorshid*), 219

identification card (ID card), 192, 193, 229
ideology
 among NGOs, 275
 among prohibitionists, 77
 anti-Islamic Republic, 285
 in the work of apparatuses, 26
 in Therapeutic Communities (TC), 26

ideology (cont.)
  lectures for recovering drug (ab)
    users, 81
  state-led, 14, 99, 106
ejtihad-e mostamerr (permanent
  interpretative effort of the jurist),
  142
Ilam, 110
imperialism, 82
incarceration. *See* prison
  alternatives to, 112
  avoiding prisons through illegal
    recovery camps, 212
  avoiding the prison through
    toleration of public drug use,
    217
  combined with forced addiction
    treatment, 80
  costs for incarcerated drug users, 199
  in compulsory addiction camps, 195
  increasing numbers, 273
  origins during the Pahlavi period, 55
  to punish addiction, 152
  use during Khalkhali's period, 76
incarceration (post), 247
INCAS, 156
India, 7, 73
inequality, 170
informality
  in tackling public addiction, 230
  in the practice of harm reduciton, 122
  networks, 125, 128, 132, 134, 210
  use of meetings outside government,
    143
  within Expediency Council, 158–9
infrapolitics, 14
injection
  in prison, 108, 110, 112–3
injection (of heroin)
  engendering HIV epidemic, 13,
    120
  impossibility to counter, 272
  increasing popularity, 134
  stigma, 105
injection (of *kerack*), 108
injection paraphernalia, 24
instability
  for the Islamic Republic
    Khomein's death, 90
Instagram, 170

intellectuals
  Al-e Ahmad, Jalal, 3, 58
  anti-intellectualism under
    Ahmadinejad, 243, 251
  during Khatami period, 134
  during the Constitutional
    Revolution, 39
  Hedayat, Sadegh, 39
  Kuhi-Kermani, Hossein, 40
  new religious intellectuals' (*roshan-
    fekran-e dini*), 99
intelligence (secret services)
  absence during fieldwork research, 4
  American officers in the Pahlavi era,
    49
  budget under Ahmadinjed
    government, 244
  coercive institutions during the
    Pahlavi era, 49
  creation and expansion with
    US support, 56, 63
  deployed in War on Drugs, 84
  imbalance with non-security means,
    93
  lack of means, 79
  rise during Ahmadinejad period, 169
  role of DCHQ, 92
  shift under post-revolutionary
    period, 86
  US knowledge of Pahlavi
    involvement in drug trafficking,
    61
interdisciplinary research, 32
international drug control, 11, 23, 45,
  52, 56, 57, 72, 281
International Narcotics Control Board
  (INCB), 179
internet, 22, 172, 173, 175
intoxication, 43, 50, 51, 272, *See*
  addiction
Iran (newspaper), 29
Iran–Iraq War, 12, 72, 78, 79, 83, 84,
  86, 87, 88, 133
  long-term effects, 110
  source of policy inspiration, 95, 154
Iraq
  Iranian foreign policy, 287
  transit country for drugs, 87
IRGC, 84, 86, 88, 146, 154, 169
Iron Law of Prohibition, 58

Isfahan, 43, 66, 67, 211
  opium production, 45, 47
  opium rituals, 66
Islamic Associations (*Anjoman-e eslami*), 89
Islamic law, 9, 76, 114, 142, 160, 181, 214, 273, See *sharia'ah*
Islamic Republic
  political structure, 8
Israel, 5, 83, 166, 172
Italy, 39, 130, 132, 167, 269, 282

Ja'far, Mohammad Ali, 59
Jahanbegloo, Ramin, 166
Jalaipour, Hamid Reza, 171
Jalaipour, Mohammad Reza, 4
Jam-e Jam (newspaper), 29
jang-e tahmili (imposed war), 79
jazirah (islands of confinement), 81
job market, 179, 252, 256
Jomhuri-ye Eslami (newspaper), 29, 82
joy engineering *(mohandesi-ye shadi)*, 173
Judiciary, 87, 100, 124, 132, 142, 198, 205, 273
Judiciary, Head of, 111, 114, 126, 145, 146, 156, 199, 274
Judiciary, officials of, 123
June 5 revolt (*Panzdah-e Khordad*), 57

kahesh asib. See harm reduction
Kahrizak prison, 232
Kakavand Tribe, 61
kamp-gardi, 215
Karaj, 47
Karroubi, Mehdi, 168
kerak (kerack), 107, 108, 111
Kerman, 66, 67, 84, 109
  opium rituals, 66
Kermanshah, 61, 109, 110, 117, 118, 210
Keyhan (newspaper), 205
Khak-e Sefid, 117, 128
Khalkhali, Sadeq (ayatollah), 71–80
  inspired by, 201
  shock therapy, 82
Khamenei, Ali (ayatollah), 86, 139, 140, 141, 147, 149, 152, 190, 235
  crisis management skills, 283

khane-ha-ye nime-rah (half-way houses), 260
Khatami, Mohammad, 131
  1997 election, 98
  coping with crisis, 135
  dialogue among civilisations, 133
  in support of Triangular Clinics, 120
  on prison management, 112
  relations with the West, 130, 133
  support for decriminalisation of addiction, 115
  support for harm reduction, 129
  support for publications and civil society, 127
  supporting workers' rights for HIV-positive people, 120
  transition to post-reformism, 147, 191, 287
  use of civil society, 121
Khiyabani, Gholam, 127
khomari (hangover from lack of opium), 70
Khomeini, Hassan, 261
Khomeini, Ruhollah (ayatollah)
  and Khalkhali, Sadeq (ayatollah), 73, 77
  and Khamenei, Ali (ayatollah), 86, 139, 141
  death, 149
  Eight Point Declaration (1980), 77
  on absolute guardianship of the jurist, 142
  on addiction, 71
  on addicts, 261
  on alcohol, 57
  on drugs, 57, 72, 151
  on expediency, 140, 144
  on governance, 144
  on opium maintenance programmes, 72
  on poppy cultivation, 73
  on smuggling, 74
  on the Expediency Council, 142, 144, 145
  on the Iran–Iraq war, 154
  opposition to Shah, 57
Khorasan, 67, 81, 198
Khorramabad, 208, 210
Khuzestan, 78, 110, 210

Komeyl Hospital, 90
Kuhi Kermani, Hossein, 40
Kurdistan, 67, 84
Kurds, 61, 84, 210

Larijani Amoli, Sadeq Ardeshir (ayatollah), 199
Larijani, Ali, 199
Larijani, Javad, 273
laughter workshops (*kargah-e khandeh*), 173
Lavisan, 206, 210
Law Enforcemnet Agencies (LEAs), 23, 126, 234, 262
Local Coordination Council (*shoura-ye hamahangi*) – DCHQ, 93
LSD, 22, 279
luti, 59

Madani, Said, 6, 240
mafia, 75, 84
Majles. See parliament
Malayer, 60
Malaysia, 180
Maleki, Fada Hossein, 241
Malekzadeh, Mehdi, 54
manqal (charcoal brazier), 38
Marco Polo, 215
margins
  ethical, 214, 264
  management of, 202
  spatial, 111, 274
  urban, 210
marijuana. *See* cannabis
Markazi, 198
market
  black, 73, 84
  competition, 65
  human organs, 7, 8
  illegal treatment of addiction, 97
  of illegal methadone, 23
  of illegal opium, 44, 66, 67
  of illegal treatment, 225
  of methadone managed by private clinics, 236
  of *shishesh* in the 2000s, 176
  regulation of illicit drugs, 7, 271
marketisation, 259, 265, 269, 275
Marvdasht, 115
Marx, Karl, 17

Mashhad, 66, 81, 87
Mauss, Marcell, 22
Mazandaran, 67, 198
Mazzitelli, Antonio, 131, 133
MDMA, 22
medicalisation, 157, 237, *See* addiction: shift towards medicalisation, drugs:medicalisation
medicine
  as frame of interpretation, 114
medicine (drug), 23
medicine (practice), 38, 47, 114, 194, 284
medicine (surveillance), 286
medicine (Western), 37, 46
Medicine, International Conference of (Ramsar, 1971), 67
Mehran Gardens, 58
melancholy, 39, 186
MENAHRA, 28
mesostrata of the state, 123
methadone
  and depression, 184
  and *shisheh*, 184
  as apparatus, 23, 24, 228
  as technology of government, 24
  in Iran, 107
  in prison, 200
  origins, 23
methadone clinic, 235, 236, 247, 257
methadone maintenance treatment (MMT)
  as a device of managing drug using population, 217
  as part of Triangular Clinics, 118
  benefits for drug users, 24
  description, 23
  during Ahmadinejad's government, 224
  failure, 195
  first centre in Iran, 117
  first discussions in Iran, 107
  first pilot programmes, 156
  in Islamic jurisprudence, 115
  in prison, 115, 200
  in the 2010 law, 193, 225
  side-effects of methadone, 184
methamphetamines, 12, *See shisheh*
Mexico, 89, 276
micropolitics, 13, 14, 17, 26, 168

Milad Tower, 189
Millspaugh, Arthur C., 40
Mini Dublin Group, 132
Minister of Health and Medical Education, 182
Ministry of Education, 244
Ministry of Finance, 41, 46
Ministry of Health
  harm reduction meetings, 107
  in organ donations, 7
  in support of harm reduction, 122, 123
  in the 2010 law, 115
  management of opium coupon system, 65
  on HIV/AIDS plan, 183
  on pilot methadone programme, 117
  providing licences to NGOs, 116
  UK maintenance of opium, 68
Ministry of Interior, 85, 126, 173, 198
Ministry of Justice, 55
Ministry of Physical Education and Training, 246
minorities, 274
Mitchell, Timothy, 69
mo'tad, 26, 66
modernisation
  and prohibition, 36
  and the demise of the Qajars, 40
  criticised by Jalal Al-e Ahmad, 59
  during the Pahlavis, 43, 50
  in drugs history, 276
  in modernisation theory, 70
modernity, 8, 35, 38, 41, 43, 58, 114, 253
modiran-e miyaneh (mid-ranking officials), 123
Mohraz, Minoo, 120, 190
Mohtaj, Abbas, 173
morphine, 23, 24
  confiscation, 103
  exports, 106
  for pharmaceutical purposes, 106
  Hamid before and after injection, 60
  high content in Iranian opium, 44, 47
  imports from Turkey, 60
  injecting, 59
Mosaddeq, Mohammad, 51, 52
Mostashari, Gelareh, 128, 132

Moulavi square, 116, 216
mujahedin (Afghans), 79
mujahidin (Afghans), 83
Mujica, Pepe, 269
Mullah Omar, 102
Musavi, Mir Hossein, 86, 146, 168

NAJA. *See* police
Najjar, Mostafa, 241, 242
Naloxone, 200
Narcotics Anonymous
  coexistence with post-reformist (Ahmadienajd's) vision, 251
  expansion during post-reformism, 174
  opposition from clergy, 251
  origins in Iran, 248–53
  status vis a vis postreformist state, 250
  vision of the founder, 254
  visit from US central office, 253
  voted the best NGO by government, 253
Narenjiha, Hooman, 122, 157
Nasirimanesh, Bijan, 115, 116, 124, 240
National Security Council, 146, 154
newspapers
  awareness campaign, 120
  HIV/AIDS, 120
  data on addiction, 207, 214
  ethnographic use of, 29
  in methodology, 28
  in the War on Drugs, 86
  list of Iranian newspapers, 29
  publishing ads on addiction recovery, 96
  scandals, 204
  sensationalism, 213
  strategic use by drug reformers, 124, 127, 272
  used by reformists, 99
nezam (political order), 142
Nixon, Richard, 63
Noori, Roya, 157
Northern Alliance, 102
Nouri, Abdollah, 127
nuclear deal, 11

Obama, Barack, 233
Office for the Coordination of the Fight against Addiction, 93
Office of the Treasury (*dara'i*), 70
opiates. *See also* opium *and* heroin
opium
    administred through coupon, 63–70
    as a key export, 43
    as backwardness, 43
    as strategic asset, 52
    banned during the Mossadeq period, 51
    banned under Mohammad Reza Shah, 52
    consumed by Shah's brother, 62
    at the end of fasting in Ramadan, 39
    high quality in Iran, 44, 45
    history of use in Iran, 35
    laws approved during Pahlavi period, 52–4
    legends related to its consumption, 38
    mythologies about opium, 70
    parliamentary debates during Pahlavi period, 53
    pipe (*vafur*), 38, 46
    place in the economy, 40, 43, 53–4
    rituals of consumption in Iran, 38
    senaturi, 65
    Shah praising the ban on opium, 54
    smoked by Reza Shah, 46
    smoked in coffeshops, 53
    special connoisseurs working at the Opium Desk, 70
    Taliban ban on, 102
    the government reconsiders reintroduction of poppy cultivation, 271
    use among children, 39
    used as currency, 45
    used as medicine, 38
opium (Afghan), 101, 106
opium burning ceremony, 234
Opium Desk, 70
Opium Monopoly, 44, 51
opium tincture, 279
opium user (*taryaki*), 40
opium, conferences on, 40, 41, 45, 48
ordugah, 196, 259
organ donation, 7
orthodoxy
    moral, 110
    religious, 251
    revolutionary, 265
    state ideology, 99
overdose, 184
Oxford (University), 3, 6, 28, 30
oxymoron, 9, 27, 31, 93, 242, *See* paradox
2010 drug law, 192

Pahlavi family
    Ashraf, 61–3
    Hamid-Reza, 61–3
    involvement in drug trafficking, 61, 63
Pahlavi state, 12
    drug policy, 35–70
    fall of dynasty, 74, 95
    modernisation, 43, 70
    opium distribution, 63, *See* opium: coupon
Pahlavi state, fall of dynasty, 78
Pahlavi, Hamid-Reza, 62
Pahlavi, Mahmud-Reza, 62
Pakistan
    criminal networks, 274
    Iran's anti'narcotic strategy, 179
    Iranian NGOs role in implementing harm reduction, 157
    lack of anti-drug cooperation, 83
    refusal to end poppy cultivation, 64
    role of Iranian NGOs in implementing harm reduction, 121
    source of drug trade, 65, 84, 272
papagna (papaverum in Italy), 39
paradox
    in Iranian Studies, 8
    Iranian politics, 6
    mechanism of government, 9
Park-e Marivan, 117
parliament (Islamic Republic), 13, 51
    discussing illicit drug regulation, 269
    impossibility to legislate vis a vis Expediency Council, 151
    informal meetings on illicit drug regulation, 272
    lack of legislative power on drug issues, 140

Index

on declaration of rule of emergency, 160
opposition to harm reduction, 126
powers and limitations, 142
Rafsanjani's quote, 139
sympathetic to Ahmadinejad's government, 243
parliament (pre-1979), 40, 41, 46, 49, 51, 54
Pasolini, Pier Paolo, 167
pathology, 40, 114, 238
patient criminal, 194, 229
payin-shahr (downtown), 208
Pentecostalism, 32
Persepolis NGO, 117, 131
Persian Gulf, 67, 81, 207
Pezeshkian, Mas'ud, 183
pharmacies, 65
phenomenology
  in the making of harm reduction, 158
  methodology, 23, 288
  of drugs politics, 15
  of postreformist society, 180
Planning and Management Organisation (MPO), 243
pleasure, 24, 58, 107, 184, 186, 272
police
  as informant, 213
  budget for compulsory addiction camps, 203
  campaigns of drug arrests, 47, 111, 117, 123, 124, 201
  force of the law, 126
  in the parks, 200–4, 224
  information regarding people involved in opiate factories, 60
  missions in Southern Tehran, 40
  number of drug arrests, 88
  reform of law enforcement, 95
  relation with addiction camps, 205, 210, 212, 225, 230
  relation with NGOs, 263
  reputation, 234
  role in compulsory addiction camps, 202
  sovreign on the grey zone, 229
  the force of the law, 229, 231
  use of medicine, 194
police states, 17

police, moral (*gasht-e ershad*), 171
police, Swiss anti-narcotics, 61
police, therapeutic, 194, 200–4, 224, 237, 242 *See*
policymaking
  and medicine, 157
  bringing the revolution in government under Ahmadinejad, 287
  community, 22, 100, 106, 127, 191
  crisis, 19, 145, 149
  debureucratisation, 242
  during Rafsanjani's government, 95
  evidence-based approach, 255
  Expediency Council's powers, 149
  inner-working in the Iranian state, 158
  NGOs participation in the debate, 254
  shortermism under Ahmadinejad, 244
  under Ahmadinejad, 243
  use of econometrics models, 282
  view among the clergy on drug policy, 31
political ethnography. *See* ethnography: of policy/politics
political order *(nezam)*, 8, 10, 39, 71, 73, 233, 239, 284, 286, 287
  according to reformists, 98, 110
  amidst instability/crisis, 142, 148
  and the place of Expediency Council, 140
  in Khomeini's 8 point declaration, 77
  in the Constitution of the Islamic Republic, 145, 146
  in the wake of Khomeini's death, 90
  legitimisation, 75
  opposition to reforms, 121, 127
  unchallenged by drug reformists, 114
political practice
  distance with intellectual analysis, 284–7
  in post-reformism, 192
  in the fight against narcotics, 95
  in the logics of crisis, 141
political practice (in methods)
  adopting grassroots lens, 286
  instead of formal politics, 31
  instead of political rhetoric, 10

political science, 16, 17
politics, profane, 135, 145, 146, 149, 159, 167, 288
politics, secular, 31, 134, 145, 148, 159, 224, 288
polydrug use, 186, 227, 238, 279
poppy
  as a cash crop, 40
  ban on eating poppy seeds, 56
  boiled skin for syrup, 39
  destruction of farms, 233
  ecotype plant in Iran, 271
poppy cultivation
  eradication in 1980s, 101
  eradication in Afghanistan, 102
  expert advise to reintroduce poppy ban, 67
  first laws in Iran, 53
  in occupied Afghanistan, 83
  reconsidering cultivation during reformism, 233
  reintroduction of cultivation in 1969, 63
  US pressure to eradicate, 48
populism, 147, 265
post-Islamism, 99
post-modern
  language, 160
  people, 180
  world, 181
post-reformism, 235, 259, 261
  definition, 191
post-reformist state, 281
  bringing back revolutionary principles, 201
  budgetary largesse, 246, 247
  drug policy, 189, 192, 194, 255, 260
  going beyond legal, bureaucratic means, 212
  government as society's younger brother, 235
  governmentality, 196, 214, 232–65
  language of power, 264
  relation with civil society, 233, 248
  relying on private sector for public duties, 237
  under Ahmadinejad, 194, 198

post-war period (Iran–Iraq war)
  and the role of medicine, 114
  anomaly embodied by Ahmadinejad, 165
  crisis, 283
  drug strategy, 91, 93, 97
  effects on urban life, 79
  governance, 113
  headquartisation, 176
  privatisation, 235
  reconstruction, 91, 172
  reforms, 139
poverty, 84, 195
pre-Islamic history, 131
prison
  as primary harms to drug users, 24
  during the Islamic Republic
    costs, 199
    drugs available in prison, 108
    HIV epidemics, 109, 110, 118, 183
    increasing population, 108, 112, 198, 199
    methadone, 200
    Narcotics Anonymous, 250
    needle exchange, 123, 124, 199
    reforms, 111
    suicide, 119
    Triangular Clinics, 121
  during the Pahlavi period, 54, 56
    costs, 63
    mushrooming, 69
  in the 1980s drug law, 80
Prison Organisation
  cost of maintaining prisoners, 199
  introducing needle exchange programmes in prison, 123
  introduction of harm reduction in prison, 111
  introduction of Triangular Clinics in prisons, 120
  Mohammad Fellah (director), 108
  plans to decrease number of drug offenders in prison, 198
  requesting the police not to arrest addicts, 108
  women's branch referring female addict to private treatment camp, 209

prohibitionist regime
  in Iran, 49, 64
  challenges to the model, 10
  Iran a model for other third world countries, 52
  origins in international conventions, 41
  use of confiscation funds, 56
psychiatrists, 66–8, 174, 197, 215, 226
  shisheh, treatment of, 184, 237
psychoactive revolution, 35
public policy, 10, 25, 114, 121, 122, 125, 192, 281, 282
public space
  as a site of drug consumption, 228
  cleansing of risky groups, 229, 260
  controlling drug consumption, 14
  during the Constitutional Revolution, 41
  Islamisation, 82
  lack of entertainment, 172
  middle class concerns, 95
  opium use, 54
  presence of homeless people, 224
  presence of young people, 171
  shisheh use, 184, 195
  state intervention to expel deviants, 81
Purmohammadi, Mostafa, 198

Qajar, 37, 39, 40, 43
Qalibaf, Mohammad Baqer, 128, 219, 242
Qavam, Ahmad, 51
qesas, 214, 273
Qom, 253
Quarantine, 80–2, 194

Rafsanjani, Hashemi Akbar (ayatollah), 95, 97, 98, 139, 140, 148
Raji, Amir Hossein, 56
Ramadan, 39
Razzaghi, Emran, 231
Rebirth (Tavalod-e Dobareh)
  creation of bourgeois recovery camps, 206
  in support of 2010 drug law, 196
  involvement in addiction recovery, 205
  methods of addiction recovery, 249

NA philosophy, 256
  origins and development, 254–65
  policy branch of NA, 253
  statements by director, 204
  use of research in policy plan, 255
Red Army, 79, 83
Regan, Ronald, 76
religion
  in drug policy, 31
  in policymaking, 9, 10
  versus expertise, 32
resistance (theory), 19, 282
revolution
  in the government (Ahmadinejad), 168
Rezaei, Mohsen, 147, 148, 154
Rezaiof, Mirza Ja'far, 41
Rezazadeh, Majid, 203
rhizome, 69, 215, 231, 262, 265, 281, 285
Rihali, Shahla, 59
road accidents, 185
Roitman, Janet, 284
Rouhani, Hassan
  2013 election, 191, 287
  centrism, 147
  crisis in power, 232
  criticising Expediency Council, 151
  effects of privatisation, 287
rural life, 170
  availability of illicit drugs, 66
  changing drug consumption, 59
  flow of time, 186
  heroin, 78, 82
  image of the addict, 51
  shisheh, 176
Russia, 31, 32, *See* URSS

sahmiyah (quota system for opium), 41
Saleh, Jahan, 35, 52, 53, 64
San Francisco, 48
sanctions
  economic isolation under Mossadeq, 51
  international pressure, 206
  international pressure on Iran, 170
  nuclear-related measures, 233
  trickled down to population, 211
saudageran-e badbakhti (merchants of misery), 83

saudageran-e marg (merchants of death), 83
Saudi Arabia, 101, 285
SAVAK, 56, 62
secular (trends), 7, 175, 253, 287
secularisation, 27, 145, 146, 276
secularity, 159, 253
Seda va Sima (Islamic Republic of Iran Broadcasting), 173
seeing like a state, 23
Sefatian, Said, 122, 123, 124, 125, 127, 132
Senate (in the Islamic Republic), 151
Senate (Pahlavi), 53
setad, 79, See DCHQ
    Counterfeit Goods, 92
    DCHQ, 91
    National Elections, 92
setadisation, of politics, 95
sex work, 7, 81, 116, 209
Shafaq (compulsory treatment camp), 200, 201, 202, 203, 204, 206
Shah (Pahlavi, Mohammad Reza), 52, 57, 59
Shah (Pahlavi, Reza), 43, 46
shahid, 87
Shahr-e Nou, 182, 217
sharbat-e baccheh, 39
Sharq (newspaper), 29, 171, 218
shekayat, 212, 230
shepherd, 185
Shiraz, 45, 82, 109, 115, 174, 240, 261
shireh, 46, 47, 58, 82, 185
shirehkesh-khaneh (smoking house for opiates), 46, 47, 50, 117
Shurabad, 81, 96, 200
Shush square, 116
Single Convention of Narcotic Drugs (1961), 23, 56, See Drugs: Conventions
Siragusa, Charles, 62
Sistan, 9, 67, 84, 201, 272
siyah-nemai, 113
smuggling
    accusations against Afghan refugees, 84
    accusations against Pahlavi Iran and Communist China, 52
    Anti-Smuggling and Counterfeit *setad*, 92
    attempts at eradication during Pahlavi period, 68
    first laws against, 45
    flourishing of routes during Pahlavi period, 46
    global network, 48
    involvement of minorities, 84
    judged in revolutionary courts, 75
    Khomeini's declaration, 74
    means of sustenance, 81
    powers of Expediency Council, 156
    tribale networks, 54
social media, 29, 172, 173, 174
social sciences, 4, 18, 114, 244
Society for the Fight against Alcohol and Opium, 49, 50, 51
sociology, 6, 18
Soltani, Fariba, 131, 132
Soviet Union, 79, 83
Spain, 11, 282
St Antony's College, 4
state of exception, 20, 212, 228, 229
statistics
    call for reduction number of addicts, 270
    death penalty, 12
    dissonance in Iranian public policy, 26, 243
    driving intoxicated, 185
    false circulation to engender crisis, 49
    female drug abuse, 207
    in methods, 29
    lack of transparency, 245
    number of harm reduction centres, 241
    perception of drug problem, 234
    shisheh consumption, 176, 238
    use in presentation in drug policy event, 280
    use in social sciences, 18
stem cells, 157
stigma
    among heroin users, 107
    among HIV-positive people, 119
    among homeless people, 117
    among injecting drug users, 106
    among *shireh* users, 47
    for drug (ab)use, 119

for female drug users, 207, 210
stigma (destigmatisation), 119–120
stigma (stigmatisation), 54, 75
sufism, 46
suicide, 50, 119, 184
sukhteh, 46
Supreme Judiciary Council, 142
Supreme Leader, 147
  and the appointment of jurists in the Guardian Council, 141
  appointment of members of the Expediency Council, 146
  approval of laws emanated by the Expediency Council, 158
  constitutional responsabilities, 145
  crisis management role, 283
  General Policies of the Islamic Republic, 241, 270
  reigning, not governing, 160
  relation to the Expediency Council, 150
  representing the maximum authority, 141
  turning into Absolutre Guardianship of the Jurist, 142
  unconventional powers, 149
Supreme Leader, Office of, 143, 243
sut *(1/10 of a gramme)*, 178, 185
Switzerland, 62, 131
Syria, 283, 287

Tabatabai, Seyyed Alizadeh, 106
taboo, breaking, 120, 124, 182
taboos
  harm reduction in UNODC Vienna Headquarters, 130
  sexual transmission of HIV/AIDS, 183
Tabriz, 60
tah-e khatt, 106
Taheri, Tah, 198, 237
Tahernokhost, Hamid-Reza, 212
tajahor, 51, 192, 194
Talibans, 101, 103, 135
tariyak shenas. See opium connoisseurs working at the Opium Desk
Tashvigi, Foruhar, 250
Tazmini, Ghoncheh, 99

technology (medical), 7
technology (Western), 59
technology, of government, 20, 24, 128
Tehran
  and US FBN officials, 56
  centres for treatment, 89, 157
  depression, 171
  drug distribution, 62, 84, 87
  during the Constitutional Revolution, 40
  during the *coup d'etat* against Mossadegh, 55
  during the Pahlavi, 51
  exodus from villages, 59
  heroin cases, 58
  opium coupon distrubution, 66
  Pahlavi family and drug networks, 62
patoqs, 116, 201, 202
shirehkesh-khaneh, 47
Tehran City Council, 106
Tehran municipality, 203, 271
Tehran, East of, 128
Tehran, North of, 170, 206
Tehran, South of, 30, 59, 81, 111
Tehran, streets of, 83
Telegram app, 29
temporary marriage, 6
Thailand, 170, 180
The Plague of Life, or Morphine (Afat-e Zendegi ya Morphine, 1960), 59
theology, 10, 14, 284
therapeutic communities (TCs), 25, 26, 30
timarestan, 118
time, flow of, 17, 59, 178, 186, 188
tout'eh-ye shaytani (diabolic conspiracy), 83
Tramadol, 175
treatment. *See* addiction: treatment of
Triangular Clinics, 118, 121, 240
tribes, nomadic, 43, 54, 61
Trudeau, Justin, 269
Trump, Donald J., 11, 283, 284, 285
Turkey, 60, 64, 84, 87, 101
  refusal to end poppy cultivation, 65

TV, 75, 254
TV, satellite, 175, 208
twilight institutions, 14, 235, 255
twilight zones, 265

uncivil society, 214
United Kingdom, 39, 52, 68, 269, 282
United Nations (UN), 3, 129, 130, 131, 132, 133
United Nations General Assembly on HIV/AIDS, 110
United States of America
    drug consumption, 59, 101
    drug policy, 25
    inside Iran, 49, 61, 62
        FBN, 61–3
    vis a vis Iran, 5n, *See* sanctions
    War on Drugs, 52, 76
universities, 156, 171, 180
university entry examination (*konkur*), 180
urban life
    divide with rural life, 185, 215
    drug price, 59
    exodus, 59, 111
    fall of the Qajar, 40
    harm reduction, 122
    heroin, 79
    image of the addict, 51
    opium coupon users, 67
    party scene, 175
    patoqs, 116
    policing, 85
    the place of heroin, 58
    youth, 78, 99, 173
urban middle class, 270
urban poor, 251
urbanisation, 78
URSS, 47, 49, 52
Uruguay, 11, 21, 269
US hostage crisis, 79, 133, 283

vafursuzan (opium pipe burning), 50
vagrancy, 82, 195
Vahid-Dastjerdi, Marzieh, 182
Vanak Square, 129
vaqf, 44
veterans, 105, 113, 152

Village Councils, 186
Vladivostok, 44

war in Afghanistan, 83
War on Drugs
    alternatives to, 216, 271
    basij volunteers, 85
    conspiracy, 80
    discoursive shift, 106
    drug war martyrs, 87, 88
    drugs as existential threat, 86
    during the Islamic Revolution, 9
    Iran
        failure, 78, 113, 234
        mobilisation, 88, 214
        role of the Expediency Council, 93
    two imposed wars, 79, 82
    United States of America, 52
welfare
    and harm reduction system, 128, 217, 276
    based on popular participation, 94
    for drug users, 6, 25, 28, 63, 100, 280
    for gender reassignment, 7
    in the post-war period, 91
    privatisation, 243
    support for vulnerable people, 116
welfare (penal) system, 80, 229, 263
Welfare Organisation
    budget in national drug policy, 245
    funding used for non-welfare purposes, 246
    in support of harm reduction, 122, 123
    licences to addiction recovery camps, 225
    lincences to addiction recovery camps, 211
    supervision of addiction recovery, 205
Weltanschauung, 167
Westernisation, 35, 53, 55, 106
Westoxification (*gharbzadegi*), 58, 106, 110

White Revolution, 57, 59
Williams, Garland, 56
Wilson, Arnold (Sir), 39
World Bank, 130
World Health Organisation (WHO), 23

yaa baa, 180
Yazd, 67

Yazdi, Shaikh Mohammad (ayatollah), 274
Yeganeh, Bahram, 123

Zahedan, 87
Zarghami, Ezatollah, 173
zarurat, 125, 144, *See emergency*
Zoroastrianism, 166
zurkhaneh, 180

CPSIA information can be obtained
at www.ICGtesting.com
Printed in the USA
LVHW081611080521
686877LV00008B/49